A HISTORY OF EUROPEAN
WOMEN'S WORK

The paid and unpaid work of women in Europe has been, and is, hugely diverse – from schools to offices, factories to domestic service, dairies to hospitals and much more. The work patterns have fluctuated in relation to ideological, technological, demographic, economic and familial changes. In *A History of European Women's Work*, Deborah Simonton draws together recent research, lively personal accounts and statistical evidence to take an overview of trends in women's work from the pre-industrial period to the present.

The author discusses the definition of work within and without patriarchal families, the status of work and the skills involved. This book examines local as well as Europe-wide developments, contrasting countries such as Britain, Germany and France. Age, class and, crucially, control are defining themes of this panoramic work.

Deborah Simonton considers women's own perceptions of work, and its place in their lives, to present a rounded account of the shifting patterns of employment and the continuities which are evident in women's own experience.

Deborah Simonton teaches at the University of Aberdeen. Her publications include *Women in Higher Education: Past, Present and Future* and *Gendering Scottish History*.

A HISTORY OF
EUROPEAN
WOMEN'S WORK

1700 to the present

Deborah Simonton

London and New York

First published in 1998
by Routledge
11 New Fetter Lane, London EC4P 4EE

Simultaneously published in the USA and Canada
by Routledge
29 West 35th Street, New York, NY 10001

© 1998 Deborah Simonton

Typeset in Garamond by
J&L Composition Ltd, Filey, North Yorkshire
Printed and bound in Great Britain by
Creative Print and Design (Wales), Ebbw Vale

British Library Cataloguing in Publication Data
A catalogue record for this book is available from the British Library

Library of Congress Cataloging in Publication Data
Simonton, Deborah, 1948–
A history of European women's work: 1700 to the present/Deborah
Simonton.
p.   cm.
Includes bibliographical references and index.
1.   Women—Employment—Europe—History. 2.   Rural women—
Employment—Europe—History. 3.   Women domestics—Europe—
History. 4.   Women farmers—Europe—History. 5.   Housewives—
Europe—History. 6.   Home economics—Europe—History.
I.   Title.
HD6134.S54 1998
331.4'094—dc21   98–9480
CIP

ISBN 0–415–05531–8 (hbk)
ISBN 0–415–05532–6 (pbk)

To Joy for a love of the past;
to Vivienne as hope for women of the future

CONTENTS

CONTENTS

ILLUSTRATIONS

FIGURES

TABLES

ACKNOWLEDGEMENTS

This project has inevitably generated many debts. First and foremost go my appreciation and respect for the scholars and researchers of the many and various studies which had to be undertaken before this book could be written. My debt is recorded in notes, but I wish my thanks also to be recorded. Without sources the historian does not exist. A special thanks goes to Meta Zimmeck and Francisca de Haan for sharing unpublished work and thoughts. My appreciation goes to: archivists at Essex and Staffordshire Record Offices; the Public Record Office; Wedgwood Archives, the owners Messrs Josiah Wedgwood and Sons Ltd., Barlaston, Stoke-on-Trent, and to Keele University Library where the manuscripts are housed, who provided assistance with original research; staff of the University of Aberdeen Queen Mother Library and the National Library of Scotland for the wealth of material they provided; Hannah Kent for tracking elusive material, and for friendship.

The book was written first for students, and my thanks to those who took part in seminars at Hillcroft College, the University of Aberdeen History Department and the Cultural History and Women's Studies groups who let me try out the ideas. Thanks also to participants at numerous conferences where ideas were tested, but especially participants at the Mackie Symposium, 1996.

Pam Sharpe, Maxine Berg, Ludmilla Jordanova, Leonore Davidoff, Sîan Reynolds, Nick Fisher, Allan Macinnes provided encouragement, inspiration and historical conversation. Flora Alexander gave her time, moral support, understanding and encouragement. While they may not always agree with me, their thoughts and stimulation were invaluable.

And to those who helped this book see the light of day: Alastair and Lara Freeman and Shona Potts for help with translation; Lucy Jack for tackling the monumental task of sorting the bibliography. Readers from Routledge provided encouraging comments and food for thought, and Claire L'Enfant and Heather McCallum offered continued faith when I thought all faith was dead. Victoria McCann read the whole manuscript in an unedited version, and she has my gratitude for her care, attention and helpful comments, and her personal support when it was needed.

ACKNOWLEDGEMENTS

Family and friends who have put up with my dogged determination, especially the Simontons, Moores and Hasties, particularly Alison who always asked and Kem who knows. Eternal thanks to David who read it, lived with it and survived it, for patience, tolerance and belief.

1

INTRODUCTION

All societies and cultures redefine the gender roles of their society. Although some argue that women's position and image in European society have always been subordinate and inferior, this is patently not the case. The concept of womanhood is complex and highly nuanced. Thus the image of woman as persistently subordinate to man was always mediated by a range of influences, while women's experience often belied stereotypes. Notions of women exist in tension with other prevailing views in society. Values and motivations of society change virtually generation to generation, often very subtly, so that perceptions of women by any given culture similarly vary. Indeed, views of women and their role are part of society's perception of itself, and not always the least important. So, while women affect the character of change as active participants, as workers, mothers, wives, daughters and consumers, their experience is also shaped by the nature of change. This is both about gender construction and about the way we view any society from our own vantage point. Views of women are constructed from a range of materials and on a number of levels. The variations and balances in these facets build up a society's view of 'woman'. Frequently, that view is constructed as an absolute, regardless of class, sometimes of nation. Values, aspirations and goals can be universally ascribed to women, so that those who do not meet, or at least approximate, an ideal are seen as 'unwomanly' or 'unfeminine' – as failures. The root of women's perceived inferiority often was due to their physical and biological weakness. Not only were they lighter, smaller, shorter and less muscular, they were subject to their own little-understood gynaecological being. They were seen as subservient to their reproductive organs, and therefore as unruly and uncontrollable creatures. These notions shaped more than medical practice; women's political, social and economic roles were circumscribed by interpretations of female physiology. Physical weakness was transmuted into a corresponding belief in mental inferiority.

The relationship between woman and her labour is similarly mediated by a number of issues. Some, such as the nature of work available, its urban or rural character and the work process, affect men as well. In addition, key issues for women concern family and female life cycle. But work is mediated by ideology

1

and concepts of gender, status and power. These are less about the work itself than about relationships and psycho-social needs which work fills above and beyond its economic role. While women's work is delineated by factors such as economy, class and demography, society's notions about woman's place and its beliefs about gender roles are significant determinants. Thus domestic roles and relationships with partners and family are central to understanding their contribution to the labour market. Similarly definitions of work reflect society's perception of the values placed on different forms of labouring activity. The most obvious of these is whether unpaid work in support of the home is construed as work. Woman's place in society is also the result of a complex of ideas about what women are capable of and should do. Thus their intellectual capacity, the character of that capacity, and their sexual, moral and religious duties shape how women are perceived. They also shape women's self-perception. In these ways, women's work, its types, locations and structures are gendered. But gender is not only the result of ideologies about women. Masculinity itself supplements and complements ideas about femininity. Frequently predicated on ideas of male superiority, the male protector, the provider, the head of the family, and on beliefs about male libido, male views of the world further define lines of demarcation between sexes, not only domestically but in terms of the labour market. Thus a number of dyads are created, such as male strength, female frailty; male provider, female helpmeet; and male wage, female pin-money. Practices and precepts of women's work are determined also by obligations, such as childcare and nurturing. Ideology is of fundamental importance in shaping perceptions of the nature and level of those responsibilities. It can be argued that the development of a notion of 'childhood' and an emphasis on the importance of early childhood influences restricted women's options for their children's benefit and not their own. Similarly, companionate marriage may have tended to subsume women under men with a resultant loss of identity. As the role of the state increased, state systems tended to perpetuate and entrench the role of women as wives and mothers. These factors, outside of purely economic considerations, influenced women of all classes, though with varied effects determined partly by class and partly by culture.

Understanding of women's activities is usually situated within male definitions of work, while important ideas about women's work were derived from their positions within the household. They often performed jobs to help support the family, such as growing vegetables, raising animals, making clothing or assisting in farm and craft work, thus having 'use value' rather than 'exchange value'. As waged labour became more prominent and wage earning came to be the measure of productivity, because women's work merged with household chores, it came to be seen as non-productive. At the same time, the term 'work' came to represent productive market-orientated activity, often dissociated from the home. Activities customarily carried out by women are often laden with a pejorative connotation. For example, when housewifery or other female activity around the household is defined as not being 'work' because it is unwaged, a status or hierarchy is automatically implied. The locus of female work does not determine its importance. Whether work is described as female or as situated at home is not by itself necessarily significant. It becomes significant as part of a cluster of ideas about women, work and family; the importance of 'work' is dependent on the cultural values associated with it. Thus what matters is the value placed on that work or the meanings ascribed to being at home. Working at home did not always imply inferior tasks or domesticity. Even where division of labour existed, it was not always couched in the cultural terms associated with the nineteenth century. Thus 'work' as a concept is both historically specific and relative to the context and value systems in operation.

Similarly, gendered division of labour is historically specific. It can be seen to derive from an idea of the 'traditional', to be based on the 'partnership of working-class families', to arise from the needs of the family economy with origins in agriculture and crafts. It is argued that this division is carried into capitalist activities and becomes more pronounced as work moves out of the home, a process usually linked to mechanization, technological change and the factory system. It has important implications for waged labour and the idea of the 'family wage'. But division of labour along sexual lines was not simply because it was 'practical'. Nor is it only about protecting jobs from cheap unskilled labour; it is about power, status, position and masculinity. We have to ask why it happens and with what language women were excluded from processes, trades and workplaces, yet included in others. Possibly, the argument should be reversed: the creation of the domestic female was as much a result of division of labour and exclusion as it was a cause.

Shifting notions of gender at work can be demonstrated in the ways that 'skill' is defined and used to redefine work patterns, in particular, sexual division of labour. Skill has been perceived in terms of strength, training, intelligence, custom and control. Analysing patterns and structures of women's work, terms like technology, skill and expertise regularly appear. There is no doubt that differing notions of 'skill' underpin many analyses. What is disturbing is the imprecision with which such terms are used, so that they obscure or undercut the argument itself and make building up a coherent epistemological argument over time difficult if not impossible. Using terms like 'skill' in relation to 'technology' leads to a limited notion of what skill might have meant. Learning theory emphasizes 'transferable skills' which include a range of abilities unrelated to technology. John refers to 'skilled tasks' which rely on 'knack, opportunity to train, experiment and experience'. This implies the importance of knowledge, while Cockburn's 'know-how' suggests a more tangible relationship to tools. She delineates it further, writing 'Women may push the buttons but they may not meddle with the works.' Connection between the language and, consequently, the concepts of skill and technology is not surprising. Since Braverman and others linked technology to deskilling as partial explanation of division of labour, male control of technology and by

3

implication their control of skill have been essential elements in analysing the gendered nature of work. Linn isolated the central point that technology is not inert hardware but a cultural product: 'it is always constituted in the social practices of language and other forms of representation, in traditions of use, with associated techniques and training procedures, in domains of knowledge, and in relations of production and consumption.'[1]

There have been few unified attempts outside of economics to deal with issues surrounding women's work. Similarly, research which places the experience of work in the context of other aspects of female experience are relatively recent. In particular, linking women, work and family has been the focus of analyses over the last twenty years at the same time as issues of gender, domesticity, femininity and family have become the centre of vigorous discussion. In 1981, John Rule justified brief treatment of women's labour in *The Experience of Labour in Eighteenth-century Industry* because 'Women already have their historian'. He was referring to Pinchbeck's *Women Workers and the Industrial Revolution, 1750–1850* (1930). For the previous century, that claim might be made for Clark's *Working Life of Women in the Seventeenth Century* (1919) and, for France, Abensour's section on 'La Femme du peuple' in *La Femme et le Féminisme en France avant la Révolution* (1923) stands as an important contribution, often unsurpassed for detail. These books, now over sixty years old, are starting points for many contemporary women's historians.

The central focus of Pinchbeck and Clark is the question of whether women benefited from capitalist expansion and how industrial and structural economic change affected women's productivity. Clark presented seventeenth-century women's activities as evidence of their vigour, competence and enterprise, stemming from their active and valued role in the pre-capitalist household, a theme echoed by Abensour. To Clark, the shift in capitalized work disadvantaged women with regard to skill and devalued them as equal contributors to the family. To Pinchbeck, on the other hand, the industrial revolution represented an advance for women. She argued that agrarian and industrial change combined to deprive women of their earning capacity in the home, but in the longer view such change was beneficial by leading to greater leisure in the home and relieving women from the monotony and drudgery of the domestic system. For woman workers outside the home, capitalism brought better conditions, a greater variety of openings and improved status. In some ways, Pinchbeck and Clark disagree more in interpretation than in specifics. In the intervening years, women's history as well as family and economic history have found new ways of framing questions, new models of economic life, new empirical bases and new approaches to evaluating their material. Historians of women have raised issues of definition, ideology, gender and periodization which cast earlier methodology into new relief. Adding significantly to historical debates about women's work was Tilly and Scott's *Women, Work and Family* (1978), which explicitly identified and analysed relationships between various role expectations for women. It addressed life cycle, demography and familial obligations and linked these to meanings of work and women's decisions about 'gainful employment'. In some ways, it was a pioneering book on a narrow empirical base. This was necessarily the case in 1978, when so much basic research was yet to be carried out. Notably it presents a European case, which is not defined primarily by British experience. One major flaw in writing about economic and industrial change in Europe is a tendency to measure growth and changes against a British yardstick. The result is that European issues are in danger of being measured and judged by British experience rather than their own.[2]

A great deal has been published on women's work and the related parameters of family, gender and ideology over the last twenty years. These consist largely of individual studies which focus on particular periods or countries, regions or cultures. Debates about women's work also figure in survey articles which highlight research developments or which argue aspects of ideology or methodology. A significant component of published material is collections, which though not always focused on work, deal with important related issues, often attempting to put female labour into context. In Boxer and Quataert's *Connecting Spheres* (1987), three substantial overview chapters synthesize European women's history since 1500. Demonstrating the interdependency of the so-called public and private spheres, they took an important step in surveying and exploring links between European cultures and women's experience. Hudson and Lee's *Women's Work and the Family Economy in Historical Perspective* (1990) made a timely contribution to a number of debates ranging around issues of proto-industry, female economic contribution and the role of women's history in relation to the established practices of social and economic history. The book gains significantly from the editors' introductory essay which tackles the need to bring key issues together and indicates the salience of notions of gender, skill and regional and temporal variation to our understanding of economic development and patterns of work throughout the European economy.

> Old questions and debates . . . all now need to be reassessed in the light of the vital role played by gender. As long as research about women's lives remains largely separate from wider issues such as these, the importance which society has attached to female activities and agency in the past (and in the present) will not change.[3]

More recently, de Groot and Schrover's *Women Workers and Technological Change in the Nineteenth and Twentieth Centuries* (1995b) explicitly grapples with many fundamental issues of technology, skill and status, using empirical research from across Europe, while Frader and Rose's *Gender and Class in Modern Europe* (1996) turns to wider issues and points to newer approaches of rewriting the record with a gendered perspective. Both of these books contain excellent introductions which contextualize their subject in current developments in historical thought.

There is a need to draw together recent research and methodological developments. Recent surveys of women's history have begun the process of rethinking women's history, notably, Anderson and Zinsser's *A History of Their Own* (1988), Wiesner's *Women and Gender in Early Modern Europe* (1993) and Hufton's *The Prospect Before Her* (1995). The present book begins to fill the gap with an overview of trends in women's work across Europe from the so-called pre-industrial period to the present. It will contextualize patterns of women's work within ideological, demographic, economic and familial changes, focusing on gender and class in defining and understanding women's labouring role in European society. In doing so it must, therefore, compare and contrast the pace and patterns of change between European countries, identifying distinct patterns while locating trends which held across Europe. Necessarily, it is a balancing act both to tell the story of women's work primarily in Western Europe and to analyse the dynamic of the gendered workplace. Thus there is relatively little detail about specific kinds of work, even quite important ones, and country histories are not attempted. The focus is on the overall picture, the characteristics of change and constants, on similarities and differences. In an attempt to put the woman's experience at the centre, the political and legal context probably has been given briefer coverage than some may wish. Despite an increasing literature on women, family and their work, and a wide range of in-depth studies, much work remains to be done. In many respects our knowledge is still patchy, so that the present book is a progress report, an attempt to use newer research to 'update' earlier significant contributions to the debate on women's work.

A historical study of women's work poses problems of periodization, since the course of life flows on without much regard for artificial points of reference. Political reference points, such as wars, elections or even revolutions can be of limited use, since women's lives were not governed primarily by these demarcations. Periods associated with economic shifts, such as pre-industrial, proto-industrial, industrial, also have problems. First, historians are not agreed about what each of these terms means. Second, if they are meant as stages in development, the stages were reached at different times in different parts of Europe. Third, when described as 'stages', these terms suggest a necessary progression from one to the other. In this way, the framework of *Women, Work and Family* highlights one debate in economic history circles: the transition from pre-industrial, through proto-industrial to industrial development. Tilly and Scott took a relatively unproblematic approach to the shift from 'family economy' through 'family wage economy' to 'family consumer economy'. However, such transitions and periodization require disentangling and re-examination with regard to women's labour. They are useful terms which focus attention on varying patterns of income and family structure. Because they are about the nature of work, the way it was organized and where it was located, they also describe the overall shape of an economy. But they also suggest progression to a 'modern' conception of family, work and women's roles which tends to obscure

6

differentials which existed at all times across Europe as a whole, but also within individual countries. There is a subtle danger in employing such terms, even as a shorthand, because they become a straitjacket which constrains the discussion, tending to exclude variations and permutations which need to be explored.

Elizabeth Fox-Genovese made the point that, 'Notoriously, historians love to find traditional society, in all its reassuring stability, in the century that preceded the one they are studying.'[4] In fact, we frequently use 'traditional' as a shorthand to refer to times we know little about, or to provide us with a model for comparison. In the same way, debates about the industrial revolution, and particularly women's role and status before, during and after, have led some to suppose that there was a golden age, when women were independent and powerful, characteristics which were destroyed by capitalism, mechanization, specialization and the 'industrial revolution'. Or they perceive 'bad old days', days of drudgery and subordination which existed before the liberating effects of capitalism and industrialization. The so-called 'traditional' woman probably never existed any more than some sort of 'golden age' for women did. Each of these views, in their own way, contains elements of modernization, implying that there is a continual progression to the modern age. Such an orientation in historical writing is dangerous and misleading. It suggests, first, that there is something perfect and resolved in our own age, which events hardly justify, and, second, tends to ignore the variations not only over time but across regions, which make it obvious that there is not just one route to the present, nor is the view of the past so simple.

This book is divided into three parts, each roughly coinciding with a century, but with blurred edges. They approximate a predominant structure and shape to women's lives, but the text also reflects the extent to which there are important overlaps. Part I centres on the eighteenth century (c. 1700–90), a primarily rural economy, but one which witnessed changes in craft and industrial organization. Several patterns overlapped so that people could be working for themselves or others, for wages, piece rates, barter or accommodation. They were mainly involved in small-scale operations, in both town and country, though larger workplaces developed and with them more division of labour and specialization. Ideas about women began to shift as a legacy of Enlightenment thought such that new and durable ideological restrictions on women's lives signalled a new direction in thinking about women and their place in society and economy. At the same time, scientific and Enlightenment thought, and the notion of 'improvement' began to influence economic concepts and society as a whole. The nineteenth century (1790–1880) saw a further evolution of large-scale industry, and the establishment of the factory system in a number of industries. Society became far more urban and consumer based at the same time, and yet a large part of the population of Europe was still rural. Mechanization had not revolutionized all aspects of life, and craft trades continued to operate in small-scale workshops. Views of womanhood became more solidified within a domestic view of woman, but the same middle-class women who had given definition to the 'Angel in the House' began to spread their wings, seeking alternatives. By the end of the nineteenth century, challenges to legal and social restrictions for women and the working classes began to bear fruit in legal changes and political emancipation. And yet, if from the 1880s people could think in terms of a more democratic and 'emancipated' society, the first half of the twentieth century saw two major wars in Europe with the disruption and destruction that they brought, coupled with shifts in living standards. They also put new demands on the workforce, and contributed to changes in women's working. Commercialization and the service sectors of the economy grew significantly, with far-reaching implications for women's work. Socially, economically and politically women played a more visible part in the society and economy while their role in the household also changed. At the same time, it could be argued that in many respects, though the context and language had changed, their role was the same one that many eighteenth-century women filled.

Class issues frequently emerge as a tension between bourgeois notions of woman's place and the reality witnessed by women who worked. Ideas of class and status are built on male position, and as shifts took place throughout the period, they also shaped concepts of womanhood and femininity and the reality of women's lives. Such beliefs were used to define appropriate work for both men and women. However, class should not be seen simplistically as a relation in which the middle classes imposed forms of social control on those below them in the status hierarchy. Much of women's history over the last two decades has been informed by the notion of the 'public' and the 'private'. While the idea of public and private spheres seems obvious, the notion is extraordinarily complex. In its simplest form, the male sphere was the public, the market, business and politics, while the private domestic sphere was the realm of the woman. Clearly this is oversimplified, but, like other systems of thought, it has evolved into a shorthand which at times obscures as much as it reveals. Throughout this study, women can be seen to be operating on several levels and functioning in a variety of ways in both spheres. Also, the demarcation between the two becomes almost non-existent when examining the organization of work and family life in many domestic industries. Nevertheless, the notions of power and status which are suggested by this dyad retain their relevance within shifting social and economic structures.

A key question was whether women gained status through their labour contribution. The view that paid work was good for women's status in society was shared by early middle-class feminists, such as Clark. Women's position was closely linked to their domestic work together with their crucial contribution to family upkeep by paid work outwith the immediate domestic sphere. However, Clark saw capitalism as undermining that valued position. This contrasts with Shorter who argues that capitalism helped enhance women's power in the household since their work brought in resources from outside, 'And the money wages that these women earned had their names written on them, rather than disappearing into undifferentiated family revenues.' It is relatively easy to take issue with this logic, since women had frequently brought money into the household from marketing activities. More important than cash itself was who controlled it and how work was regarded. Even if women's work was crucial, the gender roles of society were often about other things altogether, such as status, masculinity, power and control. Thus Fox-Genovese argues that women's work only exceptionally netted women power, prestige or remuneration like men's work did. Women's waged labour did not significantly modify the relationship between women's work and society, nor did it necessarily advantage or disadvantage women consistently.[5] The question of skill is particularly significant since women were excluded from many established routes to male-defined expertise, which were closely associated with status, prestige and political rights. Economic and technical changes altered work, while issues of skill and deskilling influenced experience. Frequently these were about gender rather than ability or expertise. Although operating within a male-defined and male-dominated world, female contexts, strategies and networks were significant in shaping their lives. It must not be assumed that women were passive recipients of their culture. There is sufficient evidence that women were active in shaping and defining their own sense of value and status.

Part I

THE EIGHTEENTH CENTURY,
c. 1700–90

2

WOMEN, HOUSEHOLD AND FARM

THE IDEA OF WOMAN IN SOCIETY AND ECONOMY

Two sets of ideas came together to shape the concept of womanhood that prevailed in Europe during the eighteenth century. One drew from the Judaeo-Christian tradition that frequently depicted women as evil and dangerous, needing to be controlled. New scientific thought and the Enlightenment reshaped that view and added new and extremely durable theoretical justifications for legal, economic, social and educational disabilities. The focus of eighteenth-century thought on Nature led to attempts to 'discover' the 'natural woman'. Once her nature was understood, her position in society, her relationships and her appropriate education could be deduced. The appeal to Nature, which translated into a liberating appeal for the rights of 'man', was a mechanism for redefining and restricting women's field of action. As Kleinbaum indicated, 'the Philosophes' light was dim and imperfectly transmitted'. Older ideas about the character of women also influenced them, and they frequently ignored the question of women's inequality or attacked women as representatives of social classes they wished to condemn. Had they followed the 'natural law argument' initiated by Jaucourt in the *Encyclopédie*, there was potential to create a clear feminist agenda within Enlightenment thought. In the event, however, those like Voltaire who could have raised its profile 'never viewed the plight of women as a critical issue worthy of his full energy and genius'.[1] Instead, except for individuals like Condorcet and Wollstonecraft, Rousseau, whose view of the female stressed sexual difference and a domestic role for women, tended to set the agenda. This ultimately was women's legacy from the Enlightenment.

The bourgeoisie was significant in creating gender roles defined in terms of public and private spheres and emphasizing domesticity for females. Although the new middle classes shared Enlightenment criticisms of absolutism, 'they adhered to tradition when it came to the role and rights of woman'.[2] Rousseau was in the forefront of this new conception of woman. Beginning from the supposedly weaker physical nature of the female, it was possible to exclude them from a range of occupations and activities. Thus, identification of women with an idealized domestic role defined the character of their activities, while it appeared to enhance their image, sanctifying as virtues characteristics arising from their 'weakness'. Yet weakness, no matter how gloriously described, meant women required not mates, but protectors. Rousseau's creations of Julie, the perfect woman, and Sophie, Emile's companion, were prominent expressions of the new bourgeois ideal. A typical mid-eighteenth-century formulation was the sermon by John Brown, vicar of Newcastle-upon-Tyne, *On the Female Character and Education* (1765). He insisted on 'pre-established Habits of Mankind' and inborn passions that had to be eradicated. Similarly, a belief in natural traits, stemming from physical weakness, shaped his view of womankind. He intended to prove:

I.   THAT the Female Frame of Person and Mind tends chiefly to fit and qualify the sex for domestic Life only.
II. THAT from this Frame of Person and Mind, conducted by a suitable Education, the Female Virtues prescribed by Christianity do naturally arise.[3]

Similarly, the civil servant Adolf von Knigge, in 1788, concluded that:

The female sex was to remain as much excluded from involvement in the bourgeois public sphere as they were from the world of employment, and politics was certainly out of bounds. Women's exclusive domain was the household or . . . the family.[4]

Thus a key element of the idea of woman was that she was becoming defined by and restricted to domestic pursuits, because her 'acknowledged delicacy and weakness of person' disqualified her from heavy, robust activity. It was 'so obvious as to not need further proof'. Innate female timidity was ascribed to female physical weakness, from which followed a desire for peace, tranquillity and the safety of domestic life. 'In all of nature, boldness is given to the strong, timidness to the weak, to argue otherwise is to contravene nature'. Notably there was significant agreement between Philosophes and traditionalists, such as Fénelon and de Maintenon, who saw education as a necessity to redress the bad inclinations of females and to guard them against the 'natural weaknesses of their sex'.[5]

Linked to sexual protection of women, ideology ultimately subordinated women to men, while women's particular responsibilities as helpmates to husbands or as educators of children defined them in relation to men and family. These views resolved themselves into a prescription of female duty in late eighteenth-century manuals. Their energies, interests and moral force were to be directed to men's virtue and well-being and to children's upbringing. Domestic love was a woman's first obligation and her reason for being. Her ultimate goal was to preserve her husband and his honour, and to respect and love him even when he wronged her. At the same time, writers claimed women could achieve a higher moral plane than men, charging them with a special role as arbiters of morality and virtue. This operated in two ways: in a private, domestic sense and in a public, global sense. Ideology entrusted her with guardianship of male honour, since a virtuous woman could reform a man through his passion for her, while an immodest woman was responsible for men's immorality. 'The vices of men often proceed either from the ill education they received at first from their mothers, or else from the passions which other women inspire into them at a riper age'. As Rousseau wrote in 1758, 'A home whose mistress is absent is a body without a soul that soon falls into corruption'.[6] Women who obeyed injunctions of modesty, piety and humility benefited society, but should their manners relax and degenerate, society would become more vicious and debauched. In this way, women were exalted and debased simultaneously.

New attitudes towards children and the identity of childhood as a formative stage in personality development modified perceptions of both child and mother at all levels of society. Whether accepting the child as born innocent, evil or good, authors of conservative and radical persuasion, such as Locke, More, Wollstonecraft and Rousseau, relied on the malleability of the child as the keystone to its development. The number and range of tracts, sermons and advice manuals that stressed the importance of the earliest contacts demonstrated the pervasive and widely accepted belief in the importance of environmental factors. The family, particularly parents, became identified as the key factor in childrearing and character development. In Germany, the term 'familie' appeared in the dictionary in 1788, while bourgeois literature clearly identified it as a sphere of social interaction reserved exclusively for marriage partners and their children. Growing emphasis on the importance of childhood in shaping adult character gave mothers primary responsibility for childcare and nurture at that critical time so that 'the soundness or folly of our minds are not less owing to those first tempers and ways of thinking, which we receive from the love, tenderness, authority and constant conversation of mothers'. Like Rousseau, many emphasized the responsibility of mothers in childcare, whereby 'there will be a reform in morals'.[7] Likewise society held her demeanour and example to account for the effect it had on her children. Emphasis on proper moral education reflected concern for posterity and the society as a whole. As the child is father of the man, so the woman was the mother of adult virtue.

Middle-class anxiety about the morals and manners of the poor was a marked feature from mid-century. In Britain in the last quarter of the century, growing conservative reaction to the spread of radical ideas exacerbated it. In France, it was part of an attempt to control 'disorderly' women of the Revolution, while in Germany, rapid economic, cultural, intellectual and political upheaval could only be managed if the emotional side of family life was preserved. Particular criticism and attention were directed to working-class mothers' childrearing: 'Instead of acting as Mothers ought to do, of watching carefully over their little Family at home, and regulating their Manners, . . . [they] are too frequently intoxicating themselves'. This literature contained two basic assumptions about plebeian girls' destiny: first, there was a specific female character, and second, they would fill positions of servants, wives and mothers. Thus it was essential to develop them in ways appropriate to their future, improving their manners and morals for society's benefit. Although the cultural and economic nexus of working-class life meant that the child-orientated, domesticated female was an alien image, advice literature firmly established that the correct province for the female of the lower orders was home and family. It was necessary 'to rivet their young and ardent attentions wholly on domestic concerns', so that they provided the right atmosphere for bringing up children. Also women would better provide for men's needs. Trimmer claimed that men became 'sots' when women worked out of doors all the time, instead of remaining at home. Thus poor women's responsibilities to husband, children and home were perceived in the same light as their 'betters'. However, this monolithic view of womankind did not run roughshod over ideas of social difference. Descriptions of appropriate schooling and training maintained social distance between classes, preparing poorer girls for a life of work. For example, women like Hannah More who supported education for the poor, saw education of different types as appropriate for different groups in society, while Wollstonecraft, though vigorous in defence of women's right to education, also maintained lines of social demarcation.[8] The character of female domestic servants merged with anxiety about the lower orders in general and female ideology in particular. The influence of servants, particularly untutored young females, on children raised problems for employers. Thus an emphasis on conduct and morals grew, and ideology began to influence the middle-class female's life directly, while it shaped ideas about how to raise girls of all levels.

Women's work took place in the context of a fluid social and economic structure. The eighteenth century was a period of economic expansion in industry and agriculture, which was an integral part of an increasing commercial marketplace at home and abroad. Expansion did not take place in all regions in the same way or at the same rate. At the same time, the stresses of economic change often determined social perceptions of women's place and their economic role. For example, Richards argued that pressure on jobs at the end of the eighteenth century and the beginning of the nineteenth contributed to the creation of domestic ideology and the withdrawal of women from the workforce, not the other way around.[9] While the late eighteenth century was a period of self-sustained economic growth, we must not overemphasize the effect and significance of changes in workplace organization by 1800. The population was still predominantly rural, and agriculture continued to be the largest single employer. Industry and agriculture were still substantially unmechanized, relying on large numbers of unskilled workers. Industrial organization continued to centre on small workshops and rural trades throughout much of Europe. Likewise, regional variation and increasing geographical specialization affected the pattern and structure of working. The economic structure could vary within a region as well as between regions, and the role of the town or countryside similarly depended on local factors. Effectively, few barriers separated town from country, industry and trade from farming or industrial workers from agricultural labourers, and there was a constant movement of people between them. The conventional emphasis on late eighteenth-century factory development especially misrepresents women's part. It implies that they newly entered the workforce, and primarily as millworkers. Yet, women had been and continued to be employed in all forms of agricultural, commercial and industrial organization, but this is blurred by overlapping changes in their work. Accelerated growth generated new opportunities for them, while losses in existing trades changed the shape of women's paid labour.

The idea of the family economy underpins almost all writing about women, their work, and their familial responsibilities in the period before factory development, centralization and rapid mechanization. In its simplest form, the family economy implies the interdependence of all family (frequently meaning household) members working towards economic survival of the unit, and one may infer that members of the unit were measured by their economic contribution, based on their labour contribution. Hudson and Lee contextualized women in the family economy, writing, 'As long as the household remained a major unit of production, the family remained the main instrument of recruitment to work and most women worked as members of a family production unit'.[10] In contrast to a later period or 'stage', described as a 'family wage economy', wages supposedly played a minor role in a family economy. The type of production and what is meant by a wage complicate this point. The family economy certainly involved money exchange, but usually income was based on piece rates, work was assumed to have taken place largely in the home, and industrial work was not necessarily the only source of income for the family.

As Berg says, the family economy was, however, frequently more than that: 'the hold of the family economy on behaviour, mentalities and social structures continued as long as all family members had some economic function'. The family economy forms part of an analysis of women's subordination that sees the replacement of the family economy by the 'family household system'. It pictures the family as dependent on the paid labour of husbands/fathers and the unpaid labour of wives/mothers in domestic tasks, and combines this with the ideology of the family, the private sphere. The assumption of an earlier historical epoch where individuals integrated work and home life underpins much contemporary research on women's subordination, so that the transition to industrial capitalism which separated home from workshop or factory is held accountable for the declining opportunities for women.[11] The danger is that theory has overrun knowledge, since we still know remarkably little of what this 'transition' meant for women.

The concept of the family economy was also imbedded in an economic system based on agriculture, agricultural trades, and a domestic system of industrial production. Work, family and household were integrally related ideas whose functions were not separable. Though not completely within an individual's control, economic need to survive and love, sentiment and affection undoubtedly coloured decisions about household formation, fertility and survival. The idea of a mutually interdependent family or household economy does not rule out the importance of emotion in shaping strategies for survival. A woman's relationship to her home and its membership, on affective, demographic and economic terms, is crucial to understanding her place within society. Used sensitively, the family economy model remains useful in highlighting the importance of strategies to a household, and stressing the interdependence of household members and the centrality of women, children and their labour to household response to economic conditions. Women's labour as wife or daughter was significant. Co-residence was not essential since one strategy for balancing household needs involved apprenticing, hiring out or sending out children. Similarly it could involve importing labour, from either kin or non-kin. This labour too was not necessarily co-resident. Women's work must be seen within this context. The frequently pivotal role of the wife meant that she was neither powerless nor dependent. Not only was she economically active, but as household manager she often determined and manipulated the strategies for survival. Strategies employed by a family were not solely in the context of family and subsistence, and other considerations, such as transmission of culture, played a part. Also, increasing reliance on wages may have changed family relationships and affected responses linked to culture, custom and control.[12]

DOMESTIC RESPONSIBILITIES

Almost always the duties required to run a household have been regarded as a normal part of women's tasks. During the eighteenth century, these had not yet evolved into a concept of 'housework' nor did they have the connotation of 'domesticity'. They were simply a part of, and frequently the primary part of, women's work. Not only were domestic tasks important to the household, they were important to women. They helped to define their scope and space, and gave value to much of their work. Paid employment for women often was simply an extension of domestic tasks. Many service occupations which employed women appropriated their functions in the home: cleaning, cooking, caring and nursing. Similarly, female domestic or farm servants were paid for tasks that they performed freely for their own family. Urban women had long taken up special opportunities as midwives, servants, laundresses, prostitutes and hawkers or market women of various kinds. This is the other side of ideology which defined the domestic female. Where women's work outside the home declined, their importance within it became more prominent, contributing to ideology. However, emergent middle-class ideas remained largely alien to plebeian women and substantially irrelevant to their economic circumstances, while at the same time their household role contributed to the mechanism that created that construction. The need for women to contribute to family maintenance was their central focus. There is no doubt that a division of labour associated women with household and childcare, but that women were subordinate *because* of gender-specific labour is less obvious. Similarly, an assumption that women became housekeepers *because* they bore children can be challenged. Indeed, Middleton argues that household tasks as women's work is the result of the underlying principle that women keep house for men.[13]

It has become a commonplace that the range of domestic tasks was far broader than our twentieth-century concept of housework. Language helps to illustrate not only how meaning and usage changed, but how ascription and status shifted. In French, *le ménage,* which has come to mean housework, formerly covered the entire farm administration. Where it once carried the sense of managing with 'masculine' connotations, these receded while retaining the 'feminine' meaning of household tasks. Indeed, as Pope explains, when 'domesticity' was coined in the seventeenth century, it referred to the household and the tasks to sustain it; only later did it develop emotional and moral connotations. German and British experience demonstrated a similar shift. The German *Hausmutter* shared responsibility for the household (*ganzes Haus*) with the *Hausvater*: 'The household was their joint domain and every task carried out – whether by the *Hausvater* or the *Hausmutter* – was important and indispensable for the farm's prosperity'. As Zedler's 1735 *Universallexikon* indicated, 'because the wife, as housemother, has also to help her husband administer and supervise the household, some authority can be ascribed to her'. But with changes in meanings of femininity and masculinity, her position became less and less defined by what she did, while housewifery became narrowly defined household tasks. The *Hausmutter* became a *Hausfrau*. In Britain, housewifery (sometimes 'huswifery'), as a term, arrived in the thirteenth century, and was used throughout the eighteenth. Linked to the masculine form, husbandry (sometimes 'housebandry'), both referred to household maintenance. The word 'housework' did not appear until well into the nineteenth century, which says as much about the changing location of recognized work as it does about the nature of domestic tasks.[14]

Fundamentally, women, especially married women, provided for immediate needs of the household. Rural women expected to fetch water, produce and prepare food, bear and care for children, mend and provide clothing. They made many items themselves, especially before the widespread commercialization of household goods at the end of the eighteenth century and the beginning of the nineteenth. As Krünitz's *Encyklopädie* of 1788 described,

> supervision and work in the kitchen and cellar, the rearing of cattle,
> pigs and poultry, the maintenance, cleaning and production of clothing

and linen, bedmaking, brewing, baking, washing, sewing, spinning, weaving and other work with wool and flax and indeed anything concerning the cleanliness of the house and the maintenance of household equipment [were the responsibilities of the *Hausmutter*.][15]

She might have been responsible for a kitchen garden as well as an orchard, depending on the size of the holding. They had charge of dairies, including care of calves and other small animals. A French peasant saying demonstrates the importance of these responsibilities: 'No wife, no cow, hence no milk, no cheese, not hens, nor chicks, nor eggs. . . .' The farm wife marketed dairy and poultry products and met various household expenses with the proceeds. In Devonshire, 'It is a common practice among them on marriage to give to their wives what is called pin-money; this consists of poultry, pigs and the whole produce of the dairy; with which supply the wife is expected to clothe and (exclusive of bread, corn and other vegetables) support the whole household.' A similar example from Burgundy highlights the overlap between domestic and market activities, both important economic functions: 'Marguerite makes some money from her spinning, from the eggs of her six hens, from the wool of her seven sheep, from the milk, butter and cheese of her cow and from the vegetables in her garden.' Acknowledged as manager of the internal budget and the provision of food, a wife handled most of the family monetary exchange, which gave her an identified sphere of authority. Often this was the only money such a household brought in.[16]

Women often took part in business management of the farm, although French evidence suggests that buying and selling land and paying wages belonged to men. Other marketing duties could fall to the husband, such as selling and trading large livestock and grain; the proceeds from these often went to meet external obligations such as taxes and rents. Thus, there is an intimation that women's budgetary control related to her particular responsibilities and on a 'macro' economic level, where men perceived their status was at risk, they controlled transactions. There are clear parallels to gendered divisions of labour. Women's position changed when men were absent, in that women undertook 'men's' marketing as substitutes. In the Auvergne, where seasonal migration meant long male absences, wives contracted the debts that carried families through the men's absence and negotiated hiring out children to itinerant peddlers. Women had more control over property and household expenditure in fishing households, as a result of male absence and risks at sea.[17]

Arguably, cleaning, mending, cooking and childcare were fairly marginal demands on women's time. Historical records of households where domestics were paid to carry out such work demonstrate how relatively minor cleaning was, with very little clothes-washing and general scrubbing or housework in the modern sense being carried out no more than once or twice a year. Similarly, domestic manuals were relatively silent on the subject. Pahl suggests 'what was a rare occurrence for the rich probably hardly occurred at all for the

poor'. The character of housing, whether in country or town, cottage or tene-
ment, with rough walls, modest or unflagged flooring, thatched roofs and
scanty, crude furniture was an indication that cleaning was of minimal value.
In many places, animals still shared some part of the house. Cooking utensils
were limited, and bedclothes frequently rough and flea infested. Food preparation was minimal, relying on bread, cheese, eggs, vegetables and boiled meat
or soup broth. Importantly, people did not keep possessions to define the pos-
sessor, nor was there the ideological reinforcement of a modern concept of
housework. At the same time, such work could be onerous, such as the carriage
of water to meet daily needs of families of eight or ten.[18]

The urban woman, similarly, retained responsibility for immediate needs of
the household. When she could not provide items directly, such as produce,
she supplied them from the market. Where industrial work or other responsibilities in the workshop demanded her attentions, she hired a laundress or servant. In the workshop setting, her domestic duties mirrored rural women's, in
that she expected not only to feed and clothe her own family, but apprentices,
journeymen and any resident domestic servants. Although many requisites
could be bought, they still required processing. For example, even in towns
women expected to make bread and butter, to preserve fruits and vegetables,
and occasionally slaughter livestock, or at least clean poultry.[19] In towns,
women were not as far removed from the countryside as today's urban woman.
Many towns were still small, retaining features associated with villages, in that
small livestock and vegetable gardens proliferated. Thus, like their rural sisters, women in towns expected to carry out similar 'domestic' functions. These
responsibilities were crucial to the successful survival of the family. In forming
a marriage partnership, society took for granted that a young woman would see
this as her province and would have the skills to carry it out. While romantic
love may have been increasingly a part of marital decisions, women's skills,
work capacity, dowry and potential fertility were all assets so that the economic
functioning of households throughout Europe depended on the active role of a
wife. Women were expected to be able to earn sufficient for their own maintenance, as the often quoted *Present for a Servant Maid* made explicit:

> Consider, my dear girl, that you have no portions and endeavour to
> supply the deficiencies of fortune by mind. You cannot expect to
> marry in such a manner as neither of you shall have occasion to work,
> and none but a fool will take a wife whose bread must be earned solely
> by his labour and who will contribute nothing towards it herself.[20]

German and French proverbs emphasize the point: not only was a woman
expected to be able to support herself by her labour, the household depended
on her. Sogner, writing about Sweden, also emphasized the importance of their
contribution to the 'crew'. Where a household depended on wages, women's provisioning was the difference between poverty and subsistence, or subsistence

and comfort. In desperate circumstances, women provided by begging or organizing their children to appeal for alms. The woman became the pivotal force in an 'economy of expedients'. Hufton describes virtually formalized instances of mothers organizing children's begging, either regularly or sporadically, in town and country throughout France. 'The importance of the mother within the family economy was immense; her death or incapacity could cause a family to cross the narrow but extremely meaningful barrier between poverty and destitution'.[21]

The larger the town and the greater the commercialization of the market, the less likely it was that a woman produced directly for the family. Research on early eighteenth-century Britain shows an overall increase in the ownership of household goods across the population, a trend that operated throughout Europe where patterns of trading and manufacturing increasingly differentiated. The ability to provide more domestic necessities from the marketplace touched all classes, and historians credited women with stimulating demand, even on a mundane level. Their desire for small consumer goods like metal pins and buttons expanded the domestic market for such products and in turn created more work for women who produced them. The implications for all women were that more goods were available and where money existed to buy them, women were central to organizing the consuming strategies of the family. At the same time, historians do not agree on the effect on women. McKendrick believed that commercialization allowed women to meet their domestic responsibilities with less personal contribution.[22] Arguably, purchasing goods and services freed them for other activities and could be one of the strategies women used to balance their work and time. Yet Berg's argument is persuasive, pointing out that the incursion of a consumer economy changed the standards required of housekeeping, putting more demands on women.

> The housewifery that became associated with the proliferation of home-produced and purchased commodities also became an indicator of a family's status. A woman's labour power was an important asset, but her consuming power for the household was also an asset of rising significance in the eighteenth century.[23]

It became a powerful part of household management, which might free women from some of the more onerous tasks and might have added to their household strategies, but at the same time it added another durable element to the redefinition of women's role.

Another consideration was the level of women's non-domestic responsibilities, that is, work specifically for the marketplace, since rural and urban women had to balance demands on their time. Although domestic duties were seen as a central part of her life, she was still expected to contribute to the workforce as and when required. Thus women developed a variety of strategies, including hiring servants and putting babies to wetnurses when the premium on their time meant that they had to pass on domestic responsibilities in the search for a living. Thompson's discussion of time in relation to life, work and leisure is helpful in thinking about the character of women's lives. He suggests that 'a community in which task-orientation is common appears to show least demarcation between 'work' and 'life'. Social intercourse and labour are inter-mingled'.[24] Where the sense of time is more flexible, so is the approach to work. In this women were not unique. But in several respects women's work was the most task-orientated of all, so that the working day expanded to meet the needs of the work. Because of the character of domestic duties, women were more likely to respond to industrial work in the same way, taking on task work, rather than jobs defined by time. Yet, it is clearly an oversimplification to state, 'Because women's work in the pre-industrial world had been home-based and largely seasonal, work had not seriously interfered with women's responsibilities in childcare and household duties'.[25] The literature is replete with descriptions of women's flexibility and the necessity of juggling a range of tasks, insofar as some work was so unspecialized as to be virtually invisible.

HOUSEHOLD, LIFE CYCLE AND FEMALE UPBRINGING

Clearly, women's domestic tasks, as with all their work, depended on their place in the life cycle. Young girls were expected to assist in the household, as they were able, perhaps looking after still younger children and to balance 'domestic' work with field or industrial tasks. Schlumbohm indicates that fam-ilies expected German daughters to work harder and from an earlier age than sons, helping in the household and the family business. This is in keeping with evidence from England, where schools regularly set girls 'work', especially 'female' work including needleworking, laundering and cleaning, while boys usually were free from such tasks. Primary responsibility for training girls in the tasks needed as adults lay with mothers, assisted by sisters, aunts, servants and other females in the household. Girls' upbringing usually included 'train-ing' in domestic skills, though for the most part it was not formalized, nor was it glorified by the term 'training'. However, the prominence of 'housewifery' in English apprenticeship records bears witness to the fact that society considered it normal and expected girls to learn these essential tasks. A farm *servante* in France found that her period of service was a superb training for the aspirant farmer's wife, as did her English cousin.[26]

Young women expected similar tasks, or moved directly into the world of paid work. Most children lived in their familial home for at least the first ten to fourteen years of life, though several routes to adulthood are identifiable. Figure 2.1 illustrates typical life-cycle patterns for English working-class children. Girls tended to follow the paths in columns A, D and E while all five patterns represented typical avenues for boys. Probably the majority of girls from labouring families followed the pattern in column E, spending their

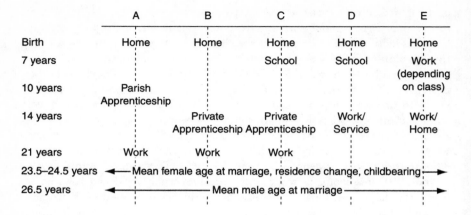

	A	B	C	D	E
Birth	Home	Home	Home	Home	Home
7 years			School	School	Work (depending on class)
10 years	Parish Apprenticeship				
14 years		Private Apprenticeship	Private Apprenticeship	Work/ Service	Work/ Home
21 years	Work	Work	Work		
23.5–24.5 years	◄── Mean female age at marriage, residence change, childbearing ──►				
26.5 years	◄──────── Mean male age at marriage ────────►				

Figure 2.1 Educative life cycles, c. 1780[27]

formative years and much of their early working life in the familial home. Many left home by fourteen, going into farm or domestic service, apprenticeship or other work. But still one-third to a half probably remained until marriage. Patterns varied in different economic and social settings. Hufton, for example, suggests that the town girl in France was less likely to leave home to work than her country cousin, partly because she could expect to be brought up in the family business.[28] They frequently found they had similar domestic tasks in another's house, as did women who never married. This was obviously true of girls who went into domestic service or apprentices in housewifery, but even those hired or apprenticed to agriculture or domestic manufacture frequently shared household work. As domestic service probably was the largest employer of women throughout the century and a stage of life for very large numbers of females, domestic obligations continued to be highly significant for them.

The end of service and marriage represented the transition to adulthood and on marriage most women acquired the responsibility of their own home.[29] Married women were primarily responsible for housekeeping and household-management duties. However, their level of independence depended on family structure. With high population turnover, most households may well have been hybrid families of parents, step- and foster-children and their own off-spring, at some time. A newlywed wife was likely to gain authority in the house only if the mother-in-law relinquished it or if the young couple set up a separate household. Families from the Béarn in the Pyrenees illustrate a mother-in-law's authority, so that the ritual of serving the soup and her reminders that 'I have not yet given you the ladle' demonstrated female rank in the household.[30] Regardless of pecking order, married women were expected, and would expect, to share responsibility for supplying the household and feeding men and children.

Mothers acquired particular responsibility for children and there is little doubt that contemporaries believed it was 'women's work', though not necessarily the mother's. 'In the large multiple family households of central France . . . one woman would specialize in childrearing leaving the others free for field work'.[31] The importance of childbearing and rearing to women was part of the context of women's lives; in many respects, a reciprocal part. The seeds of change in childcare attitudes had already been sown, with a growing interest in the social investment represented by children. The way a woman cared for her children became a key aspect of defining her as a woman. At one time, historians charged industrialization with creating child labour and exploiting children. Research has discredited that view and with it the emotionalism that infused it, while emphasizing the importance of child labour in earlier periods, usually as part of a family economy. However, some, like Shorter and Stone, claimed that parents were uncaring, with children's lives of little relative value, promoting a distinct feeling that they assessed childcare against a 'modern' model.[32] Such views give little attention to the circumstances and culture of the family that demanded a different set of values and decisions. The realities of women's lives are a necessary caveat to shifts in attitudes towards childcare. If feeding the whole family was the key to family life, mothers' strategies may have led them to decisions that 'modernists' like Shorter condemned. If children did not receive the level of attention and care that today's world asks of mothers, it does not mean that they did not care for their children. They measured the character of emotionality differently and priorities were, in some ways, far more basic. Emotional ties were not essential for the survival of marriage and family, and love and affection were not necessarily opposed to economic and social purposes of marriage even if these appeared of primary importance.

Nevertheless, the presence of children at home shaped decisions women made about rationing their time and energies. In England, the mean number of live births per woman hovered at 6.83 throughout the period 1550–1800, though Laslett's household data show an average of 2.3 to 3.5 children in households, depending on social status.[33] Because of the high unfulfilled pregnancy and child mortality rates, such figures underrate women's time commitment. Irrespective of whether a child was born live, pregnancy affected the potential mother's time, energy and approach to daily work. If a child survived, the early years were the period of maximum dependency. So even with stillbirth, infant and child mortality, many women had greater childcare responsibilities than household figures imply. However, in a period of high child employment at home or in other households, the image of very large numbers of resident children requiring full maintenance is somewhat overstated. These points converge in families of the poor, who had potentially higher mortality, a greater need to send children out to work and probably fewer live births due to maternal health. Childcare also involved far less concentration of time. Schlumbohm argues that urban mothers worked so hard that they had little time for it. Frevert echoes this image for the rural

Hausmutter working incessantly in and around the house: 'Mothers had neither the time nor did they see the need to treat children in any particular manner.' Thus a mother allocated little time to activities specifically connected with childrearing. Wetnursing is at the forefront of this debate. Far less common in Germany or Britain, in France it developed into a well-established business. Less frequently used in rural areas than in urban ones, the pattern was one of putting town children to country nurses. Workshop needs dictated that urban working mothers could not be spared for the demands of nursing and early childcare. Thus wetnursing was one strategy a mother employed to balance her roles. Significantly, wetnursing increased among urban classes, particularly in France, at the same time as Enlightenment thought, which placed high value on mothering, led to diminished use by middle and upper classes.[34]

Widows' positions depended on whether they lived alone, had children or were themselves head of a household, perhaps living with adult children. In a small English study, Wall found that the vast majority of women over forty-five who had never married lived alone as lodgers or householders. However, in Lichfield, Staffordshire, nine of the twenty women also had co-resident children, which serves as a reminder 'that a certain proportion . . . of never married women still had a familial role'. Similarly some 71 to 78 per cent of widows headed their own household, although approximately 40 per cent had no resident children. These women still had household duties. Wall suggests girls were more likely to stay at home with widowed mothers than boys, further supporting the link between mothers and daughters and the building of reciprocal female networks, while Hufton cites this as one version of 'female clustering' for mutual economic support. Hufton's evidence from the *bureaux de charité* for eighteenth-century France suggests approximately four children reliant on each widowed mother recorded.[35] Thus, not only did widows and unmarried women have their own domestic needs to think about, they had many of the same responsibilities for children as married women. Motherhood was not only a married state.

Significant to understanding women's work is recognizing the importance of 'strategies'. There is little doubt that the household, and women in particular, juggled labour needs and time to provide the most efficient use of their labour and skills. When a woman's domestic obligations were at a maximum, and when she could not be substituted, her participation in other work was curtailed. When industrial demands were of prime importance, and when she could use others in her place, she was likely to do so. With prime responsibility for maintenance of the 'home', women were often central to deciding household strategies, above and beyond the decisions they made about their own time and tasks. They were pivotal in determining roles of children, while there is evidence of women acting as mediators for men and the family in relations with putting-out merchants. In this sense, one could say they held power of a significant kind. Probably the key was their expected domestic responsibilities, and the importance of survival to the whole unit.

WOMEN AS FARM WORKERS

Continuities are a striking feature of women's agricultural labour, so that much appeared to stay the same. The agricultural community operated within an implicit value system subject to seasonal rhythms of work. Anderson and Zinsser argue in 'The Constants of the Peasant Woman's World: The Ninth to the Twentieth Centuries' that 'generation after generation their lives bear an awesome similarity to each other'.[36] While there is an important truth in this view, it also elides the real changes in women's experience that came about because of altered land practices, rotations and crops, the significance of technologies and tools which carry with them gendered constructs, and the relevance of commercialization of agriculture throughout Europe. And it overlooks the shifting social and ideological context in which perceptions of women's jobs change. The division of labour in agriculture is not universal; it varies over time and by economic structures, cultures and regions. Trends apparent in the eighteenth century clearly overlap into the nineteenth, highlighting the problem of periodization referred to at the outset, as well as emphasizing the significance of regional variation. Many changes affecting women's work came later in some areas than in others. For example, Snell places the most important shifts in the south-east of England firmly in the eighteenth century, while Lee shows that many of the same issues belong to nineteenth-century Germanic regions. Pollard and Braudel also stress the variety of patterns of change and variation in timing and conditions.[37] Important aspects of agricultural change such as introduction of new crops, changes in hand tools and enclosure of farms affected women differently depending upon their timing. Although all types of holding hired maidservants, the work which women did in the fields varied from pastoral to arable economies. Landowning patterns affected labour patterns with implications for women, particularly the application of labour service.

Farmers' wives shared in the activities and management of the farm which for them tended to focus on the house and domestic management. In many areas of France, for example, they were co-fermiers, signing legal undertakings, and selling and buying land jointly. Such was the case in Comtat, Brittany, Angoumois and the Ile de France; in Barèges and the Auvergne, a man moved into the woman's home. In other areas, particularly where Roman law prevailed, such as Normandy or Languedoc, women could be virtually servants. Frevert also confirmed partnerships in German rural families. Women shared in the work of the farm, cultivated the gardens and took responsibility for fruit, vegetables, poultry and small livestock, as described above. They prepared goods for market and took advantage of gleaning and common rights. Income from their responsibilities for the stock and gardening, together with wages from haymaking and harvest, meant that they might make as much towards housekeeping as their husbands did.[38] Single females in better-off rural families assisted their mothers, learning tasks they needed to know when they married. Peasant and cottager wives also were active in household management and farm work, but were far more likely to work in fields. Thus, the level of women's potential labour contribution on the land was often related to the size of the holding and the prosperity of the farm. A broad generalization suggests that the larger and more prosperous the farm, the more the wife was able to manage servants and day labour instead of engaging directly in field work. On smaller or poorer farms, wives' and daughters' work was far more likely to be similar to servants' and day labourers' work.

Across Europe, female farm servants and day labourers undertook a wide range of tasks in agriculture including field work. Although their work range was probably similar, the experience of these two groups had significant differences. For the servant and apprentice, the position was temporary and usually marked a transition from childhood to adulthood. They probably began the life of hired or apprenticed labour in their early teens and remained until their early twenties. At the end of her time, an apprentice might work in day labour or as a servant for a couple of years, but was expected to marry by her mid-twenties and be working on a holding with her husband. Female farm servants came from single daughters of small farmers or cottagers, saving for some years to set themselves up on a smallholding. The end of farm service tended to coincide with marriage, and often with pregnancy, and marked an important female rite of passage. Importantly, the period of service acted as a transition from the child to the woman who would have her own farming household to oversee and contribute to.[39]

As a farm *servante* a French girl could tend poultry, prepare cheese and butter, turn haymaker and gleaner, cook meals, carry food and drink to workers in the fields, tend vegetables, carry water to sheep terraces, wash and mend clothes and fill in any remaining time with domestic industry or with extracting oil from nuts, picking oakum or chestnuts, plaiting onions or garlic. The farm servant in England, Scotland or Germanic countries performed much the same tasks, marked only by differences in cultural traditions and crops. For example, a Scottish female servant in the north-east expected to be an 'in and out' girl, working at kitchen and dairying tasks and undertaking general farm work, and Pinchbeck describes similar work for English servants, with more emphasis on field work. They often worked alongside the mistress with their work mirroring hers in its diffused character rather than being focused on specific tasks. That so many women were farm servants at some time in their lives is notable because women were to lose this productive role as farm service declined. Kussmaul shows that women were a much higher proportion of farm servants than of full-time labourers, and, indeed, several accounts indicate that female day labour was a phenomenon created by changes in agriculture during the century. In the open field system, women infrequently appeared as day labourers, except at harvest and haymaking. In Sweden 60 per cent of servants were female, though Sogner includes rural domestic servants in this figure. Ankarloo confirms that females in agricultural service were always more numerous than men, and it was a normal occurrence for rural Scottish girls.[40]

Day labour was part time, usually seasonal and could occur at any point in the life cycle, instead of marking a period of transition. Abensour noted that female day labourers could be itinerant, travelling around the countryside working the grape harvest, mowing hay and tending vines, as required. In the rural lowlands of Scotland, much day labour came from seasonal hirings of girls from the Western Highlands. Many female day labourers, however, were dependants of male farmers, whether owner, tenant or cottager. Throughout Europe, married women's work was tied to the character of their husbands' tenancies and although men were personally free, landlords could oblige them to provide female labour as part of their agreement. In Scotland, it was essential for an adult male agricultural worker to bring a woman, usually his wife, to a hiring with him since farmers relied on this supplementary labour at particular times of the year, such as the harvest. It was customary for the labour of their wives to pay labourers' rent in the south-east and north-east of Scotland. In Midlothian, such women were obliged to work at shearing, carrying to the thresher, mucking-out, muck-spreading, carting and winnowing as rent payment. In Northumberland, 'They each had to provide a woman to do certain work, e.g. weeding and haymaking, at fixed wages; and when corn was threshed . . . a woman must be there to see to the winnowing of the grain'. In Westmorland, married labourers were provided with houses, gardens and a plot of ground plus higher wages than those who were not married.[41]

In continental areas with labour service, serfs, male and female alike, still paid feudal dues to acknowledge the overlordship of a landlord. Agriculture in much of France, eastern Netherlands and Germanic countries, for example, still relied on feudal service, obligations that did not disappear until after the French Revolution in many places and well into the nineteenth century for much of Germany. In Eastern Europe, remission was even later, and Russian emancipation in 1861 did not free men and women from a range of obligations. Labour service was common if not universal and frequently onerous. Wide variations existed, but women were frequently sent as part of the labour service, perhaps one to three days a week, and in Denmark even landless labourers had to provide the labour of wives for sixty to seventy days a year. In Germany, Sweden and Finland the practice remained of sending daughters into service, not to save for a dowry, but to pay parents' feudal dues. In north-west Germany wives could be required to contribute twenty to twenty-five days of agricultural work as labour rent, as in Scotland. These days were often concentrated in haying, planting and harvest seasons, leaving little time for peasants to work their own land. In many cases, the main work of the household plot fell to those women whose service demands were usually lighter. Women's labour service involved manual work, but they could also carry out domestic tasks and spin.[42]

Women's contribution was valued, and the economic functioning of the holding was largely dependent on wives' active role. A Bremen proverb underlines their importance: 'Wo die Frau arbeitet nicht, da gibt kein brodt im

Hause [Where the wife does not work, there is no bread in the house].' Much of women's work was highly skilled and depended on the possession of considerable knowledge. Particularly, dairying was recognized as a craft and involved passing on the skills and 'mysteries' associated with it from mother to daughter. Similarly, the central importance of a wife to the operation of a farm led to repeated petitions to remarry by widowers from seventeenth-century Württemberg and is demonstrated by the rapidity with which many men did so. In Sweden, Sogner found that over half of widowers remarried, and almost all the younger ones, those most likely to require additional labour and a housekeeper and mother for children. As she says, 'for all households to function well, ideally they had to have a full "crew"'.[43]

GENDER AND THE TASKS OF THE FIELD

Well before the eighteenth century, although there was a great deal of task-sharing and jobs often were 'complementary', certain field tasks were becoming identified as women's work and others as men's. The pattern and distribution of their work and the crops with which they worked, however, were subject to local, regional and gender-specific differentiation. Haymaking, hoeing, harrowing, winnowing, planting and spreading manure were usually identified with women. Commonly they were responsible for root-crop planting and cultivation, from soil preparation, hoeing and weeding to digging up, as records from Germany, Scotland and England indicate. They also processed crops after harvest, such as binding barley and threshing grain. In Norway women sowed the grain 'because people felt this would ensure a bigger harvest'. In grape-growing areas of France and Italy, women trimmed young vines in early summer. They also tended olives and undertook most of the agricultural work associated with silk production. In much of Southern Europe drought was common, and women could spend three to five hours daily watering crops by hand or carrying water to cattle and other livestock in the summer. They also ploughed, carried soil, loaded and spread dung and carted produce.[44]

Pinchbeck plays down the field work of wives, but says that 'women servants in husbandry seem to have shared the heaviest work of the farm, few tasks if any being considered too severe for them'. Mary Puddicombe recounted:

> I used to be employed when I was apprenticed in driving bullocks to the field and fetching them in again; cleaning out their houses, and bedding them up; washing potatoes and boiling them up for pigs; milking; in the field leading horses or bullocks to plough . . . then I was employed in mixing lime to spread, digging potatoes, digging and pulling turnips and anything that came to hand like a boy. I reaped a little, not much; loaded pack horses; went out with horses for furze.[45]

Also gleaning or 'leasing' remained an important traditional activity for women and children across Europe. Rather than a marginal activity, King argues that it contributed up to one-eighth of household earnings in grain-growing parishes.[46]

Despite this array of tasks, there were common features in that women were associated with labour-intensive hand work. They tended to use hand tools and not to work with animals, although tending animals clearly fell into their domain. They also performed many jobs as assistants to men, such as dung spreading, while harvesting and haying involved men and women in complementary roles. Because of the heavy reliance on women in hand operations, even as changes took place, the limited mechanization and labour-intensive character of farming meant they continued to be important in the labour force. Women had a particularly seasonal role, so that throughout Europe women, who might normally spend relatively little time in field work or farming, joined the haying and harvest. In the Caux, as in other parts of France, a large labour force of men, women and children came out at the end of summer, to cut and gather grain crops, but the rest of the year men mainly carried out field work. In Eastern Europe, people came from the hills and mountains to the plains; Scottish, Welsh and Irish labour joined in the English harvest.[47] Within harvesting activity, however, tasks were allocated on the basis of sex and age.

Women clearly dominated dairying throughout the century. As Sommestad says, 'The idea that milk belongs to the female sphere pervaded many pre-industrial cultures,' and Valenze similarly comments, 'As a ubiquitous domestic enterprise, dairying was women's work in the eighteenth-century rural world.' Sommestad draws out the association of female biology and culture with milk and milking in Sweden, while Valenze confirms that in England women were closely associated with 'the realm of nature and superstition'. They were linked with the cow and especially with the process of lactation in many cultures. In Scandinavia, 'the feminine coding of dairying was particularly strong' and the Irish counted women's dowries in cows. However, Segalen argues that in France 'the cow is not an incontestably feminine animal in the way that the chicken is'. In small scale, family dairies of north-west and south-west England, parts of Suffolk and Yorkshire, south-west Scotland and in Sweden and Denmark, female family members were the fulcrum on which dairying operated. Even when it became a business on an eighteenth-century farm, women retained their association with the dairy, and farmers valued dairymaids highly for their skill and expertise.[48]

The division of labour between the sexes in agriculture was not automatic or, strictly speaking, *natural*, but commonly there was a notional division into male and female duties, often more customary and ideal than real. Wiesner argues that task allocation rested partly on differences in physical strength, in that men were more likely to undertake tasks that required upper-body strength, such as the use of the scythe or ploughing. Women on the other hand were likely to undertake tasks located closer to the home and which they could

interrupt with childcare and household responsibilities.[49] Cultural difference
and custom also played a part in determining role distribution. What in one
area were seen as women's tasks were in another area seen as men's. Harvesting,
ploughing and threshing are discussed more fully below, but it is clear from
most accounts that women assisted rather than taking charge of an operation,
although task demarcation was variable across cultures and regions. As Lee
says,

> Given that the gender-specific division of agricultural work seldom
> reflected bio-social demands, and women were often to be found carry-
> ing out heavy physical work on the land, the precise allocation of agri-
> cultural tasks evinced a high degree of variance, both over time and
> space . . . According to Wiegelmann, 'work custom', which was itself
> highly mutable, often determined the choice of agricultural imple-
> ments, and therefore the gender-specific allocation of labour tasks.[50]

The distribution of tasks and the resultant sexual division of labour probably
fluctuated considerably over a family life cycle and was affected by the priority
assigned to a task and the availability of labour of either sex, so that a great
deal of work appears to have been substitutable. In better times, there is also
evidence that women avoided some of the more unpleasant tasks.[51]

Many women's activities were supervised by men, assisting men, or in place
of men. Threshing is one such activity where different economies have allocated it to one sex or the other, or seen it as shared. In Scotland, for example,
farmers did not employ women as threshers by the beginning of the nineteenth
century, while a contemporary account from Germany includes threshing
among women's tasks.[52] Indeed many *tasks* make up the *activity*, a distinction
that may provide a key to disentangling gender-specific division of labour in
agriculture. Arthur Young's description of threshing in the Languedoc is
evocative:

> The corn is all stacked around a firm dry spot, where great numbers of
> mules and horses are driven on a trot around a centre, a woman hold-
> ing the reins and another, or a girl or two, with whips drive; the men
> supply and clear the floor; other parties are dressing, by throwing the
> corn into the air for the wind to blow away the chaff.[53]

The passage does not indicate the sex of the winnowers, but women and girls
clearly took part in threshing and working with horses, two activities usually
associated with men. These examples illustrate that gender-specific division of
labour was not necessarily uniform. They also demonstrate regional variation
and serve as a reminder that tasks within an activity may be distributed differently. Furthermore, they reinforce the importance of using all hands and the
complementarity of work.

Ploughing, hedging and ditching as well as 'specialist' jobs, like shepherd-
ing, cartering and stockman, were seen as male prerogatives. The latter, like
long-distance marketing, required long absences from home and may have
become associated with men for that reason. If so, they reinforce female identity with home and hearth. In general, field work was considered male and
work nearer the home female, but the exceptions indicated above are sufficient
to make this an ideal rather than a reality. Where it has significance is where
status depends on what is seen as one's social role as ascribed by the work one
does. It is dangerous to fall into the trap of seeing women's agricultural work
as unskilled and men's as skilled. It would be easy to suggest this since so
many women's jobs appear to have been 'menial' or 'general' while men tended
to control more sophisticated tools and hold down the more 'specialized' positions. Many jobs carried out by both sexes were unskilled, in others the skills
were undervalued, such as the dexterity required to weed root crops with a hoe
without damage. Male work is often associated with status either in the sense
of the prestige or power carried by the job, or because the task was better paid.

Two aspects of field work which are therefore particularly interesting as
gender-specific tasks are ploughing and cutting grain. Ploughing tended to be
seen as men's work, as did mowing with the scythe, both among the more
highly paid tasks, while reaping with the sickle became identified with
women. In the north-east of Scotland and France 'horse work' was always
assumed to be men's work, and as farmers used horses more regularly, the specialized ploughman became more prominent. As the two-horse plough came
into use, the specialist horsemen who operated it assumed a higher status in a
job from which farmers excluded women. Throughout Blum's discussion of
ploughing on the continent, he refers exclusively to the 'plowman' or the peasant, by which he appears to mean a male. These ploughs could be rudimentary
and did not always rely on horse power, so the status derived from working
with horses was not always present. Women were not excluded for lack of ability. Certainly women did use ploughs. In 1794, Pringle reported in
Westmoreland that women drove teams of three and four with harrows or
ploughs, while Clarke on a tour through the south of England, Wales and
Ireland claimed it was common to see females driving the plough. In the eighteenth century, most German women were excluded from ploughing, wood
cutting and long-distance transportation of produce, though they ploughed in
the north. They may have assisted men, leading horses while men manoeuvred
the ploughshare, as described by Segalen for nineteenth-century France. The
dominance of men in ploughing does not, in any case, prove that women were
unable to plough, nor that there was anything intrinsic in the activity that prevented women from carrying it out.[54]

The increasing use of the scythe instead of the sickle for harvesting grain
meant that women reapers were increasingly replaced by men. The story
belongs primarily to the end of the eighteenth century and the early nineteenth and is taken up in more detail later. However, it is worth noting the

gendered allocation of tasks already existed in the eighteenth century, so that women became identified with the sickle, though men used it, and the scythe, a larger, heavier instrument, became identified with men. Accounts from Germany, Scotland, England as well as European surveys always refer to men using the scythe, citing the heaviness and size of the tool as key factors in barring women. Contemporaries and historians often argued that the heaviness of the plough and scythe required the strength of men to manipulate them successfully. Shorter thus writes, 'spading and ploughing the fields was too much for women to manage as a rule – great strength being necessary to maneuver a Norfolk plow behind a team of percherons'. Goody also sees physical imperatives at the root of male assumption of ploughing as well as of male control of large livestock in primitive societies, though time required away from home for herding may have partly accounted for this. This does not tally with female responsibility for dairying, however, since women not only had to manage the cows to milk and tend them, but frequently spent time away from home in highland regions where cows were put to summer pasture. Roberts maintains that the 'greater ease with which a man could manoeuvre the plough, together perhaps with the inherited association of men with stock-herding, placed greater emphasis on the value of strength'. In describing the transition to the scythe in eighteenth- and nineteenth-century Europe, he says, 'The increased size and weight of the scythe emphasized the strength and stature required of the mower, effectively confining its use to the strongest men.'[55]

Strength becomes confused with notions of skill and status and gender. The association of women with weakness was not necessarily a biological notion, since the persistence of woman as the 'weaker vessel' was as much an ideological construction as it was physical. We have seen how the idea of woman was changing and that the conception of the female as weaker and more 'sensible' (i.e. sensitive), was becoming firmly bedded into eighteenth-century thought. The resurgence of these notions with particular connotations for women's work had an impact upon labouring women, shaping ideas about what kind of labour was suitable. Pringle's much quoted comment at the end of the eighteenth century marks a new trend, but also has to be recognized as a bourgeois comment on the working female: 'It is not uncommon to see, sweating at the dung-cart, a girl whose elegant features and delicate nicely proportioned limbs, seemingly but ill accord with such rough employment.' Marshall was reluctant to hire females because 'of their propensity to waste time in gossip', but farming manuals as a whole during the century did not disapprove of women working at a wide range of tasks.[56] At the same time, a gender-specific division of labour existed with indications that it was becoming more pronounced, partly as a result of economic change. Ideological shifts also played their part, justifying changes that diminished the value of female contribution while designating the more prized and better-paid jobs for men.

A number of factors led women to assume a broad spectrum of agricultural tasks, with the underlying feature being the need to maintain the holding and sustain the household. Male absence was a fundamental reason for women taking on work which custom designated as male. Remaining European seigniorial labour services deprived peasant families of male labour at crucial times of the year, so that females took responsibility for tasks on the peasant holding. Seasonal labour migration all over Europe frequently left wives to take on the full range of tasks so that their own holding remained productive. Men from parts of Germany went to Holland or Saxony; peasants from Burgundy went to Brie for the grain harvest, returning home for the grape harvest. Also if unmarried sons worked away from the immediate vicinity, sisters may have assumed the customary tasks of the farm labourer.[57] Increased male mobility, either through military conscription or as a result of geographical expansion of markets, probably reinforced women's involvement in agricultural tasks. Therefore, women certainly did 'male' work either as substitutes or for pay. It is notable that throughout historians' discussion of 'male absence', there is an assumption that they were *his* duties to be taken on temporarily by the females of the household, besides their own work. Clearly the woman was able to carry out this wide range of tasks, and the division of labour created a high degree of complementarity as well as allowing short-term substitution of one partner for the other as required. Sexual division of labour rarely relied purely on physical capacity, since women often carried out heavy work on the land. However, customary practices and ideas about gender and appropriate roles were instrumental in delineating tasks as male work and female work.

The issue of wages is extraordinarily fraught, not only by factors of inflation and prices, but by the extent to which labourers and servants received all or part of their earnings in kind, especially room and board, or a cottage and allotment, and by the requirement to provide a female worker for no wages. Nevertheless, a few comparisons may prove suggestive. Kussmaul's survey of servants' hirings shows that from the sixteenth through to the eighteenth century, female servants' wages averaged less than males' in the ratio of 1 to 0.60, and between 1750 and 1800, in Spalding, Lincolnshire women's wages were less than males' in a ratio of 1 to 0.44. For the period 1751–1836 Snell shows women's wages to have been two-thirds to one-half of men's throughout southeast England. In these arable counties, they increasingly tended to diverge, while in south-western pastoral counties, areas where dairying was prominent, women's wages were often higher than men's. In the Scottish Borders around 1800, a female servant received food and lodging and from £3 to £5 a year depending on where she worked, while a male servant received between £6 to £10, with room and board and his laundry.[58] Differentials represented conceptions of women and men, which were ingrained by the eighteenth century. Men were perceived as workers who needed to support the family and the reproductive force of the community. Women were seen as assistants, subordinate and supplementary. Their work was also casual, in that their tasks were already becoming seen as part time. Women were viewed as temporary workers and men as permanent ones, together with differentials in status implied by that distinction. The picture that emerges is one of overlapping gender-specific boundaries and the application of divisions of labour that were frequently affected by local and regional factors including work custom, the dominant cultivation pattern and the structure of landholding. These boundaries were influenced by new work customs derived from shifting ideas, availability of male labour and changes which took place in cultivation patterns, the structure of land usage and the level of specialization.

3

MAKING, SELLING, SERVING

THE VERLAGSYSTEM AND PROTO-INDUSTRY

One of the key changes in the economy was an apparent shift in the relative importance of agriculture and industry. Significant growth in manufacturing in the eighteenth century resulted largely from a rapid increase in rural industries organized as 'dispersed manufactures'. These were located in agricultural areas with easy access to local urban or international markets. They usually required a higher degree of organization and larger capitalization, especially supplies of materials, than small-scale handicrafts and tended to take advantage of underutilized rural labour, especially women. Because of networks and urban/rural links which were forged, the system proved to be durable, lasting well after other modes of manufacture dominated. Historians have long recognized the significance of rural crafts and workshop production, and the British 'putting-out' or Germanic '*Verlag*' system controlled by a merchant or *Verleger*. However, in 1972, Mendels characterized two stages of economic development: pre-industry and proto-industry. This set off a debate that perhaps has come full circle. Proto-industrialization is a conceptual tool to indicate the dynamism of 'pre-industrial industry' that explains and analyses the route to full-blown industrial capitalism. While it recognizes prevailing rural industries, proto-industry was a 'first phase which preceded and prepared industrialization proper'. Medick's seminal 1976 article characterized proto-industrialization as 'the close association between household production based on the family economy on the one hand, and the capitalist organization of trade, putting-out and marketing of the product on the other'. He argued that the family economy of agrarian peasantry, based on land and inheritance, underwent fundamental change in motivation and function to become the proto-industrial family economy. The essential elements were interrelationship between family structure and patterns of economic development, strategies for survival, implications for division of labour, and relationships within the household mediated by economic concerns.[1]

The challenge of the approach and the ensuing debate engendered a range of research which fruitfully opened up social and economic history and pushed the boundaries of thought in important ways. Two positive results, emphasized by Davis, are that though localized studies have made generalization difficult, they have greatly expanded our understanding of the largely uncharted geography of European enterprise. At the same time, they mark the level of change that had already taken place, dispelling the notion that industrialization took place in a static economy. Proto-industrialization deals effectively with the range of rural domestic industry and suggests the array of industrial skills available for use in more mechanized and centralized settings. But it is too narrow as a description of the economic system and of the rural economy. It does not apply to mining and most metalworking, nor necessarily reflect the diversity of rural handicrafts, nor account for the interplay between dispersed and centralized aspects of the same industry. And it is too bold as an explanation of the stages of economic development, especially as rural industry had flourished since the late middle ages; it could hardly explain the industrial revolution of the eighteenth century. In many cases proto-industry simply did not develop into industrialization. Wiltshire and Essex textile industries are cases in point. In the Languedoc dein-dustrialization followed, while in Flanders and the English West Country, factory production was slow or incomplete. As a model of labour strategies based on a 'family economy', proto-industrial theory relies on kin and ignores the frequent need for labour from outside the kinship group and those outside a household unit. For many, such as day labourers, outsiders directed and co-ordinated productive activities and in ways which frequently conflicted with the interests of labourers' families. Studies by Schlumbohm on Osnabrück linen and Gullickson on textiles in the Caux demonstrate that family production decisions and division of labour could readily deviate from a model based on price and economic considerations. The family balancing act went beyond production and consumption, and took in a range of variables such as labour, leisure, marital and industrial activities.[2] The theory, then, has raised a number of questions which impinge on the way we understand women's work and familial role. It has revealed important issues about economic development, family participation, the role of rural communities, gender relations, affections and household formation. In particular, it stimulates thinking about links between economic theory and gender studies and goes beyond an historical approach to women's work that operates only in terms of participation rates.

Throughout the century a recurring theme was the variety of organizational patterns that operated, sometimes competitively, sometimes complementarily, within the industrial landscape. Coexistence was a key feature. Large firms were accompanied by a proliferation of small producing units and the continued growth of outwork. Cottage, workshop and neophyte factory organization existed side by side and with them came different interpersonal relationships. As Hudson argued:

> By overemphasising the growth of the putting-out system and the accumulation of capital by merchant capitalists, the immense variety

of organisational and domestic structures is ignored and the corresponding diversity of accumulation and change is glossed over . . .
Considerable differences of structure are found between regions,
industries and branches of the same industry.[3]

Likewise the work discipline and the value placed on industrial time varied.
The complexity of these issues has to be recognized in order to understand
women's work and their industrial role. A commonly held view is that a transition from household to workshops and ultimately to factories disadvantaged
women, particularly married women. Linked to this is the argument that
women were disadvantaged by the time discipline that operated in workshops
and factories of Europe. There are two obvious problems. First, the transition
from home to factory did not take place in such a simplistic way. A multiplicity of forms of working went on simultaneously throughout the period, with
such factories as did exist generally smaller than their nineteenth-century successors. And one form did not lead to another. In fact, the workshop was infrequently the parent of the factory. Also many people continued to take part in
mixed working, so that there were not clear-cut boundaries about the definitions of labour either. Second, the argument assumes a common experience for
women, which was only true at the most reductionist level. Life cycle, among
other things, has to be taken into consideration.

WOMEN AND RURAL INDUSTRY

Women remained active in artisanal activities, commerce and a range of rural
crafts and businesses that were the continuance of longstanding economic traditions. At the same time, new industries required a supply of labour, and
wives and daughters of men throughout the economy, such as miners, agricultural labourers, metalworkers and traditional craftsmen, took up spinning and
other domestic industries, often in an industry different from that of their
menfolk. One could argue that given the pre-existing sexual division of labour,
proto-industries opened up lucrative opportunities for women and that the
spread of proto-industries resulted from an income-maximizing strategy. This
is particularly true where agricultural change diminished women's ability to
contribute productively. Hufton indicated that between 50 and 90 per cent of
holdings in France, depending on region, were insufficient to support even a
small family of two or three children. In the Scottish Highlands and Orkney,
small-scale subsistence agriculture rather than 'agricultural improvement' led
to women taking up commercial spinning as manufacturers penetrated the
region. In many areas where domestic industries developed, there was little
other paid work for women, as in the Caux where they took part in the fields
only at harvest time. Women engaged in cottage industries on a uniquely large
scale because of the reliance on low-paid labour. Dorothy George identified the

centrality of women's and children's roles in domestic industry, but it has taken recent research to restore women as key participants.[4] An important difference is the assertion that women had a special position in domestic industry, and yet, quite what this special position was remains clouded by the mists of the past. As Gullickson perspicaciously admits,

> We know very little about the lives of the men and women who worked in these industries, and, in particular, we know very little about the participation of women in proto-industrial production, and about how their participation or non-participation may have affected their position vis à vis men.[5]

Reliable quantitative evidence of women in eighteenth-century industry is nonexistent, leading Richards to suggest that in Britain during the pre-industrial period women's participation was a 'notional maximum', and up to about 1820, the number of jobs for women rose, even in proportion to the rising female population. Arthur Young's account of the Caux, 'farmhouses and cottages everywhere, and the cotton manufacture in all', though colourful, was essentially correct.[6]

Women dominated textiles by their numerical superiority, while textiles were the largest employers of women. In particular women were primarily the spinners of all types and qualities of yarns. Gullickson has shown that 75.5 per cent of women in the Caux were spinners, as were roughly 80 per cent of adult women who worked in Scottish linen, indicating not only the importance of spinning to these regions, but the significance of women to industry. The textile industry throughout Europe confirms this ratio, such that females appear in proportionally higher numbers than men. Thousands of women spinners are reported from Silesia, Zürich canton, Bohemia, Upper Austria, Roubaix, Artois, Picardy, Maine and Alsace spinning wool, linen and cotton.[7] Some women worked directly for putting-out manufacturers as in the Caux or much of Scotland. In the Nagold Valley, women were responsible for the supply of both the wool and the yarn, which meant they bought directly from the ducal court and spun wool for the weaver of the household, usually a husband. Others worked within a family setting in which the whole unit engaged in cloth production, as in the West Riding of Yorkshire. In Scotland, most spun for linen or woollen merchants while men farmed and fished, so that sexual division of labour was reinforced even where the whole family did not engage in domestic industry. The importance of women's role as spinners should not be underestimated because it was lower paid and of less status, for it was pivotal to textile industries. Collins has shown how significant women were to the linen industry in pre-famine Ireland, not only because the household depended on its own spinners, but because linen yarn had a ready market within the linen industry and as warps for the cotton industry. Pay for spinning did not match the scarcity of the yarn, often because custom kept prices down; since it was women's work, it was invariably cheaper. In Württemberg, the rural guild and the merchant company colluded to enforce a lower wage than demand would predict. These officials strenuously prevented putters-out from breaking the price ceiling by using the authority of ducal courts. The female culture associated with spinning is illustrated by the development of *spinnstuben*, *écreignes* or *veillées*, gatherings where women came together to spin and talk, usually in winter evenings when they could share heat and light. In the Caux, women undertook an exclusively female pilgrimage to the textile market in Bacqueville to sell their yarn.[8] Large numbers of female silk workers engaged in labour-intensive preparatory stages from emptying, washing and unravelling cocoons to classifying thread or preparing it for looms. Hufton's description of silk extraction, over a basin of nearly boiling water that dissolved the sticky substance binding threads together, makes it clear that the job was unpleasant, surrounding her with evil-smelling steam and frequently scalding her hands. However, she easily learned the job; later she learned the more skilled job of the *tireuse*, assisting a weaver on the loom, but also 'draining her physical resources to the utmost'.[9]

Artisans defined handloom weaving as a skilled activity carried out by men, but the picture is more complicated. In Württemberg, guild and local courts enforced an absolute prohibition against *single* females weaving or combing wool, yet no restrictions operated against married women working in their own home. Married women also could inherit the right to weave from husbands, though they could not pass it on to children. In the Rhineland and Saxon Oberlausitz wives might prepare warps, but so might husbands, and often husband and wife wove on one piece alternately. Throughout English woollens, males tended to be seen as weavers, though it was useful for a wife to be able to take a turn at the loom. In part it may have been demand for women as spinners that kept them from weaving, because wherever there was low demand for handspun yarn, women more frequently wove. In Essex, worsted weaving declined due to continental wars affecting the Spanish market, exacerbated by the growing popularity and availability of cotton and an unimaginative response to the industry's problems. At this point, women took up weaving.[10] Women became more identified as weavers when spinning moved from home together with increased demand for cloth. But it did not necessarily increase women's status or independence, since they often worked in flooded labour markets and in the remnants of a declining industry. Linen in the Osnabrück region is interesting for the extent to which jobs were shared, with sexual division of labour apparently non-existent. The whole family took part in each activity, the main distinction being between the mistress who wove when the rest of the household returned to the fields for the summer.

> husband, wife, children, servants and maids all spin a certain amount each day. This takes until the middle of the month of April, when the mistress of the house bleaches the spun yarn with the help of some of

the servants . . . The mistress, who is the focal point of the work, spins, weaves and bleaches, each at the correct time, as do the daughter, son, father, servant. There are no particular spinners, weavers or bleachers.[11]

This supports Medick's view of the proto-industrial family characterized by 'a rather strong degree of assimilation between the production functions of men and women'.[12]

A distinctive feature of lacemaking was that women controlled all stages of production, while in most other domestic industries women were relegated to preparatory or minor finishing tasks dependent on male merchants, while the primary worker was male, for example, the weaver, the smith, the shoemaker or the framework knitter. There were centres in Ireland, south-west and midland England, Normandy, Picardy, Flanders and Belgium. It so dominated the Velay that inspectors designated it a female economy. Married women worked on their own, hired a few servants or workers or worked with daughters. Equipment and the quantities of raw material needed were modest, requiring minimal capitalization. Despite widespread male unemployment, there was no thought of drawing men into the industry, as it was regarded 'in some way detracting from quintessential masculinity'. *Marchandes* made comfortable profits between 1730 and 1770 at the height of the trade; village women did less well, earning as little as two sous per day.[13] While today knitting is almost exclusively a female pastime associated with leisure, it has not always been so clearly gendered. Throughout stocking districts, women and children of both sexes, as well as men not otherwise employed, knitted. Knitting was part of the 'accepted armoury of skills' by which women provided for their families and was a useful 'by-occupation' for struggling peasant families, as evidence from Aberdeenshire, Orkney and Shetland suggests. However, men dominated the history of frame knitting. Men worked the frame while women seamed and stitched the stockings. Boys wound bobbins until old enough to learn to knit with their fathers. This was a classic division of labour based on the sexual hierarchies of a patriarchal society in which inferior or subsidiary tasks were allotted to women, and children were trained within the family for adult roles.[14]

If cultural identification of men with hard materials is significant, it helps explain the association of men with leather, metals, mining and pottery. Leather trades were strongly masculine, particularly shoemaking. English data show fewer than 1 per cent of females apprenticed to any leather trades. They worked primarily where a process was subdivided, and were responsible for less skilled tasks including 'closing' shoes and boots, decoration and fitting laces, with 'real' jobs retained for men. Mining and small metal trades drew heavily on women's labour, but in low-status jobs. English and Scottish women on smaller coalfields worked largely within family groups, hired and paid by male kin, primarily as drawers, pulling sledges or tubs full of coal along the pit floor, or carrying full baskets to the surface. In many areas women ceased to work down the mines as early as 1780. The putting-out sector of metalwares relied on female labour as well, such as pins and nails. Around Thiers in the Basse Auvergne, village women fixed pins to cards for distribution by peddlers. In the Pays d'Ouche the number of pinmakers increased tenfold between 1700 and 1789, while the number of piece workers in small ironware grew from 1,500 to 8,000 in the same period. They worked throughout the metal trades of the Black Country, particularly in buttonmaking and japanning where their dexterity was valued. As apprentices they appeared most often in bucklemaking and locksmithing, though in tiny numbers and it is suspected they remained as assistants to a man in most cases.[15] The language of William Hutton's observation of nailers in the Black Country in 1741 creates a mixed female image:

> In some of these shops I observed one or more females, stript of their upper garment . . . wielding the hammer with all the grace of the sex . . . struck with this novelty, I enquired, 'whether the ladies of this locality shod horses?' but was answered with a smile, 'they are nailers'.[16]

Early eighteenth-century wills indicate very few female potters, confirmed in such manufactories as Whieldon's in Burslem or Baddeley's at mid-century. Women made up about a third of the workforce at Wedgwood's at the end of the century. However, they worked as assistants in the same way as in domestic textiles, not always paid or identifiable. With a frequently remarked system of division of labour, women appear to have dominated certain tasks. They were flower-makers, painters, gilders, burnishers and scourers, and were responsible for transferring engravings on to porcelain. Hiring lists of 1810 indicate that the majority of enamellers were women. Wedgwood viewed decorating as unskilled and therefore suitable for women, saying of burnishers at the Chelsea pottery, 'I believe it is neither a secret or very curious art for Women only are employed in it'.[17] Men commonly performed the more intricate and 'artistic' tasks, although he recognized individual craftswomen. Preparation stages, mainly heavy and dirty work, were commonly male, as were shaping and throwing, the latter highly skilled.

To understand women's experience we need to appreciate that the reasons why merchants transferred work to the countryside were different from the reasons why women took part in it. The merchants' primary purpose for relocating industry from town to country was the search for cheap labour, and large numbers of women and children, needing a 'casual' income, made domestic industry attractive and lucrative to entrepreneurs. In some instances, competing demands for women's labour precipitated the drive to find cheaper labour. In Scotland in the second half of the eighteenth century, commercial spinning spread beyond the main weaving areas largely because better-paid sources of

43

employment for women enticed women from the spinning wheel into muslin embroidery, the bleachfields and ultimately the mills. To meet the need for cheap yarn, more work was put out to areas such as the Highlands and Islands. Female response to the spread of domestic industry derived from women's need for household income. This decisive marginal work effort went underpaid, going primarily to the merchant as increased profit. Entrepreneurial and market controls severely restricted female earning. Married women were particularly vulnerable since both family ties and family need drove them to 'exploit' their labour, while 'her willingness, indeed frequently dire need, to work – albeit at derisory rates – determined the general level of pay for female industrial work'. The response to increasing pressures on subsistence often drove the family to increase its work effort to maintain its subsistence income, what Medick has called 'self-exploitation'. For example, following the bad harvest of 1782, Aberdeenshire stocking knitters redoubled their efforts to maintain family income in the face of a slump in demand and competition from framework knitters and overseas workers, all of which drove prices down.[18]

New domestic industries did not on the whole require apprenticeship so that access for women was easier and they were more likely to move into them from a period of informal service or training, often at home. However, there was no clear split between guild-controlled town work and 'unregulated' rural domestic industry. The longstanding proto-industries in Württemberg operated within a system of rural guilds and corporate and entrepreneurial structures that continued to regulate much of economic, and indeed social, activity. Women working in a household under the licence of a male guild member did considerably better than independent females who had very little bargaining power. Frequently, introduction of rural industry enabled the family to stay together at home, thus increasing their options. In parts of Scotland, 'the income from spinning, knitting and especially the embroidering of muslins discouraged young girls from going into service, allowing them to remain at home and contribute to the family's income or to set up on their own'. Similarly, Gullickson argues that without wages from spinning, many *cauchois* families 'would have been forced to choose between sending sons and daughters away from home to work, making the husband/father a seasonal migrant, and moving out of the region'. Also Dunlop and Denman point out that the fact that many girls could be usefully employed in industry at home undoubtedly often prevented their being apprenticed away from home.[19] The implication, of course, is that keeping women at home and the family together was a 'good thing'.

The flexibility of female labour was one factor that attracted entrepreneurs to the countryside. It was work that could be fitted in, could be described as 'casual' and like much of women's work it was largely task orientated. As the minister at Keith-Hall, Scotland, believed, a woman could knit 'and do some little things about her house at the same time. Or she can work at her stocking while feeding her cows.'[20] Much industrial employment throughout the period was irregular for a variety of reasons, and it was the flexibility of women's labour, imposed on them by their traditional position in the secondary labour market, that permitted the survival of many industrial enterprises. Such industrial labour was regarded as a by-employment. The connection with the land remained the backdrop for domestic industries, which were identified with the supplementary earnings of women and children. This precluded them from gaining recognition as a primary source of income. Proto-industrial activities were usually added to rather than substituted for women's 'normal' work, thus increasing the intensity of their labour. As wage earning became more necessary in household strategies, women needed to earn wages, besides 'normal' chores, though a cash transfer did not always occur. Domestic industry also built on pre-existent skills and was entirely consistent with women's long-standing role as spinners.

The growth of a waged female labour force, in both town and country, throughout the eighteenth century is indisputable and consistent with an increase in wage dependency throughout the economy. In the Staffordshire potteries women's and children's earnings could more than double those of the household and Whyte claims that in Scotland relatively high wages in spinning and weaving could lead to earlier independence than day labouring or service. It is impossible to be precise about earnings in cottage industry, since rates were dependent on a number of variables, including the kind and quality of work and the type of product, and on the amount of time put in, as well as local and regional economic factors. Experienced workers earned more than beginners because they worked more quickly and with greater skill. Pinchbeck was careful to draw a distinction between women who could be considered 'full-time' workers (mainly those who were single and dependent for their sole income on spinning, for example) and those who supplemented family income and their other responsibilities with spinning, knitting or lace making (see Figure 3.1). Not only are weekly wages not comparable but their needs were different. Because women's work was primarily a facet of household economies throughout the period, the level of income rarely permitted a comfortable independent living. Across Europe, the lowest men's wages are usually higher than even the best wages for skilled women in the most profitable industries (see Figure 3.2). Hufton estimated that where both members of a couple were engaged in industry, a woman's earning power was between a third to a half of her husband's for a working day of fifteen to sixteen hours. A similar ratio applies to the relationship between the earning power of a seamstress and an artisan. In Scotland, lower female wages were the norm, and Houston suggests they had become customary, decided upon by male authorities and endorsed by the men. Hufton estimated that pay for female industrial work rarely rose above eight sous per day in France, and it could fall in the lacemaking areas of the Massif Central to less than four, equal to the price of two to three pounds of bread. Such income certainly could not both feed and house a young woman.[21] The data underline the dependence of women on men's earnings and the difficulty of an independent existence.

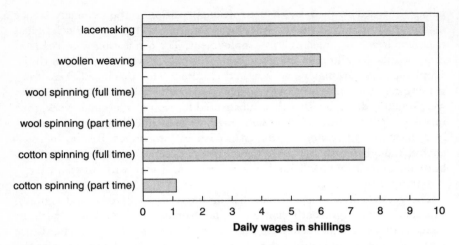

Figure 3.1 Wages of women in domestic industry in England
Sources: Eden (1797) vol. 3, p. 796; Young (1784–1815) ix, pp. 280–338, 523–24; x, pp. 554–56; xi, p. 26; Pinchbeck (1930) pp. 139–42

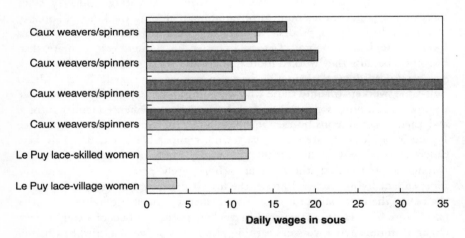

Figure 3.2 Wages in domestic industry in France (female spinners, male weavers)
Sources: Hufton (1981) p. 188 and (1975) pp. 2, 14, 16; Gullickson (1981) p. 186 and (1976) pp. 211–12

While there is every indication that an increase in domestic industry saw the employment of women in market activities on an unprecedented scale, it is more questionable whether their work became more crucial to the household than previously. A feature of domestic industry was that it operated on plentiful supplies of cheap labour, and even when there was pressure on labour, women's wages tended to remain low. This was less about the supply and

46

demand of labour and more about perceptions of women's work as cheap and low status. The low status of women's work, in spite of the acknowledged necessity and significance of cash earnings to the household, must be largely explained by their continued subordination in the family. With the increase in rural industry, there was more work available in a domestic setting. Most girls worked in a household until marriage, which on average took place earlier than in previous centuries. They then set up their own production unit, which replicated the family setting, and had their own children, probably having more of them and earlier than their mothers or grandmothers had. Thus their industrial production became even more closely associated with household formation and domestic tasks, with no division between earning activities and household duties. Although the family economy as a model was not all pervasive, a number of concepts derive from it which tended to subsume women within a specific definition of female role and obstructed their attempts to operate outside of the normative ideal. This model has at its base the belief that what men do is more important than what women do. Domestic industry, whether in country or town, brought with it a number of changes in individuals' relation to the market, but did not necessarily advantage or disadvantage women consistently. In areas such as Russia, proto-industrial activities expanded enormously without disrupting the traditional structure of the family or division of labour, so that traditional patriarchal patterns remained largely undisturbed.[22]

WOMEN IN TOWNS: THE GUILD MODEL

Throughout early modern Europe women regularly participated in the urban economy, their economic role was acknowledged, and their trading position was widely recognized. But they did not take part on equal terms with men, and the character of their work could and did vary radically. Their position in urban industrial production was gradually eroded from at least the sixteenth century, undermining their participation in high-status occupations, and it became increasingly difficult to gain access to them. Men became the artisans, while women were relegated to low-status activities. There was a steadily rising sex-ratio in the cities of Europe, and an expanding range of jobs opened to women because of urban growth and the needs of an increasing population. At the same time, aspects of division of labour and the political and economic life of many towns restricted women's access to certain trades. The extent of such constraints depended on the ability of male groups and power structures to limit women's work, which in turn depended on corporate structures. Towns not governed by guilds and corporate regulations, such as Birmingham, might have provided women more opportunities than those which were. However, women's status within a trade as well as the standing of the trade are central factors in how women related to the urban economy. The urban economy could be a minefield for women with the risk of destitution leading to prostitution, among other dangers, but it also offered opportunity. Although precarious, furnished rooms, lodging houses and networks of other women, not to mention shops and taverns with prepared food, meant that women could live alone and struggle to survive.

The legacy of guild and corporate structures maintained much of their significance. While female guilds existed, and women gained admission to some male guilds, they were essentially masculine organizations that paralleled the male life cycle, reflecting in their structure and rules male rites of passage. The effect was to link economic, social and political roles in explicit and implicit ways which had important ramifications for rank and status, but also had particular meaning for women's role in the urban society. From the fifteenth century, guilds began to impose restrictions on women's participation, derived from pressures of shifting markets and overstocked trades. For example, in Geneva, restriction of female apprentices came to a head around 1700, after which girls were not admitted to apprenticeships and it was no longer allowed to teach them *passementerie* and watchmaking. Also, a deliberate transfer of work to unregulated areas by merchant capitalists challenged guilds directly. Their response was to restrict membership further and to remove women from independent artisanship. There were two features. First, guilds were becoming more restrictive and protective of what they saw as their own interests. Although not explicitly gender based, this detrimental policy affected women's position within guilds. Second, identification of women with dishonourable work such as domestic production, and the recurrent notion of women as casual labour, housewives and mothers, and a growing hostility to women's work, contributed to specific restrictions against them.[23]

Many females entered mixed guilds as inheritors of male members. In Paris, Dijon and Caen, where guilds allowed women independent entry, they were identified as *marchandes* and *apprentisses* but tacitly excluded from office. They usually belonged to trades that included sufficient numbers of women for them to be recognized, though not on an equal footing with males, such as drapers, hostellers, goldsmiths, grain merchants and fishmongers. Indeed, women were most prominent in guilds in which selling constituted an important element, acknowledging women's marketing role. Similarly, female guilds reflected areas of the economy where women had an established footing, such as seamstresses, spinners, lingerie-makers, dressmakers, embroiderers, milliners: trades that became 'feminine'. However, others were less obviously gendered, such as hemp and flax combers, hosiers, fan-, wig- and cloak-makers. Notably, having adopted guild organization, female guilds operated in the same way as male guilds regarding apprentices, fees and passing on trades, usually restricting the position of *maîtresse* to daughters of *maîtresses*.[24]

Alongside guild restrictions, journeymen were usurping tasks like preparing and finishing which had been masters' wives' and daughters' work, thus removing them from production and further identifying females with cleaning, cooking, maintenance and selling. Also, increasing gender identification of work within guilds effectively marginalized many women's activities. For example, Abensour cites the tailors' guild, which relegated seamstresses to making undergarments, reserving to themselves the right to make skirts and bodices. On the other hand, women sometimes found an opportunity to insert themselves into a male-dominated trade with changes in fashion. With the arrival of the mantua, a loose-fitting garment requiring little fitting, women managed to become the mantuamakers and their successors, the dressmakers. Ironically, the male response was to try to force them to join the guild, which they refused to do. In many towns, women's response was to retreat from artisanal work, either into household activities, or into non-guild trades associated with the putting-out system, such as lacemakers of Antwerp and Caen, or into marketing, hawking and charring, or sewing and laundering which a woman could do at home.[25]

Both guilds and workshops were patriarchal institutions, which controlled trade, so that access was usually through women's relationship to the head of household or workshop, and they operated without full rights.[26] Most commonly, masters' widows were allowed to continue operating their husband's trade, but regulations varied as to whether they could take apprentices in their own right or pass the trade on to children. For example, in France, printers' widows were allowed to continue a shop and retain journeymen, but could not begin a new piece of work or take on new apprentices, though late husbands' apprentices could finish their time with them. Indeed, Hufton points out that 'women almost everywhere were permitted to run a printing shop, but not to pull the press, which was man's work. Hence from London to Vienna we find the widow's imprimatur on eighteenth-century books.' Similar restrictions operated in Oxford and Kingston Upon Thames, so that widows could continue working if they paid quarterage to late husbands' guilds and obeyed regulations. Apprentices might serve a master's widow as long as she remained unmarried and practised only her husband's trade. No widows took on apprentices in their own right and girls were not apprenticed. Wives' and daughters' right to work in a craft was not formally recognized. A wife's position, less formal than that of a widow, was more secure than a daughter's. Although women were admitted as apprentices to the London booktrade, they were not in France, despite no prohibition in the regulations of the Compagnie des libraires. Daughters could not gain entrance by patrimony and had no legal right to trade, although they could confer rights upon suitably qualified husbands, similar to those widows could confer on remarriage. There are no instances of married women trading in their own right in Oxford between 1500 and 1800, though they almost certainly worked alongside husbands. Neither daughters nor spinsters had a right to trade. No women were enrolled as mistresses in eighteenth-century Kingston Upon Thames, though a handful took 'tolerations' allowing them to trade as 'not being free of the town'. However, in London, city clockmakers received girl apprentices, and the

Goldsmiths' Company, among others, admitted women in their own right following apprenticeship. Journeymen's wives and daughters were usually excluded, unless trading in their own right. Like masters' daughters, if they had not served an apprenticeship they had no right to trade, but even apprenticeship was no guarantee of a trading position in a system which was essentially patriarchal and which was becoming more protective of male tradition as time went on. Thus many women in trades outside the corporate structure were from journeymen's families. Women also did not participate in the *compagnonnage*, except in the symbolic role of the *mère* who welcomed and housed participants in the Tour de France as they worked their way around the country. Thus some companies and towns allowed women to enrol and permitted female apprenticeship; others limited enrolment to widows and few female apprenticeships.

The example of Geneva is revealing, since it, like other European cities, provided economic and political advantages to its citizens. Genevan law permitted women of citizen status, that is, daughters and wives of bourgeois, to engage in trade without restriction, while severe disadvantages operated against those who were not citizens. The case of Madeleine Ducret, who was charged with illegally operating a linen shop in 1752, reveals the complexity. She successfully claimed that she was an employee of her mother, a citizen who had regained her status with legal separation from her husband. But when Madeleine inherited the shop in 1758, the Chambre de Commerce forced her out of business because she was not a citizen. The political role of guilds and corporate structures is thus significant. Restrictions clearly were part of a campaign to limit competition and to maintain an elite group of tradesmen. Howell has drawn attention to this for the early modern period in Northern Europe, where the link between political and economic power effectively excluded women from privileges and position.[27] Generally, in towns where guild power was not directly associated with civic power, women seem to have had greater opportunities to remain within the guild structure, but as secondary colleagues. In Geneva, however, the ability to achieve citizen status by birth or marriage worked in women's favour.

APPRENTICESHIP

Apprenticeship was a key element of the guild system, but also operated outside of it. As a means of gaining access to certain trades and the right to trade in many corporations, the same compliance was expected of girls as of boys, though the language is overwhelmingly male. Indeed, the overt reason for not allowing daughters to trade after their fathers' death was that they had not served an apprenticeship. In England, for example, the terms of the Statute of Artificers were frequently invoked to restrain unapprenticed women from practising trades, regarded as a means of introducing untrained cheap labour. The importance of apprenticeship probably varied with the status of the trade and the social position of the apprentice or the master or mistress. Formally putting out a child was costly because of the premium paid to masters, taxes and fees; the expense may have outweighed advantages gained in status and adult position. Certain benefits were not obtainable for girls since they usually could not gain the freedom of a corporation, nor did apprenticeship necessarily enhance their trading or political position as it did for boys. Women were largely restricted from guilds and the advantages of a collective work group and often were seen by men not as trading partners but as threats to their own position. Since they had less to gain from formal indenture, families may have been less interested in incurring such obligations. Hufton suggests that the tendency of urban families to absorb girls into work could explain the relatively small number of recorded apprenticeships. In Sheridan's examination of French corporations, women's trading opportunities and apprenticeships were sharply curtailed, although Abensour refers to it as a normal feature of a working girl's life. In Germany, by the late Middle Ages, girls were no longer formally apprenticed. However, 19 per cent of apprentices were girls in Geneva between 1701 and 1710, and in England they comprised 9 per cent in Staffordshire and Essex between 1750 and 1799, about 2 per cent in Warwickshire and 5 per cent in Wiltshire.[28] So while not as prominent as for boys, apprenticeship was a recognized mode of training for girls.

Not only were fewer girls than boys apprenticed, but the characteristics of their service varied significantly from the male pattern, with clear implications that girls' training was perceived differently from boys'. As a regulated system of upbringing, apprenticeship taught children social values and behaviour. However, economic functions seem to have diminished for girls, underrating their working position. The nature of trades open to girls, the length of service and the levels of premiums suggest a devaluation of female work and status, and reflect a narrowing of occupational opportunities. But girls' apprenticeship satisfied different aims which had value in their own right. Because apprenticeship did not mirror accurately the economic roles and divisions in society, and social roles were constructed along gender divisions, male and female apprenticeship should have reflected differences as well as similarities. The question is whether notions of skill and training were the root cause, or whether other considerations such as gender, ideology and their relationship to the meanings of work were. In this way apprenticeship reflected the prevailing eighteenth-century cast of mind and frame of reference, as we would expect.

In data from Essex and Staffordshire, three-quarters of girls in trade, rather than Poor Law, apprenticeships went to textiles, mainly millinery and mantua-making.[29] The other quarter were spread relatively evenly across the remaining trade groups (see Figure 3.3). Both boys and girls went to metalwork, but boys were apprenticed to 143 separate trades, while girls went to only 19, none considered prestige trades. Although timber and leather trades accounted for well over a third of apprentices, they included only minute numbers of girls.

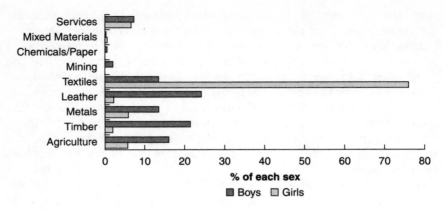

Figure 3.3 Distribution of trades by sex for trade apprentices in Staffordshire and Essex, 1750–99
Source: Simonton (1988)

Individual trades show an even more marked sexual differentiation since those commanding higher premiums and offering better returns usually were exclusively male adult trades. For example, millers and grocers demanded premiums averaging £23 and £42 respectively, yet only one pauper girl was placed with a miller and none with grocers. The same was true of cabinetmakers, plumbers and curriers, to name but a few. In 'non-female' trades where girls were most numerous, weaving, locksmithing and bucklemaking, their premiums were low, averaging £2 to £5. Terms tended to exceed seven years, though technical requirements were minimal, suggesting that they were cheap labour. Milliners' and mantuamakers' apprentices gained training and a trade in a way many girls did not. Also by apprenticeship to a trade with the potential of high status, girls expected to learn the polish and ways of a social class into which they might hope to marry. Apprenticeship of girls to mercers and drapers, with short terms and very high premiums, suggests pointedly that it was 'finishing' similar to boys indentured to gentlemen for similar sums and terms. This characteristic is a clear reminder of social class distinctions within apprenticeship. It was not a monolithic form of training with a single function.

Girls were bound throughout the economy, although some areas of work were considered more appropriate, and others were difficult for them to enter. However, their presence across the spectrum underlines the extent of their activities and the lack of a rigid definition of female work, at least for social groups from which apprentices were drawn. Despite sexual differentiation of trades, women and girls regularly engaged in work which later generations identified as distinctly non-female. They were clearly regarded as able to do heavy, unpleasant jobs. So while girls spread throughout apprenticed trades, there were ideas of where they should normally be placed. Seventy-eight per cent of English girls went to only five trades, while the twenty-six most popular trades for boys encompassed 78 per cent of male apprentices. Also, few females went to handicraft or mercantile trades associated with skill. This is confirmed for Geneva where in 1701–10, almost 75 per cent of girls apprenticed as seamstresses, and in 1750, 116 girls went to only four trades: seamstresses (55 per cent), watch chain-makers (25 per cent), laundresses and *passementerie*.[30]

Instead of the 'traditional' seven-year term, female apprentices could expect to serve under five years.[31] The brevity of their terms suggests that the institution applied quite differently for them than for boys. By custom, young men were admitted to the freedom of the guild and corporation on completion of apprenticeship, entailing economic and political responsibilities. Apprenticed at fourteen, a seven-year term meant that boys achieved 'manhood' at the end of their service, which acquired a particular significance validating their masculinity. For girls, however, there was no such consequence; they were likely to acquire more status from marriage. In practice, marriage could terminate apprenticeship for girls but not for boys. The probable reason for girls' relatively short terms was that acquisition of status through apprenticeship was far less relevant for them than for boys. Indeed, their terms might well have reflected a realistic estimate of training required to trade. Girls clearly did not follow the customary guild practices carrying with them status and prospects. While they were available for work earlier than boys, perhaps saving for a dowry, their ultimate prospects financially and socially as independent women diminished. In many ways the system worked to prepare girls for a married future, as helper to a husband, and reflected society's view of women as married and valued in relation to men.

Service of various sorts acted as a training for many girls, without the paraphernalia of apprenticeship and without some of the potential perquisites to be gained on completion. Daughters of tradesmen and craftsmen probably learned requisite 'female' jobs, helped in shops and may have been systematically trained. Wiesner argues that daughters worked alongside apprentices learning the trade and thus acquired a dowry based on skill and knowledge. Often girls were taught during service with their parents or others in an informal arrangement. Such was the case of the author Ann Gilbert, whose father taught her engraving at home along with apprentices and siblings. Sheridan's study of the French booktrade indicates that daughters and wives frequently received a great deal more training in technical, legal, financial and managerial skills within family businesses than records show. Domestic servants in an artisan household probably helped in the shop, and at the very least shared in the rhythms and processes of craft life. Many women gained a trading position because contemporaries accepted seven years' experience as equivalent to apprenticeship, although not strictly within statute or corporation rules. Schools also provided occupational training, such as charity schools which included training for work in their curricula, particularly for girls. It might have been basic needlework, but could include housekeeping, accounts and childminding, all of which would have been useful to them as mothers and servants. Writers made it clear that there was a dual purpose to schools, to prepare girls for motherhood but also provide them with the requisite knowledge and skill to work for their living. Specifically 'vocational' schools also existed throughout Europe, such as the industrial schools of Britain and Central Europe, often associated with charitable institutions.[32]

Additionally, much traditionally female work usually did not take apprentices. For example, only 32 spinners were recorded from Staffordshire and Essex out of a total of over 18,000 apprentices, while retail took very few children, and most of the girls were probably shop assistants. Prospects of setting up on their own would have been slim, since they were unlikely to have access to the necessary capital and were more likely to work in partnership with husbands. Thus, apprenticeship records are not a true indication of the extent and nature of women's work, nor do they necessarily accurately reflect their training opportunities. This is not to say that they were not apprenticed or that they did not receive similar training. Some were no doubt as carefully taught as boys. Others were apprenticed on the same conditions as brothers and served a formal term. When they completed their apprenticeship, they could set up as independent mistresses and take apprentices themselves. Nevertheless, as a training scheme, apprenticeship affected girls less systematically and less formally than it did boys. Although women's work was skilled and important, it was not recognized as such through apprenticeship.

URBAN WOMEN AND FAMILY WORKING

Although guilds dominated many city economies, the system did not encompass women's work adequately. The model is important because it helps to identify characteristics which defined work status, but it can lead to a tendency to identify women's work in a framework that characterizes what men do as important. This underplays women's contribution to the urban economy in their own right and in ways not well recorded. Women's work underpinned the urban economy through their household contribution, budgetary management and across commerce, manufacturing, trades and services. Their activities often made the difference to a family between starvation and subsistence or between profitability and bankruptcy. In most respects the urban woman's role mirrored that of her sister in the countryside. Domestic industries also operated in towns and indeed contributed to the growth of small towns into the cities of Europe. Requirements for spinners, for example, were not confined to rural areas, and in cloth centres like Augsburg, Ulm or Strasbourg female spinners were kept busy, as they were in Rouen and Aberdeen. Lace- and silkmaking often took place in towns, like Lyon and London. In mid-eighteenth-century Antwerp there were 10,000 laceworkers, a quarter of the population, while 84 per cent of textile workers in Caen were laceworkers, mostly women, children and the elderly.[33]

The point in the life cycle partly shaped women's experience in the urban economy. Many single women shared industrial or commercial activity contained within the household. Also they assisted mothers, who might carry on a separate trade. Thus, as Hufton writes, 'Laundress produced laundresses; seamstress generated seamstresses. Chocolate-maker mothers and aunts trained daughters and cousins. Tavern and café keepers' daughters helped their mothers run the business.' In Beauvais, daughters spun for weaver fathers much as a country girl did. In Paris and provincial towns, daughters of printers continued in their father's trade though it was more likely in the bookselling side and easier outside of the heavily regulated Paris trade. Daughters working at home were unlikely to receive wages so that their skill and knowledge had to serve as a dowry. Sometimes craftsmen provided daughters with household furnishings or tools. Daughters might, of course, take employment in the town, returning home at night, contributing part of their wages to the family pot. Thus they could be less exposed to risk than country girls who migrated to town without family protection. Single women with craft skills but without family resources probably hired themselves to a craftsman or woman, or worked for a tavern-keeper or shopkeeper. Daughters and wives operated as assistants carrying out minor parts of the work, for example, sewing on buttons in a tailor's shop. A branch of the trade might be allowed them, such as making black puddings and sausages in a butcher's shop, while confectioners' wives and daughters might make chocolates and decorate pastries. The group of married women most often working throughout the urban economy were wives of wage-earning men and journeymen. These women had no family workshop to rely on and had to look elsewhere to help support the family. They were industrial day labourers and turned to nursing, wetnursing and petty trading. They worked in urban manufactories such as silkmaking in England, buttonmaking in Birmingham and lacemaking in Beaulieu. The level of wages often required them to turn to whatever was available, frequently undertaking several things at once. Women who fell on hard times were often in this position. Many operated in the 'economy of makeshift', which required them to use their enterprise to make a living. An irregular, unreliable way of life, it was often unskilled and sporadic.[34]

Many women worked in partnership with husbands, taking apprentices and contributing to the firm. The dominance of economic partnership persisted in urban areas, supplemented by the dowry, the skills and property each brought to the union. Several examples appeared in the French booktrade, where husband and wife were associated equally in police charges resulting from trading activities. Women appear regularly with husbands in legal documents, such as apprenticeship indentures, often when a girl was involved. Also almost all legal documents consulted by Abensour for Paris and the Ile de France were signed by merchants and countersigned by their wives. Port books of late seventeenth-century Scotland also contain a sprinkling of wives signing for consignments instead of their husbands. Houston conjectures that other females whose names appear might have been buying in bulk for the house-hold, or women trading in their own right. Yet in most instances, 'the man governed and the women assisted . . . Custom and law combined to promote asymmetrical relations between men and women within the family, but what-ever the subordination of the wife, the work of both partners remained essen-tial to success.'[35]

In many respects the master's wife was the most important figure in the shop, with responsibility for its smooth running, providing food to apprentices and journeymen, frequently doing their laundry, keeping accounts, selling products, collecting debts, purchasing raw materials and running errands. Such was Madame Tribout who kept accounts of the putting-out operation of the family lacemaking enterprise in Valenciennes from 1748 to 1775, or women handling sales in the boutiques of Lyon. In France, 'working behind the counter of the bookshop was clearly the woman's accepted place', despite virtual 'official' exclusion from the trade. Pinchbeck saw such a woman as so well acquainted with her husband's business as to be 'mistress of the managing part of it'.[36] Guild regulations which often specified that masters had to be married recognized her contribution. In Campbell's guide for parents and aspiring apprentices, he warns that the master's wife must be considered before undertaking an indenture. He draws an uncomplimentary picture, but one which indicates her potential power in the workshop:

> Such a Woman who has got the better of her Husband, in the Management of her Domestic Concerns, must of Course rule his Apprentice; the youth must be Madame's Slave, must fetch and carry, & do all the Drudgery of her House without regard to his business, in which he is never employed but when she has nothing for him to do in the Kitchen.[37]

In Paris, Farge indicated that her position was 'utterly ambiguous', but had the effect of making her a more important person with her wide range of duties and responsibilities. She worked in close parallel with her husband, had a pow-erful influence over day-to-day matters and exercised considerable authority over workers in the shop. The character of her work could mean she was pre-sent in the shop more than he was. Indeed, her prominence and power also were her vulnerability, since they rested on convention and marriage and exposed her to grievance, a feature implied in the passage by Campbell.[38]

Women most frequently shared husbands' occupations and so worked in a wide range of trades, including printers, glaziers, plumbers, butchers, silk-makers, pinmakers and coal merchants, among others. Notably, they clustered in shopkeeping, textiles and provisioning. A wife's exact role in a business depended on her abilities; for example, a woman who could not read could hardly act as a proofreader. Nevertheless, identification of tasks as 'skilled' or simply as men's work, such as pulling the press, could keep women from undertaking them. Within the patriarchal household and workshop, the principle of male head of household and control of the workshop fundamentally underpinned the premise that men's work was high status and female work was supplementary and supportive. She was his assistant. Throughout much of Europe, law merged a married woman's legal identity with her husband's and as a *femme coverte* she could be restrained from independent trading. Thus most women found access to business through husbands and fathers, and even that was constrained by custom. As in the rural economy, wives substituted for husbands when they were ill or away, or during imprisonment. That women often worked side-by-side with husbands and substituted for them, either short term, taking turns at a loom, or longer term, managing an entire concern, suggests that some tasks were interchangeable. Women certainly learned many of the same jobs as men and could do them when required. However, if some work was interchangeable, ideas about it were not; the wife temporarily took on *men's* work. When her husband was able, she should leave it to him and get on with *her* work.

MASTERLESS WOMEN: LIFE CYCLE AND INDEPENDENCE

Eighteenth-century Europe was a patriarchal society in which men held overt political power and in which law and custom recognized the subordination of women to men. Society expected the male to be the authority in the family, and through marriage most women gained strength, position and status. Of course, *most* women are not *all* women, and a substantial population of single and widowed females worked in their own right. With average marriage ages around the mid-twenties and a high level of 'never married' women, there were many single women. In France, women born about 1700 had a mean age at marriage of twenty-five or twenty-six and 14 per cent of those born between 1785 and 1789 were permanently celibate. Wrigley and Schofield identified a similar pattern in England where 10 per cent of women born in 1700 never married, dipping to a low of 5 per cent about 1740, rising again towards 10 per cent by about 1800. Similar patterns existed throughout Europe, notably in parts of Scandinavia and Belgium. Hufton suggests 11 per cent was a nominal European norm for the proportion of widows in the female population, though Malcolmson places it lower for England, 8 to 10 per cent. Wall estimated women headed between 9 and 14 per cent of households, more likely widows than single women, while throughout the last half of the eighteenth century, Gullickson estimated that women headed 10 to 15 per cent of Auffay households.[39] This is an important reminder that not all households were the typical 'proto-industrial family'.

A woman might be an independent worker for a part of her life, fitting into a 'family economy' much of the time. Similarly, an independent artisan might have been married but operating her own trade. In both cases, her independent identity has tended to be subsumed within the idea of a family economy and her activities obscured. In this way the concept of family economy, often seen as enhancing women's position, ignored the contribution of a significant number of women to the economy, but also eliminated agency in determining their own lifestyle. Since wages and social perceptions derived from the 'model' family, these women and their households could be significantly disadvantaged. Their decision-making process comprised complex considerations which included emotional and moral values as well as economic considerations. To argue either that these women sought independence or that they were forced into it only through instrumental concerns is oversimplification. Also, few women's positions were static. Many 'women alone' were at a particular life-cycle stage, a stage that might have lasted most of their lives, but for many comprising the years between childhood and marriage; others were on their own as widows. Some would remarry, given the dependence of men on women's labour.

European society was suspicious of masterless persons, particularly women who were not controlled by a man: father, husband or employer. Regulations, work practices and legal restrictions throughout Europe reinforced powers of husbands and fathers and were used to try to force females into households headed by men. Often unsuccessful, these attempts remain a reminder that what women did was not dependent solely on economic factors. The notion of a masterless woman applied equally to young single females, who were effectively between masters, that is, father and husband, and independent single women who by choice or accident were unmarried, working in their own right. Nevertheless, attitudes towards them varied little, although ideology was harsher on those who did not marry, producing mockery of the 'old maid'. Economic change and fears of a breakdown in public order combined with views of women's proper place and emergent notions of domesticity to increase suspicion of masterless women. Contemporaries explicitly tried to control their sexuality and blamed women for any perceived sexual laxity in society. French administrators sought to channel 'disorderly' single women to the discipline of royal manufactures, new factories and *ateliers de charité*. Such views encouraged perceptions of their work as a 'stop-gap' until they attained a 'proper' married place, and helped keep female wages low, adding further pressures pushing women into male-headed households. Married *femmes seules* were tolerated, if they adhered to the normative view of women's role. In Württemberg, they could be squeezed out of lucrative sectors, but sanctioned when working in a male-headed household or substituting for a husband. In urban Scotland, also heavily governed by corporate institutions, legal and institutional constraints buttressed economic disadvantages of being single in much the same way. Most women remained in a patriarchal structure which limited their freedom of action, working in households, mills and workshops.[40] Even where women gained or retained economic rights, custom still dictated forms of service and subservience.

Single women most frequently left home to become servants, where they contributed domestic as well as industrial tasks. For many, service was an interim stage between rural roots and adulthood. For example, in Ardleigh, Essex, in 1796, 29 per cent of girls aged fifteen to twenty were servants, but only 19 per cent and 10 per cent in the two successive age groups were. For others it became a permanent job. Many entered another household for both work and accommodation, though in towns there was a greater opportunity to rent rooms and work outside of a household. Girls migrated to other villages, towns and regions in the search for work, usually following well-travelled routes, building on contacts with friends and family. Many made only a short journey; others migrated from as far as Brittany to Paris. Hufton reckons that 13 per cent of the total population of any city north of the Loire was made up of *servantes*, though the proportion was lower in Southern Europe. Some servants came into towns to earn their dowry and returned to set up house in their original community. Others stayed in the city, having gained a craft skill, and built up a dowry towards establishing their own shop with a husband. Others married another servant, setting up in an inn or similar trade.[41]

The growth of an urban bourgeoisie created demand for domestic servants, at the same time as an increase in urban work for men made male servants more expensive. Departures from schools in Essex show a clear rise in the proportion of girls who went to service, many to commercial towns like Colchester, Chelmsford and Romford, others to London; for example, Romford Charity School:[42]

1764–73	7 of 31	girls leaving school	(23%)	went to service
1774–83	12 of 51	"	(24%)	"
1784–93	16 of 43	"	(37%)	"
1793–99	13 of 29	"	(45%)	"

The integration of a servant into the family also began to shift so that in France wages were paid rather than noted for payment at the end of a year, and the relationship became more contractual than familial. They undertook the full range of domestic duties, helped in a shop or workshop as needed and usually assisted a mistress. Few servants were 'domestic' in that their duties only lay in the role of servicing a household's domestic wants, and many spent much of their time in industrial work, as the farm servant did in agriculture. In larger households, a hierarchy allowed a girl to work her way up, achieving status among servants. Some stayed their whole life in one situation, becoming part of the family, often remembered in wills; others were highly mobile, changing jobs to improve their position, or left service altogether. On the one hand, the servant was in a clearly inferior position, dependent entirely on the family in which she lived, subject to their vagaries and reliant on them to honour her wages. She was also sexually vulnerable. If she complained of sexual advances by males in the household, she was just as likely to be out of a position as not. On the other hand, service was the ideal female job, performed in private and adhering to the feminine ideology of service and dependence.

In some areas steady employment in domestic industries allowed women to create independent living arrangements, although female earnings were usually so low that this was difficult. In spinning, lacemaking and similar trades women were frequently able to operate independently, because of weak regulation, because they were identified as women's crafts or because level of demand allowed them the freedom to trade. Creating a separate household of women, or women and children, allowed production to be divided, and women could gain some control over markets and income. So could women working directly for a merchant. Though wages were dependent on economic conditions, the existence of numerous merchants in an area competing for women's labour was to their advantage compared to areas where a few or a single merchant controlled raw materials. Such was the case in Rouen and Augsburg. In Normandy, given the short supply of yarn, there were so many dealers that workers could always choose the offer of another one, or could go to the weekly market to try for an improved rate. Reddy quotes a good example of such a spinner:

> If she has enough money to pay for three pounds of raw cotton, she buys no more. She works with this small amount, and works with care. When the cotton is spun she sells it that much more advantageously as her work is perfect. From the proceeds, she subtracts enough for her subsistence, and if her small capital has now increased, she buys a larger amount of raw material.[43]

Such practices led to a royal ordinance prohibiting trade with unauthorized peddlers in April 1752. Spinners gathered at the Cloth Hall to protest about the injunction. Although the demonstration awoke other grievances, 'within the terms of market culture, it might be more appropriate to see this as a raw-material riot ... and to see the spinners as being moved by entrepreneurial grievances'. Not only were they operating in their own right, they were prepared to assert their right to do so on terms that benefited them. Such households were common in north-west Ireland where the premium on female labour for spinning linen enhanced their position. In the Caux, some single and widowed women supported themselves by spinning; in the lacemaking districts of Le Puy *marchandes* could make comfortable profits employing four or five *servantes* or their own daughters. In Colyton, the structure of poor relief encouraged poor women to live together as spinners, backed up by relief and charity when times were especially hard. This supports Gullickson's belief that spinning wages were not high enough to *encourage* women to establish independent households, but were high enough to *permit* it. The picture of independent households, therefore, is somewhat mixed. On balance, income did not provide the incentive for women to establish separate households, but a women-only household was a strategy for coping with economic necessity. If wages were too low for a single woman to gain an independent existence, then in combination with others she could ensure her room and board. Whether they wanted an independent existence or gained in standing is harder to assess.[44]

Towns throughout Europe reflected a very large presence of 'industrial' women. Many low-profit items, such as brushes, combs, candles, soap, thimbles, brooms, needles and pins, wooden bowls and spoons, were unregulated and women producers were not a threat to the craftsmen's status. As more towns grew up without guild regulations, and as proto-industry loosened their hold in others, women could gain a measure of independence and mobility. In Lyon, for example, conflict between guilds and silk merchants was resolved in the merchants' favour, allowing large numbers of women to work with weaver husbands and as day labourers. Women were active in the metal and hardware trades of Birmingham as wage earners, independent traders and members of family workshops. In the French booktrade, non-kin women were employed, many from without the trade and without skills. Genevan criminal cases from 1740 to 1760 listed seventy-seven women's occupations, including the ever-present domestic service, seamstresses, watchmaking, textile and laundresses. These comprised the bulk, 76 per cent, but furriers, silk millers and hatmakers were also recorded.[45]

Independent women could gain respect within the urban economy and sometimes defend their economic position. Usually they were wives or widows of artisans. Just under a quarter of widows heading households in late seventeenth-century Oxford ran their own businesses, and Hufton found about 10 per cent of publishing houses identified in the British Library run by women alone. In Geneva between 1741 and 1751, 50 of 206 licensed enterprises belonged to women, including 21 which were female partnerships and a further 26 which were partnerships of men and women. Modest shops selling clothing or other goods were most numerous, with the rest mainly food shops, inns or taverns. Widows taking apprentices suggest areas in which women most likely traded. Food and drink were most prominent, 20 per cent, followed by leather goods, such as gloves and shoes, 17 per cent, 14 per cent in distributive trades and 8 per cent in clothing, mainly tailoring.[46] Fifty-five occupations followed by women in Staffordshire and Essex also indicate the gendered nature of trades. Some carried on their husband's craft, such as fishing, chandlery and glazing. Female grocers took only male apprentices, a lucrative trade with high premiums, but victuallers took mainly girls, perhaps as shop assistants. The largest number of mistresses was mantuamakers followed by milliners, areas with few masters and one solitary male apprentice. This correlates with the female presence in textiles where they dominated trades like bonnetmaking, pencilling and silkwinding, and figured frequently as tailors, spinners and weavers. Even in 'male' clothing trades, women took girl apprentices as hatters, mercers, drapers, perukemakers, glovers or tanners.

Thus mistresses were overwhelmingly in 'feminine' trades, confirming limited expectations for journeywomen. The prospect of girls becoming sole mistresses, especially outside female trades, was very slim.[47]

Millinery, a prestige occupation, was recommended to girls of 'good family'. It was skilled and offered scope, attracting those with capital and some social standing. English apprentices paid high premiums of £25 to £75 for training. It was a good business enterprise for the able well-capitalized employer, but prospects were much less promising for the less fortunate and employees; for many it became a pauper trade. Contemporaries such as Campbell thought women could begin business with capital ranging from £100 to £1,000, but stressed to parents the need to provide adequately for daughters since, in spite of 'vast profits' made by mistresses, they 'yet give but poor, mean Wages to every Person they employ under them'. Mantuamakers, usually capitalized under £100, also paid poorly. The variation in premiums of £2 to £31 illustrates the range within the trade. According to Campbell, journeywomen 'may make shift with great Sobriety and Oeconomy to live upon their Allowance; but their Want of Prudence, and general Poverty, has brought the business into small Reputation'. He warned that pay was frequently so low as to make prostitution the alternative. In Essex and Staffordshire between 1750 and 1800, five firms of mantuamakers and milliners conscientiously run by women demonstrated a regular pattern of apprenticing girls and were successful enough to employ a minimum of two women and two apprentices. Premiums tended to rise as the century passed while terms continued to be short. These cases also emphasize the overwhelming female character of the trades. Campbell called millinery 'no Male Trade' and commented that 'the Fair Sex ... are generally bound to this Business', while the mantuamaker was 'Sister to the Taylor'.[48]

In towns, women were brewers, butchers, bakers, grocers, lodging-house keepers and innkeepers. They pickled and smoked meat, made mead, beer and hard cider, and baked breads, dominating the market as vendors of almost any commodity one could imagine, but mainly provisions from fruit and vegetables, fish, chicken and game, to brandy and sausage. In German towns pretzel bakers sold their wares, as did sauerkraut-makers. These activities were associated with women's role in provisioning households, so that such activities were perceived and accepted as extensions of their 'natural' activity. Many markets did not differentiate between men and women selling, as long as they obeyed trading rules, such as not selling stolen or adulterated goods. Authorities were more concerned about women who sold from baskets since it was not easily regulated. In trades where women could acquire a degree of economic independence, however, they were underrepresented. For example, brewing, where women once figured extensively, increasingly became male dominated. In 1725, only 7 brewers in Edinburgh were women and in 1695 only 10 in Aberdeen were, compared to 230 and 150 respectively in the sixteenth century.[49]

The village or neighbourhood midwife had perpetuated for centuries, and an unattended birth was 'abnormal and even suspicious'. Similarly, the village wisewoman was a constant. Local authorities could pay them regularly to tend the ill or pregnant. Such roles were not restricted to the poor or peasant woman. Charitable ladies also devoted themselves to looking after the ill, treating wounds and distributing medicines. Yet, the period saw growth in occupational opportunities for women in health care, which moved them beyond unpaid caring and nursing in their own homes and villages. The business of caring remained unprofessionalized outside of religious orders, but the growth of charitable institutions, lying-in hospitals and other forms of institutionalized care provided opportunities for women to develop their talents and find an occupation. They were employed as carers in medical institutions, such as hospitals, infirmaries, poor houses and orphanages. They might be nurses, but just as often were keepers who looked after purchases, ran the kitchen, led patients in prayer and examined them on admission. This reflected the nature of hospitals before the discovery of cures for infectious diseases. Hospitals were places for the old and infirm, non-contagious diseases and poor pregnant women, so that it was imperative to prevent those with infectious disease from entering. These went to pest houses, where they were also looked after by women. By the end of the century, with more public and private institutions, more women were paid wages for what they had done without wages in their own homes, or even community. They became identified with administration of these charities, which would eventually lead to new female occupations.[50]

In keeping with the growing distinctions between men as artisans and women as assistants, the period saw a growing divide in medicine between the professional male practitioner and the female. Training and access to formal professions like surgery and dentistry became far more male controlled and legalized. Women practised medicine illegally in France, but only after 1755 were they officially banned from specialist branches except midwifery. As training became more formalized and university based in France, women were excluded because they were explicitly denied access to universities. In contrast, Pinchbeck describes 'female practitioners', who advertised their services, while Parliament granted Mrs Joanna Stephens £5,000 on condition that she revealed her method of preparing medicines. Oculists and dentists appeared in newspapers and at least one, Madame Ranxcourt, apprenticed in France to dentistry, practised in London in 1751. Yet their access to training was no better than in France.[51]

Even though male midwives made inroads on the upper end of midwifery, a traditional midwife still brought most people into the world.[52] Importantly the notion of untrained 'aged unskilled crones' was essentially mythical. In a largely rural society, oral tradition held an important place. For most people in villages and many in towns, their understanding of the world remained local and their knowledge of the way things were done rested on verbal exchange and custom. In this context, women established and maintained their own communication links and networks. It was through an oral network that many girls learned skills they would need and the roles they would fill as adults. Thus, childbirth was exclusively a female activity among lower orders of society, with midwives, wisewomen or other women grouping together to teach and help one another. French midwives served an apprenticeship and passed an exam before practising, and though there were over two hundred in Paris at the end of the century, numbers and training were inadequate across the country. No girls were apprenticed to any medical trades in the English sample, though Burnby suggests they might have been in other parts of England, while Harley found only one provincial woman formally apprenticed. Further, he emphasizes the importance of the notion that 'midwifery had always been regarded as a skill that could only be learned by experience'. Licensing of English midwives, though not uniform, required testimonials usually provided by medical practitioners, which also attests to the strength and importance of informal apprenticeship and experience. The idea of untrained midwives stems in part from the attack on them from medical men who charged them with insufficient theoretical knowledge as part of male attempts to usurp the trade while enhancing and professionalizing their own. Women also were subject to the superstitions associated with witchcraft. Increasingly women were marginalized because of their lack of education coupled with a faith in science, on which a doctor's training and technical vocabulary allowed him to capitalize, and the opposition of surgeons. While eighteenth-century Spain instituted training open to women, 'it was not so rigorous, exclusive to women and prepared them to a lesser degree' than men, for whom sophisticated training was instituted at the same time. Despite attempts by French and English women to upgrade training and to strive for professionalization, wealthy families showed a distinct preference for male midwives.[53] The status conferred by being able to afford the more expensive male midwife, with the aura of science behind him, was an important factor marginalizing women. The issue of class cannot be ignored, since doctors and male midwives came from a social stratum that could afford education and the trappings which went with it. For example, English boys apprenticed to medical services paid premiums which averaged £80, compared to an average male premium of £18. As Harley argues,

> Women were not politically impotent, despite not having the vote, and the introduction [of state licensing] would have been more likely had it not been for articulate women's desertion of the practice of midwifery and the employment of midwives . . . in the seventeenth century, midwives were often women of considerable social status . . . in the eighteenth century, the gentry withdrew behind their park walls . . . Increasing aspirations to 'respectability' meant that affluent and educated townswomen were no longer recruited to the art of midwifery.[54]

Italy, however, shows that the experience across Europe was variable, with different political voices joining the debate. The role of the Church and different churches, as well as women's own ability to fight their own corner, contributed to different European patterns emerging.[55]

Much of what a girl learned about the life she was to lead as an adult was acquired from women around her, especially mothers and other female relatives, thus forging another link in the female network. Children's and women's work was intertwined, as was children's upbringing with women's domestic and productive role. Thus 'Women trained and supervised the younger members of the family production unit; they passed on "skills" to the next generation of the industrial workforce and they cared for their children, all as part of one process'. Formal schooling also contributed to the process, and as my research on eighteenth-century girls' education shows, women taught girls of all classes in a range of schools and at home. The importance of literacy in obtaining work and conducting a range of occupations should not be under-valued, even for service, for example, but the need for literacy was paramount in women who became teachers. The range of educational opportunities was clearly class based and often determined by religion. Religious orders played a much larger role on the continent, and Hufton suggests teaching nuns had a greater impact on literacy north of the Loire. Many teachers appear to have emerged from personal hardship, rather than career motivations. The 'distressed gentlewoman' was frequently steered towards teaching either as governess or schoolmistress. Clergymen's widows, for example, were seen as eminently suited to become charity school mistresses, and the increasing number of middle-class gentlewomen may have seen teaching as an appropriate solution to a need for support in a conducive atmosphere. As Hufton says, 'Literate and frequently used to living in homes which had books and journals, the clergyman's daughter was likely to try to edge her way into teaching or even into print.' Many also needed the accommodation which governessing provided. Virtually no training existed, the only requisite qualities being literacy and some gentility. Even this was not always required for the dame school that frequently involved an older woman tending children while she spun or knitted. Among English apprentices, more schoolmistresses than masters emerged, though apprenticeship appears to have been little used as a training route.[56] Regulations spelled out the qualifications of charity school mistresses, as for Blencowe's charity in Essex:

> The Master and Mistrefs at the time of their Election must not be lefs than 25 Years of age nor more than 45, the former must write a Good hand and understand vulgar Arithmetick the latter must be able to Instruct the Girls in reading in English and plain work, they must be members of the Church of England and must have received the Sacrament according to the Church of England within six Months before their Election.[57]

It was common for the master's wife to undertake this role of mistress. Some schools also hired a dame, who supervised girls' practical work and sometimes the youngest children. Qualifications included suitable moral standards, some-times specifying 'keeps good orders in his [sic] family'.[58] Such qualifications, while modest, nevertheless logically restricted the opportunity for such posts largely to women from respectable and literate households.

Widows frequently carried on husbands' trades, hiring workers for those aspects of work which they could not perform either through lack of ability and knowledge or as a result of customary taboos and restrictions. Of course, they required good knowledge of the craft even when they concentrated on management and sales. Some chose to resign the mastership of part of a trade, such as booksellers' widows in France who gave up the printing side but retained the bookshop, or Sarah Baskerville, widow of a letter-founder and printer, who kept the letter-founding 'in all its parts'. It was more difficult for a woman to run a printing shop, in which she probably lacked expertise and which was identified as a masculine trade, than to run a bookshop that embraced the female role of shopkeeper. In some cases, as trading widows, they gained greater economic status than other women and a certain amount of independence. At the same time, difficulties of coping alone in the eighteenth-century economy, combined with obstacles derived from society's suspicion of 'masterless' persons, meant that many widows were unable to carry on success-fully. Many survived with the assistance of networks of family, friends and hus-bands' business associates which gave widows an advantage over spinsters who tried to operate independently in the urban economy. Remarriage was one option. Her chance of remarriage improved if she had a shop and goodwill of some value, or if marriage could gain a journeyman access to a trade. Remarriage resolved a number of problems for society, since her livelihood was more certain and she was re-entering the 'natural' order of the patriarchal household, since 'the ungoverned woman was a threat to the social order'. A widow, however, was free of male control of her person and property, and a 'comfortable' widow might wish not to remarry; even a poor widow gained the right to run her own life. Reasons for deciding for or against remarriage were complex and certainly were not only about her economic well-being. Her chil-dren's position, feelings for her deceased husband, social considerations and not least affection for a new suitor were all part of the picture. It was not a simple equation between subsistence and independence, as the variables exposed in Todd's study of Abingdon indicate.[59] Notably, they were in a position to make a decision; they retained agency and were not the victims or subjects of male choice.

Throughout Europe, widows featured prominently on poor rolls and chari-table lists. For example, at Emblavès, near Le Puy, 38 widows supporting 111 dependants on low irregular pay were recorded at the *bureau de charité*; at Bayeux the *bureau* reported 70 widows with over 300 dependants on low incomes as lacemakers or stocking-knitters. Thus widows often applied to authorities to continue working because of poverty. In England and France, they successfully petitioned to continue 'civic' posts, formerly held by husbands, such as running gaols where they had been matron, as Elizabeth Prince did in 1785, though 'offices' were formally only available to men:

> That your Petitioner is left in very distressful circumstances with family of eight children, the eldest of which being a daughter of only 14 years old and 3 of them have natural infirmities which will probably render them ever incapable of gaining their livelihood.
> That your Petitioner's Husband and his Father and Grandfather have been Keepers of the House-of-Correction at Abingdon for a great number of years and your Petitioner has a brother and Brother-in-law very well qualified and willing to assist her in the future management of that prison and she confined sufficient security if required for her faithful discharge of the Office of Bridewell Keeper.[60]

Sometimes they cited their age and dependent children to bolster their case, like Prince, but they were usually successful since authorities preferred people to work rather than receive charity. Importantly though, permission to work always applied to a *specific* woman as a privilege based on the authority's generosity. Similarly, pleas were most successful if based on need and not trade ties; guilds often assisted widows of non-brothers. Prince, for example, cited dependants and family links, including male support, rather than a right to the job or that a woman also ran the Poor House in Abingdon. Her plea was an individual claim as woman, widow and mother for help.[61] Women thus had little claim to rights and status as craftswomen, but as women, widows, poor and weak.

At one and the same time the most obvious and most hidden independent 'masterless' woman was the prostitute. Certainly, resort to prostitution was a risk for women in seasonal urban trades subject to periods of slack employment and low wages, as well as to widows or other single women needing to support themselves and, possibly, dependants. Some were still children contributing to family support. Rural women too would offer themselves for a loaf, a bag of coals or other tangible 'considerations'. Thus some women fell into the 'profession' as a result of destitution. Most prominent were former servants, followed by seamstresses and textile workers. There are indications that it was seasonal, in that garment workers facing a slump in trade had few other alternatives. Many may have simply been supplementing meagre wages as domestic or industrial servants. They may have retained their amateur status, moving out again at the first opportunity, or moving back and forth as one of a series of expedients. On the other hand, numerous women followed the trade as a regular occupation. The most common, according to Hufton, were the former camp-followers. Many lived together, some in brothels and bawdy houses, plying their trade off the streets, but others operated as a female household that allowed them to save on accommodation and heating and to join forces for shopping and other chores.[62] There are numerous issues tied up with prostitution, such as social disapproval, victimization, social concern for safety and health and the double standard gendering sexual behaviour. Of central importance to this study is its role as an occupation. Prostitution was not problematized as it would be in the nineteenth century, nor was it uniformly reviled or accepted. For many it was a fact of life.

WOMAN AS WORKER

The woman's power and strength rested on her household management and the importance of her labour, while partnership involving pursuit of a common goal characterized relations between husbands and wives. Thus co-operation resulting from economic subsistence requirements has to be seen as a part of gender relations. However, the importance of women's work did not necessarily translate into improved social status, and economic co-operation only partly defined gender relations. A woman's position in guilds and her work status depended on her place in the life cycle as well as her relation to a master. Women's trading identity was often weak, because they did not belong to *compagnonnages* and did not share in the comradely activities and rituals with which urban crafts were permeated. It was not only their nearly invisible position in guilds, and the lack of political influence and identity that went with it, which undercut their position. Because the changes in women's lives, marking the transition from one stage to another, including childbearing, happened at different points in each woman's life, Wiesner suggested that women generally did not develop a strong sense of kinship with other women of their age group. Life-cycle changes could also mark shifts in occupation, so that although they sold workshop products as daughters and wives, the products might change on marriage. Thus women developed transferable skills, but did not necessarily evolve a strong sense of occupational identity, unlike male craftsmen who tended to stay in one trade. Davis points out that with their thinner occupational identity than men, their energies could shift into other work as situations demanded.[63]

And yet, through the esteem of husbands, kin, neighbours, clients and other independent female traders, women could gain and maintain a sense of craft and status. In Lyon, feminization of names noted identity, for example, Estiennette Cappin, a tavern keeper, becoming Estiennette Cappine, and by the attribution of nicknames, or titles of respect such as Dame. Such women's positions might be recognized by their frequency as godmother, by small loans to neighbours or gifts to needy women. Similarly, groups of women sometimes evolved their own internal discipline and usages, such as the *crieuses de vieux chapeaux*, trading in old clothes and furniture, who developed an extensive hierarchy and 'apprenticeship' system. They were often linked to the underworld, because of suspicion that they sold stolen goods, but in an era when few people bought new clothes, the trade was an important part of urban life. Thus women gained a sense of achievement less through the identity of skill and more through establishing position in the neighbourhood.[64]

In practice, women's work related to the family economy as a series of gradations. They could work as assistants to men in a single craft; they could work in the household at a different trade, contributing to the family income; they could work outside the household to help support the family; and they could work in and outside the household to support themselves. The notion that women functioned only within the family economy is flawed, in that numerous women operated throughout the economy in a way which, while compatible with family needs, was not necessarily predicated on shared work experience, or even shared location of work. Also, the notion that women's work was necessarily home-based undervalues the extent to which women operated outside the household situation, and in the cities the extent to which the street and the market was their milieu. Their role in trading networks was important, as was their financial role for household and workshop accounts and in organizing and managing the sale of the workshop produce. The proportion of single and widowed women trading, sometimes temporarily as *femmes soles*, sometimes permanently, has to be reckoned with in understanding female work in the eighteenth century.

The so-called decline in women's position in the eighteenth-century workplace can hardly be documented. Such a theory presupposes a golden age for women, which was not the case. Various forms of gender-based division of labour had always restricted women. Their trading role was always limited by guilds, corporations and patriarchal officialdom. The construction of apprenticeship, for example, owed less to a feminine ideal and more to a status evaluation which described girls and women as subordinate, and their work, albeit economically valuable, as inferior in status to male work. On many occasions the only way for a woman to ensure her economic and social position was in relationship to men and the patriarchal structures which the economy fostered. However, women operated in defiance of such restrictions, either by taking up new trades or operating in parallel. The increase in industrial activities that became apparent in the eighteenth century through the development of domestic industries provided opportunities for women to insert themselves into the workplace in new and different ways. For many, income was small and living precarious, whether working for wages or as independent producers. Clearly however, significant numbers of women operated in the urban economy. Indeed, official concern with unbridled women resulted partly from the visibility of independent female traders, working outwith the control of males, exacerbating the hostility to women who did not assume the natural state.

4

LOCATION, SKILL AND
STATUS

DOMESTICITY, TIME AND PLACE

In mainstream economic history, an underlying assumption is that because work was located in the home, women could do it, and work away from home was not available to them. There are two notions inherent in this thinking. One is the obvious one that women, particularly married women, had to stay at home in order to fulfil their female role. The second is that women required work which was not time-disciplined, which was flexible and they could fit into the interstices of domestic tasks. Thus historians often give the close link between domestic manufacture and family economy as the reason for high levels of female participation; domestic industry allowed women to control the time and pace of their work, and to integrate various domestic activities. Importantly, encapsulating women's strategies in such a way undervalues their work and their familial contribution, and simply does not reflect the variety of approaches women employed to balance their obligations.

Certainly the fact that a woman bore children influenced what she did, but did not restrict her to a specific set of tasks or exclude her from productive activity. There is oversimplification in the view, as expressed by McBride: 'Because women's work in the preindustrial world had been home based and largely seasonal, work had not seriously interfered with women's responsibilities in child care and household duties.' Though women were crucial to the workforce, if a woman had young children, she reduced her productive labour even if she worked at home. Compatibility depended on the character of the work, the industry, the economic cycle, her status and life-cycle position. The degree to which domestic industry could be merged with women's other responsibilities varied enormously by region, industry and over time. The experience of a spinner or nailmaker was not the same as that of a pottery worker or buttonmaker, and the lacemaker in Bedfordshire could well experience work differently from one in Le Puy.[1] Single women's experience and availability were different from married women's, and emphasis on the domestic role tends to overlook their importance in the labour force. At the same time, the married woman, and ideas about her, often established the norm in

70

terms of wages and access to the workforce. Even though certain types of work, such as spinning, sewing, lacemaking, laundering and silkworking, seem to have remained immutably in women's hands, this tendency cannot be explained simply by the need for women's work to be fitted around household and maternal responsibilities.

Certainly a great deal of women's work did fit into a task-orientated model, reliant on flexible use of time, but we should remember that artisanal work was task orientated in any case. To assume that women had 'an imperfect sense of time', imbedded in a pre-modern world in which 'task-orientation' in relation to the 'natural work-rhythms' operated instead of time-discipline, tends to undervalue women's strategies.[2] Women endured the time-discipline imposed on domestic industries by market dates, raw-material deliveries and putting-out networks, a discipline greatly amplified by the intensification of labour driving down piece rates. Shifting international markets brought spells of highly intensive labour followed by periods of unemployment. Such erratic demands, increasing the intensity of periods of work, made it more difficult to integrate housework and childcare with paid work. Single and married women, working at home, in workshops or small factories, were increasingly tied to forms of work that structured their use of time, rather than fitting between other tasks of domestic life. For women, work-discipline and the value placed on industrial time could be significant. In 1740, Mary Collier, a washerwoman, described women's use of time:

> When Ev'ning does approach, we homeward hie,
> And our domestic Toils incessant ply:
> Against your coming Home prepare to get
> Our Work all done, our House in order set; . . .
>
> Early next Morning we on you attend,
> Our children dress and feed, their cloaths we mend;
> And in the Field our daily Task renew,
> Soon as the rising Sun had dry'd the Dew.[3]

Women saw the so-called 'double burden' of productive work and domestic duty as inevitable. Because household work was task-orientated, employment centred on tasks, rather than on time, was easier to take up. Single women were not so constrained, and, as we have seen, such restrictions did not always influence married women either. Importantly, the shift to work defined almost exclusively by time would have far more effect on married women's work than location, but they adapted by deriving new strategies.

However, a view of women's work as task-orientated made it appear as though they were 'part time', supplementing the 'real' work of men. It lent credence to the idea of women as casual, non-essential labour, although quite the opposite was the case. Certainly mothers and housewives 'respond to different rhythms than those dictated by the clock, and a working week'. So did most proto-industrial workers. But women's patterns were not 'casual', they were

> orientated to care for others. The rhythm of life and work of house-wives is not just task-orientated; it is governed by a strict day by day and week by week time discipline, and continuous thinking of the future . . . Not only is time disciplined; it is spent on others in differ-ent ways, leaving virtually none of it for the housewife to 'waste' on herself.[4]

The tempos of domestic work and domestic life cut across each other. Time-discipline mattered to the proto-industrial world because industrial work for all workers was regulated by factors such as delivery times of raw materials and dates of markets and fairs. Also, other social and income-earning activities had their own time-discipline, while the availability of assistants could be deter-mined by their personal time economy. But it also mattered to women. To con-struct it as a casual world, made up of tasks to be picked up and put down, with industrial activities seen as by-employments to women's 'real' work belies the structure and meaning of their lives. Reddy proposes a similar view of spinners who did not engage in distinct entrepreneurial, labour or consumer functions; they were all of these at once. 'They were not trying to maximise purchasing power as consumers or minimize labour time as labourers.'[5] They reconciled conflicts in their daily lives between diverse functions, such as a desire for earnings against a desire for leisure, with a way of life that they sought to achieve.

Although women's activities could be described as 'domestic' in recognition of their responsibility for home management, food production and preparation, childbearing and rearing, this belies the extent of their non-family, non-domestic activities. Male work also contributed to household maintenance, blurring the distinction between public and private. The relationship of 'pub-lic' to 'private' has limited use in the eighteenth century. It can be helpful in drawing out shifts that took place in eighteenth-century thought, but can be misleading in describing women's experience. Perhaps they did not take part in conventional politics, or take pre-eminence in the more visible reaches of commerce and trade. In short, perhaps they did not occupy the seats of public power. Yet they did share the public sphere on political and economic levels. Their marketplace activities, selling, trading and producing goods, apprenti-cing and hiring, being apprenticed and hired, and public protests, all indicate a lively and important female presence. Women performed much of their work outside the domestic setting, and not only in clothing- and food-production activities, as demonstrated by the numbers in mining and metalwork. Similarly, household management frequently involved them in negotiations in the public sphere, and they also acted as intermediaries between husbands and employers, negotiating working and financial arrangements. They managed

72

the financial affairs of business and household in a number of rural and urban settings. Similarly, their shared responsibility with men for maintenance of a household and an economic concern, whether farm or workshop, attests to a gender relation obscured by the notion of public/private. These variations illustrate the divergence between reality and the ideology of women as domestic creatures.

The other strand of the domestic view is that 'Industrialization affected women most profoundly through the separation of work and home.'[6] Obviously, industrialization in the literal sense brought work into the home. However, one suspects that McBride is referring to large-scale workplaces distinctly separate from the house. For this to be significant to women, it has to clash with their other perceived roles. By now it should be clear that society usually defined men by the work they did, and women by their familial status as single or married, daughter or mother. Movement of work, any work, away from home had to be coupled with other factors such as what was expected of women and the time-discipline associated with new work. Clearly, eighteenth-century women did leave home to work in agriculture, industry and commerce. The migration of single women in particular was a noteworthy feature of the rural–urban nexus. These same females were largely unaffected by shifts in the location of industrial concerns. Married women also left home to work, either locally or at longer distances. Sometimes they migrated temporarily with children or as a part of family migration, such as those who sought work in the early factories. Certainly, however, if household maintenance was the key to a married woman's life, work that took her geographically away for long periods was not ideal.

Great variation in the transformation of manufacturing had no uniform effect on the location of waged labour. Dramatic changes brought by factory working in some areas obscures the fact that it never was the major occupation and that much industrial organization continued to centre on workshops. Indeed, local small-scale workshops might not be very different from households in terms of work and time-discipline. Throughout the century across Europe, women continued work primarily in their own homes, on land or in workshops virtually contiguous to their home. They continued to work in others' homes as servants and labourers. Thus, for most people, separation of home from work was relatively insignificant during this period. Probably more critical was the decline and contraction in some industries, such as woollen worsted in East Anglia, which removed employment from some areas completely. Technologies and concentration in some industries provided work for some women, but disadvantaged those living in more remote areas. There is an important ideological aspect to the separation of home and work, however. As waged employment came to be seen as proper work for men, and family maintenance, housework and childcare as the proper province for women, then an ideological separation of home and work took place. While this was first generated as a bourgeois ideal, actual changes in the location of work supported it.

Yet, it is important to ask how such ideology contributed to the way those changes took place, and in particular the exclusion of women from certain kinds of workplaces.

Organizational structures were important in determining the extent to which female work in commercial manufacturing translated itself into independent incomes, new status or freedoms. Entrepreneurs set up early small mills in the countryside to take advantage of skilled female labour. Many were simply large workshops that brought together domestic industry activities under one roof, like Wedgwood's, for example. Even the earliest cotton mills were little more than collections of large jennies. In domestic industries, women worked under different organizational structures. They worked directly for a merchant, were subcontracted by husbands, or worked in household production units. Much of women's market work appeared supplementary and complementary to male work, for example, carding and spinning, while men wove. The rate paid for the finished product, in this case cloth, represented the whole effort. In the process, her participation was interpreted as subsidiary and subordinate. Because their work was secondary, it was cheap. Although their status may have improved in domestic industry compared to the agrarian world, 'their labour was still far cheaper than . . . in workshops or early factories'.[7] As families turned more and more to waged activities, men continued to draw the equivalent of the 'family wage' while women regularly were paid less. The relative invisibility of their work thus tended to disadvantage women once there was a growing reliance on wages, which made it difficult for women to support themselves or dependants. Sharpe depicted an important contrasting image writing about spinsters in Colyton, where employment opportunities favoured women.

> Women's work was not a corollary of men's, nor a complement, as the current 'family economy' theory suggests. It was, rather, separate and different in terms of the type of job involved, the wages earned, and the amount of time spent in employment. The type of domestic industry carried out in Colyton did not require a family unit as the typical proto-industrial model suggests. Rather, it promoted the independence of women as wage earners in their own right.[8]

At the same time, she argues, there is little evidence that the circumstances enhanced their position or that their quality of life was significantly different from women in other regions.

Changes in organization and location are tied closely to technological developments. Their impact was greatest in the nineteenth century, but we cannot ignore the fact that domestic industry involved technology, for what are distaffs, knitting needles, spinning wheels and looms if not tools? Even hand-powered technologies could have significantly affected women. Gender, technology and skill are explored more substantially below, but in industry as in agriculture certain tools and processes were more likely to be associated with women than men. One explanation and justification for women's exclusion from productive work and their concentration in positions of low pay and low skill rests on the differential effects of mechanization upon women and men. Spinning provides a useful example of the effect of technical change on women's work. They used the distaff, spinning wheel and jenny in the domestic system, though the jenny was also the mechanism for establishing large workshops or proto-factories. The cheapness of their labour made it viable to continue spinning on the distaff long after wheels and jennies had come into widespread use. Not only could it spin a finer thread, but unused labour could be employed, including feeble older women and women walking to and from other jobs. For a similar reason it was cheaper to employ female handknitters, for whom industrial work was only part of their livelihood, than frameworkers who derived virtually all of their income from knitting. Similarly, silkthrowing machinery duplicated hand procedures. Because labour was available, manually operated mills continued in use long after implementing water and steam power. Thus, the cheapness of women's labour retarded the application of newer technologies. Calico printing adopted another strategy of accommodating existing female workers rather than developing new technologies, devising a number of labour-saving technical innovations coupled with extensive division of labour.[9]

As spinning technology responded to the growing demand for yarn, machines threatened women's work. Although jennies continued to employ them, one woman on a single jenny could do the work of several. In the English West Country, the number of women workers dropped between 1780 and 1802 to only 18 per cent of its former level. Young noted that one girl working for Van Roubaix at Abbeville could spin as much as forty-six women. Women could use smaller jennies at home, and not larger ones, but more importantly it was more efficient for a manufacturer to bring several jennies together into one place. The price paid was less than that prevailing in putting-out, and the worker was tied to a single employer in a way that she had not been when working in the countryside. Response was pronounced. In the *cahiers de doléances* preceding the French Revolution, workers condemned jennies as 'these spinning machines which have stolen the bread from innumerable poor citizens who have nothing but cotton spinning as their sole resource'. Significantly, criticism was not of the machine *per se*, but expressed the view that there should be 'a certain balance between the price of bread and the profit to be had from the spinning of cotton'. At Louviers in Normandy, 'many spinning jennies have been destroyed by the people, under the idea that such machines were contrary to their interests'. Backlash in England was similar, though delayed in textile districts, since jennies remained part of the domestic industry until machines became very large and moved into mills, disadvantaging women who could not transfer to mills.[10] During the transition, the number of women's jobs probably rose, with decline coming in the next century.

GENDER AND SKILL

Despite different economic situations, political histories, culture and language, there were remarkable similarities in perceptions of women, work and skill in eighteenth-century Europe. Constructions of skill have little to do with the training or ability required for a task. Instead, as Phillips and Taylor argue:

> skill definitions are saturated with sexual bias. The work of women is often deemed inferior simply because it is women who do it. Women workers carry into the workplace their status as subordinate individuals, and this status comes to define the value of the work they do. Far from being an objective economic fact, skill is often an ideological category imposed on certain types of work by virtue of the sex and power of the workers who perform it.[11]

Like much of language, 'work' and 'skill' carry with them immense cultural overtones from which they cannot be wholly isolated. They are terms which are historically specific and have meaning in particular cultural contexts. The English words skill and technology are essentially modern, that is, current usage and implications are not the same as for eighteenth-century men or women. From the seventeenth century, 'technology' contained the concept of systematic treatment and 'the arts'. By the early eighteenth century, a characteristic definition was 'a description of arts, especially the mechanical'. Skill meant having discrimination or knowledge, particularly in a specified matter, and described the 'capability of accomplishing something with precision and certainty', reflecting the language of eighteenth-century metaphysical certainty. It could be construed to mean 'practical knowledge in combination with ability' or 'cleverness, expertness'. To be skilled was to be possessed of 'skill or knowledge, properly trained or experienced'.[12] Thus, the notion of skill carried a sense of knowledge or discrimination, but described an ability to accomplish something, that is, a sense of not only *knowing* but being able to *do* something. While skill clearly referred to ability, it was not limited to a mechanical or technological sense as we know it today, and it paid heed to both experience and training as ways of knowing. Notably, the terms skill, technique and expertness do not appear in the language of English apprenticeship on the whole. Our reading of Adam Smith, Collyer and Campbell on apprenticeship ascribes skill to their descriptions. Defoe used the word sparingly, and when he did so, it was to convey knowledge and awareness of business practices.[13] Apprenticeship invokes mystery rather than skill. Historical meanings of mystery referred to secret or the unknowable, and most appropriately 'an action or practice about which there is, or is supposed to be, some secrecy; a "secret" or highly technical operation in a trade or art'. While mystery encompassed 'technical operation' and 'trade', it also included art. Usage throughout apprenticeship was far more about trade secrets than technical skill, as with 'art of midwifery'.

Instead of talking about work itself, eighteenth-century French workers referred to it in a personal way, so that the proficiency of the worker and the qualities of work were relatively indistinguishable. Thus they acknowledged respect to each other as *le plus fort* or *le plus gros*, thus ascribing the quality of the work to the worth of the individual. Sonenscher further stressed the importance and usage of this language to assert position within the workplace and to establish status. He identifies the importance of rituals in French *compagnonnages* in creating symbolic inequalities in order to establish barriers which protected workers' fragile claims to the work they did. In a world which relied on relatively homogeneous skills and range of abilities, rituals and ascription of status or honour were important to defend workers' places, and allowed masters a means of controlling work and journeymen. Rule ascribes property of skill to the creation of identity and standing within eighteenth-century language. Similarly, he has shown how the property of skill in the period of manufacture was at the centre of workers' self-evaluations, and ideas associated with skill spilled far beyond the workplace to enter the vocabulary of labour with its own rights and dignity.[14] Both French and English usage identify an important characteristic of skill, in that it is a linguistic device to claim and maintain control and exclusivity in the workplace. The idea that there was a secret to maintain, that there were rituals to go through, even that strength or size were aspects of the ascription of status and skill is significant to understanding women's position in the workplace.

In many industries and activities, women's work was seen as supplementary and complementary to men's, and their position depended on their relationship to a male worker. In this way, women's participation was interpreted as subordinate. Also they could be perceived as casual, part-time workers, which ignored the totality of their household contribution. Specifically, these interpretations became more important as definitions of work changed, and as men sought to protect their position in relation to other changes in the economic structure that meant that many men's independent work status was threatened and with it their personal status and value. Thus it became important not only to define skill and status vis-à-vis men who were seen as poachers, but against women. On one level debate was not about gender but about position. However, capitalistic challenges as well as shifting attitudes towards women meant that they became targets of specific interdictions and redefinitions of work. The need to define skill and redefine work probably contributed to reshaping femininity. Significantly, also, women did not begin as equal workers with men, so that eighteenth-century changes cannot be seen as a decline from some sort of golden age. The same problem exists for the nineteenth century, when some historians hark back to the golden age of the eighteenth century as a backdrop to the 'exploitations' of the factory age.

As the pre-industrial bodies mainly responsible for regulation of craftwork and workshop production, guilds were crucial to the structure of the workforce and to the language and ideology of work. Their control of access to the workplace through apprenticeship and mastership rules helped imbed masculinity into artisanal work and gradually removed women from areas perceived as skilled. These regulations were about control and exclusion. While they existed to maintain standards of production, they were equally intended to hold up prices and prevent unskilled, uncontrolled labour from undermining artisans' positions. As pressures grew from competition from work put out to unincorporated areas, new unregulated trades, governments which reflected laissez-faire attitudes, and shifts in the economic structure which undermined many older trades, guild members became more assiduous in asserting their right to command labour and production. To maintain their status, they more explicitly defined work practices with respect to masculinity. As shifting definitions of status came together with re-evaluations of femininity, women were more frequently perceived as unsuited for work, particularly skilled work.

In the Germanic world the distinction between 'honourable' and 'dishonourable' work had a central role in guild ranking, insofar as workers deemed to be dishonourable could neither join a guild nor obtain a church position. Although historians ascribed this demarcation to notions of 'free' and 'unfree' labour, Quataert argues that the concept of honourable work also referred to work processes clearly dissociated from the household economy. Only this distinction could assure proper training and guarantee that production took place under approved procedures. Equally important was an assurance that persons who learned a trade in a household would not be admitted to guilds. By denigrating the productive strength of the rural household, guildsmen equated village work with women's work. Previously, work had been belittled because it was non-guild, but after the mid-seventeenth century, such disesteemed work came to be identified as women's work. Thus in Central Europe, urban guildsmen articulated the competition from domestic industry by adopting a gender order that reserved to guildsmen sole control over production for exchange, and inextricably linked household production, that is, dishonourable work, with women's work. In the escalating guild and non-guild struggle 'a rigid definition of sex roles coincided with the effort to alienate the household from the market (exchange) economy'.[15] In this way, artisanal practice identified productive work as properly male, and domestic activities in households as properly female. Significant was the association of women with dishonourable non-guild work and thus work which was perceived as 'unskilled'.

However, reasons for male exclusivity went further. German workers, like French, linked work with the person. Wiesner has shown how to work with women could, in itself, dishonour a male worker, and guild honour was the primary reason for specific ordinances prohibiting female work. In other words, 'Women were to be kept out of guild shops not only because they had not been formally trained or would work more cheaply, but simply because they were women.' She argues that male bonding and notions of masculinity were further motives for seeing guild work as 'a learned art and given to men alone'. Honour was an important commodity to journeymen because it protected their right to work, and when prevented from attaining masterships they could become obsessed with the 'symbolic capital of honour'. They felt particularly vulnerable to dishonour, and not working next to women became an important part of journeymen's notion of honour. Thus 'skilled' work in guild shops was increasingly defined as men's work, and the 'mystery' of a 'craft', the 'secrets of the trade' as something that should not be shared with women.[16] The guild concept that the strongest bonds were those between men had implications far beyond the realm of economics, and went hand in hand with other developments which redefined male and female roles.

In France, Germany and England, women challenged tailors' rights to make women's clothes. These disputes usefully illustrate the relation of women workers to the guild trades. The arguments centred, apparently, on 'untrained' seamstresses engaged in dressmaking in their own homes for sale, but were far more complicated. With the mantua, which could be made up simply, women in Oxford seized the chance to create a niche in the occupational structure, leaving staymaking and boning to men and male guilds. Although the guilds resorted to prosecution, lack of solidarity undermined their power, and eventually led to demands that women join guilds. In Prussia, the same dispute was couched in terms of proper spheres of work, women's role defined as domestic and her work as not really work. In these cases, as in a similar dispute in Paris, where there was no *real* — for example, lack of technical skill — barrier to women, male guilds tried to establish one. In the case of women's clothes, women had ideology on their side because of the 'delicacy' of fitting them. French guilds resolved the issue by limiting women's sphere of action to the amount of cloth they could use or the persons whom they could clothe, retaining to themselves the right to make bodices, the 'skilled' end of the work.[17] In all three cases, guilds retained for themselves the right to control work and to keep the high-status trades.

The operation and language of apprenticeship during the eighteenth century were part and parcel of eighteenth-century notions of the social and economic structure. Thus it clearly reflected ideas of gender and class. In so far as the society was paternal, so was it patriarchal; in so far as social mobility remained an important feature, so apprenticeship was a key in debates about mobility and status. Where women and girls were central to defining, and redefining, place, position and status, so apprenticeship of young women was a subtle part of that contest. Ostensibly apprenticeship was about training in a craft or trade. Historians such as Dunlop regularly use the term skill in conjunction with craft trades. Rule refers to skilled workers as those seeking to preserve apprenticeship sections of the English Statute of Artificers and Apprentices in the period before repeal in 1814. Similarly, Behagg links 'skilled' with 'artisan' in referring to workers who have served apprenticeships and to those preserving the custom of trade.[18] Apprenticeship legally and in the eyes of labour conferred an exclusive right to practise a particular trade. The literature and documentary evidence are full of references to 'teaching', carrying with it the notion of ability, skill and expertise to modern eyes. However, the language of apprenticeship, the 'mysteries', 'arts' and 'practices' of trades, conveyed a sense of value or rank which apprenticeship gained for a young man; it operated as an induction into a hierarchy which had social meaning. The word 'trade' as opposed to 'occupation' implied much the same. In this way apprenticeship marked a rite of passage, not only from youth into manhood, but into a recognized status or position. He became one of them. While this had always been important, in eighteenth-century Europe, notions of social rank and order intensified, with society perceived as a series of fine echelons or strata, and regulation of social mobility was a central feature of contemporary literature. Although economic opinion which favoured removal of trade restrictions was aggressively opposed to apprenticeship, skilled artisans continued to assert that it conferred a particular property right to the exclusive exercise of their trade. The period of apprenticeship was a stage when the male apprentice moved from lad to man, a transitional period that meant far more than 'learning a skill'. Indeed, he learned the culture of trade as well as the stages in masculine development.

Crucially, gender and status were inextricably entwined. Notions of female 'nature' and role inevitably influenced whether they were apprenticed, and, when they were, the character of that apprenticeship. While apprenticeship had an important role to play in transmitting values and culture, these were the values of a male society, and it was as much about gender as about training. Apprenticeship was one mechanism for controlling women in society and for protecting male preserves and 'maleness'. In this respect, references to training and skill, when they used them, are often spurious and manipulative. We have seen how girls were limited in access to apprenticeship by the eighteenth century. In England, girls were more likely to be parish apprentices than private ones, which relates to class, status and politics as much as to ideology. Two divergent patterns suggest a skill/status differentiation between trade and parish apprenticeship. Private apprentices were strongly associated with traditional crafts, production of goods and secondary stages of processing, all aspects which could claim an emphasis on skill and were closely associated with the idea of status and the 'mysteries' of a closed group. Parish apprenticeship contrasted sharply in that the majority were split between agriculture and services and it was very strongly biased to primary stages of processing. Seventy per cent of pauper girls were apprenticed to housewifery, while three-quarters of trade-apprenticed females went to textiles, mainly millinery and mantuamaking. Parishes placed out 60 per cent of female apprentices, but only about an eighth of boys. Female apprenticeship for the parish apprentice was different from that of the private one, partly because of the clear difference in the kinds of trade girls could expect to be placed in. Implications for girls are crucial. The relatively strong female involvement in parish apprenticeship implies that girls were subject to an inferior occupational training. Rarely did a female parish apprentice find herself put to a trade with good prospects.

Pauper apprenticeship had very little status, although it could operate as an avenue to a trade with a financial future and good status for a poor boy. It also meant that training was about gendered division of labour, and about masculinity and femininity throughout society. Skill and status which boys could achieve through apprenticeship were simply not options for girls. While girls might have learned technical ability, they did not acquire the quality of 'skill'. They might learn a trade or get a job, but they did not become skilled. Underlying girls' apprenticeships were the values which society placed on status and the meaning of skill. They did not gain the attributes which went with skill and which had become, by the end of the eighteenth century, clearly part of masculine qualities. Skill and training were not the root cause, but gender and its relationship to the meanings of work were.[19]

Issues in domestic industry are not distinct from those in guild work, though the character of control and the perceptions of place, skill and status usually are not overt. There is little doubt that women's work was central to many industries, and that tasks, like spinning, required 'know-how' or 'knack' that had to be acquired. Expansion of domestic industry might have increased women's employment opportunities, but there is little evidence that it enhanced their job status or wages. In Berg's view, the status of women in new manufacturing households *may* have improved, depending on conditions that varied over time and place. Significantly, however, their labour in household production was far cheaper than in workshops and early factories. Hufton, Pinchbeck and Berg all argue that the tradition of low wages established within the domestic system contributed to low wages subsequently paid for women's work in mills. Proto-industrialists maintain that the expansion of domestic industries emancipated women by removing them from private household production, where their domestic role subordinated them, and by introducing them into public market production. Instead of their contact with the outside world being mediated through male market labour, they had their own active role in that world, giving them more control and status in the process, which supposedly led to greater parity in marriage, so that 'These were not the patriarchally organized households of peasants or artisans . . . [and] marriage was more likely to take the form of a partnership between persons participating in some common task.' Crucial is a belief that women's household contribution attained higher status and importance than their role in the peasant household or urban crafts. In contrast, English empirical history maintains that expansion of domestic industry gradually forced women into household labour so that they became effectively dependent on husbands. Thus, with increasing industrialization, even domestic production, women's opportunities became increasingly limited with a reduced participation rate, and their experience was less likely to be in the sexually shared work situation of pre-industrial times.[20] The implication is that women had held a position of independence and status that the structures and practices of domestic industry eroded, weakening their position and status.

Both views tend to overlook the complexity of household structures and to ignore the possibility that a persistent gendered hierarchy of labour may have affirmed female subordination both before and after the introduction of industrial work into the household.[21] On a fundamental level, the notion of sexual division of labour tends to rely on the position of married women, who are expected to provide free labour services for men. So while a marriage-based division of labour directly relates to only part of the adult population, it transfers to all men and women.

> It is an ideological representation of work distribution in society and extends patriarchal relations into areas where patriarchal exploitation does not exist, that is, the non-familial labour process. The sexual division of labour treats all women as potential wives–mothers – that is, dependent on men – precisely because they are biologically female.[22]

Thus gender-based division of labour legitimizes hierarchies between men and women, and integrates unmarried women into a patriarchal mode of work organization. Sexual division of labour divides discrete work processes into male and female tasks while patriarchy subordinates tasks defined as female to those coded as male. The gendered nature of tasks and work is not inherent in the job itself, but in the ideological identification and distribution of tasks. Closer examination of sexual division of labour and status has been addressed specifically by Gullickson on the Caux, by Berg on domestic manufactures in Britain, particularly textiles and the Birmingham toy trades, by Quataert on textiles in the Rhineland and Saxon Oberlausitz and by my work on English apprenticeship, among others. Such research highlights the complexity of the issues involved, and the difficulties of generalization. 'Different branches of production, associated with different organisational structures and different labour processes, make it impossible to isolate any homogeneous socio-cultural response.'[23]

Customary practices on the land and in peasant households contributed to the adoption of sexually segregated patterns throughout cottage industries; they 'made decisions based on customary sex-role concepts intimately associated with an ideal of a working household that involved a delicate balancing of moral, cultural, and biological imperatives, not a unidimensional maximizing of output or income'. Significantly, when there was pressure for more spinners, as in Essex and the Caux, employers brought more women into spinning rather than expected men to do it. However, when rural spinning fell off, women took up weaving. But the apparent sexual integration of weaving does not mean that ideas of status and gender difference disappeared. The literature is full of comments on male strength (and intelligence) and female weakness and inferiority. In the Caux, women were only allowed to take up calico weaving while men continued to weave heavy fabrics. In Shepshed, although women and men were paid the same piece rate and produced the same quality fabric, men continued to earn more. Although contemporaries commented that this was because men could turn out more work, as a result of their superiority, Gullickson suggests it was more likely the result of women's continued responsibility for children and household which allowed them less time for industrial work. The question of division of labour is therefore clearly tied up with ideas of status and gender and with notions of skill.[24]

The appeal to male attributes, such as strength and supposed superior intelligence, is common in debates about skill, and operated to maintain the low status of women as workers. Such was the case of spinning mules and scythes. As Taylor and Phillips argued, status attaches to the worker, not the work, a concept explicit in the identity of male workers in the *compagnonnages*, and implicit in the regular reworking of notions of skill when issues of gender are at stake. Berg's exploration of female skills and female technologies underlines the extent to which sexual division between trades was mirrored within processes when male workers could restrict entry, in that women tended to be confined to less efficient and more labour-intensive practices. Although constructions of skill underpinned these distinctions, the very definitions of skilled and unskilled had at their root gender distinctions far more significant than technical attributes. The skills which women had, such as dexterity and deftness, were seldom regarded as skills. They were seen as 'natural' and feminine and therefore not given the credit which expertise carried with it. Many so-called female skills were not acquired through a recognized and controlled training. They were often learned working side-by-side with other women, especially mothers. They were the wisdom and practices passed from mother to daughter. In this way they also lacked the status which apprenticeship gave to many 'male' skills learned in the same way. Credit for their work and ability remained largely, as Davis has shown, within their own world, 'their street, their commérage, their tavern, their kin – unpublished and unsung'.[25]

Part II

THE NINETEENTH CENTURY,
c. 1790–1880

5

DOMESTICITY, THE INVENTION OF HOUSEWORK, AND DOMESTIC SERVICE

DOMESTICITY

After the French Revolution, the overwhelming influence of the doctrine of dual spheres is striking. Social morality and the cult of the home overhang views of work and inevitably shaped the context within which women, and indeed men, worked. It is often taken as axiomatic that the nineteenth-century woman was the embodiment of domesticity, and that the maturation of eighteenth-century ideology colluded with industrial and economic changes to create a concept of womanhood embedded in femininity, domesticity and the private world of the home. However, a woman's position was highly nuanced. The image remained an ideal for most, and the extent to which it became real was highly dependent on cultural, social and economic factors. The 'cult of true womanhood' was pre-eminently a bourgeois ideology, which was never completely satisfactory for many middle-class women, but which had even more complex implications for working-class women.[1] Yet the normative language of domesticity influenced the way they were all supposed to operate. National, regional and cultural difference varied views of femininity. Compare women of the mercantile Cadbury family in industrializing Birmingham with those of the Nord whose origins were rural textiles, and with women of the emerging German bourgeoisie centred on civil service, commerce and education. The middle classes neither originated from a single idiom nor did they become a monolithic class; similarly, femininity could be shaded differently. Despite such variables, there is a truth to the idea of a domestic female sheltered within the private domain and a vigorous male operating in the public arena. Indeed, the words 'domain' and 'arena' suggest the gendered nature of their existence. Historians, sociologists and anthropologists continue to grapple with the dualism of public and private. On one hand it expresses a truth, and on another it can be challenged as oversimplifying social and gender relations. Women already operated in the private sphere, having primary charge of home and family, so that there was a direct continuity in their responsibilities and in social perceptions of them. The nineteenth century was different, however, in

more than degree. A clearly articulated and formulated ideology of womanhood emerged which was relevant to European women of all classes. What was
new was 'the unprecedented scale on which it was propagated and diffused'.[2]

Bourgeois ideology contained gendered sets of complementary virtues: the
cult of virile qualities such as creative energy, endurance, capacity for invention, and a taste for the rational and a speculative intelligence placed against:

> The attributes of True Womanhood, by which a woman judged herself
> and was judged by her neighbors, and society could be divided into
> four cardinal virtues – piety, purity, submissiveness and domesticity.
> Put them all together and they spelled mother, daughter, sister, wife
> – woman. Without them, no matter whether there was fame, achieve-
> ment, or wealth, all was ashes. With them she was promised happi-
> ness and power.[3]

Caroline Michaelis echoed this judgement: 'Women are judged only according
to what they are as women.'[4] Woman was dependent, submissive, frail and vulnerable, but her dependence and physical weakness were idealized so that she
was transformed into an ethereal being – but one requiring protection and controlling. While the Enlightenment model of woman, as a companion to man,
and an emphasis on rational love, might have offered more scope for individuality and personal development, instead, it placed a premium on woman as
educator of children, preserver of morality, and increasingly as creator of a
haven for men and children. Though it gave women a central role in creating
the social order and establishing the right kind of society, it placed limits on
that role, and effectively put women in a position of almost unlimited subju-
gation to men. Those limits were both psychological and spatial.

Central to this conception of social order was the institution of the family,
headed by the paterfamilias, husband, father and representative of patriarchal
authority, upon whom wife and child alike depended. Within the bourgeois
world, social roles of men and women were allocated strictly by gender. Man's
destiny was to work and participate in public affairs; woman's was to organize
the household and raise children. Thus the 'family became a sphere of private
domestic compensation for the hardworking "public" male while his wife
devoted herself to the cultivation of domesticity and the passing on of correct
cultural values and norms to the next generation'.[5] As Jules Simon, moderate
French republican, put it, 'What is man's vocation? It is to be a good citizen.
And woman's? To be a good wife and a good mother. One is in some way called
to the outside world: the other is retained for the interior.'[6] Or in the words of
John Ruskin, English art critic and social theorist:[7] 'The man's work for his
own home is to secure its maintenance, progress and defence; the woman's is to
secure its order, comfort and loveliness.'

As industrial society developed, so did the ideal of womanhood. While it
never matched reality and shifted emphasis, lack of work for women was a

defining characteristic. Withdrawal from the 'public' workplace signalled that men could support their women, enhancing the male role of breadwinner. Movement to suburbs signalled their complete removal from the workplace, to a separate sphere completely divorced from connections with the source of family wealth. This move altered women's contacts, while removing them physically from the work space. Masculinity became even more clearly defined by the idea of male breadwinner and family wage. Although businesses were 'family' businesses, they became more clearly identified with males and more firmly imbedded in legal and financial practices.

The bourgeoisie did not always see the working-class woman as female. Because she did not fit their notions of gender, she could be seen as unsexed or virtually asexual, 'le travail de la femme la déclasse [the work of a woman degraded her]'.[8] At the same time, working women probably perceived little in common with bourgeois women. As housemaids, seamstresses and washerwomen, they provided services necessary to sustain the middle-class home, and were more likely to view their middle-class counterparts in class terms than gendered ones, as employers rather than as 'sisters' oppressed by their sex. Class was a distinctive feature in perceptions of the public and private, because working-class women were likely to experience a much less pronounced separation between productive and reproductive work than middle-class women. Yet the ideal inevitably affected working-class women. Employment practices reflected bourgeois ideas of gender by the kinds of job each sex was hired for and the pay they received. Gentility was reflected in the types and locations of jobs deemed suitable for women. For example, the ascendant class promoted domestic service as appropriate female work in an appropriate setting. Large numbers of poorer girls operated in the middle-class homes and witnessed first hand the structures and practices of domesticity. The bourgeoisie also inveighed against living conditions of the labouring classes, and pressed for reform of public health and housing, pressuring working-class families to conform to their own domestic practices. Legislation throughout Europe assumed and accepted the bourgeois model, often with little consideration of the exigencies of working-class life. Education legislation is only one such example, requiring girls to attend school when the subsistence economy of many families meant that they were crucial at home. Such pressure was especially significant from mid-century, when across Europe associations, institutions and campaigns not only sought legal reform, but encouraged emulation of middle-class home life, with an eye to improving health standards.

The family wage ideology resulted in a working-class version of domesticity, so that respectability became a particularly potent concept. Families of skilled artisans who aspired to middle-class status were more likely to adopt bourgeois views, mediated by their own culture, than those further down the economic and social scale. Respectability for the working man came to mean that his wife devoted herself to household affairs without needing to earn wages.

His social status and domestic comfort were enhanced more by her dedicating herself exclusively to domestic tasks. The ultimate aim of the respectable working-class husband – to keep his wife at home 'in a lady*like* manner' – became increasingly relevant for skilled European men, although the vast majority of women were far from becoming solely housewives and mothers. Only a few of the most highly skilled workers earned enough to cover family expenditure, perhaps 10 to 20 per cent in Germany. Among peasants and out-workers in insecure and unskilled trades, there was little emulation of the bourgeois ideal. Historians must treat cautiously the idea that the better-off working classes and even the lower middle class accepted and embraced the ideology of domesticity as an 'emblem of respectability'. Their views were not monolithic, and the ways gender operated to shape their lives depended on where they saw themselves in the order of things. Their own culture and experience flavoured attitudes to gender, and specifically views of women's role. The importance of work status and hierarchy contributed to gendered notions of work and place, as did traditional views of women. As Rose has shown in some English communities, local traditions of family employment rather than ideology may have influenced the way that households satisfied labour needs.[9] Changes in the economic structure of society, and shifts in location of work, also influenced men's and women's views of work available to women. When work moved away from the home, coupled with periodic pressure on jobs, the effect was to prioritize paid work as the property of men. These views could determine whether women worked outside the home, what kind of work they did and what the pay and status of that work was.

Many middle-class women accepted the model as the norm, and we cannot assume that they felt oppressed. The patriarchal past and bourgeois sublimation of the feminine were crucial to its acceptance and internalization. Even support of women portrayed as victims, such as Caroline Norton, died slowly: 'As for me (and there are millions of us) I believe in the superiority of the man as I do in the existence of a God. The Natural position of a woman is inferiority to a man, that is a thing of God's appointing, not of man's devising.'[10] Yet, throughout the century, women for whom the model was too constraining reacted against it. In 1819 Rachel Varnhagen wrote to her sister,

> Whereas for men employment is, at least in their own eyes, not only to be regarded as important, but is also something which flatters their ambition and gives them a chance to get on . . . we only ever have before us the fragments which pull us down, the small tasks and services which must relate to our husbands' standing and needs . . . Of course, one lives, shares and cherishes the wishes of one's own family, submits to them, makes them one's greatest worry and most pressing preoccupation. But they cannot fulfil us, rally us, rest us in readiness to further activity and suffering. Nor can they strengthen and invigorate us throughout our lives.[11]

Charitable work was an acceptable alternative whereby a number of women reconciled their feelings about femininity; for others it became a positive part of their approach to femininity.

The discomfort some women felt with an ideal that was unachievable for so many led them to challenge it, others to maintain the virtues but enlarge the scope of womanhood, and from the 1840s, women began to campaign to change their prescribed role. The women's movement in Germany in 1848 built on a number of disparate interventions of women in the public sphere. In Britain, individual responses to women's position were the forerunners of more coherent movements, such as for the vote and improved education. Contributing to the process were social-reform movements and philanthropy which expanded middle-class women's contacts and scope. It became clear that if women could undertake voluntary work that profited from their femininity, then they could draw up suitably feminine job descriptions. Utopian ideas and working-class suffrage movements challenged the bourgeois view of the world, and models of women at home and abroad emerged, such as in the American Civil War or Crimea. Improving education created new opportunities. Changes in family size and in the male to female ratio affected the experience of women. In England and Wales in 1851, for example, there were 2.75 million spinsters. They could hardly achieve the ideal of marriage and family.

HOUSEWORK

As Davidoff so cogently wrote, 'it is often assumed that housework itself is a constant feature of all societies. But even though the activities may be timeless, the context and meaning are not.'[12] Thus the continuity of women's experience of household tasks can be emphasized, but it can also be seen as a new feature, one which was virtually created by domesticity and fostered by the technological changes of industrialization. There is a truth in both perceptions. Indeed, this book has used 'household tasks' explicitly because of their different relation to women and work than the term 'housework'. Household tasks were, and are, an important part of understanding women's work, because they had specific value to the society in which they were embedded. They also formed a major part of women's tasks and contributed to defining other work. A key feature of the evolving context was that increasingly tasks of all sorts became waged. As more people worked for others and for money, and earned their livelihood outside the household, money became the measure of value. As the 'family wage' became attached to men's visible work, women's household work became devalued and invisible in a way that their multifarious activities in earlier households had not been. At the same time, the character and range of household activities changed. Though childcare, food preparation, cleaning and clothing remained the essential core of women's domestic tasks, they changed in context, meaning, scale and duration. The range of tasks multiplied as housework became associated with status. The creation of the domestic ideal had important ramifications, and during the century the bourgeoisie generated a concept of housework which radically altered women's work. The period from about 1780 to 1840 probably was crucial. The birth and decline of *Hausmütterliterature* during that period marked out a transition from the *Hausmutter*, who worked in partnership with her husband presiding over operations of agricultural estates, to the *Hausfrau* or housewife who was guardian of the private sphere. Davidoff and Hall applied a similar chronology for English middle-class women, echoed by Oakley.[13]

Like domesticity, the creation of the housewife was initially bourgeois with more meaning for middle- than working-class women. In many respects the family home became for a wife what business became for her husband. A housewife's job was to maintain and direct a well-run household, in the same way as her husband ran a shop or business. In this context, commercial rationalization became a key feature of the bourgeois home, with an attempt to transfer the values of business into the home, with limited but important success.[14] Housework was professionalized, with an emphasis on order and regimen. 'A place for everything and everything in its place.' A proliferation of manuals, frequently written by women, was one consequence, while they likewise contributed to the construction of the 'correct' way to run a household, underpinning ideals of routine, thrift and good order. Isabella Mary Beeton's *Household Management* (1859–61) is the best-known English manual of nineteenth-century housekeeping, while guides were produced across Europe, such as Simon Bloquel's *Guide des femmes de ménage, des cuisinières, et des bonnes d'enfants* (1862), thought to have been written by his wife, and Henriette Davidis's, *Die Hausfrau; Praktische Anleitung zur selbständigen und sparsamen Führung des Haushalts. Mitgabe für junge Hausfrauen* (1863). This wide and copious literature found expression in women's magazines that burgeoned during the period, such as *Schweizer Frauenheim*, which claimed that a tidy linen closet was the pride of every good housewife. Notions of management and the need for study permeate the literature. As Sarah Stickney Ellis wrote, 'the perfection of good domestic management required so many excellencies both of head and heart, as to render it a study well worth the attention of the most benevolent and enlightened human beings'.[15] One presumes she meant female beings. Housework might be natural work for women, but they did not naturally know how to do it.

Manuals emphasized monitoring and controlling the household through strictures of time schedules and rigorous accounting. Women's lives in the Nord attest to the importance of record-keeping: 'My mother did this religiously, and she became panic stricken if the figures failed to tally. Although she claimed that my father would be furious, he hardly ever looked at the book, and then only perfunctorily.' Mistresses were encouraged to keep detailed inventories of provisions, linens and china. There was an emphasis on arranging the day in a regular pattern of activities with time periods allotted to each. Even in children's play 'there should be a degree of perfectness and even something approaching to business habits encouraged and expected even in these little amusements to give a worth and interest to them. Perfect play is the anticipation of perfect worth.' There was clearly a concern for efficiency in housekeeping. Thrift was a cardinal virtue with special meaning for women as household managers. The public display of family entertainment was important symbolically and if status required a family to spend money on decor, food, fashion and servants, then the onus was on the housewife to stay within budget. The ideological mission of womanhood also charged women with household frugality and thrift. Maria Marsh managed hospitality for her cleric husband in Colchester and Birmingham, 'on a scale which his income could hardly have met, but for the careful, though generous economy and simplicity with which my mother ordered her household'. To counteract such costs, women saved by 'recycling', mending clothes and linens, limiting consumption on family meals, and creating household items out of sometimes incongruous objects. Meyer cites a footstool made of carpet beaters, for example. Importantly, this side of housekeeping was to be kept hidden.[16]

Instead of simply satisfying fundamental household needs, many tasks became more complex, taking on new meaning and expectations so that the way a woman 'kept house' defined her and her family. Housekeeping became homemaking. Ideology contributed to this shift, which promoted housework and fostered the guilt of a 'dirty' house. Decoration became part of feminine image, a woman's identity and correct bourgeois form. She was expected to adorn her home with a profusion of household items, just as she adorned herself, and to create a warm cosy space through polished surfaces which reflected light, colour and warmth. In Britain, the centrality of the family hearth was sufficient to retard the use of more efficient closed stoves, common in Germany and Scandinavia. Adornment of the home conveyed moral worth, while at the same time it expressed and heightened female presence: 'The shining interior mirrored the character of the woman.' Identification of woman as mistress of the household also contained within it a significant message, because it recognized a clear concession of a sphere of power that was specifically female.[17]

Cleanliness illustrates the relationship between housework and moral worth. Previously, wealth and possessions had determined status and standing, not personal or domestic cleanliness. By 1800, cleanliness had become a way of distinguishing the better-off from the poor or bourgeoisie from labourers. Wesley's well-known dictum 'Cleanliness is next to Godliness' suggests a new view of hygiene. While cleanliness was a classed notion, it was also gendered, associated with female chastity and purity. It was an important lesson for girls in Trimmer's *The Charity Spelling Book* (1798–99), but unmentioned in the companion volume for boys.[18] In succeeding years, it took on more meaning for women, associating clean houses with pure character. Hausen's description of *Grosse Wäsche* demonstrates how Germanic concepts of housewifely cleanliness changed over the period:

Clean, stain-free, white, fragrant – even two hundred years ago these were considered qualities of freshly washed laundry worth striving for; one hundred years ago [1887], however, nobody spoke of soft and fluffy and a hundred years earlier the hygiene of the washing would not have been a criterion.[19]

Ideas about cleanliness manifested themselves in tidying and polishing anything that could be polished, for example, silver, glass, wood, brass, and extended to the front doorstep. In late nineteenth-century Denmark, the transition of women from working dairy wives to housekeepers coincided with changing patterns of domestic cleanliness. Good dairy products had required tools and workrooms which were as clean as possible. As women were excluded from dairying, 'it was as though this cleanliness had been transferred to the home'. Whereas major cleaning and washing of floors had been a twice-yearly activity, it became a central domestic issue.[20]

Of course, highly carved and ornate furnishings and the multiplicity of decorative items compounded the problem of cleaning. Also social and economic changes created new problems, including urban sewerage and water supply, along with smoke and other industrial detritus. Increasingly, working-class wives were caught up in the battle against dirt and the importance of demonstrating family standards to the neighbourhood. Sweeping away dirt, battling bugs, whitening doorsteps and blacking grates were a mixture of necessity and respectability. The shifting idea of housework coincided with the public health movement where pressure came not only from social critics, such as Chadwick in England or Villermé in France. Underpinning the debate was a body of opinion which held that dirt was a class issue. In 1876, the Berliner Hausfrauenverein (Association of Berlin Housewives) set up a school for domestic servants, typical of bourgeois women's contribution to 'civilize' the working classes by inculcating them with their norms and values. In this role, middle-class wives set an example of how to run a household and care for children, as well as acting as visitors to check the households of the poor.[21]

The wheels of industry also turned attention on the household. New devices, such as the English cast-iron stove, which were supposed to be labour saving, created new jobs of caring for the equipment. The reality was that many housekeeping tasks were laborious, and technology did not significantly alter them during the period for most women, despite the optimistic view taken by Neff in her early contribution to the debate (1929). Cleaning and polishing were not touched, and carpet sweepers only affected sweeping late in the century. Women's tasks of fetching water and fuel were not immediately reduced nor were cooking or laundry transformed. Cleaning remained a job with brushes, mops and brooms, with few improvements in cleaning materials or agents. Change came primarily in new perceptions about cleanliness so that cleaning became central rather than peripheral to housekeeping. Washing-up became an identifiable task as affordable prices made crockery more widely available.

Arguably hundreds of household conveniences were invented and diffused, but workloads did not change in ways which saved the labour of a typical house-wife. Ravetz argues that 'gadgets' probably only lessened burdens for house-wives who already had multiple tasks, while Bose argues that technology allowed wives to take on an increased workload arising from loss of servants. The implication is that technological changes, particularly at the end of the century, were a way of addressing the falling number of female servants and, therefore, may have had little effect on the housewife's work. Those most likely to benefit were the newly servantless who attempted to keep up standards established when they had servants, and the upwardly mobile who with better housing and fewer children aspired to middle-class standards.[22]

There is little doubt that industrial and commercial processes brought more goods, from basic clothing to china and decorative items, into the market. With more items available, women increasingly shaped household purchases while some tasks moved out of the household. Not only did her purchases shape household perceptions, but they contributed to fuelling the expansion of consumer-production industries at the same time. Growing dependence on the market influenced her role as monitor of household expenses, removed certain tasks from the array of 'housework', and created new tasks. Although a middle-class home produced little, women spent a great deal of time processing and preserving purchased products. Most processing became commercialized only by the end of the century. As Louise Otto-Peters described her childhood in the 1820s in Meissen:

> Bread and cakes were made at home, all the preserves for the winter: fruit from the simplest dried kind to the most complicated jellies, meat in all its various preparations, butter and eggs – everything was prepared and preserved at home for the household's needs.[23]

Rural women similarly smoked, pickled and preserved food, in addition to day-to-day cooking and baking. 'Keeping a good table' was part of their claim to respectability in the rural community. Almost all homes purchased some clothing and food, including 'made-up' meals. Overseeing purchasing contin-ued to be an important part of her work, particularly in the working classes, where food could constitute two-thirds of the budget.[24]

The impression is that women were perpetually active satisfying household needs. Some, like Meyer, argue that the activity required of middle-class housewives involved as much toil as their working-class counterparts. Although recognition of demands on housewives of all classes is important and revises prejudices about middle-class women, it unfortunately creates new myths. There remained class differences in expectations, level of workload, and such a view can miss the important demarcation between a housewife who was mistress of servants and one who carried out the work herself. Similarly, it ignores the juggling act of most working-class wives between housework and paid work. One thing is clear, despite 'improvements' to housework, most women were busy most of the time, and the strain on their physical resources left many tired and drained. Elizabeth Head Cadbury was described by her husband as able 'to bustle about all day', with water to carry, a house to keep clean, meals to prepare, servants to supervise, clothes to make and mend, apprentices to keep in line, children to nurse and teach, while keeping a watchful eye on business.[25] Frevert quotes Frau O, wife of a middle-ranking Prussian civil servant from the 1860s:

> Since but one servant was there to help keep in order a five room res-
> idence with five, and later seven, beds, with every single drop of water
> for drinking, cooking and cleaning having to be carried up and down
> the stairs; since all the laundry, including the children's clothes, was
> washed at home . . . since all the children's clothes, except boots and
> hats, were sewn and knitted at home, and since, in addition, several
> children demanded constant attention; and since two births came
> within three years without any extra domestic help: the life of the
> housewife comprised little more than toil and effort.[26]

Childcare was central and relentless, which no technology could relieve. One view of 'labour-saving' improvements was that they released women for tasks perceived as less laborious, such as childcare. As middle-class women came to have more time for children, they made childcare more time and energy consuming.

Women's perception of these changes is highly problematic. One could agree with Ravetz that new tasks were imposed on women that were more complex or involved higher standards. Yet Cowan argues that women knew what they were doing; they placed privacy and the autonomy of the family above other priorities. The conundrum is whether women were 'free' to choose, since for a variety of reasons housewives were suggestible and not free agents. For working-class women, choice was an important issue, whether they should be 'protected', stay at home, keep house and care for children, or whether the family was better off when they contributed to income, utilized shop-made pies and puddings, and had childcare, washing and cleaning done by women who specialized in those jobs.[27] That working-class women's experience varied from the middle classes' was inevitable. The need to work combined with lack of refinements and standard of living of the middle classes shaped their experience.

CONTEXT AND CHRONOLOGY OF DOMESTIC SERVICE

Although earlier traditions persisted, a distinctive development of the late eighteenth century and the nineteenth was widespread increase in domestic service which became a predominant route for girls in the search for a livelihood and dowry. In this period the domestic servant became established in popular and legal terminology, and began to be identified as a separate category across Europe.[28] Directly linked to domesticity, it became a fundamental institution with its own hierarchies and rules. Domestic service is particularly under-recorded, since servants were not always reported separately in household returns. Many were relatives, which complicated perceptions of them as either 'family member' or 'worker'. Nevertheless, there is no doubt that domestic service was one of the most important employers of women and girls. The large numbers in towns exemplified its economic significance and predominance as an urban occupation. Fourteen per cent of the population of Munich in 1828 were domestic servants; in Berlin in 1885, 32 per cent of employed females were, as were a third of women between fifteen and twenty-four in London in the 1860s; and 28 per cent of French urban working women in 1866, compared to the national figure of 22 per cent. Servants were invaluable in the grimy urban environment to carry water, goods and slops up and down tall terraced houses, and most new wealth was in cities. It is mistaken, however, to assume that domestic service was limited to urban homes. As farmers' profits increased, they responded as mercantile and artisanal households did, striving for higher standards of comfort. Thus farmhouses saw changes in the number of servants employed, with specialized domestics becoming more common, and on more farms cooks, laundrymaids and nursemaids were paid higher wages than farm servants.[29]

Three broad phases of domestic service can be identified, but with national, regional and local differences. The first corresponds to the period of transition, from the late eighteenth century through to the middle third of the nineteenth, when the meaning of service shifted. Demand for household servants grew, associated with urbanization and the diffusion of domesticity, while demand for female agricultural labour in some regions declined. The increase was linked to a rise in the number of prosperous households in expanding urban areas, population growth, and a marked increase in the number of young in the population. While artisanal and factory industry competed for young single female labour, neither could absorb those unable to find work in the countryside. Attractions of domestic service saw regular growth in the numbers entering it, while demand for servants helped hold up female wages. Many stereotypes of domestic service originate from the second period, 1830 to 1880. Demand continued to grow from the well- and modestly well-off. Numbers grew rapidly from the 1830s, peaking in the last decades of the century (Figure 5.1), as the proportion of town dwellers who were servants also increased. Indeed, the number of servants in Paris continued to rise to the turn of the century, after decline had set in nationally. Wages also appeared to grow by about 30 per cent if advertisements in *The Times* are a guide. The relative absence of alternative work contributed to a very high proportion of the young female population in service at any one time; by the late nineteenth century, the experience of service was very common (Figure 5.2). Before 1880, employment opportunities changed little, though in industrial areas, factories provided an option which girls sometimes alternated with service or substituted for service altogether. The third phase, from about 1880 to the First World War, saw domestic service peaking, then a slow but distinctive decline set in; and by 1900, clearly fewer girls and a smaller proportion of the female labour force turned to domestic service.[30]

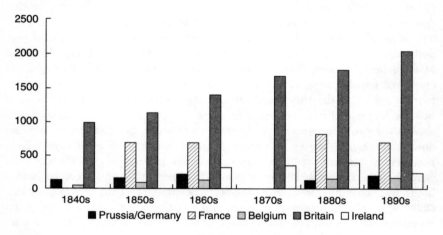

Figure 5.1   Female domestic servants, 1840s to 1890s
Source: Bairoch *et al.* (1968)

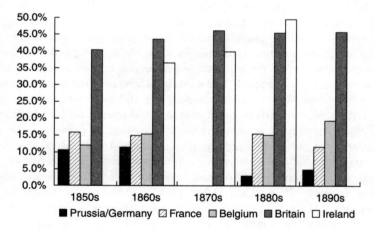

Figure 5.2   Female servants as a percentage of the female labour force
Source: Bairoch *et al.* (1968)

WHO WERE THE DOMESTIC SERVANTS?

The typical live-in domestic servant was a young woman of rural origin, aged between mid-teens and mid-twenties. The term 'servant' was synonymous with 'lad' or 'maid', and therefore, virtually by definition, they were young, unmarried and dependent. Germans almost exclusively called a female servant *mädchen*, regardless of whether she was young, single or virginal. The necessity to be single was partly a feature of living in another's household, a simple issue of accommodation if nothing else. Also, few households tolerated spouses who were independent of the household. Marriage altered the mistress–servant relationship, and created a conflict of interest. In Hamburg in 1885, only 1 per cent of female servants was married; in Ireland in 1871, less than 4 per cent were; and in London in 1851, 2 per cent were. More were married in France: 11.9 per cent in 1836. Thus it was part of cultural consciousness that 'servant' and 'single' were synonymous, especially for women. Domestic servants were young, because employers preferred 'innocents' and because it was a transition stage. In Hamburg in 1871, a third of female servants were between sixteen and twenty, and another third between twenty-one and twenty-five. In 1851 in England and Wales, most live-in domestics were single females between fifteen and twenty-five; indeed 40 per cent were under nineteen and 60 per cent under twenty-four. Nevertheless, the large number of unmarried female servants over fifty suggests that domestic service could easily become permanent. Career servants tended to work their way up the hierarchy, so that in Hamburg only 1 per cent stayed at the lowest rungs. Half of the more qualified servants, housekeepers, companions and cooks, were between twenty-five and forty-five, and the majority of charwomen, laundresses and manglers were middle aged or older.[31]

Many young women worked in domestic service as preparation for marriage. With provision of room, board and work clothes, they stood a chance of saving, provided, of course, that they did not become ill, pregnant or lose their place through bad behaviour or an employer's whim. LePlay's research and reminiscences suggest that many intended a permanent move to town, while others went to amass a dowry, in order to return home to marry someone with land. Sometimes couples migrated together, him to trade and her to service, marrying when they saved enough to set up their own household, such as Marie R., daughter of a blacksmith of the Meurthe, who entered service in 1836. In seven years she managed to save a small trousseau.[32] McBride argues that

> For roughly a third of [French] female domestics, the solitude of service ended in promotion through marriage . . . Servants . . . often were able to make 'good' marriages, that is, to men of the urban shopkeeping or artisanal classes . . . the pattern of these marriages is clear. What the interpretation of the data should be is not so obvious.[33]

It is not obvious that urban marriage was 'an improvement in their social status' since her argument relies on the notion that urban was better than rural. Marital patterns in Cambridge demonstrate that domestic service might not have been 'a significant means of achieving upward social mobility'. Servants were more likely to marry men from social classes lower than their fathers'. In the Caux, servants were likely to marry poorly paid weavers, day labourers and farm domestics.[34] Domestic service had potential for upward mobility, given the experience of a middle-class lifestyle and the acquisition of skills, but the extent to which it happened is unclear.

Most servants came from rural backgrounds. In Rochdale, between 1851 and 1871, the proportion of female servants born outside the town rose from 62 to 80 per cent. In Versailles between 1825 and 1853, 60 per cent came from the countryside, as did over half in Bordeaux, 'virtually all' in Marseilles, and 57 per cent in Melun in 1872. In Frankfurt, 98 per cent of the female domestics and 91 per cent in Berlin were born out of town in 1885. Migration patterns varied. In England, larger aristocratic households recruited from further away, while provincial middle classes were more likely to recruit from near by. In 1851, 75 per cent of servants in Colchester had been recruited within a ten-mile radius, the furthest distance it was possible to walk in a day off to visit the family. London servants of the gentry and aristocracy were likely to come from their country homes, but servants of trade and artisan classes often came from London's poor. French peasant women often found jobs as servants in rural landlords' town houses. For example, merchant Pierre Lacoste-Rigail employed a daughter of a tenant as chambermaid to his wife, and Elise Blanc was first hired as a chambermaid at the local château of Prévange in the Bourbonnais, and then went to Paris where her 'châtelains kept an apartment'. A common French pattern was for girls to migrate to provincial towns, and eventually to Paris. Well-established networks evolved for girls making the move, many arriving with a priest's reference for an employment bureau. Relatives and villagers working in cities formed an important conduit for hopeful girls. For example, in 1888, Doris Viersbeck stayed with an aunt in Hamburg, who helped advertise for a position and 'shortlist' three prospective employers, accompanied her to visit the ladies' homes, and negotiated wages.[35]

Agricultural distress, structural change and rural overpopulation could have been the impetus for girls to migrate, as in Germany and England. Such strategies were time-honoured ways of dealing with labour surpluses as well as shortages. English Poor Law authorities used service to relieve the parish of potentially chargeable girls, some assisting them to find a position, others removing entitlement from young single girls, effectively forcing them to seek one. One effect was to pauperize service, particularly in parishes, as in Sussex, which paid maintenance to girls who went into service. In France, pressure to leave came from poorer agricultural departments with high birth rates. Marginal peasant farmers were most likely to send daughters to service, and the 'Breton servant-girl became almost synonymous with domestic service in Paris'. Townspeople preferred rural servants, because of a latent mistrust of urban girls, who were not 'innocent' enough to bring into the idealized bourgeois home. They saw them as independent, less malleable, more intransigent and alert to opportunities. As a result, women of the Nord sent frantic letters to rural relatives asking for healthy, robust, moral and tractable servants. The naïveté, vigour and youth of a rural girl were advantages, her lack of ties made her more reliant upon her new household, and if she came from a distance, she would have fewer links with her own community.[36]

From servants' point of view, town service offered advantages like wider horizons, a chance to see new things, perhaps advance in the world and, usually, higher wages. It could be a secure form of migration, thus rural girls in Rome saw service as a solution to problems of lodging, employment and personal safety.[37] This is a recurrent theme. The highly traditional character of domestic service, based on familiar rural service and the availability of positions, explains much of its popularity. One asset was that it preserved the familial context of work. Young women left parental control and protection to adopt that of an employer. In fact, parents and employer could arrange contracts, though more experienced servants found their own positions.

> [It] gave secure care during the years of service, teaching and upbringing, a feeling of belonging to the Herrschaft and the family (sometimes to old age), cooperation and trust (especially with childrearing), [in] a relationship, which was not identical to that with old style 'masters' nor with new employer relationships.[38]

It was a practical solution to the fundamental need to support themselves and prepare for a future. In Wierling's study, German female servants saw it as entry into 'modern' life and a job with a career structure and 'a good ring' to it. Acceptance into a family meant a great deal, as did earning for oneself. They also saw it as preparation for life in the 'outside' world. No special skills were required, and the availability of jobs in cities meant that choices existed. For many, the first job in service was only a step to other work once they became adjusted to urban living. Others moved back and forth between domestic service and alternative occupations as the economy shifted or their personal circumstances or interests changed. In Halstead, Essex, many female weavers left Courtauld's silk factory for short periods of time, because of the 'pull of domestic service', and it was not uncommon for young girls to try both factory work and domestic service. In the Caux, domestic service was seen as less desirable than spinning, primarily because the servant lived with and worked for another family.[39] The dynamic between domestic service and other work is highly complex. Socio-economic factors, family predilections, political change, the experience of service and of other opportunities helped shape a girl's range of choices and the decisions she made.

Domestic service was highly gendered and became even more so. Women were a consistently high proportion, remaining above 90 per cent in England, rising to 92 per cent in Ireland, 83 per cent in France and well over 90 per cent in Hamburg about the end of the century. A rise in the proportion of female servants resulted from economic changes which left unskilled women with few options. The same factors created more jobs for men in the industrial sector, most of which were less subservient and better paid than service, especially as servant wages levelled off. To a former male servant, service was 'something like that of a bird shut up in a cage. The bird is well housed and well fed but deprived of liberty.' Subservience and independence were not only male issues, but there is little doubt that they contributed to men taking other work. Importantly, similar opportunities were not generated for women at the same time as countervailing pressures pushed them more and more into domestic service. The cult of domesticity and feminization of the household coincided with changes in occupational opportunities, particularly as middle classes more sharply defined household tasks as particularly suited to women, and women as particularly suited to domestic tasks. Because there were fewer permanent male servants and only the wealthiest could afford them, they became a sign of great refinement, and were 'shown off' as status symbols.[40] In this way, feminization of service probably contributed to a loss of prestige for females in domestic service.

THE EXPERIENCE OF DOMESTIC SERVICE

Significantly, the *Upstairs, Downstairs* image of a flock of servants in wealthy households with rigid hierarchies and traditions was atypical. Servants were more likely to be in smaller establishments working alone for shopkeepers, tradespeople and artisans in towns or suburbs. They frequently had little companionship, and did not live near family or friends. They were 'general' servants, the *Alleinmädchen*, or maids-of-all-work, doing whatever the household required. In early nineteenth-century Montauban, the president of the Cour des Aides employed only eight servants, and the wealthiest merchant only six. In 1851 in Rochdale, 61 per cent of servants were the only one in the household, while 34 per cent of London households had only one servant and 25 per cent had two. At the end of the century in Hamburg, over 75 per cent of domestic servants were the only employee. In 1872 in Versailles, 80 per cent of servants worked either alone, or with one other, while in Lyon, 70 per cent of servants worked alone. Typically, the maid was therefore the only servant. A small minority worked in large households or on country estates, and experienced the servant's hall with its career structure and hierarchy. Tasks were differentiated and service was a finely developed classification of duties and deference. For women, roles could stretch from the well-paid and respected housekeeper to lady's maid, cook, parlourmaid, right to the bottom of the pile, the lowly scullery maid. The large household was far more attractive for one who expected to 'get on', since they could advance with commensurate gains in wages and perks. Servants interviewed by Wierling indicate that they saw service as a way to improve themselves, and Viersbeck similarly appreciated the value of moving up the servant hierarchy.[41]

The experience of service obviously depended on the size, composition, resources and occupation of the household, while the environment in which servants worked related directly to status. Most 'servant-keepers' were middle and upper class. Whether a household employed a residential servant depended on a combination of needs and resources. Families with a number of daughters were less likely to hire, as were households headed by women and single people, which were not only probably among the less well off, but had fewer people to serve. Early in the century, one-third of the English lower middle classes were without servants as were 15 per cent of the better-off middle class. Similarly, many Parisian professionals did not hire servants; in 1856, at least 11 per cent of doctors and 38 per cent of lawyers employed none. On the other hand, some working-class families had servants, often relatives. The number and type of servant tended to rise as the demands of children in the family increased, falling off as older daughters or female relatives became available. The death of a mistress might be resolved by employing a servant. An upwardly mobile English banking family in the 1830s had two maids who did every sort of work, including gardening. By 1870, the family had three maids: cook, housemaid and nursemaid; the third generation in 1900 added a gardener and underhousemaid. Though the number of servants related to increasing wealth, the form of specialization, for example, between indoor and outdoor and between kitchen and house, is significant. This trend was also apparent in the Nord, where increasing wealth led to growing numbers of servants as well as differentiation of tasks.[42]

Differentiation of tasks did not lessen burdens, however. Viersbeck's first job in Hamburg as a cook illustrates the expectations placed on a servant.

> At half past five in the morning she would get up to provide early coffee. Two hours later, when the master had left, housework could begin: shopping, preparation of a breakfast at eleven o'clock, serving up lunch at four o'clock. Apart from her free evening, when she was allowed to go out from half past seven until ten o'clock, the end of a day's work was not fixed.[43]

A maid of all work was responsible for cleaning rooms, cooking, washing up, laundering and ironing. She was 'the soldier at the dirt-front' with brushes and mops to cope with daily cleaning of furniture, curtains and carpets. She carried heavy loads of wood, coal, laundry or food, emptied and washed chamberpots, and boiled clothes, menstrual rags, diapers and sheets before washing them. At the same time, she served the household as nanny, lady's maid and valet.

Jeanne Bouvier looked after 'two spoiled and insolent children – though their mother would not hear a word against them', and did all the shopping and housework, including the heavy laundry. Because the majority found themselves as the sole servant, the lowest tasks fell to them as well as the bulk of the work. Certainly girls fresh from the country, unschooled in the ways of the middle class, had few resources on which to draw and little support if they were overworked. Neither repeated fainting nor 'housemaid's knee' brought Viersbeck any relief from work.[44]

If new domestic conveniences created work for women, households with servants delegated these tasks. Indeed, Hardyment argues explicitly that for a complicated relationship between servant-keeping and the adoption of domestic appliances. As long as domestics were readily available, they took up the slack in the evolution of domestic technology, potentially delaying development as well as implementation of change. More significantly, she argues that the presence of servants encouraged people to think of machines as replacing servants, rather than enabling a radically new domestic management to evolve. Instead of encouraging collective strategies, such as washhouses, she believes the existence of servants encouraged the privatization of domestic work and led ultimately to the development of individualized appliances and the isolation of the female in the home.[45] An intriguing argument, it must be seen in the context of other ideological and economic developments that contributed to the emergence of privatized domestic work for women.

Contemporaries and historians considered relatively good wages as one of the attractions of domestic service. In England, wages for a general servant rose from £9.5 annually in 1833–37 to £18.8 by 1893–97, and those for female cotton workers from £20.8 to £37.1. However, the value of room and board was part of the attraction. Higgs added 5s per week to servants' wages, based on subsistence costs in Lancashire, to inflate wages for the added value of lodging, board and perks. Despite inherent difficulties, this approach provides a rough guide to comparative income levels. His calculations show that general servants were better compensated than textile workers between 1833 and 1857, but fell behind over the last years of the century. In Paris in 1883, the basic living cost for a worker was about 850 francs, including rent, light, heat and some clothing. Thus, McBride estimates the true value of a Parisian servant's wage was about 1,300 to 1,400 francs per year, in contrast to female cotton spinners who earned approximately 780 francs per year. Wage figures for industrial workers assume no stoppages and full employment, and therefore represent a maximum rather than a minimum. In many cases, servants had perks while living standards were better inside than outside service. The best-paid servants in the German Empire were in Berlin, and across Europe the largest cities paid more than provincial towns, and most towns paid more than rural domestic service. Wages in Paris were generally the highest in France, where 'average' female domestics earned 390 francs per year compared to counterparts in Toulouse, who earned 180 francs. It is no wonder that girls tended to migrate to the larger towns. Servants' wages rose throughout the century, and wages of the most skilled, specialized servants, like cooks, held up best and were always higher than those of general servants.[46] Thus the attractions of domestic service in the first part of the century were apparent. Despite difficult conditions and hard work, service held financial promise for many girls, but general servants' loss of comparability with textile workers at the end of the century helps to explain the numbers leaving service. The shift away from service came with new opportunities and as wages rose in other industries so that service began to lose its attraction.

Servants were often paid annually, and the lump sum could provide capital to invest or loan. In Montauban, thirteen of nineteen wage earners who lent money were servants, eight of whom made loans to relatives. In one case, in 1769, Durand Gasc borrowed 150 livres from his sister, Antoinette, a servant of a Montauban bourgeois, and returned for another loan of 150 livres eight years later. Thus, if all were well, a servant could accrue earnings to put towards her future. In contrast, Emmeline Pankhurst wrote of older former servants who 'had reached a time of life when it was impossible to get more employment. [Poverty] was through no fault of their own, but simply because they had never earned enough to save.'[47] Between the vagaries of service, the range of wages, and sending money to families, saving was difficult. Frequently, payments were in arrears with the risk of servants never receiving them if they were fired, quit, or if the family fell on hard times. Cora-Elisabeth Millet-Robinet, in *La Maison rustique des dames* (1844–45), is explicit:

> it is preferable to pay them each month, or at least every third month, rather than once a year as is the custom in many provinces . . . When money is at one's disposal, it is easy for it to be put to different use than that for which it was set aside, and this can become cause for embarrassment. Moreover, it is unfair to make servants wait a long time for salary that is due to them.[48]

Servants did not always receive wages directly. The merchant Pierre Lacoste paid a chambermaid's wages directly to her peasant father. Similarly, Monsieur Flahaut sent foodstuffs or coals to the parents of servant girls, or paid rents on father's farms for girls who served the Flahaut family from 1811 to 1877.[49] So, instead of saving, some girls had no funds at their disposal.

Since servants usually lived in the mistress's house they were under constant scrutiny and at the family's 'beck and call'. Summonses frequently came by bells, called 'tormentors' by Viersbeck. They worked long, hard hours, since a day could begin at 5 a.m. and not finish before 10 or 11 p.m. Employers felt a sixteen-hour day was not unreasonable, because housework included so many 'natural breaks'. Time to themselves during the day was scarce, as were days off. Holidays were only possible if the family was away. Employers frequently regulated contacts outside the household, sometimes with complete 'no followers' bans. This lack of independent judgement over friendships and association with family members isolated servants further. Employers operated from a mixture of motives, including fear of theft, but equally important was control of their household and preservation of carefully worked-out standards. Such interference created an important source of tension. Viersbeck expressed resentment of enquiries about her relations, leisure time and contact with persons outside the house, even tradesmen. Servants lacked privacy and time to themselves at a time when the household was becoming more privatized and society as a whole placed greater value on privacy. There was little outcry about servants' condition primarily because it was private, carried out in the home. Indeed, it attracted contemporary approval because it fulfilled women's domestic destiny. Another reason for silence was the fear that regulation or cost would deprive households of servants, who not only relieved women from many burdens of housework, but contributed to the identification with domesticity.[50]

Servant girls were vulnerable on a number of levels. They were away from home, with few friends or supporters, and therefore dependent on the goodwill and protection of their employers. They could be dismissed at will, without cause. If they became ill or infirm, they could be replaced. Lack of a reference limited a girl's chance of employment. Hamburg police court records reveal servants' vulnerability and deprivation. Regular reportage of bedwetting suggests the psychological damage many suffered. Given their youth, it is not surprising, and one doctor urged employers to watch the state of mind of their young 'charges', away from home for the first time.[51] Proximity and close living quarters contributed to a situation of young, sexually aware servants, often isolated and perhaps needing comfort and love. They were vulnerable to demands and 'charms' of the master as well as male servants in the house. Most female patients in the Hôtel Dieu at Montauban were servants or textile workers, often admitted in labour, or suffering from postpartum debility or infections. Few employers would hesitate to fire a servant they suspected was pregnant, or even sexually active. The innkeeper of the Auberge de la Menusière in 1790 found Marianne Dubosc, a servant, with the stableboy, Michel, in her room. He dismissed her but Michel kept his job. To the innkeeper's credit, when Marianne discovered she was pregnant, he pressed Michel to pay the costs.[52]

Many bourgeois writers were convinced of servants' immorality, and it was also widely believed that the ranks of prostitutes comprised former female servants. London Chief of Police in 1816 J. N. Lavender stated:

> many prostitutes upon the town are servant girls, who have been driven there through the caprice of their masters or mistresses, who frequently discharge them, and refuse to give them any character. I have had many complaints from female servants personally to me upon that subject; I may say two or three hundred.[53]

Many young female workers lived and worked in others' households, but servants most explicitly and most frequently. There is little doubt that former domestics made up a large proportion of prostitutes. The largest occupational group of registered prostitutes in Paris in 1830 were household servants, 28 per cent. In 1880, a third of known and registered prostitutes and mothers of abandoned children in France were former domestics. In Germany, about one-third of prostitutes had been servants, and 61 per cent of inhabitants of Magdalene institutions in Glasgow were former servants between 1860 and 1869. However, selective admission policies sought girls most susceptible to reform, such as servants.[54] Two issues emerge. First, contemporaries closely linked service and prostitution, regardless of the facts; and second, servants comprised a large portion of prostitutes.

Pinchbeck noted that 'immorality among dressmakers and domestic servants was proverbial'. Yet all working women were vulnerable to the sorts of pressure that led them to turn to prostitution, either permanently or sporadically, usually in periods of unemployment.[55] Walser argues that no particular group of female workers, including domestic servants, was over-represented among prostitutes. Instead the emergence of new independent wage-earning working-class females was in obvious contrast to their middle-class employers who were tightly bound up in the family. Thus they became the object of sexual fantasies and symbolically posed a threat to the bourgeois family. The style of the domestic servant epitomized all that society said was unacceptable behaviour for a middle-class woman. An identifiable group of former servants among prostitutes fuelled speculation that they were particularly susceptible to a life of immorality, and reinforced distrust that middle classes showed towards their domestic staff. However, servant girls were also the largest group working in cities. In English accounts, similar criticisms were made about any single working woman, referring variously to lace-runners, factory girls and glove-makers, and women workers in distressed trades often told Mayhew of being driven to the streets.[56]

However, the founding of Magdalene hospitals in Scotland, the passing of the Contagious Diseases Act in England and the registration of prostitutes in France indicated social attitudes which reached beyond fear of disease. First, police hounded, searched and subjected to forcible medical examinations and incarcerated women, not men. Second, no evidence suggests an increase in venereal disease or prostitution. 'Prostitute' was not a clear category of meaning, but was constructed out of discourses of the period, and authorities were quick to label women as prostitutes if their behaviour did not coincide with bourgeois norms. Commentators were liable to accuse young girls who dressed and behaved immodestly, unmarried mothers, mill girls, socialists and young women with no apparent means of support of prostitution. The doctor at the Lock Hospital in Glasgow said only one in ten of his patients gave prostitute as her occupation, though it was not a crime, but 'They are all prostitutes of one sort or another.' The causes of prostitution were largely put down to women's individual character flaws, such as vanity and desire for pretty clothes, with only passing reference to contributory factors of poverty and poor education. For example, the Chief Constable of Glasgow in 1870 thought there was no difficulty in identifying a prostitute: 'you may well know a prostitute as you would know a sweep. A man with a black face may not be a sweep, but at the same time you would say he was a sweep.'[57] Thus labelling prostitutes was highly subjective, charged with bourgeois morality.

There is no doubt that there were tensions inherent in the mistress–servant relationship, though perhaps these were easier to deal with when kin–servant identity was blurred. Smith argued for a reciprocity and partnership between servant and mistress that perpetuated a moral economy in the household quite distinct from the cash tie binding employers and employees in the labour contract. The bond lay in ideas of duty, obligation and correct behaviour. Although clearly a contract between unequals, it was situated in mutual dependency rather than self-interest and aimed at the good of the whole. The personal nature of obligation sometimes alleviated the worst features of the authoritarian structure. Wierling emphasized that the position of a housemaid entailed relationships with 'her' family, friendship with servants, even secret friendships with daughters of the house. Subjection to employers was a prime feature, and personal service was important to the conduct of the relationship. German servants associated service with concepts like respect, trust and personal devotion. Having been brought up to believe in respect for one's betters, service was an extension of these inculcated views.[58] Mistresses used social distance to lend authority to commands and to reinforce their control. Despite the personal character of the relationship, social etiquette maintained distance and servants knew that they were paid for politeness, while form and rules shaped relationships:

> Mother would go down and see her cook in the morning, to give orders and that kind of thing. And thereafter, if she wanted to speak to her for any reason or other bells were rung and the cook would come up. No mistress would ever go downstairs.[59]

They were to obey, follow orders and subsume their own thoughts and feelings, while appearing to unite their interests with those of the family. These factors diminished what would have been natural respect. Davidis described how servants were expected to identify with the household:

> Good honest serving maids are a reliable support for the housewife; they prove to be true, they do not allow themselves to be tempted to disloyalty . . . They hold it an injustice to steal the slightest of their possessions; similarly they also take to heart that through lethargy and carelessness time and advantages are lost, and through them the *Herrschaft* becomes just as disadvantaged as through embezzlement.

They . . . practise its precepts just as faithfully behind their backs as before their eyes . . . the honour of the *Herrschaft* is their honour.[60]

Mistresses were charged with scrutinizing staff and remembering duties towards them. Thus, in Lille, women organized prayer groups for female domestics, and bound servants to them by providing children's education, clothing, nursing care, and burying faithful servants.[61] Mistresses expected servants to reciprocate, behave according to a strict code of respectability and maintain unquestioning loyalty. Not only did their behaviour reflect the gentility of the household, their loyalty and acquiescence protected the veneer of family respectability.

Viersbeck's experience illustrates how servants regarded relationships in the household. Her first post in Hamburg showed little care for her needs, as she was hungry and overworked. She moved to a home where she felt rewarded and valued, and where wishes were expressed in a friendly way. 'Usually Frau Dahn came to see us in the kitchen in order to show her satisfaction as soon as the meal was over. Sometimes we were given a bottle of wine by the master.' She enjoyed another post since 'you did not feel the difference of rank so much because Herr and Frau Nielson were always friendly. To Frau Nielson especially I had become something like a confidante.' Tensions arose not only from close personal contacts but from inherent contrasts. Disparities were apparent to servants at the sharp end of demonstrating public respectability. They saw the body beneath the show and the hypocrisy that underpinned the system. Viersbeck became annoyed by Frau Nielson's indulgence in a life of pleasure which contrasted starkly with her own life of hard conscientious labour, and after a build up of grievances, she resigned. As Schlegel interpreted it, 'On the one hand the young mistress rejected all the outward forms which might emphasize their different status, while at the same time living out precisely this formally-denied inequality.' Servants' appearance, language and manner reflected on household image, but too close an imitation of the bourgeoisie could be explosive because it threatened carefully acquired status. Maids were expected to be clean, neat and respectable, and had cast-off clothing as a perquisite. However, wearing it could lead to criticism of mimicking their 'betters'.[62] Thus experience rather than preconceived notions influenced domestics' view of service.

Where a hierarchy of servants existed, the servant–servant relationship shaped experience. Servants' quarters reflected nuances of status and prestige within the ranks, mirroring the gender and seniority of the patriarchal household in microcosm. Thus the butler wielded patriarchal authority over junior servants, often controlling specific spatial areas of the quarters, for example, his own pantry. The cook, a 'matronly' figure, maintained control over her table and kitchen, and exercised authority over the servants' sitting area, while kitchen and scullery maids as well as 'upstairs' maids were of inferior rank, and subordinated to the will of senior servants. Lines of demarcation and assertions of place within the hierarchy contributed to fundamental friction in the household. Quarrels and thefts among servants in Hamburg regularly appeared in the records. In households studied by Davidoff and Hall, numerous jurisdictional quarrels developed because servants persisted in breaching lines of demarcation between tasks and in using other servants' equipment. With long chains of command, servants could muddle or deliberately ignore orders.[63]

Some employers 'expressed an offensive sense of possession, superiority and harassment', but not all servants were prepared to suffer without protest, as Hamburg police courts indicate. The household hierarchy, combined with high levels of demands, created a world of tension related to class and to issues of dependence and independence. Cammarosano saw the increasing number of Florentine seamstresses resulting from deliberately avoiding the 'humiliating personal subordination' of service. Ideas of independent labour shaped notions of work status, and rejection of dependence was evident in attitudes towards service by men and increasingly by women. As one commentator of the 1860s observed, 'there are few of the employed class who would not prefer a herring and potatoes in a room of their own to the choicest meals in the servants' hall'.Wierling's interviews make it clear that opposition of servants was not towards the work, since they were accustomed to hard work, but towards servitude. Indeed, they were proud of their achievements, making a distinction themselves between work and service. They could not reach self-realization through work, but the separation of the concepts of 'work' and 'service' helped their self-image.[64]

LIVING-OUT SERVANTS

Many former servants continued with similar work after leaving live-in service. Married women took in lodgers and provided services, such as washing and meals. This was useful work for former domestics, or any woman with young children, who had a spare room she could rent. Others became charwomen, took in washing, went to other homes to do the washing, or worked for laundresses with their own businesses. They worked as manglers and ironers; a good ironer who was competent with the finer types of frills and linens was valuable indeed. The middle classes frequently hired extra help for specific tasks, like laundry, 'occasions' or peak times such as 'spring cleaning'. Work was casual and irregular, but where there was employment for young women, there was a demand for older women to look after children, make the tea and do washing.[65]

Women in London could earn 1s 3d to 2s per day washing and charring, though work was irregular. Labour was hard, hours long, and most was still done by hand. A widow told Mayhew, 'My health broke about six years ago, and I couldn't do hard work in washing and I took to trotter selling.' When city missionaries complained that women constantly broke the Sabbath, the

Superintendent conceded that it was an occupation 'of so laborious a character, that the Sabbath is, in common with other days, generally devoted to that kind of labour'.[66] The work was hard enough that husbands might help, like the dock labourer whose wife

> has 3s a week for washing, for charring, and for mangling: the party my wife works for has a mangle, and I go sometimes to help; for if she has got 6d worth of washing to do at home then I go to turn the mangle for an hour instead of her – she's not strong enough.[67]

A woman who owned a mangle could earn more. A watercress seller reported that his wife earned 3s per day taking washing and keeping a mangle. He too turned the mangle when at home. In mid-century France, a soaping woman earned 2fr50 for a fourteen-hour day, while a more skilled ironer got only 2fr75 for a twelve-hour shift, despite her longer apprenticeship. The washerwomen who arrived at the Seine by 6 a.m. rarely left before 7 p.m., and exposure to weather damaged their health; they frequently suffered from bronchial or rheumatic complaints and 75 per cent from hernia.[68] Tristan described washerwomen in Nîmes, in water to their waists

> that is poisonous because it is befouled with soap, potash, soda, bleach and grease, and finally with all kinds of dyes such as indigo, madder red, saffron, etc. etc. . . . These miserable washerwomen no longer looked like human beings, habitually being in the water had bloated them – professional washerwomen are always very fat and deformed.[69]

In contrast, Octave Uzanne described the laundrywoman as clean, pretty and even coquettish, although prone to vulgar language. The work could be lucrative for a servant who was able to invest in her own laundry business and, if successful, hire several women. In London, washerwomen earned 1s to 2s 6d per day, while a skilled ironer earned perhaps 15s per week. The respectable laundress herself could earn 4s per dozen shirts and 1s per dozen small articles.[70]

6

RURAL WOMEN – FARMHOUSE AND AGRICULTURE

PERIODS AND TRENDS

At the French Revolution, women's position in agriculture across Europe was little changed from a century earlier. The effect of agricultural innovation on women's work had been limited in Britain and of little significance in the rest of Europe. Disparity continued to be a significant feature of women's contribution to and experience of agricultural work, resulting from variations in sizes and wealth of farms, the type of husbandry practised, the extent to which farming had become capitalist, the role of purchased goods in family strategies, the position girls and women held in the household, in the family and on the farm, and the role and strength of local and regional custom, including inheritance and landholding practices. To the end of the French wars, women were found throughout agriculture, in fields and around the farmyard. They reaped grain and with the introduction of convertible husbandry, more work was created for which they were thought to be especially suitable, for example, weeding and hoeing. They were engaged as permanent and casual labourers, but specialization began to have an effect on women's regular role as agricultural workers.

From about 1815 to mid-century, regional variations were particularly pronounced. In the south-east of England, demand for female labour in field work decreased except at peak periods, while in Northumberland and Scotland, female labour remained important. Enclosures and specialization in England and Germany created systems of labour-intensive farming, convertible husbandry, and an increase in crops for the market. French agricultural output was increasing substantially, and the number of female day labourers and farm servants grew in areas like the Caux, while Italian women remained only seasonal field workers. Thus women were in demand, although frequently as casual rather than permanent wage earners. From mid-century to the 1870s, some areas saw a rise in women's activity, whereas in others decline was already apparent. Rising numbers of women worked in agriculture during the last half of the century in France, Germany and Italy, contrasting with a substantial decline from 1851 in Britain. Significantly, the proportion of the female workforce in agriculture tended to decline from the 1850s in France and England, and in Germany and Italy from the 1870s. In Britain, the number and proportion of women involved in agriculture declined dramatically, from about 7 to 2 per cent between 1851 and 1901, while in France, Germany, Belgium and Italy they remained around 50 per cent (see Figure 6.1). Notably, the proportion of women in Scottish agriculture was significantly higher than in England.[1] In all regions women continued to engage in activities around the farmhouse and dairy, in seasonal work and in specialized areas of production like market gardening. While female labour was often employed on similar tasks in similar ways, significant diversity is found in the responses of women and farmers on a local and regional basis. By the last decades of the century, trends were clear. Women were far less likely to be employed in fields on a regular basis than earlier, and their options had been radically revised. The interplay of economic change and ideology helped to redefine women's position in agriculture. The prevailing ideology of domesticity and women's attitudes tended to withdraw some from the fields and heavy labour. Also, other opportunities, such as domestic service and industry, shaped their participation in agriculture and decisions about work.

Although the late nineteenth-century writer, du Maroussem, described the division of labour as 'outside work for men, indoor work for women', no clear demarcation operated for much of the period.[2] Millet-Robinet, in *La Maison rustique des dames,* listed responsibilities of a mistress:

> [She] should have all of the servant girls on the farm under her immediate supervision. The farmyard – that is, the cowshed, the dairy, the pigsty, and the chicken coop – as well as the gardens, the orchards, and the sheep, are also her responsibility. She must be aware of all the jobs to be done on the farm in order to reinforce her husband in his supervision and to replace him in times of absence or sickness.[3]

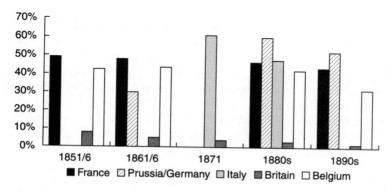

Figure 6.1 Women in agriculture as a percentage of the female labour force
Source: Bairoch *et al.* (1968)

Women undertook most tasks, but the household and kitchen garden remained their special domain together with dairying. In the Caux, farmers' wives, widows and domestic servants were responsible for the *masure*, or the farmyard and house, tasks which were mirrored in Ireland, Scotland, Italy and Russia, providing the household with fruit and vegetables from a kitchen garden. Poultry was almost exclusively the work of women who ensured 'the small-plot people make a profit of their poultry'. Even in mining communities like Larkhall, Lanarkshire, wives tended 'a good-sized garden, which was generally kept in a first class state of cultivation; and in many of them a little byre had been erected where a cow, and sometimes two, were kept'. Roubin, in her study of male and female space, argues that females were closely identified with the house as a sphere of influence which was explicitly theirs. Furthermore, the peasant household was controlled by females, no place more than the kitchen, the chief room which 'represented an organic complex minutely compartmentalized into a maze of storerooms whose contents were fully known only to the *maîtresse* of the house and manager of the domestic economy'. This female space extended beyond the house to encompass gardens which ringed the town and supplied the household. Men tended larger gardens in the fields. Related to women's farmyard work was production of goods for sale and marketing surpluses. In the 1890s, the women of Cévennes still wore the *chapsal* or *chasson*, a round pad on the head for carrying loads of sixty to eighty pounds. 'All the women of the region are trained to this sort of carrying from their tenderest youth and work with it as easily as if they were merely wearing a hat.' Women undertook a wide range of activities imbedded less in domestic ideology and more in a practical division of labour. Nor could such work be seen as 'easy' since drawing water constituted a regular aspect of women's daily work, and likewise they undertook the heavy work of milk, butter and cheese production. Similarly, carrying loads to market demanded strength and fortitude: 'The ideal paysanne needed to be robust rather than beautiful.'[4]

Daughters, daughters-in-law and servant girls assisted depending on labour requirements of the household. In 1865, Jeanne Bouvier from Isère was expected to help her mother by watching cows and knitting to keep her hands busy.[5] The daughter of a small farmer near Kielder, Northumberland, also helped.

> In those days the cows were out on the hill and they had to be brought
> in and milked up the dyke back in summer, and the milk carried back.
> We helped with whatever farm work was going on, setting potatoes
> . . . we made our own butter . . . then the water was to carry [sic] . . .
> there was always plenty work on a farm, never time to be early [sic].[6]

Experience and size of household determined tasks entrusted to a servant in Bavaria, who began helping in the house and with childcare: 'As she grows she is promoted to under-servant and starts learning farming tasks. Then she gets promoted to middle servant, who milks the cows and feeds them under super-vision. Finally she becomes an upper servant, who is responsible for the ani-mals.' Bavarian farm maids might work primarily in the cowshed, where they were in charge of feeding the animals, especially calves and other small animals, and mucking out the shed. On smaller farms, a single servant undertook the duties of stable and housemaids and substituted for the farm wife. Thus, she had to be reliable and able to undertake any household or farmyard task. Her versatility and experience were assets, and the skills learned constituted a dowry which prepared her for her own household, kitchen garden and what-ever livestock her marital farm brought her.[7]

FIELD WORK AND ITS ORGANIZATION

Women played a vital part in the fields, despite key changes in agriculture which directly influenced their 'outdoor' work. Revised practices in the orga-nization of arable, common and peripheral land such as wastes were accompa-nied by a tendency to specialization, frequently linked to greater commercialization of farming, and introduction of a wider range of crops, for fodder and market. Concentration on grain farming took place in many areas at the expense of dairy farming, and women's role also reduced in regions which shifted from crops to cattle. Simultaneously, labour-intensive farming increased, either because of crop type or new rotations. Furthermore, gradual changes in the types of tools and the introduction of machinery altered field work. These shifts determined when and where women worked and the type of work they did, and significantly altered their experience of agriculture, despite continuities in the nature of tasks and basic hard labour. Over the period male and female day labour rose markedly and live-in farm service declined. Also, whereas farm servants were largely single, both single and married women worked in day labour and became tied to tasks which were coded as women's work. Changes in agricultural practices contributed to a clearer division of labour, more overtly defined gender roles in agriculture and less shared work. Ultimately, women's status and responsibility in agriculture diminished.

It is hard to quantify women involved in field work because of the high level of seasonal employment, usually overlooked by census investigators. The wide range of women's work meant it was difficult for enumerators to allocate them an occupation, and some were not counted at all, since farmers' wives and daughters were not clearly identified as labour-force participants. Finally, the association of women with the house rather than the fields predisposed various enumerators and commentators to be blind to their field activities. As Sayer pointed out,

Women's presence in agriculture as independent waged labourers who were often strong, dressed to suit their work and beyond middle-class male control, challenged the dominant definitions of femininity. They also threatened the idea that the countryside and its people, unlike large industrial towns and their masses, was innocent and pure. The cultural image of the cottage women or dairymaid, domestic, clean and white, was the embodiment of femininity. The reality of the field labourer was its antithesis.[8]

Miller's work on Gloucestershire points to a significant gap between census data and figures for female employment recorded in farmers' wage books, which raises questions about women's participation in fields for other areas and times. The disparity suggests that more women worked both as casual labourers or permanent employees than official figures show.[9]

The prevalence of women field workers varied from region to region and from village to village. The British Poor Law Report of 1843 indicated: 'The women of one village have always been accustomed to reap while to those of another in the immediate neighbourhood, the practice is unknown. Turnip hoeing is by no means an uncommon occupation for women, yet in many villages they never undertake it.' George Culley confirmed the disparity in 1870, 'The Scotch practice differs from the English in the much more extensive employment of women. Throughout the whole of my district women are employed in all the lighter and in not a few of the heavier operations of farm labour.' In France, Martin Nadaud, in the Creuse, said 'my wife, like all other women of the countryside, was raised to work in the fields from morning till night and she worked no less ... after our marriage.' In the Caux, with a strong tradition against women working in fields, only three Auffay women were regular *journalières*, or day labourers, in 1796 when men were away in the army. Yet between 1796 and 1851, a threefold increase took place in the number of female day labourers and farm servants. In contrast, Roubin argues that Provençal fields were male space, where women went only during periods of extended irrigation or when men needed extra help. Where women had a long tradition of field work in Italy, as in the Turin hinterland with little capitalist agriculture, women made up as much as 70 per cent of the agricultural labour force by 1881. Belgian women undertook both seasonal work like harvesting and constant tending of the fields.[10]

Enclosure, larger farms, more commercial farming and regional specialization led to greater occupational specialization. This curtailed women's contribution to the full range of agricultural activities. However, consolidation of large-scale agriculture did not immediately reduce the level of women's work because farming methods remained labour intensive and mechanization developed slowly. Instead, their activity increased with the extension of production for the market, especially in mixed farming, root crops, market gardening and dairying. The wider adoption of improved methods, what Armstrong called 'neatness', involved work performed more cheaply by women, such as planting, singling, weeding and hoeing root crops, including turnips and potatoes across

Europe and sugar beet in Germany. In Sicily, women worked with new commercial crops like grapes, oranges, nuts, olives and other fruits. Not only were orchards close to town, but grape and olive harvests overlapped with ploughing which occupied men. In the Caux, artificial meadows replaced fallow fields, grain production increased and the labour force expanded, so that women were hired to work in the fields alongside men. In Scotland, commercial farming only affected main agricultural areas, but the disappearance of the commons and many smallholdings caused many women to turn to day labour. The evolution of 'market gardening' was particularly important to women since intensive labour requirements usually entailed tasks reserved for them. Thus new crops, like those of Sicily, the rise of a new soft fruit industry in Scotland in Clydeside and Carse of Gowrie, and the growing demand of urban areas like London and St Etienne for a range of garden produce created work for women. Sometimes these provided alternatives where the decay of rural industries left women looking for work. In other cases, wages were better than those locally, as for young women from north Wales who regularly migrated for the season to gardening areas of Brentford, Hammersmith and Isleworth near London. These 'ordinarily pit wenches' arrived in April to set and tend crops and then carried fruit, like strawberries, to customers in London.[11]

The seasonal pattern of women's work depended on agricultural practice, the character of crops grown, custom and women's traditional role in agriculture. The introduction of new crops increased work for women at the same time as it limited the periods in the year when they were able to find work. The development of new field systems based on turnips, grasses and new crops like potatoes required a new cycle of hiring. Snell argued that by the early nineteenth century, women's work in south and east England was most secure in the spring while they were increasingly liable to unemployment over the rest of the year. It is noteworthy, however, that the same seasonality did not hold throughout Europe nor throughout the rest of Britain, since the range of crops and tasks often meant that women were in greater demand over new periods of the year. Root crops, for example, could require ten to fifteen worker-days per acre compared to four or five for corn harvesting. In Lowland Scotland, turnips and potatoes were replacing summer fallow, leading to a significant increase in farm labour. For example, an additional 100 workers were needed on a Haddington farm, with a resident labour force of 150. In the Magdeburg region of Germany, women could find employment only during beet hoeing and harvesting. Seed drills for beets introduced mid-century eliminated an exclusively female occupation, while technical changes at the end of the century further shortened the annual cycle, so that beets were finished by January and there was no work for women until April. The labour year for men and women thus became structured differently, so that women found work later in the year than men. One of the most important implications was to create new patterns to women's field work. Because their work became closely identified with specific seasonal work, it cut down the level of shared work and accentuated gendered roles in the fields, both because men's and women's work was different and because of the types of work identified with women. The work was no less strenuous, but nor did it carry with it the sense of ownership, status or occupation which accrued to men's work. Women became associated with certain crops and specific activities, tending and gathering, whereas men retained and enhanced their association with land and stock, with an associated sense of proprietorship. Also, women's work became identified as casual seasonal labour while men's was more readily seen as permanent. This difference is demonstrated by wage books for Lincolnshire in 1851. Men were paid by the week but women's wages were by day and task, for example, 2s for harvesting, 1s 9d for lifting potatoes, 9d for weeding and planting. In wage books of southern England, women were grouped together as a 'cost', that is, 'cash paid to women haymakers, £11. 3s. 6d', which emphasizes their increasingly tenuous hold on work.[12]

Women had long been associated with harvest activities, but greater exploitation of a much wider range of crops meant that they were called upon to harvest not only roots, but fruits, nuts and other new commercial crops. Indeed, in many cases, tending and harvesting became women's work. Their long association with kitchen gardens and orchards connected them to harvesting similar produce commercially, for example, grapes, olives and oranges in Sicily. European women continued to take part in the grain harvest as reapers, gatherers, stackers, turners and binders. For many, field work was not their normal activity. In Marlhes, the demands of the harvest were met by women who normally wove. In Sicily, women joined men in distant wheat fields only at harvest. The same was true of Scandinavian women, who were primarily dairywomen, and Bavarian household servants. However, increased use of the scythe instead of the sickle, especially for corn, meant that women reapers were gradually replaced by men who, it was believed, 'were physically better equipped to wield the heavier instrument'. The key difference was that the sickle cut grain lower to the ground in smaller quantities and required fewer support workers to gather and stack it but more reapers to cut the same acreage. The scythe was considered to be a bit 'rough' but quicker. Because the sickle had advantages, the transition from one tool to the other was slow. Women's displacement from mowing depended on crops, the size of the workforce and the necessity of speed and care in cutting. In Scotland, the move from sickle or heuk, used by women, to the two-handed, heavier scythe, long associated with male strength, forced women out of work where they had been considered 'our neatest cutters', according to an Elgin farmer. The scythe was introduced in grain areas of Banffshire, Aberdeenshire and the Lothians by the 1840s, but simultaneously these areas adopted the scythe-hook, a sickle used as often by women as men. Reports from Oxfordshire in the 1870s describe 'A dozen, or maybe twenty reapers, largely women, [working] in one field, with the men following to tie up the sheaves and another group to set them in shucks.' In Germany, the choice of handtool varied considerably, even within relatively homogeneous districts. The sickle remained the primary tool in southern Germany for rye and wheat but was replaced in the north by the scythe for winter grains. Additionally, local patterns of cultivation and the state of the crop influenced the choice of tool. 'Strong' grains in Pomerania could be cut with the sickle, while in Saxony usage depended on whether the grain was wet or dry. Harvesting rye remained dependent on female labour. Also, the sickle continued to be prominent on smaller holdings, while women were reported using certain types of scythe. In Bavaria, women mowed whenever the sickle was used, as they did in France, Russia and Denmark.[13] Gradually women lost the opportunity of cutters' higher wages, although more were needed for less well-paid work: gathering, binding and stacking. However, when there was a shortage of men, women were called upon as cutters. Thus they were used as a temporary, elastic source of labour during peak seasons and could be used to depress wages, since women were almost always cheaper than men. The overall effect was to widen the differential between male and female wages as reapers. This coincided with a noticeable increase in the wages of domestic servants which contributed to a shift in women's employment from the fields to service.

An ironic feature was that women were considered by many to be more skilled in the use of the sickle than men, and one reason for the slow uptake of the scythe was difficulty in finding adequately skilled scythemen. Stephen drew direct comparison between men and women reapers: 'With a sickle, a woman is as efficient a worker as a man; indeed what is called a maiden-ridge, of three young women, will beat a bull-ridge of three men, at reaping any sort of corn, on any given day.' Many writers suggest simply that the scythe was too heavy and laborious for women, although Lee objects, citing use of the *Heidekrautsense* which was even heavier. Roberts, for example, writes, 'It should be borne in mind that strength, and the acquired skill of the mower, were both treated as scarce resources by farmers in the past . . . [These] were factors which had a direct effect on the opportunities for harvest work which would be available for women.' This is despite the fact that other work they did, such as manuring, was equally laborious and distasteful. One modern commentator on rural life expressed the view that the sickle 'was especially used by women, who are said to be physiologically better adapted to bending than men', while Hostettler suggests that the swinging motion was considered injurious to the female physique.[14] Clearly, notions of strength and skill are again confused, and the allocation of women to reaping and men to mowing is as much to do with rationalization of a masculine takeover.

Gleaning was commonly reserved for women and children and referred to as their 'work'. For some, such as Sicilian peasant women, the grain was primarily for their own use, but others sold it to buy food and essentials, or as in France: 'Sunday dresses for the girls'. By mid-century, resentment of gleaning was clear. In Suffolk, 'women will not work in harvest, only glean'. Similarly, from France came complaints that journeymen's wives refused to work at harvest and servant girls left regular work preferring *glanage* or *grapillage*. Legal and technological changes combined to bring the practice largely to an end by century's end. Enclosure and the end of many feudal rights often outlawed gleaning. In Italy, for example, with unification, semi-feudal rights ended, rendering it illegal, and the reduction of commons in southern England had a similar effect. Gleaning was curtailed, as in France and England, where smallholders harvested with greater care, cutting down grain that hired hands left and used horse rakes and mechanical reapers, ensuring little was left to gather. Also, in France, a reduction in local mills made it more difficult to sell or to turn into flour. Weber suggests that women also turned away from gleaning, preferring alternatives, such as sewing for Parisian stores.[15]

Wives and female relatives remained those most likely to work in agriculture. For example, in Ireland, 85 per cent of female agricultural labour and virtually all women on holdings less than thirty acres worked on their family farms. In Marlhes, as domestic ribbonweaving declined, wives turned more and more to agriculture. Also late in the century, families who owned enough land completely dedicated wives' and daughters' labour to agriculture, instead of daughters migrating to work.[16] In Italy, wives made an important contribution to the family labour force in farmyard, house and fields, depending on region and custom. As one peasant recalled the 1890s,

> My father and mother went to work in the fields, taking me with them like a little bundle, which they deposited under a mulberry tree. They dragged along the board with which to level the earth, my mother in front and my father behind with a rope, and once they got the ground level they began to sow the grain.[17]

Thus married women and their daughters constituted a significant if hidden part of the labour force.

As long as labour was plentiful, it was more economical to hire casual rather than permanent workers, so the century saw an increase in day labour, some of which was seasonal and sporadic. This shift in the structure of the labour force contributed to changing the level, character and timing of women's work. In the first half of the century, employment of small farmers' and labourers' daughters and wives as day labourers was widespread in England and the German Empire. Indeed, some farmers thought they had a 'prescriptive and prior right' to call on the labour of local women, especially wives and daughters of their own employees. Throughout the north-east of England and Scotland, seasonal labour was largely supplied by family hirings. Cottages were let to hinds, ploughmen or sometimes widows with daughters, in return for providing work as required at day wages. Unmarried brothers Francis and Christopher Storey hired themselves to Sir Edward Blackett in March 1865 and agreed 'our niece to work when wanted and to have 10*d* per day in summer and 1/6 a day in harvest'. In return they received their house, garden and coals free. This arrangement enabled them to provide female labour without hiring a woman whom they would have to support when she was not working.[18] As the century progressed, single women increasingly pulled out of agriculture. In England and Wales, female working relatives of farmers declined only 12 per cent between 1851 and 1871, while female labourers fell by 24 per cent and female farm servants decreased 75 per cent. In other words, permanent paid agricultural labourers were the ones who were disappearing, with a rapid decline in the numbers of females. The period also saw the invention of the female farm labourer in the Caux, rising from virtually none in the mid-eighteenth century to 41 per cent of day labourers in Auffay and 50 per cent in the neighbouring areas by 1850. Female servants became less common on large farms in Scotland, but remained important on small and medium-sized holdings, where they had to be versatile because no single task could absorb their continuous labour. By the 1860s, more attractive jobs in the towns made it difficult to keep servants or daughters on Lowland Scottish farms, so farmers built bothies and boarded servant girls from Ireland or the Highlands to meet labour demands.[19]

The need for casual, task-orientated labour led to the creation of the agricultural gang in England, France and Belgium. From the 1820s, gangmasters contracted with farmers to provide a group for a specific job, arranged and paid workers. Typically gangs were engaged for 'women's work' and comprised mainly women and children. Often, they had a long walk to the job and in inclement weather might have no work and no pay. If it was too far they stayed overnight in barns or sheds without washing or cooking facilities. Ultimately, cases of sexual and child abuse led to widespread criticism. Women from Norfolk in 1867 expressed how they felt:

> Elizabeth Dickson – . . . Some of the work is very hard, pulling turnips and mangolds, muck shaking, and when turnips are being put into the ground putting muck as fast as the plough goes along, – work which women and girls have sometimes to do. Drawing mangolds is the hardest; globe mangolds are fit to pull your inside out, and you often have to kick them up. I have pulled till my hands have been swelled that you can't see the knuckles on them. I have come home so exhausted that I have sat down and cried; it would be an hour before I could pull my things off; and I have been obliged to have the table moved up to me because I could not move to it.[20]

Another account gave a graphic description of rape by the gangmaster. Like factories, the visibility of gangs heightened awareness of conditions and played into Victorians' concern about morality. Many other women and children, working in small groups in more isolated circumstances, suffered the same hard conditions, but did not attract attention. After parliamentary inquiries of 1867 and 1876, legislation restricted the use of children in gangs and mixed-sex gangs. However, it only altered their composition and they continued in diminished use throughout the century. In Belgium, female agricultural gangs could still be seen in the fields at the end of the century, especially during planting and harvest, and the Women's Committee *Enquête* of 1892 recorded 57,000 women in gangs.[21]

DAIRYING

Women's special standing in dairy work remained in place though it shifted as dairying became part of the move to specialization. In Scotland women invariably tended cows and in Ayrshire 'unlike England, every process connected with the milk, the butter, or the cheese is conducted by women and rightly too'. In Ireland and Denmark, 'women regarded the dairy as their 'traditional' province and folklore conferred 'natural' superior milking skills on women'. During the century in Sweden and Ireland, dairying was unambiguously coded as women's work: 'Not only was it improper for a man to milk, it was considered shameful [Sweden],' and 'In days gone by cows were all milked by women. There was no such thing as a man milking a cow. Men would not consider it their work to milk a cow [Ireland]'. The association of women with milk is linked to their general connection with food production and nature. Milk, however, had a double meaning, in that not only was it a product of nature, but women were producers of milk. Hansen argues that on active dairy farms, men and women became involved in a complementary situation which was 'mutually obligating', but the importance of women's work changed the balance of power. Both men and women received cash wages, but women's wages became steadily higher with the rising price of butter. Women's importance was recognized by Scottish farmers, as far apart as Aberdeen and Dumfries, who engaged men on condition that wives would milk: 'This in many cases necessitates a second class man to be taken, on account of his supplying one or two good milkers.' Although dairying was part time on smaller farms, it was permanent since it could not be handled by casual labour. Women exercised considerable skill and influence on management and the production of knowledge in Sweden. The skill and judgement needed to assess the churning of the butter not only required experience, but retained a sense of mystery. Ancient charms were sung by women in rhythm to the churning. A Finnish account describes a woman who churned naked 'and wrapped her vest around the churn', epitomizing the association of female sexuality with butter making.[22]

Commercial farms relied on dairymaids. They were usually single, boarded, lodged and were among the highest-paid group of women workers. This was because of long hours and hard labour required by dairying, but also because of their skill and the requirement for good-quality workers upon whom responsibility fell. In 1802, Sir John Sinclair argued that a requisite for extending a dairy farm was 'To procure an attentive and skilful dairy-maid, as the whole success of the undertaking must depend on her good conduct.' In Bavaria, her value was recognized by farmers who regularly paid maids a bonus when an animal was sold. Their experience in caring for the animals, sleeping with them when a cow calved or was ill, was worth money to the farmer. In Denmark from 1836, women's position within the dairying 'industry' was enhanced, when training was introduced to enable them to take charge of butter production on a larger scale than previously. Initially only three or four from estates where particularly skilled women already worked were trained each year, but the figure rose to ten annually by 1860–70. Hansen's study demonstrates that women gained independent positions and very high wages, but especially that they also became highly responsible and confident women. They recognized their own economic importance to a large farm, where efficiency was improved by having a skilled woman and female assistants. Some women published their methods, signifying that they knew the value of their skills and felt qualified to pass on knowledge in a country where women rarely appeared in print. Indeed, Hanne Nielsen travelled throughout Europe studying cheesemaking, sharing her expertise, lecturing to agricultural groups and training over 1,000 women. Associations gradually opened to women as it was appreciated that they were essential to the economic efficiency of the industry. In Sweden, where dairying was never as important and did not constitute the same basis for economic status, farm wives also saw their control of dairying as an important source of independence. Developments on large estate farms had repercussions on women with less commercialized operations. Training was intended to improve large commercial estates by providing the best-qualified personnel, but it was soon realized that the same skills were invaluable to women who maintained their own small dairying operation. Publicity about new methods and good practice in dairying was accessible to farmer's wives, and dairymaids who had been trained on large estates shared their knowledge with friends and relatives.[23]

Dairy work was seen as appropriate for women as 'indoor' work associated with farmyard and farmhouse. It was out of public view, unlike field work. Note the distinct use of terminology: dairy maid and field woman. In the 1870s, women still held a dominant position in most of Europe; however, signs that they would lose this position were already apparent. Across England, many withdrew from managing small dairies during the nineteenth century. In Middlesex, in 1807,

> The dairy is pretty nearly excluded from the domestic economy of the farm houses in this county, as the farmers' wives for the most part, have neither inclination, industry nor skill, sufficient for management of a dairy; and in suckling, the business is performed by men, as the women (even the servants) will not go into a dirty cow-house and submit to the drudgery of milking and attending the calves.[24]

However, in Cheshire, cheese was 'almost invariably made by the farmer's wife or his daughters' into the 1870s, despite the appearance of 'factory' production. In Ireland, women in wealthier households began delegating dairying tasks to hired male labourers, beginning with milking which was conducted outdoors and more easily redefined as men's work. Indeed, mid-century editions of the *Agricultural Class Book* encouraged young boys to read the chapter on dairying in order better to perform their role of feeding and attending the cow, helping with heavy churning and supervising the women if necessary. In Sweden, the period after mid-century was characterized by men's gradual advance in dairy management and production of knowledge. Significantly, Sommestad identified that masculinization was more than mere substitution of men for women, but represented a reinterpretation of the gendered meaning of dairy work. The difficulty of finding girls willing to be dairymaids in Scotland is suggestive of a decision on their part to leave dairy work behind. Thus by 1890, 'the cry of the dairying districts is loud, that dairy-women were difficult to get at all and fully qualified dairy-women are very rare indeed'. Also in Wales and Ireland, 'Whatever be the cause, women have gone out of the business and in a great number of cases, therefore, cows have got to be milked by men and boys.' As women withdrew from the work, they also lost control of the skill.[25]

The gradual association of dairying with technical change and masculinization of dairying skill indicates that other factors were at work. In most western countries, women lost their predominant position as dairying was centralized and mechanized. Bradley argues that mechanization of milking completed the transition from women to men in dairy work, since the modern milking system was seen as highly technological skilled work. She directly associates men with machines and skill. However, we have seen that female skill was appreciated and recognized, so there was something deeper and more complex in this transition. In Sweden the association between mechanization and masculinization was not straightforward and suggests other approaches. The Swedish state maintained women's traditional position, opening vocational schools and courses for dairymaids between 1858 and 1883. The majority of them managed village dairies, but few obtained positions as 'experts'. From the 1880s, however, the state supported the introduction of men into dairying, creating the [male] 'dairy adviser'. Thus men entered the field as managers and experts, based on 'scientific' knowledge, but few made inroads into the traditional skilled practical dairy work until the end of the century. Masculinization was only completed as the association between women and milk itself was challenged. Dairy work became more scientific, so that different ways of interpreting it could be perceived. At the same time, milk itself became less conspicuous, sealed in containers, making the relationship between the skilled worker and the product, that is, women and milk, indirect.[26] On one hand there was a dearth of dairymaids in some regions, which does not suggest their being forced out. On the other hand there was a widespread trend to commercialization and ultimately mechanization, which may have squeezed women out. It could have resulted from a lack of training on new systems, though the evidence of Scandinavia tends to belie this. It could have been because the workplace was redefined by men, with a time and location framework less suited to women. While this would not have affected single women in the same way as married ones, traditional dairy work of women was associated both physically and ideologically with the home dairy.

FISHING

By and large, fishing, like most agricultural work, initially involved the whole family, but displayed relatively clear gender lines, in that men went out in boats and women dealt with the catch. Preparation could be shared, but often this was also gendered. The notion of 'going to sea' was as much about masculinity and rites of passage as it was about work. As reported in the Old Statistical Account of Scotland, 'They go to sea as boys at 14 years of age, become men at 18 and marry soon after.' On the east coast of Scotland, 'becoming a man' was linked with taking a full share in a boat, which, with marriage, gained the fullest possible standing in the community. Women usually did not go to sea and were considered bad luck. The only Scottish women on boats were those who migrated from station to station to handle the catch. However, women went on boats in Spain, Scandinavia, Brittany and other peasant communities, sometimes as cooks and as fishworkers. In southern Brittany, north-west Spain and the sheltered inner fjords of Norway, women fished from boats, while in the Baltic they used small boats to catch bait. In Scotland, however, when fetching mussels involved a boat trip, it became men's work, although women collected mussels from the shores. Another exception were women who fished where seine nets were used, as in north Norway, where '"men, women and children" would join in "the land haul" taking their proportion of the catch which was landed'. However, such accounts are the exception rather than the rule, and the lack of mention of women in a survey of fishing from around the world emphasizes how masculine fishing was.[27]

Yet, fishing was highly dependent on women's work. In the first place, most fishing communities at the beginning of the period combined farming and fishing, so that women made possible men's departure by tending the land. In the second, preparation, for example, making nets, fetching bait and baiting lines, was often allocated to women. Yorkshire women – such as those who climbed the cliffs at Flamborough Head to reach limpets and whelks – rose early and frequently took serious physical risks to find bait. Subsidiary work between sea journeys could be shared. In Stintino, Sardinia, where lobster fishing reigned, women had no part in weaving the intricate lobster pots, but made the nets; dyeing and mending them was men's work.[28] Broadly speaking, there were three patterns of work for women: fishwives working in family units; those who worked in centralized fish houses or smoke houses; and fishing girls who followed fleets as gutters and packers. There is no doubt that work was hard, as the following description from Banffshire shows.

> The fisher wives . . . assist in dragging the boats on the beach, and in launching them. They sometimes, in frosty weather, and at unseasonable hours, carry their husbands on board, to keep them dry. They receive the fish from the boats, carry them, fresh or after salting to their customers, and to market at the distance, sometimes of many miles.[29]

Processing the catch was women's work, whether gutting and packing in brine, pickling or smoking, such as herring in Scotland or shelling shellfish in Marshside and in East Anglia. Young women, who followed the fleet around the coasts to the Western Isles and down to Yarmouth, found that they could earn relatively well since they were paid a signing-on fee (*arles*), their wages and an allowance for living expenses. They worked in groups of three, often signing on together, two gutters and a packer. A woman from Embo described the work:

> Sometimes the fish, the herring would be very scarce, an' we would have nothin' to do, an' we would be browned off. 'Cause it was all piecework; an' then, no money, you see? So all we did was knit all the time . . . An' then, maybe the fishing would come good. An' there would be a glut. And we had to be up at six in the morning . . . We were away down . . . They stood at the box an' gutted the herring. An' then we carried them in two tubs, one in the middle and one each side . . . An' then I was packing them, ye know . . . Ye had to pack away to keep up with the gutters æ Ye got home then at 9 o'clock for our breakfast, wash your own dishes; we were away down again at 10 o'clock. And we would come up for our dinner and tidy up an' everything, we were away doon again, . . . and up for tea at 5 o'clock, up for tea again at 9 o'clock. An' we would come in that station at 12 o'clock.[30]

They often enjoyed the freedom that travel and independent wages gave them. With room and board provided, they could return home with a tidy sum of money. They also enjoyed the companionship and pleasure of the work groups. They are remembered as singing, flirting and joking, and one has recalled, 'it was a free and easy time, you weren't restricted – like you know, in a factory where there were bosses'. The portrait was equally valid for women in larger harbours who awaited the catch, in order to process and pack it as quickly as possible. An observer timed women at Wick gutting twenty-six herring a minute. He commented that such 'bloody' work damaged the young girls who took it up, 'still I observed several pretty and modest-looking girls who would apparently have made better shepherdesses than fish-gutters'.[31] Thus he criticized unpleasant and public work as inappropriate, but also exposed the misconceptions embodied in the rural idyll of the feminine shepherdess.

Women had a special role in marketing catches, largely before large merchants controlled the industry. Marshside women took shrimps to market in Lancashire towns, either by cart or baskets. Newhaven fishwives were well known in Edinburgh, marked out by their distinctive dress and apron. Women took great pride in their role, and accounts from Embo on the Dornoch Firth in Scotland are testimony to the respect these women commanded in the family and community. In Scandinavia, women were also indispensable to the local fishing economy as fish sellers and gutters. The shift from family to commercial organization was felt in Scotland from the 1830s, when subsidiary tasks, like gutting, packing and net-making were centralized rather than carried out in small units. Women became waged labour at the same time as more men sailed on boats owned by merchants rather than the shared crew ownership of the early days. So while some women's work disappeared, commercial operations also created jobs, especially for those who were free to follow the trade as it moved around the coast. Women moved into canning and packing factories which took work into the unseen sector, while continued commercialization changed the familial character of fishing.[32]

WOMEN'S SKILLS AND GENDER DIFFERENCES

Most of women's agricultural work fell into two patterns: care of the farmyard and, linked to it, dairying; and fussy, fiddly work which required care, detailed attention and manual dexterity. Thus biological perceptions played a part in determining women's work in ways which often contradicted ideological perceptions of woman's place. Certain work was associated specifically with women, such as dairying, because of its link with maternal biology. Many beliefs about women's work could be characterized, as Johansson argues for Sweden, by stressing it as a form of 'bestowing care' on humans, and perhaps more so on cows. There is little doubt that cattle had a great symbolic value in feminine identity. Similarly, their work in the farmyard, caring for chickens and small animals, carried with it some of the same values. Producing food from an allotment, the aptly named kitchen garden, was consistent with caring for the household. All these activities could take on enhanced significance in a market economy that was consistent with women's traditional familial role. This association no way diminished the immense value of this work to the household. Additionally, much of their work resulted from taking on new tasks that emerged from convertible husbandry, new crops and specialization. Nevertheless, there was not a universal gendered division of labour. What was women's work in one region could be men's in another. For example, Bavarian male farm servants helped feed cattle, and in the Caux, planting was men's work.[33] In England, preparing manure and loading it into carts was usually men's work, but women did it in the south-west. Habit and custom allocated certain tasks to men in one area and to women in another.

Work with their hands characterized women's field work, whether reaping with sickles, where 'women are our neatest cutters', or planting, singling and hoeing root vegetables. They were considered particularly adept at hand weeding, and their dexterity in turnip picking was highly regarded 'for a woman, though not so strong is more alert and generally, more neat in picking the young turnips with her fingers, when they are so close that the hoe cannot separate them'. It has to be recognized that this so-called natural skill was fostered by early assumptions and training. Men commonly set up hop poles, while women tied hops to them, since 'a man cannot get on' with such an 'endless' fiddling job. It was 'not the kind of work which it would answer to employ men upon'. However, work with horses or large implements was considered inappropriate, and women were unlikely to lead plough horses or to drive ploughs. In 1812, Patrick Graham wrote, 'there are few operations in husbandry in which women are not employed, except those of ploughing and threshing' in Stirlingshire. Similarly, in France, ploughing and sowing were considered men's work; so was cutting down trees, mucking out stables and use of the scythe. Irish women rarely herded or sold cattle. Scotswomen performed all 'normal operations' of the fields using 'smaller implements' not worked by horses. The association of men with large animals, particularly the status attached to horses, may account for the increasing dominance of men in ploughing. Indeed, Devine underlines the extent to which status and masculinity came to be associated with horse management, so that 'most ploughmen would refuse to do byre work'.[34]

The importance and value of women's work can be seen in two ways. On the one hand, their contribution to the agricultural economy was significant. On the other, women's skills and status acquired through their work had particular meanings for them. The Scottish fishwife gained respect both from her community and her family, for her strength, skills and reputation as a worker, as well as her marketing ability in preparing and selling the catch. They were considered prodigious workers and admired throughout their village. Likewise the dairywoman was respected for her skills in the practical side of dairy work, milking and preparing butter and cheese. Danish dairywomen valued their skill and training, and were assured enough to disseminate their knowledge. They contributed to the production of knowledge in the industry. They also saw this skill and special role gaining them a measure of independence, much as the herring girls of north-east Scotland did. The respect which could be gained by being an assiduous individual, a 'workperson', is identified by Johansson for northern Sweden. Work was seen an essential characteristic of one's identity, male or female. Since neither light nor heavy work was distinguished, a person could gain equal admiration for everything they did, their constant occupation being a part of their persona.

A central feature of women's work in northern Sweden was that it never started and never ended. Women rose earlier and went to bed later than men, so that many lumberjacks said they had never seen their mothers in bed, or resting. One component of this activity was that they did not stop working at meals, but were perpetually in attendance and control. Women's work as constant appears in a number of cultures. In Scotland, as in Sweden, women knitted or spun while walking. French women also stood while men ate. Weber insists that while this might have been practical, it was explicitly a symbol of a stubborn division of the sexes after marriage, which coincided with a persistent tendency in Manche, Maine and Berry for the man to *tutoyer* his wife while expecting his wife to say *vous* to him. Johansson's research gives another insight into this practice and supports the more positive view of Price, who does not deny evidence which suggests that women were regarded as inferior to men, but offers a different reading of the practice of standing at meals, in that it may have been simply a customary part of the division of labour. Johansson's approach implies that it might go further, linking to Roubin's notion of female control of kitchen space, in that women were not 'standing at meals' subserviently, but as women in control of their work and their space.[35] Female farm servants in Bavaria recognized that pride in work was related to succeeding in the marriage stakes. They worked to acquire not only a dowry, but the skills essential to running their own home, farmyard and kitchen garden. Similarly, gifts of flax, linen and woollen cloth given at the end of year and Christmas were a tangible measure of a young woman's worth. The amount and quality were proof of her capabilities in specifically female areas of the household and demonstrated publicly the kind of household she would run, especially to the mother-in-law. Male labourers and farm servants as character witnesses supporting maids in criminal cases indicated how much they valued these skills. As potential husbands and as men who had worked closely with the women, their evaluation was particularly revealing.[36]

In field work also, women could gain respect and assert a position of status. One such example is German female flax workers. They controlled the whole operation from sowing seeds to spinning flax and claimed the flax and all associated with it as their own. Of special importance was the harvest and preparation of flax, when they came together for a few days sharing the sense of solidarity this special work gave them. Corresponding to the great importance that flax had for the whole clothing industry, the women surrounded themselves with a wealth of traditions. These conveyed the exceptional position of women in the flax field and expressed rights the women acquired while they were there. For example, they could swear at passers by with impunity and tell rich farmers things which no one else could say to their faces. They had to be greeted by the respectful formula: 'Gott grüss Euch, Ihr Jungfrauen und Ihr Weiber, Euer Flachs soll werden wie Samt und Seide! [God bless you, you virgins and wives, your flax should be like velvet and silk!].' They also were referred to as *Herren*, 'masters', and men had to tip their hats to them. In a strongly patriarchal society, this example may be exceptional, but it highlights the special role which women could acquire and which could raise their status and give them power, even if temporarily.[37]

The continued involvement of women across a broad spectrum of field tasks, including the most arduous, undermines the notion that purely biological characteristics or maternal functions determined female agricultural roles. Societal attitudes that deplored heavy work for women were conveniently forgotten where female labour remained vital, especially when men were unavailable and led to innovations such as bondage and gangs to guarantee workers. However, to explain the apparent decline in women's participation in agriculture, many commentators relied on arguments and explanations based on middle-class notions of femininity. The tone and language reflected their bourgeois bias, while they contributed to the debate about appropriate work and the role of working-class women. Certainly some views were heartfelt and responded to the drudgery that farm work frequently was. The burdens women shouldered alarmed observers, as in Ireland, where 'it was a cruel thing to see women in the fields digging potatoes and putting them into big hampers which they had to put on their backs . . . Some of these sacks are over 2 cwt.'[38] An English visitor to Italy noted,

> The excessive hard work which the small properties entail upon the women appears at every turn . . . No one, indeed who has seen that dreadful human being an Italian old woman – wrinkled, decrepit, squalid, with 3 hairs on top of her bare skull as her only head gear – can doubt the severe life of toil and privation to which she has been condemned.[39]

At the same time, little comment was made about men's work in similarly difficult conditions, emphasizing the significance of ideological underpinning. Criticism of women's field work was part of the wider gendered debate about protection of women and children which was both explicitly and implicitly couched in the language of bourgeois womanhood. The overwhelming disapproval which most commentators evoked was because not only did such labour 'unsex a woman in dress, gait, manners, character making her rough, coarse, clumsy, masculine; . . . it generates a further very pregnant social mischief, by unfitting her or indisposing her for a woman's proper duties at home'.[40] Such work also created independence and comradeship among women which challenged the male order. As Sayer suggests, only farm women who fulfilled the ideal of working-class femininity, such as harvesters and dairywomen, were able to escape criticism. Importantly, condemnation was levelled both at the system which required women to work in such conditions and at women themselves. Their solution was not to address social conditions, but to remove women from 'inappropriate' work.

Attitudes to the working woman were ambivalent. While farm women were condemned for not conforming to the middle-class ideal, they were also criticized when they appeared to aspire above their place in life. From the *Barrow Herald*, Lancashire, 1875, came the complaint, 'a respectable farmers' daughter would be thought ignorant if she could not treat you to a selection of operatic airs on her neat instrument'. In France, observers commented that farm hands were no longer fed in the farmhouse by the farmer's wife, who had begun to adopt social graces. Tenant farmers' wives and daughters were also subject to such comment: 'But the tenant farmer's wife who made the butter and cheese and even helped to salt bacon, where is she now? . . . There are kid gloves on her hands; there is a suspicion of perfume about her; there is a rustling of silk and satin, and a waving of ostrich feathers.' Working women supported the middle-class lifestyle as cheap labour, and it was important that they stayed in their niche. A young woman who discarded the 'coarse' work dress for a night out was criticized for adopting the dress of her betters and therefore being 'unthrifty'.[41]

Rising wages for men and agricultural prosperity were credited with allowing them to forgo supplementary earnings of wives and keep them at home to add to domestic comfort. Although there is little evidence working men and women shared the sentiments of middle classes, printed materials presented them with potent messages about separate spheres. As McPhee argues, where they had resonance was where economic change also eroded the structure of the household economy. Some male farmworkers feared that women would take their jobs, particularly as they were cheaper. An early union gathering in Gloucestershire recommended curtailing women's work, because 'Farmers will send women to winnowing, to dung cart and even to plough, and they get for this 7*d*. or 8*d*. a day, but if a man does it he gets 20*d*. a day'. In the Caux, Gullickson argues that the invention of the power loom and a fall in weaving wages may have made agriculture look more attractive to men, so that they made more effort to keep women out. Such views surface particularly in the annals of organized male labour, where lip-service was paid to workers' solidarity, but when it came to the point, male delegates tended to come down in favour of the domestic female. A union official said that 'neither he, nor the leaders of the Union thought that the sixteen women [who supported striking male farmworkers] had done either a wise or womanly thing . . . they would have been far better at home minding their families'.[42] Such comments illustrate that the ideal of womanhood permeated male working-class culture, even if it was used for their own political and economic ends. They also emphasize that farm women whose actions challenged the image of passive female were seen as a threat to the men's world.

Women's response to farm work was mixed. Partly because of a decline in opportunities, many young women pursued the time-honoured route of migration in search of work. However, there is sufficient evidence to suggest that for many, leaving the farm was a positive decision. Not only were they attracted to other jobs, but there was a growing revulsion to the harshness of outdoor work.[43] Many went to domestic service but, equally, other urban opportunities drew them, particularly as wage levels increased. As Richard Jefferies commented,

> The girls go less and less into the field . . . They shirk the work of a farmhouse, especially if it is a dairy, and so it has come to be quite a complaint among farmers' wives, in many places, that servants are not to be obtained.[44]

In Ireland, migration was more dramatic: 'You cannot now get a woman to work at any price. They all go to the American mills.' Similarly, in France, rural girls felt they had greater opportunities and a chance of realizing them. Conversely, some held the view that women's work was paid so badly that it wasn't worth the wear and tear on clothes. Even very poor women rejected field work and it hardly seems likely that 'middle-class' values were the reason. Jane Hyde told the British Commissioners, 'I have worked from eight to twelve hours for 10*d* and then been grumbled at into the bargain. They pay so little we can do without it.'[45] Other testimony echoed this sentiment and made it clear that women resented being given the worst work for so little pay.

Women's comments about farm work and the experience of rural life reflect variously the burdens of the work, the effect of bourgeois values and the pride and pleasure of the work. One told the British Royal Commission, 'I never felt that my health was hurt by the work. Hay-making is hard work, very fatiguing, but it never hurt me. Working in the fields is not such hard work as working in the factory. I am always better when I can get out to work in the fields. I intend to do so next year if I can.' This contrasts sharply with another woman from the same village in Wiltshire: 'In making hay I have been strained with the work: I have felt it sometimes for weeks; so bad I could not get out of my chair. In leasing [gleaning], in bringing home the corn, I have hurt my head and have been made deaf by it.' Another reflected the belief that field work was healthy for her and concurred that she was always better when out in the field, but in the next breath said, '. . . it is a much better thing for mothers to be at home with their children; they are much better taken care of, and other things go on better'.[46] Such examples are difficult to decipher in that we do not know how accurate the reportage was, nor to what extent women, or men, said what they were expected to say. The freshness of many of the comments tends to support their accuracy. They also represent almost exclusively British experience, and evidence from continental sources is necessary to give a fuller sense of women's perceptions of their experience. To some extent we can sense what they thought by how they acted, and throughout Europe women tended to leave agriculture when there was a choice. But in some areas, Italy and Russia are two examples, women contributed more to agriculture than previously to enable men to get industrial work or because there were no real alternatives. Some women clearly enjoyed the experience of agriculture and took pride in it. Fishing and dairywomen are prime examples, while testimony suggests that all farm work was not a negative experience.

7

INDUSTRY, COMMERCE AND PUBLIC SERVICE

WOMEN AND INDUSTRIAL CHANGE

The nineteenth century demonstrates a complexity of work organization and location, urban and rural character, level of specialization and division of labour by age and gender, while overlapping patterns of work characterized the period. Despite shifts in the economic and ideological infrastructure, significant continuities in women's experience of gender, skill and status persisted. Whether one believes 'the late eighteenth century and early nineteenth century witnessed a significant socio-economic discontinuity' or stresses the 'long tap-roots of development and the incomplete nature of economic and social transformation', a fundamental question remains of how much change any single generation, family or woman experienced. Daughters' decisions may have been different from their mothers', and individual women's work options may have shifted during their lives, but on balance, much of the impact on women and their perception of choice was gradual. The classical view of industrial transformation was that it provoked radical, traumatic changes in the lives of people, implicitly over a short time. Shifts in work practices were probably more gradual than this, and 'on the scale of an individual life . . . most change came in small steps'. Historians have been revising perceptions of the speed and completeness of industrial change, but the idea that workers' experience was dramatically and rapidly altered for the worse is deeply entrenched. Until recently historians tended to adopt the nineteenth-century view that industrialization undermined the moral basis of society and perpetuated the image of female victimization. Such a view implies a break with the past and the destruction of culture. Research of the last thirty years has demonstrated the positive force of working-class culture and important continuities in work experience. Women's relationship to household and family continued to shape how they thought about work, while life cycle influenced their responses. Their work had origins in longstanding traditions of rural society, and the same rationales continued into industrial and urban society. As Holmes and Quataert have argued, old values co-existed with, and were used to adapt to, extensive structural changes, thus importing old styles of behaviour into new contexts. Earning to contribute to family income or to amass a dowry were important constants, and household or childcare consistently influenced women's work. They congregated in the same areas of work: textiles, garment-making, domestic service and agriculture (see Figures 7.1 and 7.2). Never-theless, their experience was not uniform, and social and economic complexities varied the contexts within which they operated and the ways they sought to resolve issues of family and individual well-being. As families adapted customary strategies to deal with unaccustomed situations, they

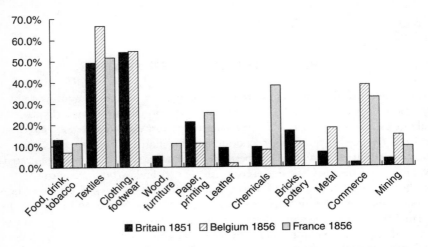

Figure 7.1 Proportion of females in the workforce, industry and commerce, 1850s
Source: Bairoch *et al.* (1968)

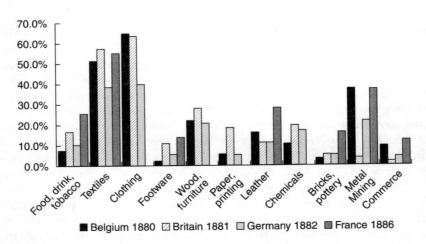

Figure 7.2 Proportion of females in the workforce, industry and commerce, 1880s
Source: Bairoch *et al.* (1968)

134

became involved in new experiences which altered relationships and perceptions of them. Yet, Accampo argues that recent empirical research has gone too far in playing down 'the extent and profundity of change that occurred in family life', and stresses 'enormous change in the family did occur with industrialization . . . [and] lost a certain measure of autonomy'. However, 'perceptions of continuity and discontinuity do not necessarily contradict one another. Instead they represent coexisting realities.'[1]

Also, there was no simple linear shift from domestic to factory industry or from rural to urban industry. Proto-industrialization often is attached chronologically to the eighteenth century. The factory system, characterized by large-scale centralized mechanized production, separation of work and home, and rigid division of labour, is seen as the major industrial development of the nineteenth century. Nevertheless, factories never employed the majority of workers, nor even the majority of women. Other production methods with their heart in workshops, rural crafts and domestic industry endured. New domestic industries sprang up as older ones mechanized or moved to large workshops or factories. Mechanization and factory development often stimulated outwork, and hand technologies were frequently cheap enough to delay full-scale mechanization. For example, industrial and agricultural revolutions in the Caux resulted in increased work for rural men and women in cottage weaving and agricultural day labour and thus delayed the full effects of industrialization on the region. Holmes and Quataert made a similar point for the Oberlausitz, where peasant–worker strategies were used to preserve the household in the face of fundamental economic change.[2] There is no doubt that important changes emerged in work practices and the location of different types of work, but continuities in approaches to work and the development of strategies by families, and by women in particular, were important factors.

The classic pattern of centralization was the textile mill which has tended to obscure the range of women's work. The image of the textile factory is ubiquitous, and women who worked in them were highly visible symbols. They represented the deviance of working-class women to the bourgeoisie; the 'girls' were too independent and unable to look after home and family properly. However, women often deliberately chose factory work for the money and independence it offered. Throughout Europe, numerous processes shifted into factories or centralized workshops, most between 1820 and 1870, yet centralization and mechanization did not always happen geographically or chronologically together. Technical innovation and centralized processes supported domestic industry, like fulling mills that underpinned woollens long before the 'factory age'. Thus, in some respects, centralization of the workforce and a division of labour which entailed specialization and 'deskilling' were the most significant changes to working practices. Wedgwood's factory at Etruria relied remarkably little on mechanization, but division of labour was significant. Mechanization was an important concomitant development, as were increasingly efficient sources of power, but was not, in itself, the key change. For women, what mattered more was a tendency towards labour-intensive practices, where they were employed as cheap, unskilled labour. As such they kept production costs down, and their labour in many domestic industries helped delay the move to centralization and mechanization.

Very generally, the period 1780–1840 remained an era of domestic manufacture, and women's work fell into four main patterns. They worked in their own 'traditional' areas, like spinning; they worked as assistants to men; they moved into work as it became less profitable or as demand increased, such as handweaving; and they made the cheaper and degraded products. They remained the hand-spinners of Europe, and in Belgium, women were so crucial to the economy that a popular proverb warned, 'Cut off the thumbs of the linen spinsters and Flanders will starve,' while silk and ribbon manufacture relied on 'an extensive, protean female labor force drawn from both town and country'. However, organizational changes began to alter work patterns, and increasingly centralized workshops took over in silk. But since throwing machinery simply reproduced hand methods on a larger scale, large supplies of cheap female and child labour delayed the shift to powered mills. Cotton, followed by wool, moved into factories, but most weaving was still carried out by hand, and parts of silk, linen, hosiery and hardware remained largely domestic processes. Women had an established position in flax, hemp and linen weaving, as far apart as Tuscany and Saxony, where, for example, in 1872, Auguste Eichler inherited the family loom while her brother received the family home, and Christiane Luise, niece of deceased weaver Johanne Schmidt, was given her aunt's loom over claims of her four brothers. In Bologna, Florence and Milan, urban women working at home wove silk, 'an ancient and difficult art'. The proliferation of rural weaving, stiffer competition, introduction of power weaving and a slump in demand for fancy silks led to an increase in rural weaving and greater reliance on hired female labour. In England and France, the spread to rural areas increased the number of women weavers as it moved beyond the more tightly controlled urban industries. Frequently they worked silk while husbands had other jobs, like silk-weavers of Warwickshire married to miners, and ribbon-weavers in the Stéphanois and Marlhes married to farmers. In other regions, weaving was chiefly male work, but powered spinning shifted pressure from spinning to weaving. Where women lost spinning, they moved to weaving, especially with the high wages which lasted until after the French wars. The demand for cotton-weavers had a knock-on effect leading to a shortage of linen- and woollen-weavers, while the wars also created a dearth of male weavers. So women moved relatively easily into a primarily male trade. In wool and cotton in the Caux and Essex, in linen in Ireland and Scotland, in ribbons in St Chamond and England, in silk in Spitalfields, women took it up more regularly. For example, in the Caux, in 1803, three married women were listed as weavers for the first time in the *Etat civil* and gradually women dominated cottage weaving so that by 1851 three times as many women as men were weavers. A similar pattern transpired in rural stocking-knitting which remained a domestic industry well after 1850, where women frequently assisted male knitters as winders, *dévideuses* and seamstresses, *couseuses*, usually from the knitter's family, as in Champagne. When he worked elsewhere, his wife or older children replaced him on the frame. Women also worked frames and seamed. They were cheaper and paid the same frame rents, so were more lucrative to employers.[3]

Despite the apparent vigour of some cottage industries, the clear trend was decline across Europe, and with it the range of women's work shrank, and a sharper division of labour emerged, since men and women often worked in distinct sectors of the economy, not only at different tasks. They also experienced divergent forms of participation, since men were more likely to hang on to skilled artisanal work, and women to become even more clearly 'operatives'. Women's work tended to remain outwork, and with centralization they often shifted tasks. At the same time, new jobs were created for women since more goods were produced for new markets at home and abroad, predominantly in textile, clothing, paper and tobacco industries. However, women who lost jobs in rural industry were not the same ones who gained new ones. Mechanization and factory production did not come to the rescue nor could new cottage industries replace the scale of employment which was lost. As time passed, choices began to alter. Instead of service, more young women went into factories; instead of domestic industry, more married women worked at tasks not shared with families, such as sewing outwork. Importantly, choices were still embedded in familial perceptions of female place and role. Timing varied considerably, so that the pattern experienced by rural France, the Highlands of Scotland, and Ireland frequently differed from England, for example. At the same time, localities experienced change differently, with local custom playing a part, so that St Etienne, St Chamond and Marlhes, for example, could present very different options for women. So, women's choices were shaped by overlapping geographical and chronological changes. There were important shifts in the life cycle of work experience, and labour experienced new gendered divisions. An individual woman was less likely to see radical changes during her lifetime, but she, her daughter and her mother could well have registered an important shift in the work available, and the kinds of choices they were able to make.

An apparent increase in the number of women in centralized workplaces did not herald an increase in the numbers of women in work. As Richards wrote, 'if the gains are balanced against the losses of work for women in all branches . . . the net consequence may have been a reduced female participation'. One-third of the entire population of Britain was adult women between 1851 and 1881, yet only one-fifth of them was in recorded employment. There was a marked decline in agricultural work, and Gullickson is clear that new work did not provide adequate outlets for women who lost spinning. Most statistical reports of the labour force are by industry, rather than by place of work; however, data from mid-century England, Wales and Prussia indicate the relatively small size of the female factory workforce, fewer than 10 per cent.[4] The character of local industry, choices available and the urban/rural context influenced women's work patterns. Desama's figures from mid-century (see Table 7.1) show the importance of woollen mills for women in Verviers, Belgium. Like many textile centres, Verviers was a one-industry town, with few other options. Where factories dominated, women felt they had little choice. A Lancashire woman said:

> The temptation is great; for, so large is the demand for female labour, that fifty women can find employment where the man fails ... Thus it is quite true that many women do keep their husbands; the men merely doing such jobbing work as they can pick up.[5]

This points to a conundrum faced by rural families, whether to move from familiar surroundings where men could get work to an unknown area where women could earn fairly well but men would probably be under-employed. Gullickson cites resistance from women in the Caux to offers from mill owners, despite higher earnings and the difficulty of finding cottage work. Many had no choice and migrated to centralized workplaces, like Verviers, Stockport and Roubaix. Yet, they did not uniformly flood into textile factories and in some places turned to other occupations rather than move. In Auffay, only 5 per cent of adult women with identified occupations worked as factory spinners in 1851. In St Chamond, they replaced centralizing silk work with domestic braids.[6]

Clearly women were in demand in centralized industries. A Rouen mill owner claimed in 1834, 'It's about one-third of each kind [men, women and children] – in the same proportion as nature makes them,' an estimate confirmed by 210 cotton spinning mills in Seine-Inférieure, where 35.9 per cent were women, 33.7 per cent men and 30.3 per cent children. Frequently women were more prominent, as in three Rouen area mills where they constituted 46.9 per cent of workers and at Heilmann Frères in Ribeauvillé, Alsace, where they comprised 66.9 per cent in 1822. At Courtauld's in 1838, females made up 83 per cent of the workforce, and 89 per cent by 1861, and in the

Table 7.1 Female factory workers in Verviers, by age[7]

Age	% of age group working in mill
12–14	19.2
15–24	50.0
25–34	48.3
35–44	34.4
45–54	28.6
55–64	22.5
over 65	14.4

Comasco, 88.1 per cent of silk workers were female. In Lancashire, they accounted for 52 per cent of adult cotton operatives. In other centralized industries, women usually formed a sizeable minority, particularly in pottery and hardware trades. In Birmingham screw-manufacture girls constituted from 80 to 90 per cent of employees, and over a third of pottery workers in Staffordshire during the 1860s.[8]

The image of factory and workshop labour is the 'mill girl', which reflected a nominal reality. Of the 260 employees at Heilmann Frères at Ribeauvillé, 39.2 per cent were females between sixteen and twenty-five years of age. In Manchester and Salford in 1852, 76 per cent of fourteen-year-old girls were in the mills, and 82 per cent of the female textile workers of Roubaix were under thirty. In Lancashire, 75 per cent of female workers were single. Similarly, in St Chamond, the braid industry relied on young women, just over half under twenty-one, who migrated from the countryside, as did workers who went to silk workshops for the season. In the time-honoured way, young females carried on the migratory patterns of their ancestors. Thus, the factory became an alternative route, instead of service. Their income remained important to families, as well as to dowries, and families played an important role in sending daughters to factories. In Marlhes, parents wove ribbons at home and farmed, but sent daughters to spinning and later weaving factories. Similarly, Biellese domestic weavers sent daughters to wool-spinning factories. Jeanne Bouvier explained how her mother sent her to a silk factory outside Lyon, and when she did not get a pay rise, her mother beat her, assuming it was her fault. The relative certainty of better wages in such work was a factor leading parents to send daughters to factories instead of domestic service.[9] Many factory managers provided housing, and supervision of young females and their morals, as in silk mills around Lyon, while at the bonnet silk factory in Jujurieux, nuns were employed to supervise 400 young girls constantly. Some employers arranged marriages and provided dowries for long-serving girls. Similar arrangements were established at Tarare, La Seauve and Bourg-Argental in France, as well as in Switzerland, Germany, Britain and Ireland, and in St Chamond for silk and braid workers. Though publicists emphasized them as ideal living conditions, with good regular food and protection from male steel workers in St Chamond, critics saw them as freezing, humid dorms, which 'choked the flight of dreams and left shadows over their minds'.[10] There is no doubt that such paternalistic arrangements served the interests of capitalists, as a guarantee of a substantial young female workforce. They also suited the paternalism of society by transferring familial duties to factory managers, and perhaps reassuring parents in the process.

The image of the mill girl obscured the fact that married women often took up factory work. In some major cloth centres, such as Roubaix, relatively few married women (17 per cent) were employed outside their homes, and among ribbon-weavers of Marlhes, the proportion of married women dropped from 37.8 to 1.3 per cent between 1851 and 1911, as the industry became firmly factory based. Yet, married women and mothers certainly did work in them. Accampo cites an estimate that 'after age twenty-one, three-fourths to nine-tenths of women workers are married'. In braid factories in 1885, 49.4 per cent of the 3,777 female workers were over twenty-one, while numerous women complained about the lack of sufficient crèches. Between 48.3 and 28.6 per cent of women aged twenty-five to fifty-four worked in factories in Verviers, suggesting that income earning and factory work continued to be important for those women most likely to be married. In Prussia in 1875, 31.9 per cent of the female factory labour force were over twenty-five, and 56 per cent of those were married. Approximately 28 per cent of women workers were married in Lancashire, mainly in northern weaving towns, while 34.9 per cent were in Reddy's Rouen mills. In the Belgian mines, only the arrival of the first child signalled the departure of women from the face. In contrast, 82 per cent of married women in the Potteries were listed as not employed in 1861, and only 21 per cent of potters' wives worked in the industry. Male craft traditions survived, while potteries provided more opportunities for men than textiles did, and the division of labour placed a premium on younger girls.[11] On balance, as long as legislation did not restrict girls' work, the majority of females in centralized units were young and unmarried. However, the number of married women in mills and workshops was sufficient to make it clear that women utilized whatever strategies suited their own specific needs. Since demand for female labour was great, and jobs were scarce for men in textile towns, it placed an even greater premium on married women's work. Many single mothers also worked in mills. If women needed income, and work was available in a mill or workshop, they were likely to take it up. We should not be blind to the variety of patterns and the strategies employed by women who had to earn. From their point of view, it was pragmatic to continue in the work one knew to make ends meet, provided childcare could be found.

The working life cycle of wives in Roubaix showed that childless ones were most likely to work, and wives worked but at a lesser rate while the youngest was under five years old. The level of wives' employment declined as children grew older and more able to contribute, so that a tiny percentage worked when all children reached eighteen. Thus, there is an indication that mothers and daughters traded off work roles. Similarly, married women working in pottery were likely to be childless. The pattern of women employed in selected Lancashire cotton mills supports this model (see Figure 7.3).[12] From the Comasco, a different pattern of late marriage and large families emerged:

> from the age of twelve – if not nine – to the age of twenty-five and over, a girl in the Lecco *circondario* would work in a silk factory, to help support her family. When she married, she would carry on working until she had one or two children. Around the age of thirty she would stop working in a factory, bear a few more children, and continue working on and off the land, to help her husband.[13]

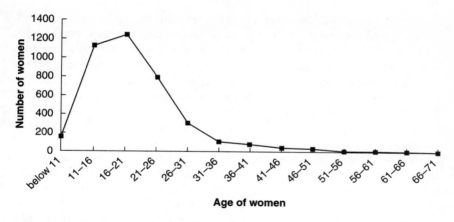

Figure 7.3 Women employed in selected Lancashire cotton mills, by age, 1834
Source: Evans (1990) p. 251

Employers were ambivalent. Some Scottish factories refused to hire married women; others, like Cowan's paper mill in Penicuik, in 1865, 'With a view to prevent the neglect of children in their homes, we do not employ the mothers of young children in our works.' The manager made an exception for 'widows or women deserted by their husbands, or having husbands unable to earn a living'. Quite the opposite was expressed by local bourgeoises in Verviers and Ghent. They worried that women who left work would lose their skills and taste for work, and would place an additional burden on families since they had to be fed. Although primarily self-seeking rhetoric, Belgian factory women were expected to stay in work rather than leave when children were born. In Halstead, no one expected married women to give up mill work when they married or had children, even women whose husbands were the most skilled and best paid. In northern Italy the expectation that mothers would look after home and children generated a diffidence about women's work, expressed succinctly by Vittorio Ellena: 'it was a source of many problems. When a woman sets up home, either she abandons the factory or she works there irregularly.'[14]

TECHNOLOGY, SKILL AND GENDER

Domestic industries were in transition throughout the eighteenth and nineteenth centuries, and an urban–rural distinction developed, which sometimes led to gendered differences in work, and often relegated rural women to the poorer end of manufacture. Towns were associated with artisanal craft and honourable trades while the country was associated with domestic production and 'dishonourable' trades. This tended to mean that different types of product were associated with each area, and rural production became linked with poor-quality products and low-status work. This geographic difference reflected skill and gender issues, since the most skilled artisanal work tended to be located in the towns. For example, by the 1820s, a contrast in silk-weaving existed between women in Coventry who worked on, and sometimes owned their own, engine looms, and those in the countryside working on the poorly paid hand loom. Also, production of patterned ribbons became centred in St Chamond, because of the need for supervision and regulation of patterns. Weaving in the city became predominantly male, while in the countryside it became exclusively female. Despite rural stocking-knitting producing higher-quality hose, it was the more marginal branch of the trade. More and more women took up narrow frame knitting just at the time it became more peripheral relative to the town trade. By mid-century, 40 per cent of knitting frames in many hosiery villages were in the hands of women.[15]

Gendered division of labour is often cited as the cause of female subordination at work, but the real issue is that, as Bock has said, 'Sexual division of labour is not just a division, but a hierarchy of labour.' This division, and hierarchy, may have arisen out of a practical solution to the economic needs of the household, but it is equally the result of ideas about work and women. The nature of work which women did as their part of such a partnership was frequently determined by a perception of their inferior status and of the female role at work. A proto-industrial family is usually characterized by a high degree of collaboration and co-operation between its members. Certainly it relied on division of labour based on age and sex, but such divisions had remained flexible and jobs could be distributed as need arose, but as the scale and location of work changed, a new rigidity developed in gendered divisions of labour. In nineteenth-century Como, silk-throwing and spinning was 'characterised by a rigid and static division of labour between its male and its female members, and more importantly, by a rigid subordination of interests and needs of its female members to the interests and needs of its male members'. In hosiery, wider frames began to be collected together into workshops, while seaming remained a domestic operation, and hosiery became more sharply divided along gender lines. Men knitted in centralized workshops and women seamed stockings and other garments at home, so that household and workplace remained synonymous for women, while they diverged for men. It was not simple exclusion by employers. Instead, as Osterud has pointed out, it resulted from interaction between 'the customary division of labour within working-class families and the transformation of the labour process . . . but its incorporation into the social division of labour changed its meaning'.[16]

As the identification of weaving as men's work and a longstanding sexual division of labour broke down, women did not necessarily acquire the status it had represented; instead, weaving was redefined so that women's weaving was always perceived as socially inferior, easier and less skilled. In part this was achieved by allocating women to 'simple' looms and men to more complicated ones, just as women's technologies of distaff and spinning wheel were seen as simple and unskilled while the mule was defined as skilled and a male technology. In the Caux, women were only allowed to take up calico-weaving while men continued to weave heavy fabrics. Retaining this sexual division of labour enabled male weavers to maintain craft superiority as well as their status in the household, the pecking order which had existed when men wove and women spun. Male weavers identified the new division of labour as a function of natural sexual differences and therefore as confirmation of their own superiority. As one weaver said, women

> make the articles that are the most easily made and consequently the least lucrative, *because* they are more suited to their [weaker] physical strength and their inferior intelligence ... [Men] are *naturally* inclined towards the articles whose construction is more laborious and difficult because they procure higher *benefits*.[17]

A similar process took place in knitting whereby women continued as hand knitters and worked on smaller frames, or were relegated to seaming only. Even where men and women worked at the same task, women tended to work on inferior products and with simpler tools. These distinctions were imbedded in concepts of technology and skill, both of which are gendered cultural products. Men tended to dominate better-paid sectors, such as fancy work which required greater skill and experience, while women made coarser gauge stockings on older narrow frames. Men commanded newer wide frames, and because more could be knitted at once, they generated higher earnings. When couples worked together, men worked the legs on a wide frame and women the tops and feet on a narrow frame. Walter Upton, a Leicestershire knitter, explained,

> I should apply of course for the best work for my own hands, because I am most expert in the business, and if my wife worked, she would not work above half her time ... They are not so much consequence as we, therefore it is in that way that we look out for the best jobs for ourselves.[18]

Although tasks were complementary, there is little doubt that men saw themselves as more skilled and women's work as inferior.

Rarely did employers and men question that 'skill' and the ability to run large, complex machinery were 'natural' masculine traits. Women were hired, conversely, to do work already defined as women's work; it was paid less and perceived as requiring less technical ability or training. In silk-weaving, for example, females were not seen as technically able to 'programme' patterns on to looms. In Spitalfields and St Chamond, they usually wove on low warp and tambour looms which produced plain ribbons and narrow silk, while men worked on broad looms for larger silk pieces and produced fancy work on improved Zurich or Jacquard looms, which earned twice the rate of plain work. Looms for patterned ribbons became increasingly difficult for women to operate because shuttles with decorative and metallic thread weighed at least 130 pounds, while plain ribbon weaving was considered 'a pretty light trade and fit for lads of a slender make, or even girls'. A decline in trade and new looms which could weave more, faster, meant that those relegated to single hand looms had very little hope of a good income. An exception to the persistent degrading of women's skills occurred with the inclusion of women in the Spitalfields Acts in 1812, protecting trained labour. They benefited some women, who in the early nineteenth century worked in skilled branches of the trade. In 1838, the Commissioner reported 526 women weaving silk velvets, which required 'peculiar skill', one wove Jacquard velvets, the most highly skilled of all, and 78 worked on other Jacquard and figured goods. Skilled women could earn good wages, and one weaver indicated that his daughter earned even more than her husband.[19]

It is sometimes claimed that mechanization was the cause of women's exclusion from a range of work. It should be transparent by now that women did work with machines, and in some industries and processes they were preferred. They were power weavers, tended powered braid and knitting machines, carding and rolling machinery, and spun on smaller mules, throstles, and in linen and worsteds. They operated turning machinery for potters, used machines to stamp out small objects in the toy trades, and closed shoes on sewing machines. So machinery did generate jobs for women. This is probably the wrong point. The meanings associated with machinery were the important factors. The relationship of women to machinery is complex. In some industries they operated machines, usually under male supervision, while in others, men used machines with female assistants. These practices further associated men with skill and women with cheap labour. Similarly, many new technologies and machines were designed for women and children. Rose argues that

> Machines designed to be worked by skilled workers were built to be operated by people with the hands, height, and weight of an average male, unless a manufacturer had in mind reducing labor costs by replacing men with women and therefore contracted with a machine maker to build a machine that would be suitable for female bodies.[20]

Berg has shown how spinning jennies, for example, were designed for operation by young girls, since they were uncomfortable for adults to use for any length of time. The British Children's Employment Commission (1816) heard that girls were hired in silk-throwing mills for the suppleness of their fingers, while a cotton mill at Emscote reportedly dismissed girls after apprenticeship because their fingers were too big to go between the threads. Processes were broken into labour-intensive technologies to take advantage of a female and child labour force and often to bypass an existing 'skilled' male workforce. Calico printing was broken down into a series of operations performed particularly well by teenage girls with manual dexterity learned at home. Pencilling was also done by women who were seen as unskilled, and by implementation of a laborious approach to the work, employers circumvented highly skilled, organized and paid 'gentlemen journeymen'. Lacquering and japanning, buttonmaking, piercing and handpainting were seen as the special provinces of females with their small hands, deftness and concentration learned from needlework. With exceptions like nailmaking, women worked primarily in lighter, newer and unskilled branches of toy trades, and operated large presses, while girls used smaller ones, as stampers and piercers.[21] Arguably, many industries were transformed by labour-intensive methods, with a greater impact on women's work than machines, using female homeworkers, who were both so prominent and so hidden in the industrial workforce.

Four interrelated issues are important in assessing the interplay between machinery and women's work: strength, skill, authority and control, and technical know-how. Mule spinning illustrates the way all four could operate. Women had been domestic spinners, brought relevant skills into water-powered spinning mills and used the first small mules. Jordan argues 'the direct link between the proto-industrial workforce and factory operatives was broken by the employment of pauper labour in water-powered mills. When new steam-powered spinning mules first arrived, they were placed in the hands of male operatives, who employed their own sons as their piecers.' Thus, women spinners acquired a minority position. Their craft position was not completely lost since they retained spinning on small mules, and manufacturers hired cheaper female labour to replace men between 1819 and 1833 in Britain. So women's marginalization was not a simple question of skill. More significant was the 'discontinuity in female craft traditions' with the development of steam-powered mules. Arguably strength played a part, since mules became larger and heavier to operate, although women were used on short mules of 250–300 spindles in the 1830s, deemed too heavy twenty years before. As manufacturers continued cost-cutting, and 'doubling up' on mules, strength continued to work against them.[22]

The self actor should have made it possible for women to work larger mules, but a number of factors led to their exclusion. Freifeld argued that mule spinning did not, in fact, become deskilled, 'but the handicraft skill of the mule-spinner was reconstituted in a new form' and tasks 'remained skilled labour, mastered only by long practice'. Reddy confirmed that 'mule spinners practiced an art that took very special skills and long experience'. Important throughout is the issue of gendering machines, and the creation of new male monopolies. The transference of coding spinners as male was significant for women's place in the industry. Gullickson argues that in the Caux, the reversal in sex-typing of spinning, that is, female hand spinners to male mule spinners, could take place because men could argue that it was a new occupation based as it was on technological change: 'Mule spinners could view themselves not as entering a previously female occupation, but as taking new jobs that only men could adequately fill.'[23] With the creation and imbedding of a new male monopoly, not only was female association with the trade lost, but so was the transmission of female craft skills from one generation to the next. Their minority position was fragile and insufficient to retain a place for them, and they could no longer bring experience to the job. In this way, mechanization reinforced the exclusion of women from spinning and other trades.

Machine lacemaking and factory hosiery knitting provide parallel examples. In Leicester hosiery, employers attempted to replace men with cheaper female labour from the 1860s. Because women refused to accept an equal wage, fearing dismissal, the 'solution' proved to be an agreement between employers and men, in 1888, restricting women to six-headed frames and reserving eight-headed frames for men. Thus, as Rose concluded, 'the solution to gender conflict . . . was to "gender machines" in effect creating a gender segregated workforce based on which particular machine was considered a "man's machine" and which was considered a "woman's machine"'. Until the end of the nineteenth century, only men worked lace machinery. Although the machines were heavy, that was not the determining factor, since young boys turned wheels on hand machines, and continued to be employed as minders when steam-powered machinery was introduced. Despite the fact that women dominated hand lacemaking, early machine manufacturers were men who had worked as skilled mechanics before buying machinery and employing operatives, creating a close link between the twist hand and the entrepreneur since 'In boom times, twist hands became entrepreneurs, and in bad times manufacturers became twist hands again.'[24]

Throughout centralized industries men claimed a particular place as machinists, building, repairing, tuning and overseeing machines. Men in the braid workforce were mainly a small group of machinists to tend steam engines and repair looms. In metalwork, men inserted tools into the stamping and piercing machines and maintained them. Mule spinners attributed some of their skill to their knowledge of tending and repairing machines, so that they could claim technical know-how which women did not have. Tacklers claimed their position as repairers and their ability to balance loom weights. Yet women argued that they were every bit as competent at mending looms as the tackler, and given the chance they could have developed the ability to balance weights. Women were less likely to have been trained in the mechanics of the knitting frame, as men were, and at Courtauld's those males who remained at the mill over the age of fifteen gained a position of high status because they were mechanics or clerks, positions which also represented authority. Similarly, employers usually filled entry-level positions with boys, so that they gained training and preparation for future jobs. Deliberate practices provided 'passage' through trades for boys which further imbedded their monopoly. Women were seen as lacking competence in handling machinery; they lacked this expertise because they were not given training; and they were not trained because they were thought to lack technical aptitude.[25] Such tactics excluded women from technical knowledge which gave status and mastery to the job. The control and authority generated by men stemmed in large part from a sense of ownership of the machinery and technical knowledge.

Probably just as important, if not more so, was the issue of authority and control. The workers who actually used machinery in the potteries were men, as turners, throwers and printers to whom women were assistants. In silk mills, millers who had oversight were men, while women operated simple machinery under their supervision. The association of gender with supervision is also evident in Nottingham hosiery, where women worked for husbands and fathers, and when it became a factory industry, some women worked powered frames, under male supervision. In spinning factories, the subcontracting system gave spinners the opportunity to maintain a considerable degree of control over the division of labour on their mules. This hierarchical division of labour meant that the male mule spinner had a supervisory role which enhanced his position in the hierarchy. Many subordinate workers were also family members so that a man's head of household position and work status reinforced each other. Although women working smaller mules also brought piecers into the mill, they gained less than men from the supervisory role. They controlled a minority of spindles and their position was degraded because they still were supervised by men. In mines across Europe, their main task was to carry, pull or push baskets of coal from the face to the shaft, and sometimes, as in Scotland, transport it up steps or ladders to the surface, with men holding the positions as hewers of coal. Women were a more persistent feature on the surface; yet again, their main task was carrying coal, stone and ores around the site or into markets. Rarely did women hew or 'get' the coals, but exceptionally there are instances of women doing so in Britain, usually substituting for men or assisting husbands to increase their work rate.[26] Women weavers were excluded from jobs as overlooker, and were under tighter and more frequent supervision than males, since employers believed women could not tune machines and they were discouraged from learning. Cleaning, carding and stretching in French mills were carried out by women, with male foremen and mechanics watching. At Courtauld's, women overseers assisted males in the winding department, where the youngest and lowest-status workers worked. Lazonick argues that the minder was a supervisor and 'men in general were more productive in this function than women, because they could command more "respect" from their assistants, particularly the younger ones'. Supervision itself did not create status, but retaining a supervisory position reflected aspects of control and status which were linked to men's economic and social position, their craft and family status. The expectation was that in most industries men would monopolize the jobs involving responsibility and skill, while women would assume subordinate positions.[27]

Women clearly were not admitted to the labour elite, and remained in lower-paid and lesser-authority positions throughout their careers. Not only were they relegated to subsidiary textile jobs except for weaving, they did not gain supervisory positions. Potters also instituted demarcations between male and female work, which corresponded with perceptions of skill and ensured that men supervised most processes, whereas women seldom supervised men but frequently acted as assistants and 'go-fers'. In mining, particularly in Belgium where female miners carried their own title, *hiercheuse*, with pride, there is a recognition of female culture and status. As cleanliness became central to womanliness, it is noteworthy that mining women's status and pride was based on strength. Only Belgian surface workers defined status by strength *and* cleanliness.[28] But because women 'never became getters' their position remained subordinate to men's. Similarly, within female workspaces, painters, weavers and female supervisors gained some status, but always within a female context, not in relation to men. Centralized workplaces introduced complex hierarchies of procedures, skills and status. These relied at times on practices and relationships brought from the domestic workplace; other times hierarchies shifted and were redefined with mechanization and new work practices. The gendered character of workplaces shifted accordingly. Women were predominantly engaged in preparatory stages and subsidiary tasks, and were restricted in gaining access to supervisory positions, which reflected patriarchal structures extant in other forms of work as well as in the experience of most women. The gendered division of labour also resulted in almost uniformly lower wages for women compared with men. At Courtaulds, Lown argues 'from the time they entered the mill boys and girls were subjected to a policy of deliberate and self-conscious gender segregation'.[29] That there was a gender issue, and not simply a cheap labour one, is demonstrated by the number of workplaces which strove to keep men and women apart. In shoe factories, there were separate entrances and dinner times, and Wedgwoods kept paintresses apart from decorators.

HANDICRAFTS, HOMEWORKING AND SWEATING

The line between domestic industry and homeworking is relatively fine. Trades like shoemaking, glove-making, tailoring and dressmaking had roots in handicrafts and guilds; some homework derived from putting out industry and others from centralized industries. In some instances, 'homework' was itself collected into 'sweated' workshops. So while we have a commonsense view of homework, the industrial origins and outcomes are not uniform. 'The sweating system and the factory system were the two endpoints which the textile industries reached by the latter half of the nineteenth century.' Late nineteenth-century German historical economists contrasted the homework of proto-industry as a male-dominated family system with that of the nineteenth century, where men left home to work, while women and girls took in work at home to augment men's income. The key distinction between old and new was the gender of the workers. Though underestimating the role of women in

148

proto-industry, they highlighted that, 'In short, the "new" home industries were dominated by female, usually married, labor.'[30] Because of its diverse character and location, there is no single satisfactory idiom to encompass it. What is clear is that much of it came to belong to women and to shape and confirm women's place in the labour market.

'Sweating' originated in a system of tailoring subcontracting that used agents for distribution and collection of goods where the lowest prices possible were paid. However, as Franzoi pointed out, any work at home with little or no equipment, that used repetitive, manual labour, could fall into this category. A feature was long hours and emphasis on poor wages, usually piece rates. It is also associated with dilution of skills and sexual division of labour. Characteristic of homework was irregular market demand. Centralized work-places had to operate regularly year round to recover capital costs, whereas a dispersed domestic workforce allowed flexibility, so that merchants could respond better to irregular market demand. Thus seasonal consumer goods were particularly reliant on homeworkers and sweating workshops. 'This type of work presented an example of casual labour and its main features; which included ineffective regulation, lack of security and rights, and low pay. In these respects, homework mirrored the larger labour market for women.'[31]

Women in homework or sweated trades are the most elusive group of employed women. They were virtually uncountable, because they moved in and out of work, because statisticians did not always consider them as workers, and because they were 'hidden' at home. Only specimen statistics reveal the strength of this workforce. Garment-making ranked among the top three non-agricultural jobs for women in France, Britain and Italy, with domestic service and textiles. By 1840, the numbers of seamstresses in cities of northern and central Italy were almost equal to numbers of domestic servants, and far out-numbered female weavers and male tailors. By 1851 in Auffay, sewing was the largest single employer of women, offering work to 20 per cent of adult women. Yet sewing underestimates the range and character of homework, since numerous other objects were assembled by women at home or in small workshops, such as artificial flowers, bonnets, sacks, boxes, tassels, ties, fringes, dolls' clothes and feather decorations. Glove-making, footwear and umbrella covering were also put out to homeworkers, and women's *kustar* work in Russia included a panoply of tasks, from lacemaking and embroidery to weaving rope sandals, nets and reins, gluing cigarette tubes and plaiting belts and straw hats. Like domestic service and factory textiles, homework was highly femi-nized. For example, in 1866, 78 per cent of the garment workers in France were female. The range and growth of women's contribution to the sector is illustrated by Aminzade (see Table 7.2). As homework industries moved into workshops, women moved with them. Particularly after the implementation of sewing machines in mid-century, women increased their share of the work-force. In Toulouse, the proportion of women in tailoring and trouser-making grew significantly, as it did in shoe- and boot-stitching. In Britain, the same

Table 7.2 The division of labour and female labour in Toulouse, 1830 and 1872[32]

Industry	1830			1872		
	Women	%	Total	Women	%	Total
I. CLOTHING						
Tailor (tailleur)	130	21.3	610	1,160	71.2	1630
Garment Cutter (coupeur d'habits, coupeur-tailleur)				0	0.0	20
Seamstress (couturière)	1,340	99.3	1,350	2,580	99.2	2,600
Stitchers (brocheuse)				40	80.0	50
Sewing Machine Operator (piqueuse à la mécanique)				10	100.0	10
Waistcoat Maker (giletier)					0.0	240
Trouser Maker (culottier)	0	0.0	10	340	100.0	340
Shirtmaker (chemisier)				80	72.7	110
II. SHOEMAKING						
Shoemaker, Bootmaker (cordonnier, bottier)	30	4.1	730	0	0.0	1500
Cobbler (savetier, sabotier)	0	0.0	10	0	0.0	90
Boot stitcher (piqueuse de bottines)				350	97.2	360
Shoe stitcher (piqueuse de chaussures)				40	100.0	40
Shoe edger (bordeuse de souliers)				10	100.0	10
III. HATMAKING						
Hatmaker (chapelier)	10	6.7	150	190	40.4	470
Hat Workers (ouvrière en chapelierie)				10	50.0	20
Hat Trimmer (garnisseuse en chapelierie)				10	100.0	10
Hat Dyer (teinturier en chapelierie)				0	0.0	10
Hat Ironer (repasseur de chapeaux)	0	0.0	10	0		0

trend is obvious: from 15 to 51 per cent in tailoring and from 12 to 21 per cent in boot- and shoemaking between 1851 and 1911.[33]

Homework emerged as an important source of income for both married and unmarried women. Many perceived it as a solution to the need to work and care for children simultaneously. However, it was not necessarily congruous with childcare, since mothers often had to work continuously to subsist. The system did allow women who worked in shops to continue in the same work, often for the same manufacturer, after childbirth. They saw advantages to working at home, and it could be a positive feature in quality trades. In cities such as Naumburg, Lübben and Zeitz, young women in *confection* apparently preferred the relative freedom of manufacturing at home to the constraints of domestic service. Cammarosano argues that young women in Florence and Rome preferred sewing, and many with comfortable posts in service left to sew for tailors' shops even though they were hardly able to make ends meet. Francesca F, a young Moravian woman, having been a domestic servant and a wool apprentice, began sewing gloves for a small manufacturer. She worked at home, a boarding house where she shared her bed with another young woman. She left to live with a young cabinetmaker, sewing gloves at home, while she had a baby and saved for marriage. Three years later the couple married, with Francesca paying for the wedding and providing her own dowry of household linen and furnishings. She continued glove work while she raised five children and kept house. In 1853, when she was thirty-six, she worked the equivalent of 125 days a year, sewing a part of most days. Another assumption is that unmarried women had no dependants. In 1841, the London Statistical Society surveyed 354 single people in east London, of whom 229 were 'unprotected' women; two-thirds had families wholly dependent on their earnings, many being abandoned wives. In France, Sophie Ternyck, of Lille, was such a woman. A shirtmaker, one of 800 listed in 1856, she worked first in a shop and then in her own home. Her work required long hours and she still earned little, while her seven-year-old son had to run errands and shop.[34] For many, need coupled with family responsibilities made domestic industry the best alternative to destitution.

Homeworkers were drawn from across the economic spectrum, including wives and daughters of labourers, tailors, artisans and merchants. In the formative years of the trade in Central Europe, the majority of seamstresses were from middle- and lower-middle-class backgrounds. By the 1870s, women of limited means had come to dominate it. One firm, Mezner and Sons, in 1842 operated eight sewing workshops for ready-made garments and employed 200 seamstresses working at home. In one shop alone, 272 middle-class girls were apprentices.[35] While the bourgeois ideal dictated that 'a lady, to be such, must be a mere lady, and nothing else', the problem of 'surplus' women made it even less plausible, and some women attempted to make a living at a 'respectable' trade requiring familiar skills. Needlework at home seemed to answer this need, though overstocked and low paid. European evidence shows that neither married nor single women fitted into a single pattern or idiom, and homework was a strategy adopted by a wide range of women. They took whatever work there was, altering strategies and domestic responsibilities as necessary to ensure their income.

Needlework was synonymous with women, and expansion of garment and leather trades, demanding various levels of skills from seaming to fine embroidery, contributed to the growth of women's work. Even in bookbinding, where they carved out a skilled area, females sewed pages together. They sewed garments, accessories, gloves and shoes; they decorated fabric with embroidery, jewels, feathers and fine ribbons; and they knitted. The invention of 'ready made', or *confection*, opened up jobs based on needle skills which women had long dominated. As big merchant houses began to produce ready-made articles parallel to the bespoke trade, they put skilled artisans under pressure. Since *confection* required less skill and was aimed at a low-income market, it cut costs of production by circumventing master tailors and putting work to semi-skilled workmen and women in Milan, Rome, Berlin, London,

Leeds, Manchester, Glasgow, Paris and Lyon as well as other cities across Europe. As waged work increased, master tailors, subcontractors, husbands and fathers brought in women as low-paid or unpaid assistants. Fundamentally these women were subordinates, filling a position that neither journeymen nor apprentices had filled. Thus a sexual division of labour developed where certain tasks were separated out and given to women. By 1848, in Paris, two-thirds of the bespoke trade were still in shops, but 83 per cent of *confection* was *'en chambre'*. Women constituted the great mass of *confection* workers, which expanded tenfold between 1830 and 1848: women were probably an inconsequential proportion in 1830; by 1848 they constituted nearly half. By then women had also become an important component of the bespoke trade, as tailors relied on them to help combat competition from *confection*. Needlework also developed outside of tailoring, like the fine embroidery work of Ayrshire and Ulster and shirtmaking in Toulouse, Berlin and Derry, which grew out of new factory outwork.[36]

The proliferation of women in these trades challenged former male superiority. Importantly, men saw the root of the problem in the transformation of the industry caused by the ready-made sector, not in wage-earning activities of women. There was no problem with women as seamstresses. The association of women with needlework was strong, and it was seen as an essential training for girls as *housewives*. Indeed, the state and tailors supported sewing schools in Central Europe. Resistance arose when they trained *workers* and were *de facto* manufactories. Debates about family wage and the balance of sexual relations in the marketplace and the working-class family all surfaced. Skilled male workers with roots in guild traditions had a strong preference for shop-based, controlled work, clearly separate from 'homework'. As Parisian tailors stipulated, 'all work must be done in the shop, and nothing outside, so that each person can practise his craft and live by his work'. The distinction between home and shop was crucial to protection of male control of tailoring skill, and as Quataert has shown, the struggle resulted in attempts to alienate the household from the market economy.[37] The protection of the workshop linked

> economic deterioration and deskilling . . . with a move from male space (the shop) to female space (the household). To the extent that definitions of maleness were associated with skilled labour and skilled labour with a location separate from the household, the protection of the workshop invoked notions of gender that were hierarchical and spatially distinct.[38]

As the 'dishonourable' sector of tailoring grew at the expense of the 'honourable', the number of women workers increased at home and in workshops. Because their labour was cheaper than men's, men were often forced to accept lower wages.

Skilled female trades existed alongside tailoring, in millinery, mantuamaking and dressmaking, offering respectability and reasonable wages to skilled women. Unlike tailoring, location was not central to the structure or skill of female businesses. Single women were likely to work in a shop while trained dressmakers with capital tended to set up their own business on marriage. Seamstresses were more likely to be piece-rate outworkers than more skilled dressmakers. Importantly, women's position, status and identity with skill rested on their personal and professional reputation. Mayhew divided London dressmakers into 'those belonging to the "honourable" and those belonging to the "dishonourable" or "slop" part of the trade'. He subdivided the honourable trade between those who put out work, whom he considered the better sort, and those who worked on the premises. Outwork virtually destroyed the skilled end of women's needle trades. Fashion and 'fitting' meant that dressmaking held on longer to its skilled label, while lingerie and underwear went first to ready made. By the 1840s, competition from *confection* was undermining all but the most exclusive dressmakers. Skilled women were less able than men to resist pressures from ready made, because the structure of their trade tended to undercut craft solidarity. They worked in dispersed locations, often from home, were usually self-employed, and had not developed the strong guild and union identity which tailors used to resist *confection*. With subcontracting, a fundamental gender change also took place. Men became owners and subcontractors. Usually, they had greater access to capital, but society also closely identified men with supervision, ownership and management, making it easier for them to take control. Thus women lost the distinction between skilled and unskilled workers and a claim to craft status. Instead of controlling their trade, women became subject to the work, with the loss of control over time which that implied. They could not command good wages, since less skilled women undercut them. As Scott made clear, the issue was loss of craft and low wages, not the location of the work.[39]

Patterns of subcontracting varied, but usually to the same effect. In Berlin, merchants set up sewing schools next to shops. After training, women sewed shirts and underwear for the school's owner, and after marriage, sewed at home to make ends meet. Thus, a pattern developed of single women sewing in shops while married women worked at home. Scottish merchants also set up industrial schools and urban warehouses from which they controlled training and putting out embroidery in Ulster and Ayrshire. In Armagh city, one firm employed over 400 girls between 1837 and 1843, who sewed at home for the manufacturer when they left the factory. However, schools and shops were only viable where there was a large supply of local labour, as in Berlin, Glasgow and Belfast. In rural areas, like for shirtmaking around Derry, or Ayrshire, where Glasgow merchants put out flowering to seamstresses, they employed commissioned agents, so in the 1850s about fifty Scots and Irish warehouse owners employed 400 to 500 agents. Also, women in Derry shirt factories were encouraged to take work home for themselves and their families to sew. Merchants also set up out-stations, particularly for underwear sewing, and some women worked there while others collected materials to take home. Shirts relied less on fashion and merchants were able to keep large stocks, so work was regular. In 1875, an estimated 4,000–5,000 worked in the Derry factories and 12,000–15,000 in the countryside. The two systems reflect the urban–rural context. In Berlin, Belfast or Glasgow, the workforce needed to be captured, given competition from other opportunities, whereas in Derry or Ayrshire, a relatively large workforce with basic sewing skills existed.[40] The trick was to get the work to them. Yet the system put women in a particularly vulnerable position, since employers dictated pay and completion dates. Agents were paid on commission, so wages were further reduced, and fines were levied for 'unsatisfactory' work; seamstresses had little recourse.

The division of labour in leather trades combined 'skilled' work for men in centralized workplaces with 'unskilled' homework and outwork for women. The first processes, including cutting, decoration and making lasts, were carried out at tanneries by men, with female outworkers sewing, lining, binding and ironing gloves. Production was broken down so that a sewer rarely completed a whole glove; she sewed sides, tamboured backs, sewed backs or welted the bottom. In 1833 in Milan, a 'very large number of women were employed by leather firms to make gloves of every sort', as 5,000 to 6,000 women and children did in the 1840s around Yeovil and Worcester, Somerset and the English West Midlands, and around St Petersburg and Moscow, as well as at Millau in France. Regular workers were mostly single women working long hours, for example, 6 a.m. to 10 p.m., but wives of labourers and small tradesmen also worked at odd times, completing 'as much in three days as they will at other times in a fortnight'. Eventually, even small workshops were replaced by factories, especially with the innovation of the sewing machine, and by 1870 some factories made shoes almost entirely by machine using a female workforce. This challenged male perceptions of their craft, perceptions which persisted even when it was clearly overstocked and low paid. In 1860 the Select Committee was told that in Leicester and Kettering, 'people who knew nothing about the shoe trade whatever, and, if I am rightly informed, girls and boys and women who never saw a shoe made, scarcely, now work these machines in making shoes'.[41]

The sewing machine altered needle trades on a variety of levels. It allowed semi-customizing of shirtmaking in Ulster, where it was introduced in 1856, at least a decade earlier than in London, and allowed rapid expansion of garment-making in Paris after 1860. Obviously it sped up sewing, but because it was first limited to straight sewing, it shifted the division of tasks, so that 'a large amount of the best work was done by hand'. Since garments were only partly made up in factories, outworkers continued working at home. The proportion of the workforce who were outworkers dropped only gradually, remaining at three to one until 1914. Sewing machines were used in factories and in homes, where women rented or bought them on hire-purchase. Women were expected to provide a machine, and what with other overheads such as heating and light, they became an even more attractive workforce. The sewing machine facilitated decentralization of sewing, but certainly did not cause it. It was introduced into workshops on a large scale after mid-century, well after dispersed homework had taken firm root, so that by 1860 garment-making was mechanized and centralized like other industries. In Italy, it brought even more women into industrialized work, especially in the Milan leather trades, where factory and outwork was combined. Even so, it raised expectations of productivity, and contributed to increasing hours of work, stress and exhaustion.[42]

Women working at home were a flexible labour force, moving in and out of the workforce as demand for labour ebbed and flowed. They provided an elastic labour supply, usually available on short notice, hired as needed, let go when there was no work. They usually worked long hours for little money. As Franzoi says, the system created a fit between capitalism's search for abundant cheap labour and women's need for wages. Employers justified low pay on the assumption that women who worked at home were married, and homework was designated low skilled partly because it was seen as just housework. In 1833, a British parliamentary inquiry was told, 'The masters prefer giving out the work to those women who keep young children, because it can be done at the lowest price.' They relied on women's tendency to self-exploitation. Scott and Tilly argue that married women retained a pre-industrial ethos long after their children and husbands had begun to adopt more individualistic values. Thus they were inclined to be self-sacrificing and self-exploitative. Precisely these characteristics contributed to a view of women homeworkers as casual labour, earning 'pin money' rather than as real workers. The incursion of women into previously male-dominated industries and the proliferation of homework was a real and symbolic threat, which generated implicit and explicit resistance of men towards women workers. Criticizing them as poorly skilled and cheap, all labour unions addressed the problem of homework. In 1822, tailors of Naumburg an der Saale complained that more than seventy untrained seamstresses were engaged in dressmaking in their home, even though guild statutes established male monopoly over this kind of work. These 'bunglers' threatened family livelihood, undermined apprenticeship training and overturned (male) tradition. In the guild view, employment of women in manufacturing contravened nature; their proper role was as a housewife or servant for others.[43] Lines blurred between household and market production and this ambiguity was a general characteristic of women's work.

BUSINESSWOMEN AND PUBLIC SERVICE

Businesswomen again pose problems of occupational identity. Not only did women take up a range of work across their lives, sometimes doing several things at once, but much of what they did does not fit occupational categories as they are usually understood. This is in part because such categories are artificial, created by statisticians for census purposes, and partly because they are generated by notions of what men do. Additionally the contribution of many women to commercial activities remained unpaid in family enterprises, or as part of an informal economy which is difficult to assess, the 'hidden-woman' factor. Sometimes work was not reported by women, for fear of tax collector following census taker.

Commercial activities involved women from across the status boundaries. Usually the image of middle-class women is the lady of leisure, but even with increasing luxury and comfortable homes many worked. As Davidoff and Hall point out, 'The largest single occupation of middle-class women earning their livelihood in their own right as well as assisting their male relatives was in trade.' Usually in partnership with men, and frequently relying on them for legal identity, many women carried on business well into the century, and widows continued to do so even later. Etienne Jouy commented in 1809 that everywhere in the Nord, 'one generally sees women directing businesses and exercising great authority in the *ménage*'. Pauline Motte-Brédart (1795–1871) virtually ran the enterprise herself, while her mother, mother-in-law, sister-in-law, daughter and granddaughter all were engaged in building business fortunes. Rosalie Parent, who married Henri Cuvelier in 1847, 'proceeded to organize the bookkeeping system and serve as office manager for Cuvelier's extensive wine trade based in Haubourdin'. Some women in Montauban conducted business themselves. Rachel Huegla carried on her father's financial business, and in *négotiant* families, daughters and sisters used family ventures to run their own mercantile business. Widows actively carried on a husband's trade; one such was Marie Vidallet, while her daughter became a merchant. Women were often responsible for records and bookkeeping, such as Motte-Brédart, who set up business accounts for one of her sons. These women's knowledge and understanding of business allowed men to leave on trips, confident in the knowledge that the firm was in good hands. Some women also took sales trips. Madame Holland-Dubois of Valenciennes was groomed by her father, and by the 1820s she and her eldest brother travelled throughout France for the Maison Dubois. From Derbyshire, Elizabeth Strutt went to London to canvass friends and relatives for orders for her husband and brother, while checking out potential sources of supply. Her grasp of business and knowledge of the trade testify to her importance as partner in fact if not in name. In Birmingham, Elizabeth Head Cadbury oversaw the business during her husband's absences, checked on orders, received news from him on wholesale purchases and dealt with callers. She helped out in the shop and was on hand to assist in the business. However, by mid-century, as bourgeois ideals and removal of the home from the business environs became more prominent, fewer women actively involved themselves in commercial enterprises. The second generation of Cadbury women did not help out. Candia Cadbury, who married in 1832, lived over the shop for a time, but never engaged directly in the business. In 1861 Mme Vrau-Aubineau retired after thirty-four years in the linen business. Her daughter and the daughters, daughters-in-law and granddaughters of Motte-Brédart slowly moved to complete domesticity, to be praised as good, sweet, excellent wives. Only Adèle Dazin-Motte (1819–93) continued in her mother's footsteps. Her daughters did not.[44]

Family enterprises were informal partnerships whereby wives remained essential, providing lodging, food and laundry to the workforce. They managed the household, dealt with customers and supervised the workshop in husbands' absence, while LePlay noted that wives of cutlery workers acted as intermediaries between husbands and masters, twice daily carrying the weight of 210 kilos as far as a kilometre. In Montauban, Darrow identified a greater tendency for husbands and wives to act together after the Revolution, with increasing numbers of property transactions notarized by both, and appearing more frequently as joint borrowers and lenders. Wives were chosen more often than sons to act as business representatives. In 1809, Jean Negre authorized his wife 'to direct and administer his goods and affairs, to receive and furnish receipts for any sums that may be due him for whatever reason, to pursue his debtors ... to sell and buy' in his absence. In 1788, Krünitz expected the wife of a master craftsman to 'be able to help her husband in his business, and ... learn how to sell his wares skilfully and at a profit', and until well after 1848, wives of German artisans were involved in the day-to-day running of family businesses.[45]

Retailing ranged from highly capitalized enterprises operating with extensive credit chains to the less formal end, with quick turnover and less credit. Women were more likely to be found in the latter, especially as independent traders. It was Poor Law policy in Manchester to assist women, especially widows with children, by supplying them with a small stock so that they might 'turn their industry to best account'. Widows were frequently village shopkeepers. In the Borinage and Lille, women kept small shops to eke out a living, as well as street trading. Women who had a little capital often invested in independent enterprises, separate from family business, and turned to selling on their own account. Marie Laplange specified in her marriage contract to a journeyman carpenter that she reserved six hundred francs as her own 'with which she intends to begin a little trade in groceries, *mercerie*, or something else'. Widows of artisans commonly used the return of their dowry as an initial investment to do the same, usually running very small businesses, capitalized with less than five hundred livres. Late eighteenth-century English trade directories list widows and single women as agents and manufacturers and demonstrate a range of women's commercial activities from linen draper, haberdasher, perfumer, glass and china dealer, mercers, hatters, stationers, hosiers, chemists, publishers, booksellers, to shopkeepers and pawnbrokers. In Colchester, female milliners and dressmakers were the main exception to male command of the quality retail trades, dominating women's clothing trades. Wedgwood's archives are replete with letters from women shopkeepers throughout the country ordering goods.[46]

The strong association of women with domestic victualling gained them a commercial niche doing the same things for sale. They were prominent in grocery and provision trades, and women from Anzin, Roubaix, Lille, Stockport, York and Preston, for example, earned livings as peddlers of food, kept inns and lodging houses and ran cabarets, cafés and eating houses. They were butchers and bakers, but less frequently brewers. The London census listed female greengrocers, bakers, confectioners, dealers in vegetables, licensed victuallers and a few grocers. Some 6 per cent of female household heads in Davidoff and Hall's sample ran inns, and every male innkeeper who made a will in Witham (Essex) left his business unconditionally to his wife, as did most of those in Birmingham. These were important commercial activities, at the centre of several subsidiary activities, including the coaching trade. Thus women's 'domestic' role enabled them to enlarge their activities and influence. Deborah Gooding ran the Chelmsford Machine fly on the lucrative Essex to London route in 1790, terminating at the Bull, Aldgate, also run by a widow, 'the all powerful Ann Nelson who had found means of making her name known on almost every road out of London'. However, inns became less respectable and increasingly stratified by rank and status, seriously constraining women's activities and creating a dilemma for those who owned and managed them. Similarly, the arrival of railways diminished business, while remaining livery stables became more closely associated with the 'masculine monopoly of horse culture'. In England, the increasing tendency to hire pubs from breweries, however, allowed women to maintain an important role providing food, drink and lodging, and Davidoff and Hall suggest women were explicitly recruited to provide a home-like atmosphere and control disorder. A conundrum existed however. On one hand, lodging and services like food and laundry replicated the feminine model, the woman carrying out domestic tasks in her own home even if it was for pay. On the other, with privacy increasingly identified with gentility, letting rooms represented a loss of caste. It is no accident that young men were the majority of lodgers, because for females to live in lodgings was even more reprehensible. The contradictions inherent in the characteristics of lodging meant that the relationship of landladies and lodgers was problematic, and the provision of personal services to lodgers was not clear cut and could include sexual services: 'the position of landlady very easily ran into common-law wife'. Indeed, the gendered character is clear from the meaning of landlord, who owns property and collects rent, contrasted with landlady, who provides rooms and services for cash.[47]

Streetsellers were only one step removed from modestly capitalized shops. They required little capital outlay and many fresh goods upon which towns increasingly depended could be brought to customers. Living was precarious and the work hard, and with a taint of poverty, street selling was also part of the economy of expedients. Females of all ages could be found selling on the streets, some regularly, others as a temporary measure. Mayhew divided English women in London into four categories of seller: wives of streetsellers, widows of former streetsellers, mechanics' or labourers' wives who went out to help family income, and single women. They sold all manner of goods, including food, fish, fruit and vegetables, small ware, laces, millinery and flowers, fresh and artificial. A German miner's wife went twice weekly to the city to buy wheat, potatoes and similar items, which she carried ten kilometres home. Some was for her use, but the rest was sold at market. Such women also operated as networks of exchange and information which helped shape the neighbourhood.[48] Such a woman was Antoinette Corbières, a cheese peddler:

> Without a shop, a stall, or even a permanent bench in the market, she made the street her place of business. Along the Grande Rue Montauban and through the side streets around the *Couverts* she hawked her wares from a tray that hung around her neck. Between customers she gossiped in doorways with her friends and flirted with the butcher's son from across the street. Once a week she walked twenty kilometres to the country town of Molières, where, on market day, she shared a bench with her sister who sold bread.[49]

Reddy notes that songs of the community show a fascination for market vendors, revealing deep affection and sense of intimacy. He argues that most vendors began as labourers who saw vending as an escape and a realistic alternative to the mill, requiring only about 100 francs to set up.[50]

Philanthropy was another route for middle-class women for whom not to 'work' was a mark of gentility. Notably, growth in women's charitable activity occurred parallel to middle-class women leaving the workplace. Individuals, such as Florence Nightingale, Octavia Hill, Elizabeth Fry, Josephine Butler, Flora Tristan, Amalie Sieveking, founder of the Weiblicher Verein für Armen- und Krankenpflege [Women's Association for the Care of the Poor and the Sick] as well as groups of women and women's organizations, like the Elisabethvereine [Associations of Elisabeth], the Société Maternelle of Paris and the Rheinisch-Westfälischer Diakonissenverein [Rheinish-Westfalian Association of Deaconesses] at Kaiserwerth, who trained nurses from 1836, took on the task of assisting the poor, sick, needy and vulnerable, such as prostitutes and pregnant women. Philanthropy could be justified within moral codes of the day and perceived as consistent with women's domestic role. It could be described as transmitting the values of their class to their social inferiors, as a mission. As Hannah More insisted, women had a moral duty to be benevolent: 'The care of the poor is her profession.' The selfishness and narrowness of the bourgeois conception of the female also became clear to many women. Nightingale wrote in *Cassandra* that 'The family is ... too narrow a field for the development of an immortal spirit, be that spirit male or female.' Such a realm also became too confining for many women. Some have suggested that women undertook philanthropic activity because they were bored; however, as Summers says, this is insulting and far too simple, suggesting only a negative motivation. Active religion, emanating from evangelical principles, played an important part; but 'women who took up charitable work were tacitly or openly condemning ... the growth of a self-contained bourgeois culture'. It gave women a sense of purpose and accomplishment, where the domestic ideal had seemed vacuous, selfish and unproductive. 'By committing themselves to causes of this kind and actively helping to solve the social problems of the day, women such as Amalie Sieveking, and those who joined her struggle, found they could upgrade their marginal social position, and compensate in a meaningful way for the fact that they were single and had no children.'[51] The philanthropic role had to be fought for, and many women were criticized for abandoning their families to undertake activities which exposed them to undesirable aspects of society, traipsing through the dirt and debris of society. There was a fundamental tension between the 'charitable enterprise and domestic duty'.

An important difference was the pursuance of 'active' philanthropy, that is visiting the poor, sick and others, ultimately becoming patronage, support and social welfare in which self-improvement came to play a bigger role, with the 'visitor' monitoring progress and providing guidance. This shift and the settlement movement helped turn philanthropy into social work, by establishing full-time centres in areas of need, such as London's East End, or proletarian sections of Charonne and Levallois-Perret. On a number of levels, philanthropy changed women's views. They learned skills of management, fund-raising, research, finance, communication and campaigning, and gained a competence which lent them authority as experts. They also realized that they required training to take it further and to contend with men who, seeing the opportunities in such work, brought all their power and standing to bear, 'quick to treat women as auxiliaries fit only for subordinate roles as nurses and social workers'. Women also acquired a radically different view of the world to the one from their front rooms. They visualized new horizons. The first steps were not easy, and required women to overcome fears and prejudices on their own part, while raising their social consciences. This led to further action and a more politicized role for some, such as campaigns for work opportunities for middle-class women, better education, better working conditions for the poor, and the women's movement and suffrage.[52]

Many bourgeois women had to work, especially surplus female relatives, for whom roles as governesses and companions were deemed most appropriate, being private, domestic and in keeping with women's caring role. From the middle years of the century, opportunities, such as teaching, nursing and white-collar work emerged, offering new scope for middle-class women. New attitudes to middle-class girls' education developed, arising from their own enforced idleness and a diminished need to assist mothers. As part of the creation of gentility it seemed that preparing a girl for marriage was the most appropriate use of her time. This led to establishing female boarding schools to teach accomplishments and new demands for women to teach girls at home. Thus, the respectability which prevented the middle-class woman from working also contributed a solution of sorts to the dilemma of a distressed gentlewoman, by requiring teachers and governesses of some gentility and modest educational attainments. One of the most notable women, who faced the conflicts 'between the conception of feminine duty that custom and her family imposed on her, and her own ambitions and desires', was Florence Nightingale, whose achievements in the Crimea and long-term efforts to professionalize nursing practice and training were to open a legitimate career option for many of her successors.[53] Nursing had long been an unformalized feminine role, but Nightingale was to challenge the untrained character of nursing at the same time as demands for higher education for women were gaining strength and medicine was undergoing significant change with a greater understanding of disease. Gradually over the period, as feminism put pressure on a number of social issues, including education, more opportunities would emerge and middle-class women's work would become more acceptable. These options are taken up in more detail in the next chapter, but it is significant that such choices began to emerge as more and more married women left family businesses behind. Given the state of reportage coupled with ideas of who should work and how work was defined, it is impossible to quantify this activity, but there is a lingering thought that far more middle-class women, single and married, worked during the century than one might expect. Despite the fact that most women worked most of the time, women's work was uncharted by many statistical accounts, was considered casual and part time. Often it was piece work and low paid. The concept of skill was blurred by association with women, homework and casual work. It was not considered real. Eugène Buret in 1840 summed up the dilemma: 'Woman is industrially speaking, an imperfect worker. If a man doesn't add his earnings to the insufficient wage of his partner, sex alone constitutes for her the cause of misery.'[54] Contemporary views thus denied the fact of women as workers as well as their identity as workers. Within such constraints, numerous women strove to create their own meaning out of work, and a sense of identity.

8

CONTINUITY AND CHANGE
Gender, skill and status

WOMAN AS WORKER

During the century after the Revolution, when hiring for wages became far more the norm than it had been, attitudes to women workers were shaped by conflicting notions of womanhood and sexuality on one hand and by the needs of capitalism and of working-class families for paid labour on the other. Female employment was not new, but as it became more visible, more clearly 'women for hire' and clashed with notions of domesticity, it became grounds for debate. To many minds, women were not workers; the terms were mutually exclusive. This view shaped the context of women's work and contributed to perceptions of women as casual, temporary employees, who could and should be treated differently from men and paid less. As women, they were seen as docile, malleable creatures, subject to a well-established patriarchal regime, subordinate to men and masters. Belief in different male and female natures coincided with a belief in different abilities, such that women were seen as nimble-fingered, dexterous, careful, meticulous and quick. The combination of cheapness, docility and 'special skills' made them desirable employees, especially in areas of work where they had been for generations, in agriculture, service, needlework and textiles.

Spinning machines and power looms required someone to reattach broken threads precisely and swiftly, a task thought suitable for 'nimble-fingered and dexterous' women. In fact the major prerequisites were sharp eyes and, in the case of looms, sufficient height to reach. Thus in central and northern Italy, as in England and Scotland, women were thought to be most adept at this task. Similarly, these attributes qualified them to work in silk mills, since 'The working of silk requires little physical force and our women, as befits this most delicate of arts, have good eyes and swift fingers.' Employers of St Chamond emphasized how well machine tending suited women because it did not require physical exertion. With a desire for cheap labour, the suspicion arises that employers adopted that part of the feminine ideal which matched their needs, describing women's 'delicacy' in terms which justified employment. Ellena's association of women with delicate fabrics and soft textiles carried this

162

allusion further. Calico printing was broken down into a series of steps, performed best by teenage girls who had learned manual dexterity at home, in needle skills. They were employed in silk mills, 'because their fingers are supple and they learn the skills more easily'.[1] If girls were more suitable, it was because work was planned to take advantage of their cheapness and skills they were expected to have learned from mothers. Such gendered descriptions of jobs appeared throughout contemporary literature, contributing to creating a category of women's work. It was obvious that the feminine ideal could hardly have applied to working-class women in the same way as to the bourgeoisie, but the battleground centred on the *nature* of female and male. At the same time, workers were needed, so they adapted the character of work.

Women's natural steadiness and docility were cited as key factors making them better employees. Miners claimed, 'Females submit to work in places where no man, or even lad could be got to labour in. They work in bad roads, up to their knees in water, in a posture nearly double.' They were praised for knowing their place, 'they make better drawers than lads. They are more steady . . . A lass never expects to be a coal-getter and that keeps her steady.'[2] Feminization of the Lombard silk industry was said to result from women providing a more pliable workforce than men. They had no mutual aid societies, very few strikes, no union-organized stoppages nor any other open manifestation of discontent. Similarly, spinning entrepreneurs considered females to be more docile workers than males, arguing that they were less prone to collective action, less likely to cause work slowdowns or stoppages. Gaskell explained that the master, 'finding that the child or woman was a more obedient servant to himself and an equally efficient slave to his machinery – was disposed to displace the male adult labourer'.[3] If women were accustomed to a patriarchal world in which male authority ruled, it is not surprising that they behaved in an obedient way. And, if a woman needed work, she was unlikely to risk losing it, especially if there were no obvious alternatives. Female self-exploitation suggests that a woman with few alternatives would take whatever pay and conditions offered in order to feed herself and her children. This would easily make her more pliable. At the same time women were largely excluded from collective action, especially as men came to believe more and more that their interests were not necessarily the same.

Feminine health and physical stamina were central to debates about women workers. In Belgium, investigators for Ghent and Verviers arrived at diametrically opposed views in 1846. In Verviers, doctors concluded that women were less, not more, able to withstand factory labour, arguing that the sedentary nature of mill work was particularly hard on the female physique. Lack of exercise caused *ouvrières* 'to grow pale and fall into a languorous state, leaving them particularly susceptible to disease'. In contrast, researchers in Ghent decided that 'women endure work just as well or better than most men', contrary to perceptions of women as the weaker sex. They believed that the imperative for females to reproduce had caused important physical changes which allowed

163

them to tolerate factory labour: 'We can thus regard it as a demonstrated fact, that despite widespread opinion about the delicacy of her organization and her inaptitude for work, woman supports the influence of the manufacturing regime better than men.' This was, of course, in the context that few Belgian voices were raised against female industrial workers, while Hilden argues that working women were widely and openly admired. Issues of health as well as the appropriateness of mine work led to exclusion of women from mineshafts in much of Europe. One woman in Dour in the Borinage told a reporter that she went down at 5 a.m. and returned to the surface at about 9 p.m., during which time she had loaded between sixty and seventy chariots and pushed them a distance of between fifty and one hundred and eighty metres. Scottish women reported carrying loads of three hundredweight, when a basket of 170 pounds required two men to lift it on to her back. One commented that 'lads are no fit to stand the work like women', and a Welsh woman said men refused the windlass, it being 'too hard for them'. Many were pleased to be out of it and would have agreed with fifty-three-year-old Scots woman Isabel Hogg: 'You must tell the Queen Victoria that we are guid loyal subjects; women people here don't mind work, but they object to horse-work.'[4] Yet in Belgium, where Hilden says it was 'ungendered', no legislation banned them, unlike virtually everywhere else. Munby's depiction of women at Charleroi in 1862 contrasts with his own diary entry from Wigan, in the second account:[5]

> Two things struck me at once; the comparative cleanliness of these girls and their white clothing . . . I saw only one or two whose faces were really blackened, and the hands alone were black in all: and their good looks. Most of them were extremely pretty, and feminine too; scarcely one who looked like a man, even in trousers.

> . . . in burst the two wenches, Ellen Meggison and Jane, shouting and tumbling over one another like lads at a fair . . . those two young women in men's clothes, as black and grim as fiends and as rough and uncouth in manners as a bargee, and yet, to those who looked deep enough, not unwomanly nor degraded . . . their talk had nothing flippant or immodest in it.

Reports on agriculture also pointed to mixed images, as did women, one saying, 'I never felt that my health was hurt by the work', another that 'In making hay I have been strained with the work . . . so bad I could not get out of my chair.' Heller and Imhof cite rising burdens on country women due to escalating demands for women in field work, continuing claims on them from the farmyard and increasing pressure from new expectations of cleanliness and housekeeping as causes of a growing higher female mortality rate. Lee concurs that 'the overall effect, in terms of various demographic indicators, was generally negative, especially as the increased involvement of married women in arduous outside work was not accompanied by any realignment of domestic responsibilities'. Urban women felt much the same pressure, as rapid urban growth led to increased labour and poor working and living conditions together with additional shopping tasks.[6]

Throughout all branches of work, whether in cotton factories, silk mills, workshops, homework or domestic service, poor working conditions are frequently cited as having a debilitating effect on women. Two features of these critiques are important. Women's work had become more visible and the woman worker had become a problem to the middle-class social and moral conscience. Her 'visibility followed from the perception of her existence as a problem ... [which] involved the very meaning of womanhood itself and the compatibility between womanhood and wage-earning; it was posed and debated in moral and categorical terms'.[7] A central aspect of the debate was not only femininity, but a growing concern with women's abilities to carry out domestic duties in an appropriate fashion, manifested in protective legislation. At the same time, there was concern that such women were out of control, too independent, reinforcing fears of 'masterless women'. Concern with women's health, their working conditions and their femininity all expressed a male anxiety about control of women.

DOMESTIC ROLES, FAMILY ISSUES AND WOMEN'S WORK

There is no doubt that contemporary rhetoric reflected a basic *right* of men to work and no such right for women; they had a *duty* to the home which could include earning. The family was perceived as a governing concept for social relationships. It shaped the meaning of middle-class life and was a frequent metaphor for the proper relationship between classes. Lown has shown how a patriarchal regime was constructed on a family motif running throughout Courtauld's factory. Domesticity stressed the significance of woman's place in the home, her moral responsibility for home and children's upbringing and the conduct of a range of domestic tasks in ways which enhanced the family's gentility and respectability. They were seen as dependants, subject to control, reliant on men. Working women were influenced by these views in terms of their domestic obligations and paid work. If earning money became necessary, women, single or married, were expected to take on paid work for whatever period required. But it was not her real work. As Alexander has argued, her skill was based on her household responsibilities and 'her property in the virtue of her person. Separated from the home, her family and domestic occupations, or outside the bonds of matrimony, a woman was assured of neither skill nor virtue.'[8] Her identity rested in the home.

Persistence of ideas about 'family strategies' underpins much writing on women's work. A view which argues that families operate to maximize income, making decisions about deployment of family members based on economic considerations, tends to overlook the power of the ideological arguments which

165

had great potency during the period. Such a position was taken by Nardinelli, writing 'division between market production and household production for any given member of the household does not depend on attitudes, affections, customs, sexual stereotypes or outside coercion; it depends only on relative productivities'. Pure economic considerations would suggest that in times of difficulty it was always preferable to send women rather than children out to work, given that women usually could bring in greater income, and yet such was the power of domestic arguments that often children went before women.[9] A range of other variables could be present, such as the type of work available and obligations in the house, but the importance of gendered notions of women and the role played by views of women's place were crucial.

Many women worked intermittently, with regular waged work more likely during their single years and more periodic and part-time work likely during years of marriage and childrearing. This archetypal pattern helped to reinforce ideology. During the century, marital status gained new significance: debates surrounding protective legislation, the cult of the family wage and ideology of domesticity emphasized gender inequality and created a hierarchy in waged work which proved very durable. Married women were overtly marginalized in the labour market, while young single women predominated in more visible workplaces. Ideologically this was acceptable, given that young women were seen as earning dowries to establish new families, and married women as nurturing and sustaining existing families. The upshot was that domesticity crystallized in an overwhelming concern that working-class women's primary responsibility was to provide the back-up needed by male workers, attending to hearth and home. Gray argues that protective legislation aimed to balance the domestic role against waged work, not to exclude women, but to define terms for their participation in waged factory labour. Voices from both working and middle classes increasingly articulated these views. For example, Reddy cites male songs used to air complaints against women, frequently referring to their idleness, ruining family budgets by drinking coffee, forgetting to make soup for dinner, trying to dominate men and having too many babies. He says it is no accident that complaints about unmade soup were most frequent. Repeatedly they dwell on women wasting time while men worked hard away from home comforts. Perhaps a protest against factory routine, they also expose an ambivalence about separate spheres, adopting a notion of separation of work and home, male breadwinner, female housekeeper, arguments which were brought to bear in pressures for a 'family wage' by working-class men. The desirability of women being at home is echoed by one woman's comments to the British Commission on agriculture, who despite feeling that hard work did her no harm believed that it was 'a much better thing for mothers to be at home with their children; they are much better taken care of'. In the view of one commissioner, 'A girl brought up in a cottage until she marries is generally ignorant of nearly everything she ought to be acquainted with for the comfortable and economic management of a cottage.' Gaskell made the same point about manufacturing: 'father, mother, son and daughter, are alike engaged [in the mill]; . . . No clean and tidy wife appears to welcome her husband – no smiling and affectionate mother to receive her children – no home, cheerful and inviting, to make it regarded.'[10] These views reveal the idea of separation of home and work, the tendency to perceive married women as the norm and disregard of life-cycle difference, and the male breadwinner/female housekeeper dyad which underpins debates about the family wage.

Historians often argue that women were disadvantaged by a separation of home and work which came with industrialization, capitalization and mechanization. The crucial hindrance is usually ascribed to work leaving the home so that women could no longer take part 'equally'. Underpinning this position is that domestic duties prevented women from following work out of the home. McPhee, for example, describes the separation of home and work as the most important turning point in the history of urban working women, with the consequent trend towards domesticity among married women with children. Similarly, Accampo sees the 'key change' as 'the removal of work from the home and its reorganization outside the context of the family'. Gullickson shows that agricultural women faced the same conflict: 'Mothers who left their cottages to work in the fields as day labourers or in factories as spinners faced a new problem because they could no longer integrate childcare with their work.' There is truth in these interpretations, but to analyse women's disadvantages in the workplace as a straightforward result of the 'separation of home and work', as some have done, is to simplify a complex situation.[11] It ignores realities of work in earlier periods and the influence of attitudes to domestic duties, and overlooks other factors which reshaped gender relations at work and home.

A fundamental flaw in this argument is the assumption that, in previous periods, work had been located in the home, giving women equal access to it. Few historians today accept such a blatant reading of the pre- or proto-industrial period. The complementarity and mutual dependency of men's and women's activities did not mean that they were 'equal' in the workplace, and it is patently obvious that not all work was in the home. Women's status in the workplace was not necessarily determined by their participation in it, nor by their access to work, but by gendered meanings attached to it. Thus work at home did not gain status for women, nor was status eroded by removal of work from home. At the same time, the married woman probably was the least likely member of the household to spend large parts of her time away from home. She always had some domestic responsibility and was accustomed to reconciling family and work functions, seeing them as much the same thing. As Dupree argues, 'there was no dichotomy between work and home or family; instead there was a continuum of women's occupations from paid industrial employment outside the home, to domestic service, to sweated labour inside the home, to unpaid home work'.[12] A more useful approach is to recognize that the shift was 'not from work at home to work away from home, but from one kind of workplace to another'. Industrialization did not create a division between home and workplace, nor did it create the pressures on childcare and domestic duties. Women had always had to make arrangements for childcare. Changing ideas of housework and Enlightenment views of motherhood generated as much influence on married women and mothers to concentrate on childcare and housework as changing workplaces did. In any case, impact was delayed until the second half of the century for the most part, and one must ask whether some historians have not adopted nineteenth-century ideology. 'If there were problems associated with this move – a new time discipline, noisy machinery, wages dependent on market conditions and economic cycles, profit-driven employers – they nonetheless were not caused by the removal of women from their own home and family settings.' Indeed, factory work could allow girls to live at home who might otherwise have boarded with employers. Scott usefully argues that the story of separation of home and work contributed to the creation of woman worker as a problem by legitimating terms and expressions which minimized continuities with the past, assumed the sameness of women's experience and stressed differences between women and men.[13]

Certainly the shape of work changed with more centralized workshops, factories and farms. However, movement was not all in one direction. With a resurgence of piece work and an increasing reliance on outwork, production continued to be carried on at home. Such developments are cited as allowing women to reconcile domestic functions with wage earning and to comply with the feminine ideal. Beier believed that the main reason that mothers and married women were prepared to take on homework under poor working conditions was because it offered an answer to the dilemma of earning and looking after children and household. Franzoi and Frevert argued that, 'Outwork offered these women the chance of tying up paid employment, housework and childcare in the same place, though the price paid was self exploitation.'[14] The bourgeoisie approved of women working at home, and some working-class men and women may have seen it as appropriate. As Quataert put it, 'what had once been class-appropriate behaviour ... became more generally gender appropriate'. Beier maintained that married women saw themselves as housewives and mothers and did not appear to have felt the double burden of work to be discriminatory. They suffered if they could not perform their household duties as well as their factory work. Taylor argues that 'The "ideology of domesticity" was not just a set of oppressive ideals foisted on a supine female population; it was an ideology actively adopted by many working-class women as the best in a very narrow range of unhappy options.' A boot sewer, cited by Tilly, who worked when her husband was unable or out of work complained of the necessity for married women to work '12 or 14 hours for pitiful wages, forced to leave their children or aged parents untended'.[15] Thus domestic roles cannot be identified as simply a middle-class pressure on working-class women.

The circumstances of homework challenged the idealized view of work at home and threatened to leave household chores and children neglected. Wages were so low as to make living difficult – the pace and timing of work was intense – and to achieve a subsistence income, women had to work long hard hours which allowed no time for domestic responsibilities. A London shirt-maker told Mayhew in 1849 that she usually worked from four in the morning until nine or ten at night in summer, 'as long as I can see'. Sophie Ternyck, shirtmaker of Lille, similarly worked long hours to earn inadequately, while her seven-year-old son ran errands and shopped. A tailoress wife stayed up half the night to do housework after her husband had gone to bed, while the boot sewer often found her work interrupted by children's illness. Only better-off working women could afford to work at a modest pace and juggle domestic and work responsibilities. Nevertheless, women utilized choices open to them to suit their own needs and preferences, such as an English lace runner: 'I like it better than the factory, though we can't get so much. We have our liberty at home and get our meals comfortable, such as they are.'[16] Many women chose to work at home precisely because it allowed them a degree of choice, despite the conflicts involved.

Time and work discipline probably imposed as much pressure on women as location of work did. The shift from being able to move from one task to another to being subject to factory discipline altered experience significantly. They had been accustomed to long hours of hard work, and commercial pressures had shaped demands on their time. However, required to work to set routines and to the dictates of overseers and machinery, food preparation, shopping, gardening and mending had to be fitted in before or after shifts, instead of being inserted into a pattern determined by a woman and her own judgement of her time expenditure. Shifts of twelve hours were common, whether in an English cotton mill, even after the Ten Hours Bill, since meals and breaks were additional to the hours of work, or in a silk or braid mill in St Chamond where employers insisted on twelve-hour shifts, around the clock. Indeed, they claimed that half-day, half-night shifts were organized precisely for the benefit of married women and mothers, who 'could tend to household chores, especially the mid-day meal, as well as contribute to the family income'.[17]

A key difficulty with the 'separation of home and work' perspective is that it obliterates differences between women. It emphasizes married women, especially those with children and overlooks single females who constituted the majority of the visible workforce. Single women found different sets of choices in the more commercialized economies of the nineteenth century than previously. On one hand, large numbers worked as domestic servants, so that work and 'home' were not any more separate for them than for their predecessors. On the other, single women comprised the majority of factory workers, preferring it because it paid better than many alternatives and through it they gained a semblance of independence. Such theory also assumes gendered work patterns: that men worked in an occupation for the duration of their working life, and that women experienced interrupted and temporary work in a number of occupations. While these archetypes may be true, they do not adequately express the variety of patterns experienced by either. Some women had stable 'careers', gaining skill and status in their work; others worked much of their lives in the same or similar jobs, while many men had the variable and peripatetic experience usually associated with women. Representing 'the skilled craftsman as the exemplary "worker" . . . repressed differences of training, job stability and tenure among male workers and thus also similar patterns of irregular and changing employment for male and female workers'.[18] Also, married women worked at a full range of activities. Often they continued at the same jobs as before marriage, or found new options, like residential servants turning to laundering or charring. Silkworkers and agricultural labourers frequently worked much as they had before. Women did not necessarily leave factory work on marriage or at the birth of children. They weighed up their preferences, making decisions which were multifaceted and which did not rely solely on domestic duty or economics.

THE FAMILY WAGE

Broadly speaking, women tended to be defined as dependants, whatever their productive role, while men were classified according to the nature of their labour.[19] This perspective contributed substance to demands for a 'family wage'. In its simplest conception, the family wage describes a man's wage which is sufficient to support all members of a family. It therefore relies also on a notion of woman who is not only dependent but removed from the workplace. The interplay with domesticity is obvious. Wages, like the gendered character of many jobs, rested on custom rather than real labour value. Demand was high for female labour 'precisely because the price was unresponsive to demand pressures. The cultural presuppositions that women's and children's labor was far less valuable than an adult males' put an artificial ceiling on their wages.'[20] Thus, hiring women meant reduced labour costs. Female wages across the economy and throughout Europe tended to be one-third to two-thirds of male wages, with most commentators agreeing that half was typical. Heywood reckons that in France, 'in the mid-nineteenth century the typical pattern was for adult male wages rarely to fall below the range of 1.25 to 1.50 francs per day; for female wages only exceptionally to exceed 1.10 francs; and for those of children to be between 40 and 75 centimes'. Berg makes the differential greater in Britain, where 'it is generally assumed that women by custom received one third to one half the wage of men'.[21] Three caveats are necessary, however. First, it is virtually impossible to compare like with like, since not only jobs, but status was gendered. Second, not all men or women earned the same, and women could and did earn as much as some men. Third, because of reliance on piece rates, earnings depended on time spent. High earnings required not only good wages but steady employment. Although

170

women's wages were nearly always lower than men's in any branch of manufacture, there was considerable variation according to region, season and business cycle in both male and female wages.

Pinchbeck and others saw the family wage as a notional reality of proto-industrial practice where the effort for the whole product, a length of cloth for example, was paid by the piece. Therefore, the work of all members of the household was paid a 'family wage'. However, not all members of the production process were family members, while the model was not uniformly followed, and individual work was compensated for individually. Pinchbeck showed that when a woman substituted for a man, or wove the same cloth, she could be paid the same wage and 'it sometimes happened that husband and wife were employed by different clothiers, in which case the wife earned and received an individual wage'. Also, one suspects that employers did not see rates in terms of labour value, but as paying for the piece which is exactly what they were doing. They may have seen it as a wage to a man who happened to have assistants, many of whom were family. Viewing the effect of industrial changes on women's employment from the vantage point of the 1930s, when child health and allowances were crucial political debates, inevitably helped shape Pinchbeck's vision of the family wage for married women. She argued that women moved from a position of partnership to one where married women lost economic independence through the industrial revolution and the increase in waged work. Unless she went out to work, she lost the ability to contribute to family income and retain some independence and if she did, 'Her earnings rarely balanced the loss to the family from the non-performance of more important domestic duties; her own labour was often exploited and in many cases women's earnings only served to keep their husbands' wages at the level of individual subsistence'. She thus argued that the industrial revolution marked an advance, because ultimately 'it led to the assumption that men's wages should be paid on a family basis, and prepared the way for the more modern conception that in the rearing of children and in home-making, the married woman makes an adequate economic contribution'. A single woman also gained in social and economic independence, she argued, since, with the payment of individual wages, she 'received her own earnings as a matter of course'.[22]

Hilary Land wrote, 'It is assumed implicitly that men's wages should be sufficient to support a family whereas women's wages are supplementary to others or at most need be sufficient to support an adult. Men earn a "family wage" and women earn "pin money". If jobs are in short supply, men should have prior claim to them.'[23] Conceptualization of a family wage owes its derivation to changes in the gendered character of work during the nineteenth century and to attempts to reconcile readjustments in the relationship of men and women to work, to home and to each other. One strand looks like bourgeois morality and certainly some arguments originated in the middle classes. More importantly, working-class attitudes to domesticity and women's work come from a struggle over male wage and status. These resolved into demands for a family wage and exclusion of women from many workplaces. Other factors which contributed to women's workplace position, such as mechanization, skill, status and division of labour are, of course, not separate from the family wage debate. Essentially, there were three issues:

1 the status of men in the workplace in relation to employers, their craft status and their wages;
2 male control of the home and gender relations;
3 notions of good housekeeping and its value to the working class.

Nevertheless, the family wage was no more than an ideal and a bargaining tool since few working-class men earned adequately in the conditions of industrial capitalism to support wives and children. It was also notional in that many people did not live, or work, in 'families' and families were of varied shapes and sizes with members of different ages and sexes who contributed more or less depending on circumstances.

The main group of workers for whom the family wage was a real issue comprised skilled men, inheritors of the artisan, who constituted the first trade unions. These men believed that a family wage, by which they meant *their* wage, would reduce women's participation in the labour market leading to less competition for jobs. Men's position would then be enhanced absolutely, but also in relation to employers. This line of argument is not very far removed from earlier claims for protection of skill and status deriving from guilds and artisan craft work. On one hand, it was not about women, but about protecting their craft position and independence vis-à-vis capitalists who wished to control labour supply. On the other hand, it clearly was about gender, because the workers against whom it was aimed were women, since they perceived female labour, not unskilled male labour, as the threat.

Opposition to capitalism and state control of workers were important features. German Lassalleans opposed women's labour on the grounds that 'it undermined the economic and social strength of workers to fight capitalism', while the family wage was an assertion of control by the first national miners' union in Britain, seeking improvements in working practices on men's terms rather than on the government's. While gender was clearly important, so was class. Thus another view of the family wage is to see men and women working in concert, employing a family strategy to maximize household income. The need to oppose control of capitalism and sustain the family's position is then regarded as paramount. For example, Thomas Winters, Chartist, trade unionist and frameknitter, insisted that if work performed by a family were concentrated in the hands of adult males, 'they would receive the same amount of money in the family and save the expense of [frame] rent and charges, which would add more money to the general income of the family, and therefore they would be benefitted [sic] by being out of work rather than being in work'. Thus the family wage was one of a repertoire of strategies employed by the working-class family to maintain its independence from capitalist employers. This view harks back to the family production system with its collectivist approach that places the family above competitive individualism. There was, of course, no evidence to suggest that employers were prepared to pay such a 'family wage', especially if it raised men's wages. As Fine says, it was at best an ideological construct to justify higher wages for men, irrespective of the effects on lowering female wages and removing them from the workplace. From the perspective of many workers, the family income argument was relevant; and yet there is no doubt that patriarchy and notions that women had no right to work played a part in the rhetoric.[24]

Men were concerned about their status and patriarchal role in the workplace vis-à-vis women. Notably they did not necessarily attempt to exclude women from work, but to remove them from areas where they did the same work as men, or worked in the same industries so that they undercut men's wages, status and control. As individual wages rather than piece work or collective pay emerged, women who received wages could be seen as competing with men, threatening not only job security but their position as men. Thus, German opposition to female labour was most vociferous in those trades, like tailoring and cigar-making, where both sexes worked. In 1848, the Association of German Cigar-makers called for a ban on female factory labour. Cotton printers also reasoned that competition from cheaper women harmed their position and would induce the industry's collapse. The West Riding Short-Time Committee likewise demanded 'gradual withdrawal of all females from the factories . . . [It was an] inversion of the order of nature and providence – a return to the state of barbarism, in which the woman does the work, while the man looks idly on.' In the Aude, the male agricultural union fought to exclude women from local vineyards. Supporting these views were philanthropists, such as parliamentary investigators, who accepted that when men and women worked in the same jobs, wives undercut husbands' wages. Such a position was very much predicated on a male right to work and earn. This patriarchal control was perceived as the natural order and one upon which social order was based, despite its weak foundation.[25]

Construction of the family wage was central to sexual stereotyping and to defining women's work as secondary: 'In the last half of the nineteenth century, the size of his wage packet linked a man's status at home and in the community with his masculinity at work.' It was important to ensure that women's work was paid less well and kept inferior to men's. So, women had to be prevented from taking men's jobs and if they worked, they should be directed to appropriate work. 'Appropriate' had a double meaning. First, it simply meant work that men did not want. Second, it meant work suited to the supposed feminine frame and delicacy and situated in an appropriate place, usually the home. As one cigar-maker wrote, 'If all women socialists promise to keep well away from our businesses, then we also shall solemnly avow not to become cooks, cleaners, lacemakers, needleworkers, flower girls, knitters, seamstresses, etc. etc.'[26] Lord Ashley also relied on 'nature' when he argued that the practice of women working long hours

> disturbs the order of nature and the rights of the labouring men, by ejecting the males from the workshop and filling their places by females, who are thus withdrawn from all their domestic duties and exposed to insufferable toil at half the wages that would be assigned to males, for the support of their families.[27]

There was no campaign for a 'family wage' for female heads of households, nor any attempt to 'protect' women exploited in needlework trades working at home. As Rose said, 'Family wage rhetoric was silent on the subject of women as *workers*.' The ideal of a family wage bolstered patriarchy because it was firmly attached to the image of a breadwinning male supporting a dependent wife. Seeing separation of home and work as the cause of women's inferior work status misses the point that there were important changes in the balance of the sexes at work which affected domestic relations. For example, replacement of handloom weavers by power weavers meant men were supplanted by wives and daughters, making skilled men redundant. There was bitter resentment that they had to rely on earnings of women and children. As Rose argued, 'demand for a family wage was founded on an ideal of masculinity that required a man to be the sole support of his family . . . [and] was premised on the desirability of his wife being a full-time homemaker and mother'. It was not 'natural' that women became housewives. Instead it was part of the attempt to establish the idea of the hardworking man responsible for support of his wife and children. Gray argues that ideas about the 'respectable artisan' relied on constructions of the family as much as work identity. Economic change and domestic ideology reinforced each other in perpetuating the sexual division of labour in industry, home and society.[28] As Henry Broadhurst said at the 1877 Trades Union Congress,

> it was their duty as men and husbands to use their utmost efforts to bring about a condition of things, where their wives could be in their proper sphere at home, instead of being dragged into competition for livelihood against the great and strong men of the world.[29]

Appeals aimed to restore the 'traditional' balance in gender relations at home and at work. Archaic ideals lay behind resistance and claims for family wage, not commitment to bourgeois womanhood.

Men coupled the claim for the family wage with the case for domesticity. Cigar-makers of Leipzig wished to remove women from the workplace to promote standards of behaviour. Others demanded barring women from factory work and sending them to domestic service to turn them into good housewives. The Gotha Congress concluded that female labour should be banned 'where it might be deleterious to health and morality'. In British coalfields,

174

miners sensed that their wives were entitled to the same home comforts as employers' wives. Indeed, the *Northern Star*, the Chartist paper, linked the argument for women as homemakers with the labour-market issue succinctly in October 1843; 'Keep the women at home to look after their families; decrease the pressure on the labour market and then there is some chance of a higher rate of wages being enforced.' By the end of the century married respectability was increasingly associated with dependence on a sole male breadwinner. The family wage became the 'bedrock of respectability' and a woman's chief identity was as wife and mother, regardless of her work commitments. 'In effect, though her job may have been a source of pride, it was still viewed as secondary to, or even a detraction from, her femininity.'[30]

Women tended to see men as breadwinners, but the gap between reality and ideal, not direct confrontation with the ideal, caused their irritation. Taylor shows that tensions arose wherever working-class women took on productive roles which contested the expected division of labour.[31] However, not all women welcomed domestic duties. A widow in Nottingham said, 'I believe a married woman that goes out to work has more spirit and energy than one that always stays at home; and when she does return and she has no lace work to do at home, she can devote her time to her house and family.'[32] A single Birmingham woman argued the case for women's abilities:

> If a woman is cleverer than a man and she can go out and earn as much as her husband, I do not see why she should be prevented from earning what she can to bring up her children in a better way than she could if she did not work. Why can't a woman make a pattern of chandeliers? There is no reason whatever . . . I would rather make patterns; I can do it and do it well and would very much rather do it than stay at home and scrub.[33]

The assumption that the breadwinner husband and housekeeper wife was the natural result of the development of industrial capitalism ignored the potential for choice. In areas like Lancashire and Paris, with a high level of female employment and high household earnings, families relied on purchased ready-made food, infant day-care, charwomen and laundresses for domestic services.[34]

The effect of the debate about family wage was double edged. Efforts to drive women out of certain kinds of work further decreased their earning power, married women's dependence on males increased, and single women's position was undermined. So, many women continued to work in jobs with low status and income, further defining women's work as cheap, unimportant and of little standing. The effect was that whenever jobs became feminized, they lost status. Women's position in the labour market became even more disadvantaged, weakening their right to work. 'Low wages, dependence and housework for women are a trio of mutually reinforcing ideas, each justifying and producing the conditions for the others.'[35]

GENDER, SKILL AND CRAFT TRADITIONS

Constructions of work and skill enhanced men's productive role and diminished women's in favour of reproduction. By the nineteenth century, male craft traditions were under significantly more stress as capitalism expanded and the balance of power shifted in favour of owners and employers. The master either joined the entrepreneurs or his workplace position was eroded. The increase in waged work and large-scale centralized production together with mechanization contributed to the erosion of craft control and led to men adopting whatever strategies they could to protect their position. In the process, technological change produced a reworking of the sexual division of labour and with it ascription of status. 'Men usually retained the ability to define their superior social status through their work. Women, denied parity of status through work were just as likely . . . to seek their social definition through their domestic and mothering roles.'[36] The interplay between gender, skill, division of labour and technological change shaped the work situation of women in nineteenth-century Europe.

Whether women worked in centralized workplaces or in domestic industry, there were apparent constants in the type of work they did and the industries in which they worked. The disparity between textiles and metalwork provides one example, in that they were found in numbers in textiles but were a minority in metal trades. Within these industries there were notions of the types of task women could and should do and it is commonly believed that as tasks were mechanized, women were put to them, because they demanded less skill or ability. However, the relationships between women, industries, tasks, machinery and division of labour are neither simple nor straightforward, nor are the ideological constructs which underpin them. A number of studies have suggested that occupational segregation by gender was one result of articulation and transference of traditional gender roles into the emerging industrial workplace. Alexander, for example, argues, 'Manufacture provided the economic conditions for the hierarchy of labour powers, but it was the transference of the sexual division of labour from the family into social production which ensured that it was women who moved into the subordinate and auxiliary positions, within it.'[37]

On one hand, jobs and tasks were gendered and on the other, industries were gendered, so that women were prominent in some and virtually non-existent in others. Jordan argues 'androcentric blindness . . . prevented [employers] from considering the possibility that some of the tasks within their industry could be performed just as well and far more cheaply by women'. She argues that responsibility lay with employers who did not hire women, rather than women rejecting such work as unfeminine. Notably, women continued to work in industries where change was gradual, but in new fields or where change was radical they were most likely to be excluded. Richards suggested and Jordan's data tend to confirm, that women were employed in industrial sectors which stagnated in the second half of the century, since sectors which employed the majority of women (domestic service, garments and textiles) were stagnating and the expanding sectors (conveyance, mines, metals, and food and lodging) had very few women. They were particularly likely to find work in domestic industries which transferred to factories and in industries founded on a subcontracting and family-hiring basis where women comprised an important part of the workforce. Jordan argues, 'if an industry did not build on a pre-existing workforce and division of labour, the employer's conception of women's place being in the home meant that they considered only men as potential employees'. Domesticity cannot be ruled out as a factor, but the connection is not straightforward. Exclusion of women was certainly a result of gender ideology, but not strictly because of moral inhibitions about domesticity. 'Androcentricity' in hiring practices surely played a part.[38]

Women were most likely to be restricted where men had the strongest craft traditions or could assert those traditions in a new context. Craft in textiles was already undermined by proto-industrial strategies, while leather, wood, pottery and metalwork retained a measure of their customs and were not seen as trade routes for females. A useful example is shoemaking, or cordwaining, which was overstocked and poorly paid, but which retained status as an honourable trade to which girls were not apprenticed. In the nineteenth century, it continued to be a minority employer of women, usually family members. For example, in France in 1866, 17 per cent of the workforce in leather and footwear were females, though they comprised 34 per cent of manufacturing workers. In Leicester in 1871, with a higher female workforce than other English towns, 11 per cent of working women worked in footwear. In Central Europe, the strength of craft traditions meant that almost no women worked in shoemaking trades.[39] Thus industries with a strong handicraft base were more likely to retain a masculine character, despite introducing females into particular processes and tasks. Stitching, with its strong association with female skills, created a niche for women in footwear which the sewing machine reinforced, but it did not open the trade to them. In sectors like pottery and small hardware, which employed an increasing proportion of women, they worked primarily as assistants, since specific 'female' skills gained them an entrée. To identify reasons for female exclusion requires a highly nuanced explanation which considers both industries and processes within them.

Men continued to claim a skilled craft position that specifically operated to exclude women as a means of protecting their own standing at work. 'The crucial factor maintaining mulespinners in their position was the reconstitution of craft skill . . . In the transition from the hand mule to the "self actor", the specific tasks performed by the mule spinner changed, but not their craft status.'[40] Reddy draws a parallel between the mule spinners' way of working and the artisan, substantiating the link in artisanal craft between them. He emphasizes the extent to which new mill life was community transposed and that 'division of labour, the levels of pay and the pace of work were attuned to centuries-old popular custom and current collective needs'. Craft traditions were integrated into male workers' approach to work and even in unskilled and overstocked trades, workers relied on artisanal pride to control their work.[41] When we note that men resisted moving into factories as weavers, and shoemakers refused to use a sewing machine because they feared losing control of their craft, craft authority and control, in other words status, become central issues and appeals to skill, strength and technical know-how become pillars with which to support this claim. There is an important continuity in the reference to craft skills of workshop and guild customs, so that workers used 'tradition' to oppose women's access to skills that guilds had protected. Rule argues that the ability to preserve status and well-being was the chief concern of most artisans, not an ideal of self-employment. For example, as more untrained men and women took up hand weaving in the English West Country, male handloom weavers adopted values highly congruent with those of urban craftsmen. They demanded enforcement of apprenticeship regulations and sought to prosecute 'illegal' weavers, thus resorting to craft solidarity.

> The vocabulary of grievance which underlay . . . public speech was that of skilled men and it responded to their sense of disinheritance of the right to practise their trades. In mind too was their status as fathers and heads of families as well as their independence through 'honourable' labour and their property in skill.[42]

Throughout the period of industrialization, craft skills were reconstituted as a crucial determinant of masculinity. The sense of craft was as real as any new skills, and helps to explain the necessity of defining women's work, and skills, as not skilled. In this context, machinery contributed to men's sense of masculinity. Thus machines used by women had to be defined explicitly as 'women's machines' and depicted as 'deskilled' processes.

The same concerns were echoed in the notion of the family wage because if a man could not control the better work and command the higher wage, he could be seen as not providing for his family, thus undermining his household reputation. Sarah Wise, a knitter, testifying to Parliament in 1845, explicitly linked the importance of work and household status: 'We consider every head of a family in our village to be the head of his work.' Male workers inextricably associated their independence as workers through honourable labour, property in skill and their trade identity with their status as fathers and heads of families. Perceptions of masculinity centred on 'a man's capacity to direct and organise his family's economic contributions because of his possession of skill'.[43] Broadly speaking, we see a solidification and crystallization of gendered attitudes emerging from the eighteenth century. These took on new life, sublimation and much more widely permeated nineteenth-century society, reflecting in a striking way perceptions and definitions of women's work.

Part III

THE TWENTIETH CENTURY, *c*. 1880–1980

9

HOME AND WORK

THE SHAPE OF WORK

The political complexity of the twentieth century, two major wars and the rise
of extremist political ideologies have tended to overshadow changes in economy, family and work. These factors interacted with underlying currents and
nineteenth-century inheritance to create revised attitudes to women, work and
home. A plurality of approaches coloured the period after 1880 as countervailing ideas about women's rights and place in society asserted themselves. The
volume of information increased, as oral history and sociology, emanating from
nineteenth-century enquiries and enquêtes, created new ways of looking at
women and hearing their voices. Though still mediated, at least they have an
avowed intention of hearing women. Two apparent trends were an increase in
the number and proportion of women working and a shift from domestic service and industry to the tertiary sector, such as shop and office work. Yet, there
were important cultural, geographical, temporal and life-cycle differences, frequently depending on the economic infrastructure of where women lived and
their social position, while there were important continuities in the character
of their work.

Across Europe the numbers of women in the formal economy increased. This
simple statement however must be tempered by an understanding that construction of data colours official statistics. During this era, increasing reliance
on statistics engendered a belief in their veracity. We want to think that we
have a clear grasp of how our society is structured and that we know how many
people were doing what. However, censuses define the activity they include,
because statisticians need to decide what they will count. An underlying
theme of this book has been that work has multiple meanings, and as Reynolds
indicates, the terms 'work' and 'labour' are elastic and not synonymous with
employment or economic activity. Enumeration requires choices and is not
neutral; these decisions eliminated facets of women's work as conclusively as
less comprehensive earlier censuses had. As Zerner explained, 'activity' came to
be understood only as forms of work which can be measured statistically and
were 'visible' in the political economy.[1] Women in the informal economy,

working in a family work group, or sporadically, were still most likely to be excluded. With compendia of data, statistics become even more seductive. It is tempting to create a 'European' data set, yet definitions are not consistent across nations. For example, German censuses counted family assistants as economically active, though not always successfully. At the same time, they used the narrower term 'employed' to refer to those whose jobs entailed joining state insurance schemes. The British Ministry of Labour took a similar line, thus excluding domestic servants and women in other uninsured jobs. Parameters also changed. For example, in the 1925 German census women had more latitude defining their role, so they could register as gainfully employed if their main subsistence came from working in household business. Thus family assistants doubled to a third of working women, 4.1 million. Denmark counted the whole household before 1900 but not after.[2] National boundaries produced a different problem: they moved. Germany, Austria, Ireland and Russia, for example, were not always the same territory. These vagaries mean one data run is impossible.

Census data indicate a significant rise in women's recorded employment in Russia, Germany, Sweden, the Netherlands, Denmark and Britain, and a modest rise in France, Spain and, after a drop, in Italy. Countries such as Belgium and Austria show a more erratic pattern, though more females worked in recorded areas in 1970 than in 1880. Across Europe, a cumulative rise is apparent, topping 100 million from just over 30 million in 1880. However, such increases have to be set against the rise in female population and a concurrent rise in male workers. Within the framework of a generally expanding recorded workforce, women's increased participation was not spectacular. Numbers were most likely to have increased in countries which industrialized first and fastest, largely Northern Europe, such as Denmark, Sweden, Norway, England, Scotland, Germany and Finland. The southern countries often began at a very low level of recorded female employment, and in general rose only very slightly, if at all.[3] Because increase was not consistent across the era, it is useful to look at three periods: before the First World War, the interwar period and after the Second World War, usually referred to as post-war with a sense of optimism. These periods are not ideal, but as with so much twentieth-century history, these breaks and the concomitant shifts in policy cannot be ignored.

Before 1914, a pattern emerged which suggested that women would increase as workforce participants almost indefinitely. In Germany, France and Britain numbers grew rapidly, with steady growth in the Netherlands, Belgium and Denmark. However, male workers also increased so that females did not significantly increase in relative terms. German and French women workers increased as a proportion of recorded females and as a proportion of the workforce, reflecting economic growth and industrialization following the Franco-Prussian War. The Netherlands showed a similar pattern. Women declined as a proportion of the workforce in Britain and Sweden and in Spain and Italy where the proportion of working women also fell. Between the wars, labour demand was variable with cultural factors playing a part. In some countries, women were required to help recovery, and thus numbers continued to rise for a short time, as in France. In others, such as Britain, official policy and the return of men from war meant that many women left work, or were ousted, very quickly. Unemployment also meant that numbers of women workers may have fallen, but their proportion held its own since men too were laid off. Regeneration in the 1930s, particularly as countries began to return to a war footing, had some impact in drawing women into work. Certainly governmental policies, economic needs, perceptions of men and women with respect to work and the kinds of opportunities available all came into play.[4]

Following the Second World War, Europe was faced with two images: horror of war and need for wide-scale reconstruction coupled with an optimism and faith in progress leading to policies of full employment. In every country of Western Europe, more women were recorded as part of the labour force in the 1970s than in the 1940s, except in France and Ireland where the drop in recorded agricultural workers was not compensated for by other occupations. Lagrave asserts that in 1975, Europe 'passed an economic and sociological milestone: independent labour in its traditional form virtually vanished, and women no longer stayed at home'. After 1939 women rose to over half of the Soviet workforce, and over 40 per cent in Austria, Czechoslovakia, Denmark, Finland, Hungary, Norway, Poland, Romania, Sweden and the UK. Again, female contribution was higher in the north than the south, though Italy, Greece and Spain all saw rapid increases. Ambrosius and Hubbard draw out the significance of these increases with their 'coefficient of the utilization of potential female labour' based on the number of active females as a percentage of the total female population aged between fifteen and fifty-five. Thus in 1920 the coefficient was seldom 50 per cent, but by 1980 in ten European countries it was 66 per cent and less than 50 per cent in only six. Similarly, in 1920 women comprised a third or more of the working population in only nine countries; by 1980 this was true in nineteen.[5]

The most important change in women's experience was a shift in the structure of work. Decline in domestic service was dramatic and exacerbated by the First World War, which provided a way out for many disenchanted young women. The move away from homework was more gradual, affected most by the collapse of textile and clothing work combined with increased mechanization. Paid agricultural work for women also diminished, although outside Britain, numbers remained high, usually unpaid family members. Figure 9.1 illustrates the shape of the main changes. Patterns in manufacture are less clear because decline in textiles and garment-making, especially outwork, was offset by new processes and products. Women continued in family businesses and shops, particularly in France, but the emergence of the large *magasin*, or department store, and shop and office jobs provided alternatives to domestic service. Professions and careers opened in academia, medicine, law and business but 'the glass ceiling' tended to bar women from the highest echelons. A key issue was 'equal pay for equal work', but when it was achieved, other forms of discrimination still operated to

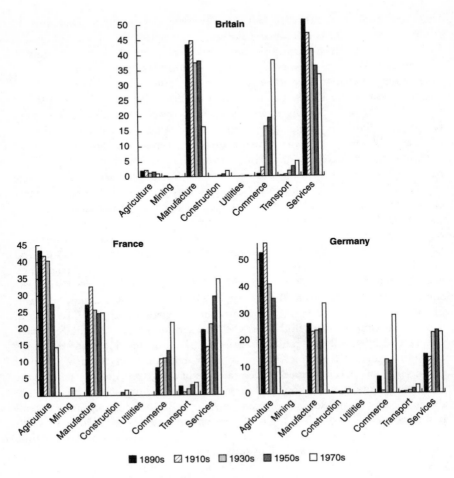

Figure 9.1 Proportion of female labour force in each branch of economic activity
Source: Bairoch *et al.* (1968)

prevent equal participation of women in work. Not the least of these is that women are still not perceived as workers. Masculinity is bound up with men's work, while femininity is still tied to domestic role. As Lagrave summed up: 'labour in Europe was still men's business'.[6]

THE MEANING OF THE WARS

Marwick argues 'that two wars have played a substantial, though unequal, part in furthering social change in twentieth-century Britain'.[7] Furthermore, on the effect of the First World War he wrote,

Whatever might or might not have happened had there been no war, only the war could have provided the concentrated experience which both gave to women a new confidence in themselves, and showed up the absurdities of the many preconceptions about what they were capable of.[8]

A key historical debate of the twentieth century has been the impact of war on social change in general and on women specifically. The controversy is polarized between those who see the wars as catalysts for change, as watersheds, and those who stress continuities, seeing them merely as interruptions. However, boundaries between the two camps are blurred, with differences of emphasis shaping the contours of their positions, and with most historians agreeing that both elements of change and continuity nuance their accounts.[9]

Both during and after the First World War, contemporaries believed a new dawn was breaking for women. In 1923, Célestin Bougle, Sorbonne sociologist, asserted 'a hundred thousand of surviving barriers to women fell at a single blow', while Montague, British Minister of Munitions, declared in 1916, 'Women of every station . . . have proved themselves able to undertake work that before the war was regarded as solely the province of men . . . [Where] is the man now who would deny to women the civil rights which she has earned by her hard work?' Responses across Europe granting women the vote, excluding France, Italy and Switzerland, and making welfare provision were seen as harbingers of a new age. The question for historians has been twofold: did women's situation improve and result in 'emancipation' and, because it quickly became apparent that it did not, then why not? Related, of course, is a comparison with the Second World War, particularly as it appeared that more 'progress was made after 1945 than after 1918'. Higonnet argues that the First World War seemed to offer more opportunities than the second, since it shattered what remained of the 'stifling nineteenth-century consensus' on women's role in society. Yet new employment and votes did not readily translate into social, political or economic power. Higonnet offers further insight by contextualizing women's participation in the wars. 'Wartime propaganda exhorted women to brave unfamiliar work, [but] these appeals were contained within a nationalist and militarist discourse that reinforced patriarchal, organicist notions of gender relations.' Women were encouraged to 'help out' 'only for the duration', 'for the nation in its time of need'. They were being asked to behave 'like men' in roles which were not 'natural' for women.[10]

Belief in wars as catalysts tends to obscure continuities and achievements of the decades before 1914. For example, Hause argues that it is more accurate to see war as only one factor in a longer and slower evolution of attitudes than as a momentous change. In doing so, he highlights the importance of weighing up all the evidence.

It is hardly surprising that women physicians obtained wider acceptance during four years of fighting when casualty rates averaged over

1,000 per diem. The important fact is not that the French public accepted doctoresses as replacements, that women received appointments at new levels; it would have been stunning if they had not. Rather it is the gradual entrance of women into medicine during the previous forty years and the efforts of feminists to open the profession to them.[11]

There is little doubt that war brought more women into the workforce. In Britain numbers rose from 3.3 million to 4.9 million between July 1914 and November 1918, a 50 per cent increase, shifting the workforce from 24 to 38 per cent female. In France in 1918, women constituted 40 per cent of workers compared to 32 per cent before it. In the Second World War, Britain and the Soviet Union conscripted women; Germany and Italy did not. Women's participation was more useful, since about twice as many women worked in war industries or armed forces in Britain than in the First World War. Soviet women virtually replaced men in agriculture, and were a majority of industrial workers by 1945.[12]

A common image is the female munitions worker, and 684,000 French and 920,000 English women worked in munitions factories in the First World War. Many jobs were in military supply, like shell filling, where women had always worked. As Reynolds says, the munitionette has a special claim because of her peculiar visibility and symbolic status. They also made uniforms, worked as canteen staff, clerks, radio operators, telephonists and administrators in a wide range of workplaces. Others replaced fathers and brothers in offices, banks, transport or shops. The Paris Métro went from employing 124 to 3,037 women. Britain, Serbia and Russia had women in the military. During the Second World War in Britain, '1,500,000 more women were working in "essential industries" in 1943 than 1939. These included every branch of engineering, as well as chemicals, vehicles, transport, gas, water and electricity and shipbuilding. Nearly 60,000 more women were working in commerce and national and local government, 500,000 were in Civil Defence and over 450,000 women were in the forces. The Women's Land Army had grown to 80,000.' Attitudes had to be influenced by 'Thousands of nurses and clerical workers in the masculine work of warfare, business and government plus tens of thousands of female factory workers.' It would be wrong, however, to suggest that women simply dropped other jobs and flooded to the ranks. In the First World War, women's employment was hard-hit. Certainly, many domestic servants turned to war work, but at the same time many were dismissed, and a fall in demand for luxuries hit trades like millinery and dressmaking. It was estimated that 44.4 per cent of the paid female workforce was unemployed in Britain at some point during 1914. One practical significance of women's wartime employment brings us back to munitions and engineering. A legacy of the First World War was the introduction of new working practices, particularly new divisions of labour. With virtually no training, processes were broken down into minute tasks so that an unskilled worker could quickly and correctly complete a task. Such procedures would have met with far more resistance in peacetime, and indeed lent themselves only to large-scale production. But employing women as virtual novices in industry using this system created an important precedent.[13]

War may have accelerated trends already under way in terms of women gaining a stronger foothold in the public workplace, but to see the position of working women in a single continuum with the wars as catalysts is problematic both for the longer-term historical picture and for the role of the war. Women in engineering and explosives industries replaced men, and issues of dilution and substitution are well known. Women often engaged in repetitious work, but they were able to demonstrate abilities which allowed them to take on more skilled work, allowing more men to be released for the forces. Whatever resentment this caused, it nevertheless revealed to employers, and male workers, the skills and potential of a female labour force. While it led to backlash in some instances, in the longer term it was another tiny step in women's move towards becoming 'workers'. Perhaps as important as the visibility of the female worker was the effect on women themselves. Nursing exposed large numbers of single females to experiences which challenged their sensibilities; they mixed far more freely with the opposite sex, and moved about much more often without mothers or chaperones. Some women moved from close-knit communities and rural surroundings into a world of factories and work, mixing with women with other histories. It could be a coming of age. Such was the story told by a woman from Scotland's central belt, who found herself transported to 'secret' work in the Dumfries area in the Second World War. Such transitions marked much wider transformations. Women came to appreciate their own abilities more, gained confidence, and developed a belief in a right to work. They acquired skills and an assurance in those skills. These issues are developed further in the chapters which follow.

DOMESTICITY AND BEYOND: REDEFINING WOMEN, WIVES AND MOTHERS

The period is often perceived as one of female emancipation. Legislation gave women more control over their earnings, better protection at work and pension rights. Gradually many gained equal rights with regard to property, income, divorce, childrearing and domicile. Fashion trends, including hairlines and hemlines, gave women more physical freedom of action. Yet, the pun can hardly be avoided that many changes were cosmetic. Fundamental shifts in attitudes and practices were far slower; there was no continuum of 'progress'. Domesticity continued to have vibrancy, with a subtle shifting of ground, while feminism argued for women's right to equality, opportunity and independence. That household and family should come first for both single and married women continued to be strongly held views. The marriage bar which operated across Europe in many occupations clearly affected women's right to work. Education authorities and the Civil Service in Britain enforced it, while many industrial employers operated discrimination against married women, such as Boots Drug Company, 'You got your cards – oh yes . . . They didn't believe in married women working, not then . . . Oh no, as soon as you got married your job went . . . – you got your cards.' In the 1950s it was common practice for women in the Ruhr to be dismissed on the day they married, 'because the employers think it is enough if the husband is earning'. In France, however, a marriage-bar policy was not implemented. Single-women clerks in Germany were expected to help mothers with housework. Spinsters of all classes were often expected to look after fathers, brothers or mothers. For example, Gittins describes Lizzie who was left to support and look after her mother; when a brother became a widower with a young son, he expected her to help him. She commented, 'I didn't feel too good about it. No, well, I didn't want to leave mother.'[14] In contrast, radicalism redefined what women wanted, though feminists were often more radical than society or their own class. They embodied different political and economic approaches: suffrage tended to be more important to middle-class activists, while socialist feminists concentrated on ameliorating the double burden of housework and paid work, through maternity insurance, day-care, on apprenticeships to improve access to better work, and on equal pay for equal work.

Political agendas underpinned domesticity with a dramatic increase in child health and pronatalist policies. After the Franco-Prussian War, the falling French birth rate together with fear of the new German imperium led to pronatalism, while feminism insisted on maternity as a distinctive and common female attribute in the struggle for women's rights. Sweden prohibited information on and sale of contraceptives in 1910. A drop in middle-class family size, unsuitability of recruits for the Boer War and heightened international tensions produced a debate in Britain which expressed fears of 'the race' against other nations but also a dread that the more prolific working classes would swamp the middle classes. Such apprehension of the 'multiplication of the "poorest and least fit classes" at the expense of the "more prudent middle classes"' also led to heated debate in Norway, Holland, France and Germany about voluntary motherhood. Neo-Malthusians claimed, 'The rights of women increase. But what is their great duty: to give birth, to give birth again, always to give birth . . . Should a woman refuse to give birth she no longer deserves her rights.' These anxieties rebounded on women who were encouraged to have more children and to expend time and energy in their care.[15]

One of the most distinctive changes was the role of the state in underpinning ideology. Protective labour legislation became more prominent as proponents condemned women's paid work as undermining physical health on moral grounds, as causing neglect of home and family, and because it contravened the 'natural' division of labour of the sexes. Government welfare provisions also contributed to constructing perceptions of women's place. Importantly, maternalist policies were promulgated across Europe, not only in fascist countries. States took a leading part in promoting child welfare through efforts such as clinics, free milk and the expansion of maternity hospitals in Britain. In the new British Ministry of Health in 1919, one department was dedicated to maternal and child welfare. The French government forged medals for mothers and decreed penalties for promoting contraception. Offen underscores the intersection between nationalism, pronatalism and politics, and entanglement of women's employment and reproduction in an impassioned debate over the strength of the French nation. During the 1930s, regular postnatal care was introduced in Denmark. Revolution law in the Soviet Union granted maternity leave, access to divorce and abortion, but entrenched values, practical realities and conservative reaction unravelled the legislation and created subsidies for women with large numbers of children as the government sought to increase birth rate.[16] Italy depicted mothering 'as woman's natural destiny and means of fulfilment, and as a responsibility: a task that has to be learned if it is to be carried out properly', and Germany glorified it 'as the contribution of women to the survival of the German people' which underpinned Nazi concepts of racial superiority and world domination. Both regimes adopted a wide range of policies, which defined the normal place of adult women as wives and mothers at home. They introduced allowances and other supports to mothers, and placed disincentives in the way of mothers who went to work. Germany introduced child allowances for women who had been in employment and awarded medals to mothers with four or more children, while in Italy, family allowances were paid to men as were fertility prizes which replaced maternity benefits. Both improved welfare and maternity services, though only Italian women who breastfed were assisted.[17] Maternalist policies across Europe significantly undercut the idea of a 'brave new world' for women.

Changes in legislation, fertility and infant mortality colluded to make children more significant in domestic life, while women became more clearly seen as mothers than as wives. Interest in child psychology coincided with a more 'scientific' approach to society, a devaluing of women's instincts, and a behaviourist approach to child training. Rapid decline in family size affected all classes, in one way reducing mothers' obligations, but with increased regulation of child labour and state schooling children were more likely to be dependent longer than previously. These changes interacted with other cultural shifts, such as encouragement to breastfeed and a rise in standards and expectations of childcare. Health measures and family 'visitors' contributed to establishing new targets in child nurture. Mothers became even more firmly defined as moral, physical and social guardians. In Italy, 'being good mothers was equated with being first and foremost good and orderly homemakers . . . There was dual stress on children as objects of systematic education and on women as mothers and housekeepers.'[18] After the Second World War, the focus turned even more on affective relationships, entailing stronger commitment to children and heightened concern over the quality of care. In response to wartime conditions, a 'restorationist' approach aimed at 'reconstruction of the family'. Women expressed concern with 'putting things back to rights'. One wrote to a German magazine,

> My husband came back after nearly five years in a prison camp. For the first three or four weeks we were very happy. But now it's one row after another. The reason: he orders me about and is never satisfied. I've changed so much, he says, I'm not a proper wife any more . . . I've been on my own, and I've had to get by as best I could. Now that he's back he should be giving me some help. But he insists on my looking after the entire household . . . He says he's entitled to a comfortable home. But to my way of thinking he's not 'entitled to' anything. How will we ever get things back to rights again?[19]

Similarly, in Britain, 'The war was over, peace was here but in 1946 the longed-for era of "plenty" had not come. The world of women was at its lowest ebb.' While the government tried to get women into work, Mary Grieve, editor of *Woman*, reflected that with rationing often worse than during the war, the foulest winter on record (1947) and generally inadequate housing, women had little desire to go to work when they had work enough to keep the household going. As the economy improved, some women believed that they had earned a right to stay at home. Winship argues, 'feminism and equality were envisaged as about a complementarity between husband and wife', they had 'the right to be equal to but different from men'. The focus shifted to 'the burning concern and proud burden [of] . . . how best to make marriage, family and home all that had been hoped for during those long years of disruption and deprivation'.[20]

Gradually, however, women without small children entered the workforce, and childrearing increasingly became part rather than the whole of a woman's life. Studies across Europe identified that 'the unspoken social assumptions' of the 1950s reversed in the 1970s. Of 1,000 German working mothers interviewed in 1956–57, only 13 per cent worked because of economic necessity. Half worked to make special purchases or improve their standard of living. By the 1970s, Pross found the woman who was 'only a housewife' had become 'problematic' and 'whenever employed and non-employed women are together, the latter tend to go on the defensive'. Homemaking no longer counted; a social view that judged people by their position in the occupational hierarchy increasingly pressured women into working. While the 'partnership household' exists, the dual burden of housework and paid work continued to dominate the experience of most European women.[21] The history of domestic values has taken many twists and turns since the Second World War, but shifting expectations allowed more choice, coloured by changing attitudes to work itself and the rise of unemployment. With a high number of childless and single parents, often women, a wide range of patterns exists. A fundamental difference between the post-war world and earlier centuries is the level of choice. Certainly, a range of reasons shape choice, and we often feel constrained to a particular option, but in reality a number of routes are now acceptable for women. Previously, the options were far fewer.

LIFE CYCLE: 'BIRDS OF PASSAGE'

Three important life-cycle changes took place in the period 1880 to 1980. First, very young girls were removed from the workplace by legislation, which ensured that they were less likely to work overtly and were most likely to be at school until their teens. Second, the number of single adult women increased in the workforce as middle-class girls and women came to see work as appropriate and joined the fray. Third, there was a greater tendency for married women to stay at work or to return once children had grown. Married women had often continued to work after marriage, but in this period they were increasingly less likely to quit on marriage itself, delaying departure until children came. Importantly, as Glickman shows for Russia, the rise in the married female workforce was greater than simple replacement of children who were prohibited. Thus working was not 'something they do just until they get married'.[22] The proportion of the fifteen to twenty-five age group continued to rise until the 1920s, while there was obvious decline in girls under fifteen in the formal economy. A snapshot of participation is shown in Figure 9.2. Clearly the majority of single women worked, and increasingly middle-class parents accepted daughters going to paid work as the ideology of feminine innocence was eroded. Changing perceptions of the world, the feminist movement and examples of pathbreaking women contributed to lessening restrictions on single middle-class women. However, 'among some upper working-class parents it was regarded as something of a status symbol if their daughters remained within the parental home', but assisting in housework.[23]

Before the First World War, though few working-class wives were in a position to stop work permanently, many clearly saw their main role as housewife. Unmarried working-class women interviewed by Pennington and Westover accepted as common sense that they would marry and leave work. Faced with the drudgery of work and a double burden, family demands were translated into a desire to remain at home as far as possible to concentrate on the contribution that housework made to family welfare. In the Kaiserreich, workers' memories emphasized partnership in the family, and the autonomy of workers' wives in running the household, while in Ireland, 'The increasing movement of women into full-time housework was a sensible strategy for reducing the risk of poverty and for maximizing control over their own lives and the lives of their family.' Roberts's interviews indicate an ambivalence among married women towards waged work. 'Those who worked were proud of their skill,

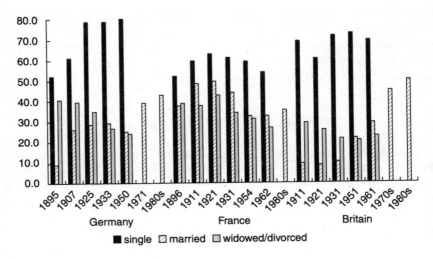

Figure 9.2 Women workers by marital status, 1890s–1980s
Note: The data represent the proportion of the cohort in work, not proportion of the workforce
Source: Bairoch *et al.* (1968)

their efforts, and their contributions to the family budget. But they rarely had any ambition to go on earning wages all their lives, and regarded it as a matter of social progress and status to be able to give up paid work.' As a constant throughout this study, when men's income did not cover household needs, women took paid work whenever they could. In Lille, for example, in 1899, 31 per cent of all women with infants worked in mills, often the only wage earners; in 1931, the same applied. In Armentières, 80 per cent of women continued to work until after the birth of their third child; in many cases a woman stayed until the oldest replaced her, as in Roubaix. British reports and surveys also revealed that husbands' low wages were key reasons for women going out to work. Nevertheless, real wages improved from about 1880 to 1910 in France and England, so that more families could have survived on a single income, and wives of skilled workers especially had a choice. The household also supported a smaller family after the 1880s.[24]

Between the wars, the workforce remained very young and single. Work prior to marriage was a norm, but after marriage depended on family size and economic factors. In Italy, women tended to remain in the formal workforce only when young and childless, though a sizeable minority remained longer. Increasingly, middle-class women turned to paid employment, many for the first time, but participation was less likely for working-class married women. In Artois, marriage usually marked the end of 'officially recognized' work, and in working-class Soleil, 'after marriage, and even more so after the birth of the first child, only a minority of married women worked as *ouvrières*, shopkeepers or *employées*'. In Germany, young mothers with small children were less likely to hold down a job 'in a society which did nothing to help them to do so'. Women assisting husbands tended to remain, but white-collar workers were discouraged from returning following a break, because the longer they worked, the more expensive they became. In Britain, the press was hostile to working women, and more so to married ones. However, the number of married women under twenty-four in paid employment increased by 5 per cent, and Beddoe suggests that high male unemployment in depressed areas may have spurred them into taking available jobs. A feature of the period was an important minority of women who never married, working throughout their lives. Those who did work after marriage usually perceived that they had to. They continued to repeat that the main reason for going out to work was the need for the income: 'I couldn't stop at home really, you had to go to work you know, because I'd a extra mouth to feed, really.'[25]

Married women workers rose to unparalleled levels in the post-war period, and much of the increase in the female workforce was drawn from married women. From the 1960s, the proportion of married women working increased sharply in most countries, and by 1985, over 55 per cent of married women under fifty held jobs in West Germany, Belgium, Britain, France, with a remarkable 87 per cent doing so in Denmark. More than a third of women with a pre-school child held full-time jobs in Denmark, Belgium, France and Italy. The pool of single women had shrunk because of earlier marriage, rising school-leaving ages and more higher education, encouraging employers to target married women and mothers. Married women found allies of a sort when governments tried to 'encourage' them to leave work. Employers argued that it was not in the corporate interest to release them, largely, of course, because women were seen as a cheap and pliable workforce. Austrian businessmen, for example, said that the cost of living would rise because men would have to be hired to replace them, and men were paid twice what women received. Also, surveys from France, Italy and Spain reported that 'working mothers were more level-headed employees than young women'.[26]

At the end of the century, a new pattern emerged comprising working coupled with 'family breaks'. Smaller families meant that childbearing and rearing were finished earlier. In Scotland, the childrearing period dropped by ten years between 1900 and 1980, with a 'bi-modal' or 'M-shaped' profile in women's life cycle. A typical pattern was eight to ten years in work, then a period of unpaid work in the home, rearing children, and then a return to paid work, either part or full time until retirement. In general, Western Europe displayed three patterns. In Germany, France, England and Scotland, many women returned after rearing children, creating a model of career breaks. In Sweden and Finland, married women and mothers tended to remain at work. In Spain, Ireland, Portugal and the Netherlands, women stopped work either on marriage or at the birth of the first child. Thus by 1975, marriage was less an obstacle to working, while childbirth and rearing remained more so. Widespread lack of appropriate childcare facilities contributed to this feature.

The rising divorce rate, which accelerated in the 1960s, pushed more mothers into the labour market, as data from Belgium indicate. In 1961, whereas 20.5 per cent of married women worked, 48.6 per cent of divorced women did, a figure similar to the participation rate of single women, 49.2. Courses for 'women returners' has been a growth area in adult education explicitly targeting women confronted by 'the empty nest syndrome'. Work was one activity that could help fill the void. The character of work and peer-group expectations did, however, influence women's views of work and marriage. Pollert's study showed that young single assembly-line workers intended to work until marriage, though their romantic views were tempered by boredom with the job and ambivalence towards marriage.[27]

The virtual invention of formal part-time work promoted participation by married women. 'During the inter-war years part-time work, in the sense of working for several hours in the day or several days in the week rather than the full working week, was unknown . . . you either worked for the full 48 hours or not at all.' Between 1951 and 1981, the proportion of female part-time jobs in Scotland rose from less than 5 per cent to 41 per cent. As one would expect, the great majority of workers were mothers, clustered in low-paid work. The same trend was experienced across Europe, so that in 1986, 40 to 45 per cent of working women in Scandinavia and the United Kingdom, 25 per cent in Belgium and France, and 30 per cent in Germany were employed part time. Employers used the flexibility of part-time work, the same elasticity as in homework, to reduce labour costs. It could be a boon to women who needed flexibility. The 'down side' was that such work is insecure, is not treated as real by most administrative systems, including pension schemes, and is usually poorly paid. Job-share is one solution because 'real' jobs are shared.[28]

In the post-war period, married women increasingly worked to pay for special goals, house or car purchase or longer holidays. Rising prosperity put expensive consumer durables within the aspirations of the working classes, providing a major incentive for married women to seek income. And in the twentieth century, the mother, not children, went out to work.[29] Financial need did not, of course, disappear as a strong motivation. Women reliant on 'housekeeping' often supplemented household income, because men's work was unreliable and they believed husbands kept too much for themselves. These women's earnings did not go for luxuries, but on basics like food and shelter as women from Preston indicated:

MRS NUTTALL: It went on food for the table.
MRS PRESTON: You got nothing out of it, it all went back on food.[30]

A UK survey in 1984 showed that homes with working married women were 35 per cent better off than homes without, but women spent a greater proportion on necessities than men.[31]

Women were better educated, resulting in proportionally higher earnings.

Kolinsky found a clear generational difference in 'career breaks' in West Germany. Women since the 1960s enjoyed and used educational and vocational opportunities; they were motivated to gain qualifications and use them in the labour market. Incentive to work shaped their lives and they returned as soon as possible; those with higher qualifications were least likely to interrupt work.[32] One feature is women's view of work as a positive factor in their lives. A desire to work for their own satisfaction and 'not to exist exclusively for the family' always existed to some degree, as earlier testimony indicated, but it is a sentiment more readily articulated in the twentieth century. Interwar women said, 'I mean, I don't know as I ever wanted to stop home – but when I could work I did so.' 'Oh it were a hard life, but I think I'd rather – I liked weaving, I used to like weaving.'[33] Dairymaids in Sweden also indicated pride and pleasure in their work: '[Cheesemaking] was a rather tough job. But it was fun. Somehow you were independent . . . And it was enjoyable at the same time . . . [Another said] And it was fun, too, there were only womenfolk, we had no men with us.'[34] Kolinsky's evidence also attests to a sense of satisfaction and self-esteem arising from work. Women since the war frequently said that they worked because they liked companionship and found it more interesting than staying at home. Rowntree and Lavers noted in 1951 that 21 per cent of their sample worked for the 'pleasure of meeting people instead of being cooped up in their homes all day'.[35] Women at 'Churchmans' in 1972 told Pollert, 'Well I've enjoyed every minute. More friends, like. When you're at home like that, you are lonely, 'cos like all your friends are out at work – it's awful lonely like.' Certainly not all felt this way, and disillusionment with mind-numbing tobacco work was evident. Some believed they were 'trapped' and felt they should have left years before, but the work was there, and the 'temporary stay' became permanent. One responded in 'feminist' language:

> You move from one boring, dirty, monotonous job to another boring, dirty, monotonous job. And then to another boring, dirty, monotonous job. And somehow you're supposed to come out of it all feeling 'enriched'. But I never feel 'enriched' – I just feel knackered.[36]

HOUSEWORK

Standards of living and housing improved, while housework became cast in terms of freedom from drudgery as the affective dimension of homemaking came to the fore. Housework in the first half of the twentieth century was often conducted in the context of social and economic disruption, housekeepers facing the effects of war, rationing, depression and poverty, as well as benefiting from rising standards of living. Magazines, doctors, social workers, teachers, health visitors and the media socialized women to adopt the pivotal role in family care, education and economic strategies in a consumer world. Making a good home for children and husbands was defined by a well-kept house. The growth of scientific management directed attention towards home management and childcare, while rationalization emphasized efficiency. In Germany, a penchant for organizational planning caught on in homemaking, while the British debated the 'ideal home'. Unquestioning faith in a domestic vision inhabited by domestic appliances contained a belief in reducing the drudgery of housework, replacing burdens which servants had undertaken, and enabling housewives to enter the creative and pleasurable side of 'homemaking'. Women operated as household managers on a much bigger and more complex scale, as the consumer economy produced a considerable range of goods for an international market, especially factory food and home furnishings. Availability of goods and services raised expectations and further complicated housekeeping. Despite 'convenience' foods, meals consisted of more courses, had more variety, and involved more preparation. 'Homemakers' became more important consumers than ever before and advertisers targeted them, promoting synthetic fabrics, hair and beauty preparations, gas and electrical equipment, prepared food and cleaning preparations. Erna Meyer's *Neuer Haushalt* (1926) had thirty print runs, and 'scores of women's and family journals sang the praises of the modern housewife who wielded a battery of domestic appliances in her practical and luxurious home, where she contentedly and apparently without effort fulfilled her social reproductive duties with dexterity and diligence'.[37] Rising standards of living and real wages meant such purchases became feasible across social classes.

Women controlled domestic finances, if not household accounts. They kept records, dealt with shopkeepers, merchants, insurance men and other administrators of public and private services which proliferated. Usually mothers liaised with teachers and officials, and were instrumental in choosing schools, although fathers often retained formal authority. Their domestic function meant becoming the family's public representative. In interwar Artois, they were the 'lookouts', the ones responsible for watching over the survival and well-being of the family, the nurses, the 'clothers', the 'maintainers'. Some women received 'housekeeping' from their husbands, while others had the whole pay packet and returned an 'allowance' to him. Such money was often the source of strife, as women had to cover household expenses as well as clothes, insurance payments and school expenses. In Welsh mining communities the transaction took place outside the front door 'so that neighbors could guarantee fair play'. Similar tension is described in Armentières or working-class Paris where 'The housewives wait at the windows or stand in the doorways, and sometimes in their impatience one sees them walking towards the factory to meet their husband.' Sometimes husbands helped out with 'gifts' of boots or clothes for children. Members of the household might 'pay' mothers, like factory girls and women clerks living at home in Berlin and Vienna. One mother in London explained that she provided her daughters with 'a half fit-out' so they could go into service at fourteen, and until they were seventeen they gave their wages to her. Women continued to apply numerous strategies to make ends meet. They organized credit and financial help in Armentières. They went without, ensuring that first men and then children were provided for. In Vienna (1896), 'the men ate the meat, not the women'. A woman in York explained: 'If there's anything extra to buy, such as a pair of boots for one of the children, me and the children goes without dinner.' 'Stealing' was another strategy, taking 'extra' money from husbands. Another was pawning, which was well organized in pre-war London. In Armentières, women smuggled. They were creative, 'mending and making-do'. Roberts cites working-class wives in interwar Lancashire who made 'pillow cases and towels out of flour bags, babies' cots out of banana boxes, or [sent] children to pick up coal fallen from carts'. The creativity that post-war shortages brought out of German women is staggering: mending clothes with human hair, washing clothes in potato peelings or ox gall.[38] Reminiscent of Hufton's 'economy of expedients', such strategies confirm how important neighbourhood was to women in meeting commitments to home and family.

Housing changes revised still further the context and definition of housework for women. A variety of schemes by employers in France and Britain towards the end of the nineteenth century provided workers' housing. Although progress was slow, erratic and sometimes dubious, such as high-rise housing in the 1960s, greatest strides were made after the First World War, when attitudes and town planning began to alter housing for the majority of people. There were more rooms to clean, and the ideology that went with new housing and social aspiration meant that expectations similarly increased. In rural Maroeuil, best rooms were created, and many 'housekeeping' activities moved to back kitchens or bakehouses. Many moved to suburbs and new neighbours so that networks had to be rebuilt. Though new estates provided better living conditions, women's isolation was greater. This together with the loss of servants helped foster the more interior-looking domestic unit, which in turn put even more onus on women to make a house a home. 'Women worked at home in housing estates and suburbs; men worked elsewhere.' Nevertheless, the impact of changes in housing, water supply and electricity was uneven. In Britain, working-class areas of London still shared outside taps in 1934, while as late as 1961, 22 per cent of Britain still did not have hot-water taps. Urban slums continued, as in Liège, central London, Glasgow and Roubaix, where housewives had to function under difficult conditions. Mme Santerre, in Roubaix, pointed out that water came from a well fifty metres away, which 'served all the families in our *coron*'.[39]

Pre-war Europe witnessed an increase in consumer durables such as sewing machines, clocks, bicycles, stoves, cooking utensils, followed by electrical appliances like irons, toasters and vacuum cleaners, promoted through expositions in London, Paris and Berlin, stimulating a woman-orientated consumer world. Yet diffusion of household appliances was slower in Europe than in the

United States, and consumers prioritized improving quality of discretionary time rather than using appliances to reduce the burden of housework. Families of the 1960s were more likely to buy a television over more expensive washing machines. Several authors argue that new technology has had virtually no effect on the organization of household labour and on saving women's time. A multinational time budget study by UNESCO in the 1960s concluded, 'There is little sign . . . that the gains from an abundant labour saving technology receive much translation into leisure. Variations in time devoted to household obligations . . . are not spectacularly large.' The reasons were not technological, but social and cultural. Women were identified with housework and rising standards of domestic care. The availability of appliances and better houses encouraged more exacting levels of comfort and hygiene. 'In the age of the washing machine and vacuum cleaner, spotless homes, fresh laundry and immaculate clothing moved into the realm of possibility.' A washing machine might make washing easier, but clothes were washed more often. Yet, the diffusion of appliances which save time ran ahead of income, suggesting that the drudgery of housework pushed forward acquisition of appliances which made it easier, even if there was more of it. In fact, the decline in time spent substantially lags behind the diffusion of appliances across Europe. Investment in household goods substantially increased the amount of work women performed by altering expectations and increasing the time maintaining the new products. For example, floor coverings became more common but so did the belief that dirty carpets spread disease and required regular cleaning.[40]

Laundry offers a typology of women's domestic work. The notion of moral worth tied up with clean, white laundry helps to explain the persistence of women's association with their laundry and the way it acted as a form of display. In Artois, washing and ironing were far more important than cleaning house. By the twentieth century notions of dirt and cleanliness meant that a major wash was on every housewife's agenda, whether she worked or not, ranging from daily with small children to fortnightly. Washing machines were available relatively late, because problems of supplying hot water and motive power were not solved until the 1920s and 1930s. Public wash houses were never very common. They were non-existent in the three villages of Artois studied by Allart; in Britain, they operated only in London, sixteen provincial towns in England and nine in Scotland. Most women washed at home, a survey of 1942 showing that 73 per cent did so, despite the drudgery involved and the availability of commercial services. In Ireland, women's newspaper columns and domestic education courses argued against commercial laundries on the grounds that they tore clothes and spread disease. Some housewives trusted laundry to small family laundries in German cities, but the number of housewives who coped with laundry alone or with a single servant increased. Women continued to do their own laundry as far as possible or with the help of a laundry woman. In Artois it was described as 'the task which takes the most time and is most irksome; . . . a harsh and exhausting task, effectively solitary and without the boisterous entertaining atmosphere of the wash-house'.[41]

In the context of technological innovation, working-class women continued to battle against living conditions with modest resources. They benefited less from domestic appliances and housing improved more slowly. Two images coexisted, both of which are true: new estates in the suburbs, healthy, clean and airy, with appliances and all the 'mod cons'; and substandard housing, women coping with little knowledge, few resources and drudgery. The stigma against laziness or dirt was as degrading to working-class women as to any other, and Leleu reminds us that women of Armentières were very house proud despite conditions. Clean steps, sidewalks, windowsills and hearths marked out women's space. 'The whitened circles, squares, or oblongs outside house doors all over working-class London . . . are poignant attempts by housewives to extend their turf just a bit beyond their own four walls.' The importance of housekeeping in demonstrating woman's worth was pervasive. 'Standards' and 'duty' were embodied in the basic tasks of good cooking, keeping an orderly house and providing husbands with comfortable homes with budgetary efficiency. Also, scientific and 'modern' views began to overcome some traditional attitudes, shifting the purpose of cleaning. For example, in Ireland, sweeping became less ritually linked with visiting fairies and became a movement to combat disease with prizes awarded for cleanliness.[42]

During the Second World War, housewives across Europe were called upon to 'do their duty' and 'make do and mend' became the order of the day. In the face of shortages, rationing and dislocation, they were expected to 'keep the home fires burning'. These phrases capture perceptions of women's role. The post-war world continued to see housework as a problem requiring intervention. In the 1950s magazines and 'experts' extolled housewifery as a worthwhile career for women of all classes with the intention to reduce drudgery and enhance domestic work for women so that they could prioritize the stimulating and rewarding aspects of childcare and beautification. In 1968, Pfeil believed 'The image of the mother as homemaker who devoted her life to her children and her husband continues to be powerful.' Class differentials also began to diminish. In the 1930s the middle-class housewife did approximately half the housework that a working-class housewife did; by 1961 the difference was insignificant. Gradually the economy reasserted itself and by the 1950s, most consumer items were available, although many goods remained out of the reach of many. In Britain between 1955 and 1965, the proportion of families owning televisions, refrigerators, vacuum cleaners and washing machines doubled. In the Federal Republic of Germany after 1952, the massive injection of US capital through the Marshall Plan meant that by 1962, 79 per cent of private German households had radios, 65 per cent had vacuum cleaners, 52 per cent had refrigerators and 34 per cent had washers and televisions. In the 1950s, running water, electricity, washing machines and refrigerators penetrated middle-class homes of central-north Italy, yet exacerbated the inequalities of continued widespread poverty. For example, in 1958, 84 per cent of families remained without a washing machine or refrigerator. Change was under way, however, and by the 1970s, these were almost universal items in the household. The availability of equipment paralleled media messages so that 'women began to hope for the nice house, the washing machine, the floor polisher and the vacuum cleaner they saw on television'. Not all of this was affordable on men's income, so the irony was that 'occupation housewife' led to women going to work to finance household acquisitions and an increase in their physical standard of living.[43]

Importantly, women adopted the ideology of homemaker and expressed pleasure in the role. One who had been a domestic before marriage commented, 'I did all the same sorts of things in a small way . . . and I was very happy doing it, I like a house and I like doing things and having things nice.' Most important for her was that she should keep her husband happy: 'I was always at home when my husband came home for a meal, . . . everything was always ready and I think that's what brought us the happiness.' Others who accepted that they should leave work at marriage were, nevertheless, not so content, often missing the factory and the company of co-workers, and expressing deep-seated frustration and loneliness. However, Tilly and Scott point out that while women were often discontented, they conceded the necessity of housework as men accepted their work, and thus concurred in a family division of labour.[44] In a context where the domestic idiom is sublimated and so overwhelmingly accepted by society, it is difficult to articulate and deal with such feelings.

DOMESTIC SERVICE

The decline in domestic service reflected a major restructuring of women's work. Demand for servants was influenced by middle-class financial difficulties, while the cost of accommodating servants became prohibitive. Reduction in family size reduced need as did the number of women who left paid employment and could undertake their own domestic tasks. However, demand continued at a high level. The 'insatiable demand' resulted in some villages losing virtually all of their young women, such as Welbourne, Norfolk, where only two of fifty-six girls on the 1881 school register remained in the village by the 1890s. A fake advertisement placed in the *Neue Hamburgerische Zeitung* in 1901 by a fictitious servant looking for a place specifically illustrated the strong bargaining position of servants. At least sixty answers were received, each clearly designed to entice a servant. Before 1900 about equal numbers of servants and employers advertised in the *Irish Times*, but after 1901 there were about 1.3 positions for every servant looking, while periodical literature is full of difficulties in finding and keeping them. Bourke, however, suggests that shortages were not universal. Wealthier women found the supply inadequate because of

200

poor communication links and because they would not hire 'rough' rural girls who required too much training. Rural employers, on the other hand, demanded 'superworkers' who would feed pigs, milk cows and take care of children.[45] Indeed, such evidence suggests that there was a mismatch in what servants and employers expected.

The numbers in service peaked in the early years of the new century, then a slow but distinctive decline set in. Clearly fewer girls as well as a smaller proportion of the female workforce turned to domestic service (Figure 9.3). On the eve of the First World War, it remained the largest employer of women across Europe, but after the outbreak of war, many left to take up war work, and contemporary comments indicate that service was increasingly unpopular with young women. Numbers rose slightly as a result of interwar government policy, but there is little doubt that service as it was known in the nineteenth century disappeared rapidly during the twentieth. Several factors account for the decline. Independence came to play an increasing part. Political changes, pressures for female emancipation, working-class movements, and middle- and working-class activism collaborated to change the climate of opinion. There can be little doubt that they contributed to shaping a more independent spirit among servants. One suggestive statistic is the increasing number of German servants who took legal action. In the 1880s, cases involving dissolution of contracts rose to 1,500–2,000 in Hamburg. More significantly, an increasing proportion of servants were prepared to appeal to regular courts, only 10 per cent in 1880, but over a third after 1885.[46]

Rapid expansion of white-collar employment led large numbers of young

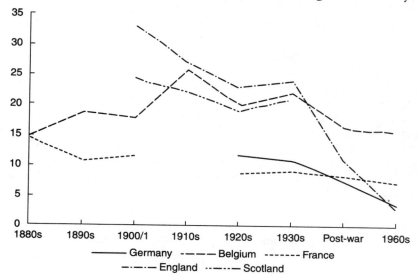

Figure 9.3 Domestic servants as a proportion of the female labour force[47]

women to take up openings in retail, government offices and private businesses, attracting those who might otherwise have gone into service. For most, the increase in personal freedom, daily contact with other young women and greater opportunities to meet men were influential. Increased education kept younger girls out of service, while at the same time it provided them with skills to improve their prospects. These changes in opportunities meant domestic service lost the status which it had maintained during the nineteenth century, a loss of status probably more acutely felt by urban than rural girls. They were more likely to be aware of the range of options and differences in conditions, so that service came to be seen as personally degrading and restrictive by comparison. Lilian Harris and Dr Marion Phillips, of the British Women's Advisory Committee, felt women shrank from conditions of servitude, lack of freedom associated with living in, low wages and long hours. As long as wages stayed significantly above other jobs, the nuisances counted for less, but by the early twentieth century, they were no longer much higher. There is little doubt that when young women had real choices they left service. Indeed, they did not always choose better-paid or higher-status work.[48]

At the same time, the servant population aged, partly as a result of changes in schooling and labour legislation. For example, in England between 1881 and 1901, the number of servants under fifteen fell by 34 per cent, while the number aged twenty-five to forty-four rose by 33 per cent, and those over forty-four increased by 20 per cent. In France, between 1906 and 1936, there was a pronounced increase in the number of servants over thirty, especially those over thirty-nine, and a decrease in younger servants. Fewer and fewer women between twenty and twenty-four entered service in Ireland. Another indicator was a generational shift. For example, mothers of interwar clerical workers were likely to have been domestic servants. This speaks not only about new opportunities for working-class women, but of the loss of servants' status. Roberts's respondents who did become domestics did not enjoy the status their mothers' generation had, were more likely to change jobs than other girls and frequently moved to other jobs altogether.[49] Increasingly, households relied on non-residential servants. They were cheaper and fitted with notions of privacy, but charring also suited women who did not wish to, or could not, live in. Expanded opportunities for 'daily' service meant that more married women entered domestic occupations, or retained them when they married. The shifting balance of live-in service and charwomen, or *femmes de ménage*, is demonstrated from France:

	1906	1936
Live-in domestic servants	688,000	422,000
Femmes de ménage	96,000	153,000[50]

Frequently, women whose household fell on hard times resorted to such work. For example, in Glasgow, it 'is often the only means of support when the husband is ill or out of work, and much gratitude has been expressed by women who have [been] helped over times of severe distress'. In Birmingham charring appealed to older women with large families. In Artois, women filled in throughout the year with occasional laundry work. Regular charwomen who enjoyed a reputation as reliable and trustworthy also gained benefits in kind. Charring carried better status than domestic service during this period, because of its independence and a woman's control over her own home. She was less tied to it, using it for her own ends.[51]

Domestic servants still came mainly from rural settings. As Winifred Foley, a miner's daughter, explained in 1914, it was 'the common lot of every girl in our mining village' since there were no other opportunities. In Armentières before 1920, domestic service paid better than factories or fields, but jobs were frequently temporary, young women preferring to become shop assistants or council workers, or to marry. There is little doubt that urban opportunities continued to draw rural girls, but it is less clear that the 'pull of the towns' was due to service. Since, 'white-collar' work was usually more available to urban girls, many rural girls used service as a stepping stone, 'Once settled in a town ... [they] were more likely to look to factory work or shop work than to what was increasingly considered a low status occupation, fit only for country bumpkins and orphan girls from the Poor Law Institutions.' In France, servants increasingly came from further away and less developed areas, first from Brittany, later from rural Italy, Spain or recently from Portugal. England increasingly drew on Scottish or Irish girls to meet the demand. Ultimately, ethnic-minority women, often former colonial subjects who became the new underclass, took these jobs.[52]

Conditions changed little before the First World War. Servants experienced little personal freedom, long hours and poor living conditions. Amalie Seidl, arrested for industrial action in 1893, reflected, 'I still remember how pleasantly surprised I was when I entered "the cell" . . . I fared a lot better than during the time when I had been a servant girl with a monthly wage of Kr. 6.' German servants in 1919 revealed that over half worked sixteen hours per day. There was, of course, great variation depending on whether they worked alone, and on the status and wealth of the household. Also, there was an increase in locations for work, including hospitals, shops and pubs. For the most part servants remained unprotected. The *Gesindeordnungen* remained in force until 1918. In France, no worker protection related to domestics, such as laws covering accidents at work, rest periods, limitations of hours, rest for pregnant women, or retirement or insurance benefits. Only legislation relating to references (1890) and placements (1904) offered them any assistance. In Britain and Ireland, Old Age Pensions (1908) and National Insurance Acts (1911) applied, but did not alter conditions. The National Insurance Acts were strongly opposed by both employers and servants because of the 3*d* weekly contribution each had to pay. Protective legislation of the 1920s did not restrain domestic servants, clerical or shopworkers from night work. Italian legislative reforms culminating in the 1902 child and female labour law excluded domestic servants who did not work in units covered by the legislation.[53]

The hallmark of the period was struggle between employers and servants, a genteel struggle but nonetheless real. Housewife employers argued vehemently against changes in conditions of service while liberals, socialists and not a few servants pressed for reform. In Weimar Germany, the Domestic Servants Union wanted specified hours of work rather than it filling all available time, while the Housewives Union strongly opposed limiting hours to 13 per day. In 1900, the French feminist congress refused to allow maidservants one day off a week, contending that they would only earn extra income working as prostitutes. They also rejected wage agreements and protective legislation. Socialist and liberal women supported domestic servants, called for rescinding the Servants' Law in Germany and promoted free bargaining.[54] Servants themselves became more confident in the use of their power. The *Woman's Leader* complained in 1920:

> Throughout the country distraught and injured mistresses are giving free expression to their feelings with regard to the servant class that has suddenly dwindled to astonishingly small numbers and has begun to demand unheard of conditions . . . unwilling service, ill performed, higher wages demanded than can be paid, principles of cleanliness and orderliness violated, appearances having to be kept up and rigid rules adhered to for fear 'the girl will give notice.' It is tyranny.[55]

Middle-class housewives bemoaned the servant problem in the 1890s and it remained the great issue in the 1930s. In the face of declining numbers, they wanted to hold on to whatever service they could, instead of striving to make it more attractive and comparable to other women's jobs.

Departure, or even the threat, was an effective and frequently used expression of servant power, since they could expect to get work readily and always obtained conditions at least as good as their previous position. A study in 1894 showed that 54 per cent of servants in Britain had been in post less than two years, while advertisements indicated that they thought two years a very long time to stay in post. Five years later, another study showed that 36 per cent of servants had held the same job for less than one year. Sauget admitted that she liked 'changes and it took very little cause for me to decide to leave an employer'. Domestics in Armentières also frequently changed jobs. In late nineteenth-century Hamburg, the numbers moving were twice as high as the number of servants employed. Those in Dublin and Hamburg between 1880 and 1920 who demanded rises with or without the threat of departure got them. There were risks, however, indicated by the numbers out of work. In Hamburg in 1895, 1,560 servants were registered unemployed. Demarcation was another point of contention where servants' power told. The subcommittee of the Women's Advisory Committee (1918) reported that a servant could not be allowed greater leisure unless 'she is prepared to accept as part of her conditions of service far greater interchange of duties with her fellow [sic] workers than has hitherto been the custom'. Advertisements explicitly spelled out tasks since, 'mistresses found it difficult, either by persuasion or threat, to get servants to undertake tasks which were not seen by the servants as part of their "proper" duties'. Irish servants restricted the range of tasks: some would do no washing, others insisted on working only in small families, others demanded a minimum wage. Indeed, the average wage demanded by servants was 18 per cent higher than offered by employers.[56] Though the relationship of servant and mistress had never been one-way, there was evidence of a shift in the balance of power.

The First World War probably sealed the fate of domestic service. Many servants went to war work where money was good and they enjoyed the camaraderie of other young women. They became accustomed to the money and to deciding how to spend it and their time. One young woman reporting to the [London] City Exchange after two and a half years in munitions said, 'I feel so pleased that the war's over that I'll take any old job that comes along,' but when offered service, she laughed, 'Except that!' The war also exacerbated the problems of employers, who in a period of uncertainty and shortage felt that letting servants go was sensible. German households were encouraged to think twice before laying off servants, and to 'try and ensure that staff are adequately fed'. Nevertheless, many replaced servants with 'dailies'. Several servants in Scotland 'believed that the First World War had struck service a body blow and that the Second World War put an end to it'. Their testimony demonstrates the perception that 'Nobody had maids after the [first] war.'[57] Although an overstatement, it sums up the general impression that service was virtually dead. An informal investigation by *Woman Worker* in February 1919 outside a labour exchange revealed:

> 5% would accept domestic service if wages were £40 p.a. for living in, 2 days off per week, and they could choose their clothes unless purchased by the mistress. Like German servants, they had to buy and greatly resented their uniform.
>
> 30% would accept it if they could live out, have one meal a day provided, finish before 6 p.m. and earn 9*d* per hour, double on Sundays.
>
> 65% would not accept it on any terms[58]

Following both wars, governmental policy was used to put force into middle-class demands for an increase in servant supply. The Weimar Housewives Union promoted a 'year of service' for every girl, and local employment offices tried to channel demobilized women into service. British Employment Exchanges demonstrated that domestic service was seen as appropriate for any woman, and virtually the only suitable placement. In one instance, an official entered a room where forty women were waiting and asked, 'Who's for domestic service?' When none replied, all forty were disqualified from benefit. Women with children and a home were refused when they would not take residential service. In Manchester in one week 1,000 appeals were refused. These strategies supported the numbers of servants until 1931. Weimar created the Freiwilliger Arbeitsdienst (Voluntary Labour Service) in 1931, expanded by the National Socialists. From 1934, all female school-leavers wanting to go to university had to serve six months as an *Arbeitsmaid* (maid of labour), and the compulsory *Pflichtjahr* (Year of Duty) was introduced in 1938 for single women under twenty-five, usually in domestic service or agriculture. It was seen as *hauswirtschaftliche Ertüchtigung* (training through service). According to policy 'what matters in girls' employment today is not the income but the concept of service'. Such policies, together with reductions in insurance contributions by servants and income-tax relief for employers, aimed to increase participation of young women in appropriate employment 'compatible with their nature'. As in Britain, intervention temporarily halted decline and in 1939 there were 250,000 more servants than in 1933. Instead of improving conditions and wages, governmental practice utilized punitive measures to try to force women into service. Ultimately these strategies failed. For economic and ideological reasons, domestic service was seen by the middle class and officialdom as logical work for women. Working women had other ideas. In the aftermath of the Second World War, many interwar themes were reiterated, such as the Labour government attempting to help restore the popularity of domestic service through training schemes, better wages and improved conditions. But numbers continued to fall in Britain from 750,000 in 1951 to only 200,000 in 1961. Despite its promotion as appropriate training for married life, as a 'skilled craft' requiring training, and as specifically women's work, servants shared few of the official views.[59]

10

CONTINUITIES IN COUNTRY
AND TOWN

AGRICULTURE AND RURAL WOMEN

During the twentieth century there was a dramatic decline in the numbers and proportion of women working in agriculture across Europe (see Figure 10.1). Although occasionally the recorded participation level rose, by 1987 only 7.3 per cent of women were employed in agriculture across the European Community. Only Greece (35.4 per cent), Portugal (27.3 per cent), Spain (13.0 per cent) and Italy (10.6 per cent) had over 10 per cent employed. These figures do not account for two features: the invisibility of women's unwaged farm work and the local significance of their agricultural contribution in farming regions. Indications are that throughout the period, female relatives provided an important counter to the numbers of hired women leaving farming. For example, in Germany during the 1930s, agriculture became increasingly dependent on female family labour as male labourers declined by 25 per cent, together with a slight decline in hired female labour. However, an increase of over 10 per cent, 360,000, in the number of female family assistants more than

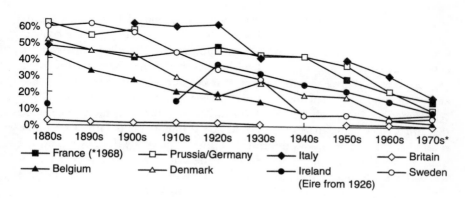

Figure 10.1 Women in agriculture as proportion of female labour force, 1880s–1970s
Source: Bairoch *et al.* (1968)

compensated for this drop.[1] While some increase was due to better counting, nevertheless the gender balance shifted during the decade.

The flight of young women from the countryside was as much a positive decision as a function of economic change, due to lack of real opportunities in esteemed work. In Scotland by the 1890s, and Sweden in the late 1930s, a typical strategy was to leave for cleaner, lighter and more genteel jobs in towns and cities, turning their backs on farming and dairying, while in Denmark lack of opportunity in the centralized dairy industry encouraged young women to leave. Russian women gave lack of technology, including milking machines, poor educational opportunities and poor working conditions, as their main reasons. In Finland, Greece and Germany, daughters had no desire 'to stay and become like their mothers'. Farm work was stigmatized and young women wanted a better deal. Their intention was to have a job 'contrary to the idea of staying at home to look after the family and the cattle, which is perceived as equivalent to having no job at all'. Where primogeniture operated, many young rural women chose to emigrate rather than marry into a farm family.[2]

Community studies make it plain that women did not cease to play a part in farm life. Wives, least likely to be recorded, remained the most likely to be drawn into field and farmyard work. As family farms became more labour intensive, and economic factors made hiring outsiders unprofitable, they assumed an increasing share. Women were usually responsible for three areas of work on a family farm:

1 men's 'traditional' field work, often including ploughing and using machinery;
2 women's 'traditional' farmyard work looking after small animals and gardening;
3 upkeep of the household and childcare.

For example, Segalen cites virtually unchanged farms in France between 1835 and 1945, 'and one can assume that the organisation of labour had hardly changed either'. In Tarn-et-Garonne in 1946, mother and daughter cooked, kept house, fed poultry and milked. In summer they worked with men in fields in afternoons and mornings when they had time. Between the wars, women were so central to farm upkeep that peasant wives in Germany worked an average of 12 per cent more hours a year than their husbands, and 40 per cent more than hired help. In the 1970s in Baden-Württemberg, men believed that unless they could marry they would find it impossible to farm. One told a researcher, 'If I want to go on farming, I have to have a wife. On my own, I can't do it. The work in the fields and in the stable, and on top of it housework—that's too much.' In Norway, women's burdens increased, with demand for higher standards of cleanliness, hygiene and quality of dairy products despite a lack of running water in cowsheds. Cows were milked more frequently and the average farm did not have milking machines until the 1960s.

On Scottish Border farms, women's contribution remained important until at least the end of the Second World War, which was a watershed 'between what could be termed a traditional way of life on Border farms and the emergence of a new industrialised one'.[3]

The strong association of men with the land, fields, commerce and enterprise of the farm dictated that even within a shifting rural economy, women remained associated with the farmyard and men with the farm. Notions of women's place drew heavily on perceptions of natural endowments, the gendered abilities and skills of men and women. Thus the view persisted that women did jobs requiring dexterity better than men, such as pea-picking and flower-cutting, but were less able to match male outputs in jobs demanding strength and stamina. That this translated into women being seen as unable to drive tractors confirms the underlying gendered associations of men with machinery. Where women took part in tasks outside of 'female' jobs, they were constrained to a narrow range, usually the most tedious and repetitive, and barred from specialized 'skilled' tasks where men retained a monopoly. Women were less often *hired* for field work, which was male and full time, and usually only assisted or substituted. The boundaries of divisions of labour varied between communities, based on cultural difference and perceptions of gender. In Portugal, men were responsible for things growing above the ground (*produtos do ar*) and women for things growing in or near the earth (*produtos da terra*). Women were 'rooted to the ground; they were also considered to be less mobile, for they are attached to a particular stretch of land, their *terra*'. So, as elsewhere, men had primary responsibility for cattle, fruit trees, woods, vines (on trellises), women for pigs, poultry, beans, potatoes, pumpkins and kitchen gardens. Indeed, cultural prohibitions meant men were proscribed from women's terrain, and she did not climb trees or prune vines, only assisting him. Much farm work was complementary and separation of tasks more apparent than real, although each gender carried authority in their own special area. In Finland, a traditional gender split between male responsibility for field and forestry and female responsibility for the dairy was still broadly respected. As herd size increased and contributed more to household income, divisions became less rigid, and men worked alongside women. However, the herd remained women's responsibility. In Minot, 'No one made fun of a woman who went to work in the fields with her husband and then went ploughing and the rest of it. Oh no, on the contrary this was thought to be perfectly natural. "She's his wife after all, and there is no reason why she shouldn't do it." A woman must do everything.' On German family farms in the 1980s, labour-intensive commercial activities, like milking, tended to be shared.[4]

During the two wars, the decline in the number of women in agriculture was temporarily reversed, in an exaggerated case of 'male absence'. Shortage of male labour and government policies encouraged women into fields to keep up food production. They were involved across the skill spectrum, ploughing, using tractors, working with horses, and in timber trades, areas usually coded as masculine, and making the lie of women's lack of skills. In the Second World War, women coped with highly mechanized agriculture, operating cultivators, threshing machines, and mechanized spraying. In the Soviet countryside, for example, peasant women led labour brigades and chaired collectives, and the proportion of female collective farmers soared to a record high of 76 per cent. Women's reluctance to work in German munitions meant that farm women found their heavy workload became even greater as men were drawn away for war and industry. Until prisoners of war and conscript labour were sent to the countryside, there was no assistance. In the Vaucluse, one young woman ran her parents' farm single-handedly, ploughing, harvesting and looking after horses, goats and sheep.[5] Across Britain, rural women were joined by members of the Women's Land Army.

At the end of each war, official and private rhetoric quickly reverted to the myth of gendered skills, with a decline in hired women on the land. Soviet women lost most managerial posts, since military officers were encouraged to chair collective committees. Increasingly, administrators and equipment operators were male, while field hands and livestock tenders were female. Agriculture employed 34 per cent of women in West Germany in 1950, by 1985 it employed only 7 per cent. For Scots women, the Second World War promoted two key changes. First, the process of mechanization accelerated rapidly, transforming horse to tractor power, so that 'by the early 1950s the traditional Border farm scene of men with horses (and with attendant women workers) was giving way to a lonelier picture of one-man with machine'. Second, the introduction of Land Army 'girls' bringing with them new ideas, broke down rural isolation. As in other parts of Europe, the movement of people, and new ideas and ways of doing things changed the rural scene.[6]

In many countries after 1945, rapid industrialization, or re-industrialization, placed heavy demands on male labour, drawing men away from farming. In Romania, for example, rapid collectivization relied on a large increase of women between 1949 and 1962, a phenomenon which meant by 1978 that women overtook men as the bulk of the labour force. Also in many countries, like Norway, which was 'a land of many small farms and few large ones', small family farms were increasingly unable to support a family, leading to 'part-time' farms, as family members moved away to work. These farms became effectively full-time work for women. As Besteman points out, the concept of part-time farms obscures the important role of the woman, by describing them in terms of male commitment. The label 'housewife-farmer' similarly implied these women were housewives first and farmers second. Despite an increase in farm size, family farming still predominated in agricultural production, and women became the primary farmers. Farm work was not significantly reduced, although mechanization may have helped. Mechanized farming tended to require fewer supplementary workers, and viticulture was less intensive if wine was made in co-operatives. Data from Russia suggest that technological progress provided more opportunities for men than women, men shifting into work with combines and tractors while the proportion of women working with cattle increased. At the same time, women made little progress into better-paid jobs associated with operating machinery. Women in two German communities were equivocal about whether machinery made farm work easier. They thought that hours had not increased though fewer hands shared work, and that tractors caused physical problems. Some believed they made work easier, especially lightening the heaviest work, such as loading manure. Older women said machines destroyed old work rhythms and created tensions.[7]

Poultry and dairying, with strong symbolic links with females, were fundamentally influenced by machinery, though women retained their position longest. Portuguese wives of peasant-workers for the first time participated in the market economy through dairying. Nevertheless, as dairying and poultry became big business subsidized by states, they became male dominated. Male possession of technical knowledge and perceptions of managers as male moved them into key positions in the Danish co-operative dairy industry. In Hartland (Cornwall), villagers regarded bulk milk production as men's work, a perception increased by state intervention, mechanization and centralization. Sommestad drew out a similar trend in Sweden, but one which 'must be analysed not only as a mere substitution of men for women in the dairy work force, but also as a reinterpretation of the gendered meaning of dairy work'. Between 1890 and 1950, men began competing with women as practising dairymen, leading to the almost complete disappearance of dairymaids in Sweden. Sommestad argues that 'People who basically perceived dairying as feminine, drawing on the female dairy tradition rooted in agriculture, nevertheless seemed to make sense of the appearance of dairymen, understanding their arrival in relation to the expanding urban–industrial culture.' Her analysis points to the importance of understanding masculinization and marginalization of females in dairying as not simply a process of substitution. Shifts were also about the meanings associated with masculinity and femininity in relation to work and place. In some respects, it was tied less to mechanization and more to longstanding beliefs about males 'in charge' and female assistants.[8]

Women continued as net-makers, fishsellers and processors in fishing communities of Northern Europe, across Scandinavia and Britain in particular, as fishing, like farming, became more centralized and commercialized. Commercialization was not new, but there were fewer independent fishers, and thus less work in a family venture. Processing became 'factory' production and women became more concentrated in processing, retained their role as gutters and packers, and worked in larger units:

> despite the shift from family living-room or open yard to factory production, and from door-to-door hawking to self-service from the supermarket freezer, it is still women who provide most of the workforce in contemporary fish processing and distribution.[9]

211

The assumption that women's work was land-based and men's was on boats witnessed a new twist when traditionally women's jobs, such as processing, moved on to boats, so that female gutters and filleters appeared on Russian factory ships. Women wage-earners played an important role in Icelandic and British disputes during the early years of the century. Indeed, Aberdeen female fishworkers struck for increased wages in 1913, setting off a wave of strikes across the industry.[10]

In twentieth-century Europe peasant–worker strategies became permanent ways of operating small farms and providing the supplementary income to make it feasible. For example in 1980, two-thirds of French farm households benefited from a second income, one-third from industrial sources. In practice, most migration was male in long-term, seasonal or daily 'commuter' patterns. In two Portuguese communities in 1979, the proportion of female farmers was suggestive of the level of migration. In Couto, 74.2 per cent of self-employed farmers were female, and in Paço, 68.6 per cent were. In Romania, Cernea estimated that 60 to 70 per cent of rural households had at least one absentee, while in a Basque community a third worked off-farm: half of the men but virtually no women. Italian men from Grassano left for decades, while in Friuli from 1911 to 1961, between 8.9 and 15.2 per cent of the population were absentees. Thus a major post-war trend was the extent to which agricultural production was feminized, a trend most pronounced on 'part-time' farms as a result of women taking over work previously performed primarily or exclusively by men. As First-Dilic shows, male exodus only minimally disturbed working patterns on farms because of the 'existential imperative' which makes women make up for labour shortage. Women could be expected to carry out every activity, sometimes with hired male assistance, but often without. In Norway, investigations in 1939 and 1949 revealed that women did more farm work than men, while men often had other income, sometimes from fishing or factory work. On Scottish crofts where men worked away, women were responsible for cultivation, although men did the digging before they left and returned in time to cut the peats. In German and Basque communities, men worked in early morning and late evenings on the farm, going to outside jobs during the day.[11]

In some communities, however, women increasingly took off-farm or non-farm work. Thus Mørkeberg noted an increase from 6 per cent of Danish wives working off-farm in 1960, to 26 per cent by 1975, 12 per cent of the latter not assisting on the farm at all. Hours worked off-farm by women between 1979 and 1989 in Norway rose by a third, and in Holland they increasingly worked outside the home: 6 per cent in 1982 and 18 per cent in 1989. Women valued off-farm work for a variety of reasons. While economic need certainly counted, social contact and positive feedback were significant factors. As Gasson argues, working on a family farm was 'unlikely to meet the woman's needs for income, financial independence and security, social contact and recognition'. Irish women said, 'it is a great feeling knowing you are doing something useful and getting paid for it', 'you are more your own person'. For some, farm wife trans-mogrified into 'countrywoman'. Women in southern England tended to hold clearly gendered views of division of labour and role specialization; they iden-tified with a myth of rurality and defended their rural heritage. Such rural women were more likely to be less involved in direct farm production and more active in tasks like bookkeeping. Increasingly, they lived in a village rather than on a farm, controlling and managing household consumption. Shopping, freezing and storing became paramount. Some moved into tourism, running *pensions* or 'bed and breakfast'. In Hartland, medium-sized and all local 'big' farmers' wives took in visitors. Similarly, country shops, tea shops and small cafés were increasingly taken up by women, as were 'rural crafts'. In Artois, women ran the post office, inn and grocery, all central to community life. Women gained visitors' appreciation of their work, giving value to what they did. They also attained positions as mediators between the community and visitors; they referred them to shops, events, beaches. It was important for women and an important link to their community.[12]

In communities where widespread and regular separation took place, gen-dered notions of place and role were undercut. Though women remained at home, they could enhance their control over the household and power within the family. Conventional ideals were undermined by their increased responsi-bility for finances and home, while men acquired self-sufficiency and inde-pendence from familial values. Such emotional alienation emerges from communities like Aberdeen in Scotland, in Brittany, Normandy, and coastal regions of Scandinavia, Iceland and Galicia. Also, overlapping roles devel-oped, so that men helped with domestic chores while at home. Sometimes, while men owned the boat, or a share, women owned the land. These charac-teristics taken together gave women the 'possibility of achieving, within the fishing family, a degree of power and independence which is unusual'. Similar tendencies were evident in areas of northern Sweden where men were away for logging, and in central France, such as Creuse or Limousin where men took seasonal jobs away from the farm. Cernea makes a similar case for Romania, where women's threefold role and the fact that they undertook traditionally men's tasks during their absence enhanced their decision-making authority. In Poland, '[Her] prestige is positively correlated with the farmers undertak-ing work outside agriculture.'[13] However, Pina-Cabral suggests an important counter-shift which off-farm work introduced into power relations. As the economic importance of émigré work increased and the peasantry became more wage dependent, men's economic position and personal authority were enhanced. Women's significance rested on the crucial role of agriculture, and as this diminished, so did her authority. Even in agriculture, men usually managed the main commercial activities. Shortall noted how rural structures created a less powerful position for women. Key was the invisibility of their work, particularly the contribution of the farmhouse in farm business; the domi-nant view was that she was dependent on the farm, making no reciprocal return. Thus Irish women commonly referred callers to their husbands, saying, 'he would know best'. So thoroughly had they internalized their sense of low esteem that they widely condemned the one visible female-farmer in the community.[14]

Women played an important part maintaining rural cohesion through their caring and networking. Often activities were mutual aid, but they also had an 'overseeing' role, believing they had a 'duty' to know even what they did not see and hear themselves. They exchanged information at public places, shops, on visits and at church, which travelled through feminine networks to other neighbourhoods and villages. Stebbing found that English women placed emphasis on consensus, seeing differences as divisive. In Iberian rural ideology, kinship, neighbourhood and village are female concerns, and in many rural communities, women faced social pressures rising from the expectation that they should use their caring skills for community benefit. With a relative lack of social services, including a deficiency of transport, and childcare, care falls on women. In Fróneyri, women's mutual support systems constituted stepping in during crises, like when a housewife was sick, lending items for a party, or picking things up at the shop. The most formal networking was childcare, with women working alternate shifts in the fish factory and taking each other's children. The level of networking and its impact depend on the character of the community and women's link to it. In Stebbing's and Bouquet's studies, there is an implication that 'incomers' are less well networked and may in fact perceive it as negative and 'nosy'.[15]

HOMEWORK AND SWEATED TRADES

Homeworking and sweated workshops at the turn of the century were little changed so that in many respects these jobs sat at the 'turning point between a domestic economy and industrial activity'. It expanded around the turn of the century with increased demand for popularly priced clothing, toys and luxury goods previously only available to the leisured classes, accompanied by a reduction in prices and sophisticated division of labour in the workshops. Department stores that created 'dream worlds' for mass consumption, and a burgeoning white-collar labour force together with skilled and semi-skilled workers' families created a vast, new internal market for such goods. Flower-making in Paris, French and German garment-making and rural outwork in Ulster grew between about 1881 and 1910. The range and quality of products were vast. A list from Glasgow indicates the variety: dressmakers, shirtmakers, seamers, tailors, milliners, umbrella-, parasol- and stick-makers, staymakers, paper-, box- and bag-makers. In London, women homeworkers predominated in clothing trades, as quill and feather dressers, as jam-, preserve- and sweet-makers, chocolate- and cocoa-makers, and tobacco workers in addition to making up a large proportion of the upholsterers. The luxury trades, particularly those of Paris, formed one end of the range, while others, such as making cigarette tubes or cigar tips, marked the sweated end.[16]

At the same time, one of the most important female occupations, garment-making, began to decline, so that by 1910 the trend was apparent across Europe. For example:

Table 10.1 Decline in garment-making as a proportion of the female workforce[17]

Country	Dates	Percentage change
Germany	1895–1907	11.2 to 8.8
Britain	1891–1911	16.9 to 15.2
Belgium	1890–1910	15.8 to 15.2
France	1896–1921	14.9 to 10.5

By 1915, Belfast Health Reports reported 'outwork in the city has been reduced as employers prefer it to be done on their premises because of punctuality, combined with sending it to the country districts where it can be embroidered at a cheaper rate'. In Norway, the number of married women employed as seamstresses was in decline by 1900, while Boxer places the crisis from German competition in Parisian flower-making at the same time, and in Glasgow, homeworkers in garment trades declined by a quarter between 1901 and 1911. In Moscow province by 1911, demand for domestic handwork had diminished dramatically, 'as the machine continues to bear down relentlessly on home industry'.[18] The First World War added new work, such as army clothing and kitbags for British soldiers, but government rates were lower than commercial rates had been, while subcontracting and economic dislocations exacerbated problems for homeworkers. In contrast, the German army introduced a minimum wage for the first time for commissioned clothing outwork. Indeed, good pay in war industries lured women away from homework, so that the war exacerbated decline. Yet women continued as homeworkers throughout Europe, even if in diminished numbers. During the interwar period, a combination of homeworkers' invisibility, a reluctance to declare all income, and the equivocal position of dependent women clearly led to under-recording. Reynolds suggests that there were as many as a million French outworkers in 1936, though only a quarter were returned by the census. They were common in rural Artois, sewing for local residents, or occasionally, for retailers. Although in 1921, lacemaking and embroidery employed numerous women, dressmaking and linen work fell radically due to the end of certain types of production and the effects of mechanization. In Germany, outwork also survived into the interwar years, although the proportion of recorded women workers declined from 8.8 per cent in 1907 to 6.8 per cent in 1933. British dressmaking and millinery declined due to shifting fashion and economic hardship, so that the per centage of women in apparel and footwear dropped from 15.2 per cent in 1911 to 8.6 in 1931. Decline also affected provincial areas, Barrow dropping from 14 per cent of the female workforce as dressmakers, tailoresses and milliners in 1891 to only 4 per cent in 1931, with a similar drop in Lancaster.[19]

Even after the Second World War, homework did not disappear, though it became even less visible with public disinterest. The bulk of homeworkers still worked in machining and finishing clothing and related areas such as hats, belts, ties and buttonholing. A study in North London in 1972 identified a range of outwork including packing crackers, stuffing toys, pasting jewellery, knitting, crocheting, making hooks and eyes, carding buttons and thread, wiring batteries and making or mending netting. New homework evolved in electrical component assembly, inspecting and packing goods and clerical tasks, including copy typing, stuffing or addressing envelopes. Technology created employment using electronic office equipment and 'teleworking'. Country differences existed in the prevailing types of homework. For example, in Italy, most remained manufacturing, such as knitting, shoemaking and assembling automobile transmissions. In Scandinavia and England, word processing or database work became prominent. A black economy made these workers even less visible, since many were paid 'off the books'.[20]

Many homeworkers were married or at least women with dependants. A survey in Paris in 1907 showed that 50 per cent of needleworkers were married, 37 per cent widowed and 16 per cent single, 12 per cent of the last with children. Flower-makers were similar: 52 per cent married, 22 per cent widowed or divorced and 21 per cent single. In Glasgow, the 1911 census reported 34.9 per cent of married women workers as homeworkers, while two earlier surveys demonstrated high proportions of married or widowed women: 8 per cent married but 84.3 per cent widowed in 1900; and in 1907, 45.4 per cent married and 26.7 per cent widowed. In Birmingham, 46 per cent were widows or deserted wives. Such a high proportion of married and widowed women underlines their need for income and the probability that they had dependants. Women might continue to take homework when a subsistence crisis lifted, but at that point they were more likely to make deliberate choices about what they were prepared to do. They could move in and out of the system, or they could be virtually permanent 'full-time' workers. Whether women undertook homework was highly dependent on the level and reliability of a husband's income; this could also determine what sort of homework they did. In Glasgow, when men were laid off, became ill, or worked irregularly, wives turned to homework. Homeworkers also clustered in areas of Glasgow where 'male' trades of heavy engineering, dock work and shipbuilding concentrated and where local work for women was limited. French government investigations into homework in 1905 and 1911 revealed that married women's earnings provided up to 50 per cent of total family income.[21] Nevertheless, from a Glasgow firm came the disparaging remark,

> the outside workers who do our shirts are generally the wives of artisan and other workmen, who have nothing to do at home in the

absences of their husbands, and is so much money earned when other-wise they would have gone idle.[22]

The Scottish Council of Women's Trades, however, pointed out that numbers working for 'pin money' were 'so small as to be absolutely negligible'. Lower-middle-class women formed a significant part of this workforce, but are difficult to distinguish since their class meant that they were not identified as workers, either in common perception or records. Many such women took up homework precisely because it was more acceptable and discreet. A minor official's income differed little from a working-class man's, but he spent more on public consumption. Thus wives did not work for euphemistic 'pin money' but to maintain a lifestyle linked to social position. Often they too were widows.[23]

At the end of the twentieth century, the main reason for working at home remains unchanged: women work because they need the money and they adopt homework because of their perception of their needs. These include a wish or need to be at home, a lack of skill or confidence to do other work, and a belief that they retain some control in doing so. In interviews after the Second World War, women seldom figured how much they earned an hour and were simply grateful for work. Many worked in fields in which they were trained, often with factory experience, and were more likely to see themselves as 'self-employed'. On one level, freelance work is homework, but suggests a greater degree of choice as well as a different labour pricing structure which allows compensation for overheads. These workers were more likely than traditional homeworkers to receive holiday and sick pay. Another key change is the number of ethnic minority women who rely on homework. Reflecting the legacy of a post-colonial world, large numbers seeking work frequently remain at home to avoid issues of cultural and language difference, as a result of discriminatory practices, or the sheer poverty and need that many women in these communities find they are facing. Ethnic-minority women are also found in greatest numbers in urban areas where this work remains a major option.[24]

Not all homework or home workshops deserve the opprobrium which sweated labour attracts. Small artisanal and artistic production with its fine line between employer and worker, such as the luxury trades of Paris, lasted well into the twentieth century. For example, though flower-makers did not control conditions and administration like men did, they clearly exercised more control over their work than many women, retaining the role of 'mistresses of production'. Some flower-makers worked directly for manufacturers, others for *entrepreneuses* with a few apprentices and employees in the high season. Importantly, this group of workers, even when they were 'small hands', felt they had a *métier*, demonstrating that work at home 'in an industry requiring taste, talent, and time for careful work might enhance a woman's self-image, while filling her pocketbook'. Artificial flower-makers, the 'aristocrats of female labour', were highly trained in a three-year apprenticeship and

217

developed quality skills. The profession required sophisticated artistic talent, considerable training, and long experience.[25]

Increasingly, craft and quality work was lost, as was its status. For example, apprenticed workers comprised only 1 per cent of Parisian flower-makers by 1900. Milhaud's survey in 1912 found that a very good living could be made, but many were at risk. Thirty-two per cent of workers and 8 per cent of *entrepreneuses* depended on public aid, due to seasonality.[26] The survey reflected the disparity across homework, and Oliunina commented on the difference in status of work in Moscow:

> Those who are employed in workshops in the downtown area dress comparatively neatly and have fashionable dresses, hats and overcoats. The women in subcontracting workshops almost always look untidy. They wear kerchiefs. Many women, especially the older ones, have faded, dirty and torn dresses.[27]

The Viennese *Enquête* of 1896 also revealed such divergence. A skilled seamstress sewed men's shirts for a *Zwischenmeisterin* (literally 'between mistress' or middlewoman) with two other women. The workroom was pleasant, she had her own apartment, made her own clothes and only did overtime when she felt like it. She ate out, attended the theatre and went on excursions. In contrast, a semi-skilled woman sewed ties in the residence of a *Zwischenmeisterin*, but work was seasonal so in summer she earned only 2fl. a week, though with overtime she could earn up to 8fl. a week in winter. She liked to go to the Volkstheatre, but could not do so often because her family, with whom she lived, was in debt. She had to buy all her clothes 'on tick', paying high interest rates.[28]

Fashion and seasonality meant frantic toil at the height of the season, often followed by unemployment. Top dressmakers in Paris could count on between 260 and 300 days work a year, while second hands were lucky to have between 200 and 260. In off seasons, only the most persistent and regular workers found work. Most flower-makers had unemployment between March and September, and umbrella coverers expected to be out of work for four to six months each year. Dressmakers worked long overtime hours, *veillées*, before a Grand Prix, funeral or ball.[29] In Moscow, the month before Christmas or Easter was the push.

> I have seen women workers come into the refectory and fall on the benches in utter exhaustion, unable to even eat. They only wanted to lie there for a quarter or half an hour in order to rest their tired limbs and ease their headaches. By the time they are thirty, most of these women have been sapped of their strength through such long hours of labor and have lost the capacity for sustained work.[30]

Fluctuations in work had the same effect on wages so that women had to take work to compensate for fallow periods. Changes in fashion caused the decline in many trades during the interwar period, such as corset-making and artificial flowers, and the *lingère* fell out of favour because it became too expensive and unfashionable to have linen embroidered. There was also a fall in demand for work by women. Fewer young women went into homework, because of options in offices and shops. More male employment provided regular rather than casual work, with a slight improvement in wages, diminishing the need for the 'extra' earnings of a wife.[31]

The relationship between factory and homework was complex. For example, in the 1880s, women in Moscow province made cigarette tubes (*gil'zy*) and fitted mouthpieces which were returned to factories for filling. By 1904, tubes were made by machine, and rural women fixed mouthpieces. In fact, tubes could have been made by machine all along, but it was cheaper to put them out as homework. Similarly, the numbers cleaning fruit and vegetables, sorting peas and peeling shallots increased as food processing expanded, peaking at the turn of the century. But in the next decade, sorting beans, cocoa, coffee and peas was mechanized. Homework was commonly a buffer between factories and seasonal fluctuations, since at peak periods factory workers could be sent home with work to finish. Sewing machines made it possible for employers to tap the labour of those who would not or could not work in factories. Some saw the sewing machine as benefiting women, representing the break-up of the factory system and allowing them to stay at home to work. Others saw it increasing productivity, and, though reducing piece rates, increasing homeworkers' income. Perrot described how sewing machines, which seemed to promise reconciliation of housework and industrial work, became themselves 'the "instrument of [women's] servitude," establishing "the factory at home"', creating the typical homeworker as one who 'lived continually under the fear that if they did not complete enough work, they would not earn enough to ensure their family's survival'.[32]

Homework increasingly represented a 'fractured' manufacturing process whereby only part of production was carried out at home, because manufacturers were interested in the quickest turnover of goods to increase profits. An apprentice tailoress interviewed by Roberts emphasized that piece work exacerbated the pressure. Beier argues that the pace did not result from keeping up with the sewing machine but from breaking down the production process, which meant that the skill content deteriorated, while the worker lost control of the process. Most did not own materials on which they worked, and they increasingly became dependent on 'outwork' from manufacturing houses. The effect of piece work and subcontracting was that women who needed money competed with each other for as much work as they could do, and sometimes more, to retain the preference of a subcontractor. 'You do as much as you can; there's no minimum, but if you aren't quick enough you might lose your job. They return badly sewn stuff.'[33] It also exacerbated the boring, repetitious character of the work and simultaneously raised the level of alienation, as Baader indicates:

> I then bought myself my own machine [after leaving the factory] and
> worked at home. Thus I got to know well enough the lot of the home-
> worker. A session lasted from 6 a.m. to 12 a.m., with one hour pause
> for lunch. I got up at 4 a.m., tidied the flat and prepared the food. I
> had a small clock in front of me while working, and so it passed that
> one dozen collars took no longer than another, and nothing gave me
> greater pleasure than when I could spare a few minutes . . . Sometimes
> I had had more than enough of it: year after year at the sewing
> machine, always just collars and cuffs in front of me, one dozen after
> another. Life had no value, I was just a work machine and had no
> future prospects. I saw and heard nothing of what is beautiful in the
> world: I was simply shut off from that.[34]

Though mechanization might increase opportunities for women through more
division of labour, it also meant less casual work was available. Yet as the
persistence of homework suggests, it retained its economic vitality despite
mechanization.[35]

The rationale for employers was availability of a cheap labour force which
could be maintained for no cost, and which could be called upon when
required for as little or as much as required. It was flexible and self-exploitative,
especially at the lower reaches of skill and the most impoverished. What
Boxer says of flower-makers held for most outwork trades: 'The presence of a
large, partially skilled labor force ready to work in season and fall back on
other employment . . . family resources, or welfare payments out-of-season,
enabled manufacturers to follow trends in fashion and fluctuations in demand
at minimal cost.' Glasgow employers were explicit: 'the employer's responsibility lies in his frequently doling out work as people dole out indiscriminate
charity, and in his desire to have a reserve of labour, which costs nothing for
the upkeep, and which he can count on for a few hours, or days, or weeks as
it suits his convenience'. French opinion agreed that it was a deliberate policy not to pay a living wage. Treated as a marginal economic activity, they
forced wage rates down, and homeworkers became even more attractive to
employers. The policy drew on homeworkers, part-timers, temporary workers,
a secondary workforce characterized by low pay, lack of unionization and few
employment rights. Employers found the system avoided legal restrictions
and saved on overheads. The British Select Committee on Homework stated
in 1908: 'The imposition by law of conditions and obligations upon owners
and occupiers of factories and workshops tends to encourage employers to
resort to Home Work.'[36] Very little changed, as a letter to *Woman* in 1979
indicates:

> Since the asbestos scare a couple of years ago, stores personnel . . . are
> not obliged to handle anything made of asbestos. So all asbestos parts
> are collected by an outside contractor and returned individually

bagged. Who does the bagging? You've guessed it – homeworkers.
It's a very simple job, the children could help.[37]

The workforce was characterized by the sex of the worker, that is, female. The employer was relieved of basic overheads, rates, rent, heating, lighting and only paid for productive time.

During peak years, homeworkers came to the forefront of concern about women's working conditions, replacing miners and mill girls in the public conscience. Obviously, some argued that it was the most appropriate work for women, especially married women; however, the rise of concerted opinion against conditions very gradually led to restrictions on hours. As Boxer says, 'The plight of suffering seamstresses appealed to the sentiments of all classes', and 'domestic industry was officially "discovered"'. A typical sentiment came from Belgium: 'The idyll of the labouring household is no longer anything other than a sad irony; it is disenchanted work, a life which unfolds in a milieu without sun and without rest, in the centre of leprous *impasses*.' This description harks back to a mythic rural idyll of the domestic system. They also focused on isolated women, when many homeworkers were married. The debate was not clear cut, of course, since philanthropists and priests in France, defending the family, continued to support homework, while welfare workers concerned for women unable to work outside the home condemned it. But the strongest defence of the system often came from women workers themselves: 'they feared the loss of their independence and, most of all, their income'. Protective legislation generally excluded homework until the second decade of the twentieth century. Regulation of hours in Parisian homework only came in 1910, followed by supporting legislation in the following year, when German controls of *Hausarbeit* were also introduced. The Weimar Republic instituted the eight-hour day, incorporated homeworkers into mandatory social insurance provisions and officially established collective bargaining. However, they voted against a minimum wage for homeworkers, and it only became fully regulated in 1934 when the National Socialists made the system of standard wages a matter of state administration. Many sweated trades declined or disappeared during the first quarter-century in Britain, and the Trade Boards, initially established in 1909, probably played a part. They not only covered homework and set minimum rates of pay for trades under their jurisdiction, but included women members.[38] When the value of homeworkers was diminished by regulation, other factors such as control of the workforce and centralization could become more important.

One frequently cited reason for women working at home is the perception that homework gives them control over their work and time. Flower-makers, whose skill set them apart, preferred home industry because they believed 'it allowed them to control the rhythm of their work and their lives, and it enhanced their status within the family'. Roberts and Chinn argue that wage earning in the home was better than outside work 'because it meant less disruption to home routines' and conformed 'more to the ideal of the woman's place being in the home' and 'perhaps most important not to be at the beck-and-call of an employer'. Pennington and Westover call this the 'myth of freedom of time'. On one level, it is not necessarily a myth. For more skilled trades, luxury trades, and some newer homework, bordering on freelance, it holds a truth. It depends on what extent women were prepared to contribute to their own exploitation. However, for most, homeworking did not create a familial idyll. Plenty of evidence indicates that the burdens of women's labour at home severely impinged on quality of family- and childcare. For example, McMillan argues that it was nonsense to say that homework preserved the family when a 'little girl of ten [is] kept from going to school and made to do the housework and look after the smaller children, while the mother sews at her machine'.[39] Allen and Wolkowitz identify the employer and not the employee as the one who exercises control through a range of mechanisms, some of which are comparatively indirect. The work task itself, located in a system of division of labour, leaves the homeworker discretion over only most trivial aspects. Those who retain some of their craft, such as knitters, comment that when they do not have the satisfaction of completing the job by sewing the garments, 'they miss it'. The employer controlled output in a way that allowed very little flexibility, by determining how much was given to the worker, and by piece rates, which as Braverman says, made the worker 'a willing accomplice to his or her exploitation'.[40] Where the employer owned the machine, he operated another level of control. He similarly monitored quality through piece work, since inadequate work was not paid for. Women had to balance their perceptions of benefits of the work, and its location, against restrictions it placed on them. For many women it was not a matter of choice. For others, however, there was a degree of choice, where financial need was not so great, where they worked at home for other reasons and where their skill or trade allowed them room for manoeuvre within the system.

MANUFACTURING AND 'NEW INDUSTRIES'

The period since 1890 reveals a major shift in the industries in which women worked while the character of the workplace altered with the introduction of new methods of rationalized production. The number of women in manufacturing rose mainly as a function of population growth, though as Figure 10.2 shows, there were important national differences in employment trends reflecting differing economic structures or governmental policies. Most obvious was the clear decline in the proportion of women in manufacturing in Britain. Similarly, as Figure 10.3 indicates, there was relative stability in women as a proportion of manufacturing labour, though decline is obvious in Britain and France, as is a distinct rise in Germany. The post-war experiences of Italy and Belgium also represent contradictory trends. These figures hide the fact that

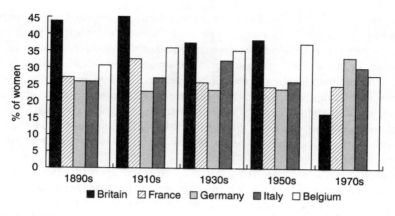

Figure 10.2 Proportion of female labour force in manufacturing, 1890s–1970s
Source: Bairoch *et al.* (1968)

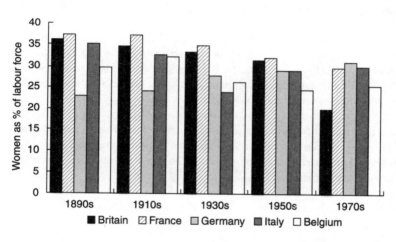

Figure 10.3 Women as a proportion of the manufacturing labour force, 1890s–1970s
Source: Bairoch *et al.* (1968)

the composition and distribution of women's jobs changed. More significant than this overview, however, was the shift in the relative importance of industries and the location of work. Local variation is evident throughout the period, especially during the interwar years, but older 'traditional female' industries, such as textiles, declined as employers of women. In Germany, the number and proportion of women in the industrial workforce rose, but in textiles, during the First World War and the interwar period, there was widespread short-time working. Change was so pronounced that only half as many worked in clothing and textiles in 1918 compared to 1914. In Britain, whether in cotton in Lancashire, silk in Cheshire, jute in Scotland or linen in Northern Ireland, depressions of the 1920s and 1930s hit them hard, and cotton never recovered, with loss of markets to overseas competitors and competition from synthetics. In Coventry, the decline of ribbon-weaving meant that it was the end of an era. Between 1921 and 1951, the proportion of women in textiles fell from 14 per cent of the female labour force to only 3 per cent. A loss of jobs occurred in France, so that despite the fact that textiles still accounted for about a third of female workers and remained a large industry, as Reynolds puts it, they were 'prey to stagnation, while all around flourished'. Decline continued after the Second World War, though women remained the overwhelming majority of textile workers.[41]

Women were less likely to be restricted to a few areas of work, and were 'increasingly successful in finding employment outside the traditional "female sectors", so that they are less at risk from the economic fluctuations, crises and decline tendencies of single branches'. In many, women came to predominate. As textiles stagnated and declined, women became the majority of the workforce as men left. They constituted 55 per cent in Bielefeld linen in the early 1860s; by 1900 they were 70 per cent. Over half of the total Belgian textile labour force was female between 1875 and 1914, in wool, cotton, jute, linen and hemp. In Armentières, the female proportion of the textile workforce grew and passed 50 per cent by 1910. In Bremen jute from 1888 until 1914, two-thirds of workers were female.[42] Glickman's work on Russia, however, demonstrates the importance of local variation.

> For example, in the Kazan factory district, where women were 40 per cent of all textile workers, one of the two largest textile factories (590 workers) employed no women, and in the other (653 workers) women were a third of the workers.[43]

In other older industries where women had been a minority, like leather and shoemaking, they became a substantial proportion, for example, in the 1950s, in leather, 37.1 per cent were women in Britain, 37.6 per cent in France and 27 per cent in Germany. Technological change in older trades, such as printing and pottery, increased opportunities for women. Belgian glassware factories witnessed a similar increase, especially in crystal manufacture. Russian women moved into industries previously employing only men. For example, in 1885, no women worked in pottery, ceramics, glass and brickmaking; by 1911 they comprised 37.5, 41.5, 29 and 16 per cent of workforces respectively. Several industries transferred from a male preserve to a female one, such as tobacco and printing in Belgium. Printing was not the battlefield which it was in France with the Coriau affair, or in Edinburgh in 1910, when 'history froze the numbers of women compositors'. German leatherwork transformed itself from a masculine trade reliant on craft work to a female domain with mechanization and division of labour. In other instances, women were utilized on new work which theoretically replaced no one. For example, introduction of wrapping machines in the Dutch margarine industry coincided with expansion of the workforce, mainly by female labour. They did not replace men, and in fact further technical change reduced the labour force, with machines replacing women.[44]

At the same time, a number of new industries developed together with new manufacturing processes. Many became important employers of women, though as Bridenthal points out, 'the branches of manufacturing traditionally occupied by women declined more rapidly than the new ones that employed them expanded'. Introduction of newer industries and rationalized production began around the turn of the century. For example, French textiles 'modernized' before the First World War, and food processing expanded with new methods and products. The war, however, gave added impetus to new methods when unskilled labour, especially in engineering, was required. Introducing women into so-called men's jobs caused disquiet and discontent and 'made female employment seem threatening', leading to a range of agreements with unions and skilled labour to ensure that women left after the war. The interwar period witnessed the most dramatic implementation of new processes, as peacetime economies turned to greater production of consumer goods. For example, in Germany, the boom in rationalization began after 1925, while in France it was during 'the post-Poincaré boom that serious efforts were made to modernize the more advanced sectors of French industry, in a context of general industrial expansion'.[45] These industries can be encapsulated by the phrase 'light industry'. As products for domestic consumption, most did not need to be near ports, and since they relied on electrical power, did not need to be near coalfields. In Britain, therefore, industry shifted from the industrial heartlands of the north to London and the Midlands.[46] The growth of Birmingham and its architectural heritage are testament to the rise of the automotive industry, with estate upon estate of 1930s houses.

New industries are perceived as taking on large numbers of females; with mechanization and automation, however, the gender balance was less clear cut. Primarily industries already relying on women expanded their female workforce, especially those which had rationalized first, such as chemicals, paper, duplicating industries and metalware manufacture. Though theoretically women had been hired for 'female skills' of patience, precision and dexterity, but in reality for docility and cheapness, it was logical to expand with a proven workforce. Certainly, the numbers and proportion of women in newer industries and processes increased, and many were highly reliant on a female workforce, though Bridenthal reminds us that of the 1.5 million new jobs created between 1925 and 1933 in Germany, 77 per cent were taken by men. Thébaud and Reynolds ascribe growth to a shift of women from traditional sectors into newer, more modern branches of the economy where Taylor's principles of scientific management were applied. In particular, 'the move into light metal working was a cultural transfer – made possible by the war – breaking with the old tradition of having women work on "soft" commodities, men on "hard" ones'. Many of what Stockman calls 'typical modern female expansion fields' overwhelmingly involved businesses which were highly mechanized and relied on division of labour. The proportion of German women in light industries expanded rapidly. For example, in electronics, where women made up only 1.9 per cent in 1882, they increased to 26.1 per cent by 1925; in chemicals from 13 per cent to 27.2 per cent. Taylorism was associated with women from the outset in France. Thus in St Etienne, women appeared in large numbers in interwar equipment factories producing individual parts, in machine polishing and nickel plating. The number of women in metal trades, chemical, food, paper and cardboard manufacture increased dramatically after 1906, and the number of women in metalwork increased sixfold between 1931 and 1954. Glucksmann identifies a similar shift in Britain, with a decrease of 12.9 per cent in the number in textiles between 1923 and 1937, and a further decrease of 36.6 per cent to 1947. In the same periods, engineering registered an increase of 62.5 per cent, and a further increase of 159 per cent. At Magneti Marelli, founded in 1919, 'the two factors which are most important to explain this pattern were management strategy and the large numbers of women in the labour force'. New industries, with new production methods, had a vested interest in tapping what Glucksmann calls 'green labour', a workforce with little industrial heritage, so that 'women were a preferred source of labour in the large monopoly firms producing new products by new methods of production for a new market'.[47]

Despite more options, segregation and gendered workplaces did not evaporate. A key feature was a 'lumpy' occupational pattern; that is, men were far more likely to make certain products or work in particular industries and women in others. As Reynolds indicates, cultural factors helped to reintroduce segregation, for example, in food processing, women worked in dairy and sugar-production processes, while men handled meat. The automobile industry stands out as a key area which remained largely male. It was still seen as an artisanal domain reliant on craft skills, even with assembly lines and large complex plants. In a survey of the Paris suburb of Puteaux in 1914, with six car plants, women made up no more than 0.45 per cent of the workforce, and at Renault in Boulogne-Billancourt, 6 per cent. In Coventry, the car and engineering industry employed 37 per cent of the male workforce, but the gendered pattern emerged here too. Around 10 per cent of women workers were employed in metal manufacturing between 1920 and 1945, but they clustered in specific factories which hired mainly women; there were only a few which hired both sexes on the shopfloor. In 1931, 9.6 per cent of metalworkers in Coventry were female; in 1935 women comprised 16.2 per cent of shopfloor workers in companies affiliated to the Engineering Employers Federation. Women workers in car plants were a tiny proportion, usually machinists sewing trims, car cleaners or canteen workers. A similar split can be seen within other industries. Although Magneti Marelli employed more women than other engineering firms in Sesto, they remained less than half, and different products were manufactured by each sex. For example, expansion in radio production led to increased recruitment of women, while accumulator batteries were made by men.[48]

The greatest influx came from single women, often preferring factories to domestic service. They were particularly enthusiastic about the higher wages and increased freedom which factory work represented. They found 'more life' there, a partial escape from parents and from looking after younger children. They had money to spend, especially on clothes and increasingly on recreation. Most also paid a contribution to parents. They experienced pleasure in the collective experience, as women from Belfast indicate. One who started at age twelve in 1898 said, 'We were happy . . . You stood all day at your work and sung them songs'; another agreed, 'you got a wee drink, got a join [pooled money for food], done your work and you had your company'. Factories and workshops in Berlin at the turn of the century drew from a younger female population than industry in general, so that 69 per cent were under twenty-five, compared to 46.4 per cent overall in the female workforce, and three-quarters were younger than the mean age at marriage for women in Berlin: 26.1 years. Approximately a third had left home and lived as lodgers. Only 13.8 per cent lived alone in their own room or apartment. Similarly, at Magneti Marelli, between the wars, new recruits were overwhelmingly young: 45.9 per cent were aged under twenty, with a third aged twenty to twenty-five, and only 22 per cent over twenty-five.[49]

In contrast to these young women were those who wished to work only until marriage. After 1945, in France it was perceived as 'a necessary evil, to be endured until marriage might allow them to abandon it'. Mason described the same for women in Weimar factories. Choice, of course, is a complicated concept. One person's freedom is another's prison. Cultural and peer values play an important part. Where work was necessary and factories provided the best option, it was likely to be viewed differently than in a culture where marriage had highest value, factory work was boring and repetitive and there were no other options. Hilden says that Belgian women always found factory work preferable to working alone, or in squalid rooms, and chose factory work over sweating wherever possible. Similar evidence comes from the Mass Observation survey begun in Britain in 1937. Women at Renault in 1920 agreed that the main incentive was money, since wages were comparatively good, but a peasant woman, who entered because of the wages, commented, 'I am glad to have found good people here. I had been told that a factory only attracted rabble.' Again, women felt the factory gave them a more varied social life and comparative emancipation. They went so far as to argue that it helped create a more equal marriage with shared respect and household tasks. One married woman went back to the plant because of money and boredom at home. Factory inspectors' reports collected by Fourcaut also indicate that women were attached to factory life for income and for conviviality: 'Factory life, with its gossip, incidents and camaraderie, amused them . . . [and] work gave them independence from their husbands.' Interwar Scottish women also recollected factory days with affection, citing job satisfaction, pride in work and an identity with one's machine.[50]

Employer preferences clearly shaped the age and marital structure of the workforce. At Van Houten's chocolate factory, there was a strong preference for girl employees. Since there was little difference in wages and it was difficult to get girls, Schrover suggests, 'he only had employment for young workers . . . there were few possibilities for getting ahead. As women usually left after a few years, Van Houten was spared the uneasy task of laying off workers.' Employer preference at Magneti Marelli also kept average age down 'as the young often made stronger and quicker workers'. One who felt she had been rejected on account of age begged the works manager 'to see if it is possible to make an exception to the rule'. British electrical engineering confirmed a preference for very young women, because 'the younger the girls, the cheaper they were'. In contrast, Bremen jute employers preferred married women, because 'single women in Bremen are, on grounds of the shipping traffic, unreliable, while the married ones are solid and dependable'. The classic way to determine life-cycle structure of the workforce was a marriage bar. Women were frequently criticized for lack of a commitment to employment, but 'employers took active steps to ensure this was the case by sacking them on marriage if they did not leave voluntarily'. Often bars were informal, but a formal bar was operated by firms like Peek Frean or Courtaulds, who aimed to control the local labour market. In Scotland, disappearance of marriage bars after the Second World War helped reshape the workforce in instrument-making and electrical engineering: in the early 1930s women comprised 20 per cent of the workforce; in the 1970s they had become almost 50 per cent.[51]

The persistence of gender stereotypes as a rationale for employment was pervasive. During the 1930s the German Labour Front's 'extreme protective superiority' towards women underlined the double standard. On the one hand, they described females as fragile, valuable and responsive to personal attention, and on the other, as unreliable, feckless and uninterested. In Armentières, women were hired after the Depression instead of men, because they were paid less, were more fearful of being laid off, and were therefore more docile. Rationalization and increasing mechanization are usually given as reasons for introducing women into new industries. The trend for greater division of labour, where work was broken down into small, mechanical, repetitive tasks, more machinery and more automated production lines, implied that skilled workers could be replaced by semi-skilled and unskilled labour, which usually meant women. But as Glickman says, they did not make employment of women necessary or inevitable. Mechanized jobs required less strength and skill and therefore commanded a lower wage. So fundamentally women were employed as cheap labour. Guilbert argues convincingly that employment of women in the lowly tedious end of metalworking was based partly on the profitability of division of labour and partly on gendered images, especially the stereotype of the woman worker in the minds of family, male workers and employers. The ideas of woman as worker and woman as woman clearly contributed to determining whether they would be employed. Their submissiveness as well as a view that they were calmer and steadier contributed to making them an attractive labour force. Thébaud argues that women were better 'agents of modernization', better able to accept innovation than men stunned by the pace of change. Certainly, many employers felt that women without a collective craft experience were more likely to be docile and accept new conditions of employment.[52]

Women's work could be summarized as production of lighter, smaller articles, often in a mechanized or automated setting, which was usually routine, boring and part of a fragmented work process. Guilbert described their tasks in the French metallurgical industry in the 1960s as physically easier, less complex, more repetitive, more manual, involving longer series of operations at a faster tempo than men's. The fact that it was usually paid less than men's work is a virtual truism which had as much to do with the worker as the work. Indeed, characterization of women's work cannot be disentangled from their sex, since perceptions of what women could do were inextricably tied to what employers and male workers perceived women to be. For example, in pottery, Wedgwoods stated that 'the smaller articles and, therefore, the lighter moulds are given to the women . . . Heavy and more responsible work is performed by men.' In an interwar German metalware factory, the inspector noted that women worked at lighter presses 'which operated faster than the heavier ones worked by men, who could take time to be careful'. Mechanization meant that women moved into new fields and occasionally took on tasks originally perceived as male. For example, during the First World War women undertook men's jobs in pottery, but only 'mechanized versions of those tasks', and between the wars, women took on newly automated tasks like throwing and turning. They also moved into the mechanized end of bicycle manufacture, while men retained their position as craftsmen. In fact, women were increasingly associated with non-qualified jobs using a machine, to soldering and managing presses. They were certainly given work on new machines, and though they did not necessarily replace men, it was often the machine and the woman which replaced them. For example, in the Viennese sheet-metal industry, larger factories with the most machinery relied exclusively on women, though small firms still used men.[53]

Division of labour was a feature of domestic industry and of the emergent factory-based processes. However, in Taylorized processes, division of labour took on new meanings. Reynolds captured the essence of the new systems in her succinct description:

> It is generally known as Taylorism, after its inventor, but is also known as *la rationalisation* or Fordism, and sometimes as *OST*, *l'organisation scientifique du travail*. The basic principles of *OST* were: the

standardization of equipment used in production; the breakdown of the production process into a series of consecutive operations; the devising of a series of production norms, obtained by time and motion studies; and the application of these norms. In its eventual full-blown form, it meant introducing bonuses for improving on norms, and penalties or docked pay if these were not met. This was the Bedaud system of payment by results (performance related pay, as it would be called today). It depended on a workforce of 'semi-skilled' or 'special-ized' workers, trained on the job rather than serving apprenticeships.[54]

The greatest impact was on a radical division of labour which capitalized on perceptions of the 'woman worker' and which further defined and delimited her place in the industrial workplace, as new strategies and processes increased the segregation of the workforce and division of labour along gendered lines. There was a significant merging of notions of skill, technology and division of labour into a workplace for women which was segregated, repetitious, monot-onous, unthinking and required rapid detailed work at high speed. 'Although the association between women and repetitive manual work was not unique to assembly industries, the lines of division between male and female workers and the form of subordination of women to technology, managerial control and men were new and characteristic of this type of work alone.'[55] Gendered segre-gation of the workplace operated in two ways. Men and women often did not work on the same shopfloors within the same industry. They also often worked in different processes carrying out different tasks, and frequently in different industries. Some of this was about areas of work allocated by gender. It was also the result of deliberate segregation to avoid comparison, to allow men to claim their special position and wages. For example, at Magneti Marelli, female employees were virtually confined to the A plant, then to the N plant when 'their' work was transferred; the B and C plants with mostly heavy work remained predominantly male. They did at times work in mixed teams, and women describe using men's tools to help the team gain a bonus, but mainly work was segregated spatially by gender. Indeed, they worked to a different timetable, in the winding shop which was virtually all female, headed by a woman, because she 'didn't want her workers to have any contact with the men, so they had that special shift and that was all'. Even when men and women in the pottery industry appeared to be doing similar jobs, they often worked in single-sex groups, often in different rooms, a feature apparent in hosiery right through to the 1980s.[56] Though men and women seldom did *exactly* the same task, there was little question of considering or implementing equal pay for equal work. The principles of vertical and horizontal segregation that operated were always mediated by specific factors in a particular work-place, including previous gender distribution, and pre-existing cultural or occupational traditions. They were not absolute, nor did they exist in the abstract.

Division of labour was fundamental to the new processes, particularly assembly-line work, in that jobs were broken into minute steps undertaken in succession. A process could involve hundreds of actions, leading to a specifically fragmented work experience. Significantly, assembly lines in both old and new industries were seen from the outset as women's work. Division of labour and mass-production techniques did not require female workers, but this was what happened. Repetitive, fragmented work with a minute division of labour required what were seen as women's special abilities. For example, Zerner linked the attributes of women accustomed to sewing piece work to new assembly processes. Almost uniformly, women were assemblers, men the supervisors and maintenance staff. An inquiry in 1929 concluded that conveyor-belt techniques employing a detailed division of labour suited women because, 'females were apparently unaffected by the monotony of the work'. Some have been listed by Beddoe: wiring up radios, fixing collar studs on shirts, cutting out chocolate shapes, sewing leather bucket-seats of cars, spreading cream on sandwich biscuits, filling tubes with toothpaste, canning meat and fish. At Philips in Mitcham, Surrey, forty-five women worked on a conveyor belt half a mile long assembling radios; each worker had forty-five solder joints to do. At Cadbury's Chocolates in 1937, 'piecework has been abolished and the girls have been set to work on a conveyor. They now pack, on the conveyor, 60 to 63 dozen boxes of chocolates in the time in which they formerly packed 25 to 30 dozen.' Women did labour-intensive intricate work requiring 'finger-tip precision and flying speed' weighing, stripping, spinning and packing cigarettes. With new machinery for portioning Dutch margarine, a more detailed division of labour was introduced and more girls were hired to supplement and substitute for boys. In machine shops, women manufactured components, operating a wide range of stamping, pressing, milling and grinding machines, and assembled components, fixing them with solder, screwdrivers or by hand. This created a rigid sexual division of labour on the shopfloor whereby, as Glucksmann puts it, they were never engaged on the same work, never in the same grade and never on the same wages as men.[57]

Introduction of assembly lines and increased division of labour was not unchallenged, and led to disputes with male workers during both wars, and to gender conflict as women came into more and more workplaces as a visible threat to men's view of themselves and their rightful work. In Armentières in 1912, the question of modernizing textile equipment was the main cause of the male workers' opposition, because it raised a new possibility for employing women, undermining the profession of male weavers. In hosiery, struggle between male trade unionists and employers over female labour continued right through both wars. Leleu argues that men feared if women were given the status or dignity they deserved and gained autonomy through work, they might take on a more independent position within and outside the couple. Chenut confirms that French unions 'in many trades clearly expressed the notion of a skilled male worker whose identity was increasingly threatened by technological advances and by women's employment. They reasoned that because skill was defined as masculine, the employment of women and children destroyed the notion of skill.' In the British East Midlands boot and shoe industry, similar male fear was evident. Their specific concern was the 'constant attempts that are made to CUT down wages by trying to introduce women's labour in the departments that are rightly looked upon as for male operatives'. At Magneti Marelli, Willson found that, 'Women do not appear to have been allowed to threaten the male monopoly of better-paid, more interesting work and learn trades such as fitting.' Work regarded as skilled was carefully preserved for men.[58]

The employment of women was contested in a number of different settings, but it was not uniformly condemned. As low-paid workers on piece rates, women posed a certain threat to male wages, but a number of conditions moderated gender conflict, and in some cases rendered it non-existent. In Germany, Frevert argues that 'the topic was manifestly uninteresting for the 1920s . . . as long as the expansion of production continued to create new opportunities for men too, the competition for supremacy on the labour market did not become a hot political potato'. Reynolds notes that sexes were segregated in the critical period of introducing new processes while at the same time employment was high, so that the threat was not clearly perceived. In any case the work experience and identity of male and female workers was totally different. She says that 'they lived on different planes' at home or at work. Frader notes that in trades where women were well represented, such as cigarette- and match-making or food processing, or where there was sufficient division of labour so that men did not perceive the women as a threat, they did not even appeal to the family wage ideal to protect their jobs. That is precisely the main point. Women did not enter most new industries as the majority of the workforce; they were usually segregated either by task or spatially, and they did not tend to replace adult men. If they did replace males it was boys, who would have outgrown the work anyway. These points are brought home in Willson's discussion of gender conflict – or rather the lack of it – at Magneti Marelli, where she says the 'men seem to have been singularly unworried by women's presence in the factory'. As she explains, 'so long as women only did "their" jobs and did not attempt to get men's jobs, particularly the more desirable ones, the men accepted it'.[59] This point is important, because women were more present, but 'ghettoizing' them into less desirable work helped to retain and imbed an even more vigorous gendered division of labour, and to preserve men's position in the workplace at a time when the character of their work was also undergoing change.

11

NEW WORK

White blouses in the tertiary sector

THE TERTIARY SECTOR AND 'WHITE BLOUSE' WORK

The main development in women's work since the 1880s has been the virtual creation of jobs associated with offices, shops and professions. The shape of men's work changed at the same time so that the creation of new work as well as the expansion of sectors, such as clerking, operated as a focus for gendered debate about work and heightened contests about women's rightful place. The first point of departure is the issue of work for middle-class women which gained momentum as the nineteenth century progressed. While marriage and family remained the ideal state, there were those for whom this was not possible. 'Respectable' single middle-class women were constrained by cultural objections and education from working, and only those with adequate education and contacts could find work as a governess or companion. Others, who wished to 'do something meaningful' and remove themselves from a state of dependency, directly challenged the established bourgeois view of womanhood, and became a more vociferous group with the growth of feminism. The second point of departure is improved education. It led to a better-educated workforce, which had the potential to accommodate a range of tasks requiring literacy and understanding. It also meant that many were less interested in manual jobs, feeling that 'something better' was worth aiming for.

The third point of departure is change in the tertiary sector. Economic, social and cultural changes during the nineteenth century expanded existing occupations and created and transformed many others. Clerking was viewed as a male craft occupation with a developed work culture which included personal advancement and social mobility, and offered a respectable opportunity to advance in what was clearly seen as a male culture. The character of office work changed dramatically after about 1870, with an expansion in record-keeping and correspondence resulting from multiplying business and industrial activity, requiring educated workers to run an increasingly urban society, to manage and record foreign trade transactions and to operate financial services. The typewriter shifted the nature of correspondence and copying which was the mainstay of many offices, while clerical and administrative tasks multiplied.

Many workplaces became larger and more complex, which meant the creation of hierarchies and increasing organizational complexity.

Department stores and revised marketing practices altered the face of retail, and the scale of operations required more staff who needed less training and expertise. Merchandizing took a new turn with the development of bazaars, large shops, chain stores and co-operative shopping. The rebuilding of Bon Marché in 1869 marked a new departure: 'for the first time a store was being constructed that was formally conceived and systematically designed to house a *grand magasin*'.[1] It signalled a shift from the small specialist shop, with goods in boxes on shelves, requiring expert knowledge and handling, to open stores with a range of goods, with clearly marked prices, through which customers could wander.

> Expositions in the spacious galleries of the stores, large display windows, publicity through catalogs and newspaper advertising shaped illusions and stimulated the public's desires for the items offered. The sales person was herself part of the presentation, helping to create an atmosphere of service and contributing to the seductiveness of the merchandise.[2]

Others followed quickly, including Les Grands Magasins du Louvre, Printemps and Galeries Lafayette in Paris, Bourne and Hollingworth's, Harrods, William Whiteley's and Army and Navy Stores in London. Numerous provincial stores sprang up, such as Bainbridge's of Newcastle, and several in Glasgow. Urban centres like Hamburg, Berlin, Nürnberg, Augsburg and München had several department stores by 1890. Like in the office, workers no longer learned a whole operation, and therefore the prospect of learning the trade and opening one's own shop largely had gone. Many continued to work in smaller shops, some relying on traditional methods for a time, retaining their specialist character and clientele, others as general 'corner shops'.[3]

Like the rest of the tertiary sector, professions demonstrated important changes in numbers, size and composition. In addition to the traditional 'learned professions' of divinity, physic and law, other occupations gained recognition as they succeeded in protecting access and creating special preserves so that civil servants, architects, engineers, chemists, veterinary surgeons, actuaries and accountants, among others, gained the standing and credibility of professions. Rising standards of living and an increasing complexity of social life led to an escalating call for services of professionals and specialists. Some, like science and engineering, experienced 'boom conditions' between 1921 and 1966. Medicine gained from improved medical knowledge, which helped to create a medical discourse grounded in knowledge and training, which would have implications for nursing and doctoring. Protecting their position gained in importance, as professions attempted to retain status and political power in the face of pressures for social mobility, democratization and educational improvement.[4] This tension clearly increased resistance to women's entrance to many professional careers. Status continued to be a crucial measure of success, especially in professional families, and erosion of male position and standing was keenly felt.

Most literature on women in the tertiary sector derives from debates about women 'entering' white-collar work between about 1870 and 1914. Frequently this debate is couched in terms of 'feminization'. However, feminization may be the wrong perspective. The concept of feminization stems from greater numbers of women and their increased visibility. It implies that men owned the work and the workplace and poses the question of whether women substituted for men. In fact, much work in the expanding tertiary sector, whether in offices, shops or professions, was new and many areas were female from the outset, although workplaces often operated around a particular culture which had been largely male. Men owned the old work, such as administration, copying and shopkeeping, and possessed the status or lack of it that went with it. With new work, men needed to assert their claim over it, as did women, while women were involved in the transition of the workplace as much as men were. As a relatively undeveloped sector, the sexual division of labour in white-collar work was not yet clearly defined.[5] However, women did not have equal opportunities for higher-status work with men, and were not 'introduced' so much as 'allocated' to 'new' work. The story is highly nuanced and surrounded by issues of gender, custom and control. Sometimes substitution was the issue, other times stratification and segregation were at the heart of the matter.

Girls and women had often helped in shops, and wives were often responsible for the retail end of artisanal work prior to the mid-nineteenth century. Shopkeeping was not regarded as inappropriate for women, and the 1851 census identified more female than male shopkeepers in England and Wales. Frequently their activity was informal, unrecorded and unrewarded. Women declined as proprietors only at the end of the century as retailing came to be seen as less genteel, and as there came to be no necessary link between girls' work and their futures. The shift in retailing virtually created a new job for vast numbers of girls: the shop assistant. Similarly, women had frequently undertaken clerical tasks, usually informally in family businesses, keeping books and records. In France, post mistresses operated during the *ancien régime*, and in England, girls and women were employed as telegraphers from the 1840s. In 1870, a Dutch feminist tract claimed that in Switzerland, 'middle-class women are employed as postal and telegraph clerks' and 'in France many girls wield their pens . . . as bookkeepers; at Swedish Post and Telegraph Offices, a great number of women hold jobs . . . and women have been put in charge of several second-class post offices'.[6] In some respects professional work has a longer feminine history than office work and a more independent one than shop work. Healing, nursing and midwifery have ancient origins, and 'dame schools' were pervasive, if largely unrecorded, throughout the seventeenth and eighteenth centuries. Philanthropy and charity work have long been considered the province of 'ladies bountiful'. Thus it could be argued that women's professional roles became formalized rather than created around the same time as clerical work expanded. It would be foolish, however, to ignore the strong male craft traditions such as for surgeons and apothecaries, and the intellectual traditions which allowed men to dominate clerical and educational positions of standing.

A slow increase in female white-collar workers accelerated from about 1870 to 1914. In France, women comprised 39.8 per cent of commercial workers by 1906 and 43.2 per cent in 1921. In Germany, the number of female white-collar workers grew faster than the female labour force, and they made up 30.5 per cent of the whole in 1907 and 35.6 per cent in 1925. In Britain, a similar increase took place, so that women rose to 17.5 per cent of the commercial workforce in 1911, and 39.4 per cent in 1921. The proportion of women in professions rose from above a third to almost half in Britain and France between the 1870s and 1920s, though many were teachers whose increase reflected changes in education. Male white-collar workers also increased, of course, but women made more spectacular gains. For example, in Britain, the number of men rose sevenfold, but women by eighty-three times. Lockwood thus declared, the 'white-blouse invasion of blackcoated work was well underway'.[7]

CHANGE IN THE TERTIARY SECTOR

Gradually, as new modes of retailing emerged, females became far more prevalent and visible. In Britain in 1861, only 19 per cent of recorded shop assistants were female; by 1911 the proportion had risen to 31 per cent. At Zola's visit to the Bon Marché in 1882 there were only 152 female clerks among the 2,500 employees. Several hundred others worked in mail order and correspondence. Although male retail assistants in Berlin complained in 1848 about growing competition from 'young madams in our shops', in reality, only in the last third of the century did they become normal places of employment. Yet, in contemporary eyes, the female clerk was a dominant image, and women were obvious in department stores by the turn of the century. In 1908 in London, a third of Harrods staff and two-thirds at Derry and Toms were women. Numbers continued to increase, and after the Second World War women spread more generally throughout retailing, especially as men found other more lucrative work in the post-war boom. In Scotland, 75 per cent of employed women worked in non-domestic services by the mid-1970s, though jobs stagnated with growth of giant stores and microchip technology. Over 40 per cent of female shop assistants were part time.[8]

Tasks were different, however. The craft dealer who cut, measured, weighed and finished the stock declined so that shopkeeping became 'keeping the stock tidy and showing merchandise across the counters and receiving payment'. Lancaster argues, however, that expansion, new products and a greater range of merchandise created customer demand for advice and competent and well-informed sales staff. This led to in-house training, and hiring 'trainees' not apprentices.[9] At the same time, a high degree of segregation emerged, and females tended to work in departments catering specifically for women. For example, men sold male clothing and household furnishings, while women handled yardage and dresses, or as at the Bon Marché, ladies' lingerie or trousseaux. Male roles remained linked to craft and apprenticed trades, with strong continuity between the 'traditional' manufacturer, that is, the artisan, and the new salesman. Thus men sold jewellery, gloves and women's stockings, and were butchers and fishmongers, while women worked in provisioning and women's clothes. Changes in merchandise also altered the gender of the workforce:

> Whereas in the nineteenth century chemists normally employed male assistants, the spread of mass-produced cosmetics and luxury toiletries brought women into this branch, although qualified dispensers still were male. Sweets and chocolates were now described as 'primarily a girl's trade'.[10]

Holcombe argues that men worked where training was required and goods were expensive, or work was rough and heavy, while women predominated in light and untrained work, reliant on female customers but resulting in low pay. Of course, pay could have been low because assistants were women. Male assistants and 'floor walkers' held their own, retaining positions of status in 'select' departments, and supervisor and head of department posts. After the First World War, the National Union of Shop Assistants reported a 'fairly clear line of demarcation' between men's and women's work, though the union, known as socially progressive, admitted that there was a place for women in some jobs requiring 'skill, method and brains'.[11]

Women entered retail relatively easily during the First World War because of labour shortages, and 'normalcy' brought expanded consumer production together with new mass-distribution techniques. Thus, as Bridenthal noted, there were thousands of cash registers for women to staff. As department stores evolved, so did women's experience. Those who held supervisory and management posts during the war acquitted themselves well. The *New Survey of London Life and Labour* in 1930 confirmed that female buyers outnumbered men, and women increasingly reached higher-status posts with responsibility. Nevertheless, segregation continued in products and status. In Croydon by 1931, for example, women penetrated bakery and grocery trades but remained largely absent from meat, fishmongery, furniture and ironware. Men tended to retain work with a craft component, where processing was part of selling. Webb's study in the 1980s highlights continued segregation. Men still held

top positions, such as management, training and stock control, and still dominated in departments with expensive or bulky consumables. Women, more
visible on display counters, were prominent selling women's clothing. In
1985, 1.5 million women worked in sales and distribution in Britain. They
were shelf-fillers, cashiers, store clerks, and, with new technology, their roles
echoed the repetitive and 'assembly-line' characteristics of new industries. By
1981 in Britain, women outnumbered men six to one in the least skilled work
of sales clerks, assistants and shelf-fillers, while at the top of the hierarchy men
outnumbered women two to one.[12]

A related area of expansion was mail order. The Army and Navy Stores relied
on it from early on and the Bon Marché ran a service from 1871, while females
staffed a correspondence bureau to answer written queries. They were expected
to have a modicum of education, sometimes a foreign language, and to write a
respectable hand. The real growth in mail order has come in the twentieth century. Nearly half the women in the United Kingdom place an order each year.
The catalogue houses that dominate this market employ 'a massive pyramid of
women, built and dominated by men'. The women are usually part-timers,
married women and mothers, and include agents who work from home. A typical British firm operates in the north, based on a female workforce unemployed by textile decline, often using the redundant factory building. It relies
on a disciplined workforce, but 'often this has meant a step down in skill and
certainly no gain in earnings'. Highly dependent on technology for handling
orders, nevertheless warehouse work remains a labour-intensive job which is
exhausting, with a woman's pay dependent on the rate at which she can select
goods for dispatch.[13] Reminiscent of new developments in manufacturing, this
is the face of work that emerged at the end of the century.

On 7 December 1871, the Board of Directors of the Prudential Assurance
Company 'Resolved: That the employment of Ladies as Clerks be tried as an
experiment.' Jordan calls this decision 'an historic and almost unprecedented
event in the employment of women in clerical work in Britain', as they moved
into large public-sector offices. Until then, women were more likely to work in
smaller offices and less likely in the financial sector, such as insurance, banking,
stockbroking, or in railways and law firms in Germany and Britain. In France,
female *employées* most rapidly increased in manufacturing industries commonly
associated with women, like those producing or marketing clothing, those
'suitable' for women, or light industries as in Germany. Banks, insurance companies, shipping firms, and big merchant houses began to hire women, but
often for routine clerical tasks. For example, less than half the women
employed in German banks were entrusted with actual banking work. The
Prudential employed female staff to copy out letters and other documents connected with new working-class insurance and for some correspondence.
Women's clerical work grew in towns and cities, particularly where firms were
small and less modern. Adams argues that 'small businesses were less likely to
pay good salaries and offered fewer opportunities for training and advance-

ment; in these circumstances women were hired'. The influx of women meant the Manchester Business Young Ladies Association in 1895 felt impelled to take on the role of finding respectable lodgings for 'a small army of Nurses, Teachers . . . Typists and Clerks' coming to work in Manchester.[14]

Civil services were the largest employers of female clerks. Women entered telegraphy, while telephonist services were virtually all female from the outset, except for night work. In France, from about 1835 the Post Office increasingly reintroduced females in rural offices, and amalgamation of postal and telegraph services in 1878 saw the beginning of a rapid rise in business, requiring massive increases in staff. They were hired in the Postal Savings Banks which opened in 1881, and in the telephone company after it became a state monopoly. In October 1873, 'at the suggestion of her Royal Highness, the Crown Princess, the administration of the Telegraph Centre [in Germany] decided to employ ladies . . . to open up a respectable branch of business to ladies of the upper middle class, the daughters of officials and officers'. It promised permanent pensionable employment, housing benefits and bonuses. In the event these promises proved hollow, though women were indeed hired. Dutch women were formally admitted to telegraph and postal services in December 1878. In 1850 the Chairman of the Electrical and International Telegraph Company in London heard that a station master's daughter had 'for some years' handled her father's telegraph business 'most efficiently'. Accordingly, 'as an experiment' the company began to train and employ women. Having proven able, they were taken on as telephonists from the outset in 1879 and in the private sector as commercial premises installed telephones. Women became Civil Service typists in 1879 when the Inland Revenue employed two to keep copies of indexes at Somerset House. While this decision was related to gender issues about the appropriateness of women as typists, it arose also from Treasury views that temporary male copyists were structurally anomalous, since they were not subject to Civil Service rules. They had also become expensive, having become regular rather than casual employees. Gradually women were employed on other clerical and quasi-administrative work throughout the service, but only in 'women's posts, classes, branches, departments and with special terms of service such as unequal pay, the marriage bar and restrictions on mobility'.[15]

The First World War provided some opportunity for advancement previously blocked by separate gendered promotion structures, and some who had left at marriage returned for the war. Afterwards, many kept these jobs. Increased opportunities in France came with the return of full employment for men and expansion of the service sector. Modern industrial methods, such as Taylorism, called for more central administration and expanded office staffs. In Germany, women took over jobs during the war, and in the 1930s, replaced men who had been dismissed because women were cheaper. Britain experienced a similar increase with lasting gains after the war, and, as in Germany, women proved 'more flexible' during the Depression and as promotion structures deteriorated.

Employers sought to fill low-level, high-turnover and temporary posts, and saw typists, file-clerks and office-machine operators, that is, women, as the solution to staffing problems. Women were perceived to be dispensable, and in 1921, when the Marine Insurance Company made savings to compensate for cost of living increases for permanent male staff, it released thirty-seven temporary female clerks. Despite competitive Civil Service exams, a feature of the period was the continued increase in lower-level work, so that most women filled routine positions at the bottom of the hierarchy. From being a male occupation, clerical work shifted towards numerical parity between the wars. Certainly, 'white-bloused' workers became more visible. The public saw a modern woman who was ubiquitous in cities, was depicted in films and who became the symbol of young, working females. 'The presence of women office workers commuting at rush hours created the impression that they were massively entering what had been the all male world of paper pushing.' Germans saw white-collar work as a typical occupation for the young single woman. In 1925 almost all were single and two-thirds were under twenty-five years of age, so that the 'hotly-disputed prototypes of female emancipation were in fact young clerical workers . . . The modernity of the Weimar system seemed to acquire the shape of secretaries, shorthand typists and shop assistants.' Office work, associated with modernity and the big city, was one of the best options open to Dutch women and the female office worker was seen and depicted as a new independent woman.[16]

Key features after the Second World War were a rapid rise in the number of female white-collar workers, often surpassing men, and the introduction of far more married women as marriage bars, real and customary, fell. Gradually, more women reached administrative levels, though the 'glass ceiling' continued to restrict opportunities. Additionally, technological explosion altered the character of the workplace, adding new twists to very durable constructs about gender and technology. Career breaks and part-time work, including 'job-share', coloured the texture of the white-bloused world. Between 1931 and 1951, the number of British female clerks more than doubled to 59.6 per cent of clerks. By 1981, they accounted for 77.7 per cent, over 2.3 million (nearly double again) and comprised the largest single category of female employment. In West Germany, the number employed in offices and the Civil Service increased two and a half times between 1950 and 1980, to become 55.9 per cent of all women workers. French *employées* rose from 52.8 per cent in 1954 to 60.8 per cent in 1968, and from 16.3 per cent of the female workforce to 25.8 per cent in those fourteen years. In Dutch manufacturing in 1991, 32 per cent of female workers had clerical jobs. Rapid growth not only conclusively altered the shape of female work, but was a contributory factor to the overall shift towards a salaried labour force as a whole. The clerical workforce reflected changes in the economy, but also echoed aspects of gender which preceded the war, and indeed which have recurred throughout this study. Secretarial work was clearly a feminine occupation from the early days of the typewriter, and showed no significant change. Over 96 per cent of secretaries were female in West Germany, Britain and France. Women increased, even in sectors like finance which had been difficult to enter in the days before the First World War, and in public administration and defence. However, gendered notions of industries still played a part. In Britain, for example, in 1961, male clerks predominated over women in manufacturing (52 per cent), but female clerks dominated in textiles (62 per cent) where a high proportion of female manual workers also worked.[17]

Middle-class women's need for paid work coupled with demands for better access to education provided the impetus and means to professionalize some of women's traditional roles and to generate access to male-dominated professions. Women recognized the potential for turning familiar activities into paid work. For example, 'they did not view becoming a professional social worker as a radical departure from acceptable women's roles. Rather they believed it was an extension of their concerns and duties as wives and mothers.'[18] By their very character most professions operated by segregated, stratified and exclusive access routes. Education was one key, but status and cultural tradition were others. Gender was another. The need to preserve exclusivity contributed to restrictions on women entering many professional fields.

Increasing formality of professions meant that women first had to obtain the right to higher education, then access to professional training and qualifications. Access to higher education and to the same education as males was the first step. British higher education admitted women to degrees slowly, but progressively after the University of London broke the barrier in 1877, the last being Cambridge in 1946. However, after the Robbins Report in 1963, just over 7 per cent of girls entered higher education and the assumption was 'that for the majority of girls the strictly academic education suitable for boys was wholly inappropriate'. Only by 1994 were half of British higher-education entrants female. The fact that mature entrants comprised over half of all students suggests the level of failure of the system over previous years. In France, the Sorbonne refused entry up to 1880 and equal access was denied to women until pressure for the Baccalauréat succeeded in 1924. French women also struggled to gain access to the prestigious and professional training at the *Grandes Ecoles*, because preparation was not provided, unofficial quotas operated and teachers directed the best girls towards 'suitable' work in teaching. Only after the Second World War were women grudgingly accepted as part of professional elites, but even in the 1960s two *Grandes Ecoles* were still closed to women, and only handfuls attended the others. They gained the right to matriculate at German universities only after 1906. Women's claims for better work coupled with demands for appropriate education were, as Albisetti says, 'more than just a call for expanded job opportunities; it was an assertion that women could handle and should have access to the elite courses of education that prepared for these careers'.[19]

Educational achievement opened doors, but was not the solution. Lack of higher-level attainment is testament to the role that specific structural and cultural barriers played. Suzanne Borel made a highly publicized entry to the French Diplomatic Service in 1931 as the 'first woman to pass the foreign office exam', but was not allowed to undertake consular duties abroad 'on account of having no political rights'. Borel reflected, 'Few women are better placed than I to appreciate the cunning, often combined with treachery and persistence, employed by men to place obstacles in the path of those unfortunate women who stray from the beaten track.' Not until recognition of women as citizens in 1945 were they eligible for foreign postings. Yet, two qualified women were told, 'You can come to us if you like but you will never be posted abroad.' This was in 1952. Indeed, very few women made it to real top jobs in France until after 1968. Crompton and Sanderson also suggest that the goalposts changed. That is, wide availability of academic qualifications devalued them as access routes to professions. In France by 1964 more women were obtaining degrees, but found that they were not worth as much, and that their studies ill-fitted them for the job market. Indeed, recent concentration in Britain on validating vocational credentials, either as part of a first degree or as a postgraduate qualification, have helped retain the notion of a 'licence' to practise, and fostered the image of professional–client relationship.[20]

Specific prohibitions against female admission to professions were powerful deterrents, more robust than customary gendered practices in other fields of work. Dame Margaret Booth described the near entry of the first woman to Britain's Bar: 'In 1903 Gray's Inn, having admitted Bertha Cave to its Honourable Society, probably by mistake, they refused to call her to the Bar simply because she was a woman.' Male monopoly was not broken until 1922. In France, the first woman lawyer qualified in 1890, but was prevented from practising at the Bar until 1900. The profession remained largely male by statute, as reported by Gabrielle Letellier in 1934, because 'men alone could aspire to be judges and magistrates in most courts, solicitors, attorneys, clerks to the court or recorders'. In Germany, Bayern was the first region (in 1912) to allow women to take state exams, but barred them from traineeships. Such prohibitions were not unique, and regulations of professional bodies were often called into play to prevent women's entry once they obtained requisite credentials. In France, Reynolds cited the difficulty with which women acquired private medical practice, so that 'a disproportionate number of women doctors were obliged to seek posts in the expanding public health sector'. Formal obstacles were strewn in their path. '"Externships" were easier to find than "internships" and the latter were long jealously guarded by closing them to women.' Similar struggles were fought in pharmacy, but in 1879, at their third attempt, two women, Isabella Skinner Clarke and Rose Coombes Minshall were admitted to the Pharmaceutical Society on 'considerations of natural justice'. Indeed, the debate focused on the Charter which did not include the male personal pronoun. In a similar case regarding accountancy, the Charter did allow exclusion.[21]

Deeply ingrained factors of culture including language provided the third barrier to women in gaining admission to, and then status in, professional fields. Elizabeth Russell, Professor of Social Medicine at Aberdeen University, explained women's position within the medical profession:

> First is the pattern of attitudes to and expected roles of women in society in general: the nineteenth century 'shock horror' that women could be present at anatomy lectures, the still present attitude that women are not physically strong enough to be surgeons, and above all the view that women should put child-rearing before careers and that therefore, for the sake of the family, the irregular and excessive hours of medical training make it an inappropriate career for women. It would not be an exaggeration to say that until recently women in medicine, as in most other professions, have been tolerated with con-descension rather than welcomed with open arms – in the professional sense.
>
> The second factor has been less overt over the century, but nonethe-less real; it is the threat that women posed in medicine, as elsewhere, to the employment and financial prospects of men. The only times before 1975 that women were admitted to medical schools in in-creased numbers were during the two world wars – and the percent-age of entrants who were women dropped rapidly thereafter.[22]

Geyer-Kordesh and Ferguson argue that women's aims 'involve other values and wider considerations for women's work than the single-minded focus of coming out on top'. Also, the drive for equality was fought on men's terms and resulted in no breakthrough to top jobs, nor a tradition of top-level female role models. Nor did they achieve restructuring which would allow a more open and diversified profession accommodating other objectives than those of white middle-class males.[23] Professional language further imbeds cultural percep-tions. When Elizabeth Butler-Schloss was appointed to the British Court of Appeal in 1988, law did not allow her to be referred to as Lady Justice, so

> Counsel addressing the Court were therefore driven to refer to her as 'My Lady, Lord Justice Butler-Schloss.' On 25 April 1994, The Master of the Rolls, Sir Thomas Bingham concluded that 'This usage is plainly absurd.' Accordingly . . . Dame Elizabeth, as a matter of prac-tice, is now known as 'Lady Justice' and in due course the Statute will be amended.[24]

Thus perceptions of what it meant to be female were joined with the narrow-ness and protectiveness of traditionally male professions to restrict not only women's entry in the first place, but their movement within them. Duchen argues the liberal professions were not liberal; they were hostile bastions of

243

reaction. It was the same in Germany: 'In a society where most lawyers were civil servants and most upper level civil servants were lawyers, even strong supporters of increased employment opportunities for women had great difficulty imagining them in legal careers.' As Booth shows, the professional world remains very masculine, and the public perception is still of a man: 'many aspects of the legal profession so closely resemble an eccentric male club that it can be difficult for women to cope with it'.[25]

Some professions became female dominated and stereotyped as women's work, such as teaching, nursing, social work and librarianship. The predominance of women has implications for the status of a profession, pay, conditions, and its relationship to allied workers. Initially these occupations provided access to 'good' jobs and careers for women. They drew from the lower middle class, and were promoted as socially and morally acceptable careers for young women. As largely female professions, however, they did not gain the status, or pay, of old liberal professions, or even newer male professions such as engineering or accountancy. Teaching and nursing were 'traditional' areas of women's influence, usually untrained, often unrecognized and closely related to persistent views of women's 'natural' caring and mothering role. Both were also associated with female clerical orders. During the period, they developed as fully defined professions with specific recruitment and training, a career path, unions and organs of expression.[26] A fundamental difference between them was the development of divergent gendered hierarchical structures.

Nurses became positioned separately from but as auxiliaries to doctors. As Leroux-Hugon explained, the medical discourse which developed in France, akin to that in other countries, assigned women a place as collaborators, dedicated and competent assistants, but with a belief that initiative taken without medical backing was dangerous. The nurse–doctor relationship could be described as one of care by nurses, cure by doctors. The doctor's role was one of diagnosis, as Gamarnikow puts it, 'monopolising the initial intervention which designates the patient *qua* patient'. As the doctor's role became more clearly diagnostic, nurses undertook more duties which by virtue of their transfer to women became devalued. The ambivalence in their position was perpetuated by perceptions of nurses as caring creatures at the same time as their role and duties expanded, and their increasing organization and training led them to professionalization. As Gamarnikow writes, 'The female dominance of the nursing profession and the male dominance of medicine are of obvious relevance to their situation, the implications of which more or less obtain in the "anomalous" instances of women doctors and, particularly, male nurses.'[27] Thus despite the aims of nursing to establish a single stratified profession, and notwithstanding their clear expertise, the subordination of nursing to medicine and its gendered character left nurses in a devalued, low-status and poorly paid profession.

Teaching, in contrast, was not initially dominated by women, and in higher education, they were virtually non-existent. Since training systems introduced with compulsory schooling were open to women, it might have been an opportunity for parity with men. In the event, vertical segregation existed from the outset, with men gaining greater access to training, certification, better pay and higher-status positions. In addition there was overt discrimination in hiring practices, as in Glasgow in the interwar period where 'most male applicants were offered appointments while only a proportion of female applicants were considered'. Bradley argues this was primarily the result of two views of teaching which assign men and women different attributes as teachers. Women were associated with childcare so that care of children's education was ascribed to women. Academic concern with acquisition and transmission of specialized knowledge was fostered by male universities. Men were thus cast as 'academics' and women as 'carers', assigning women to primary teaching and men to secondary levels and academic subjects. Transmission of gendered culture also permeated the system. The National Association of Schoolmasters (NAS) argued that the 'crucial part of the elementary schooling process was to instil gender characteristics, that is to say masculinity and femininity into pupils. They were especially anxious that boys should be taught to be men.' Vertical segregation was fostered by views of men as supervisors; the image of the *paterfamilias* was not far away. In 1926 the NAS cheered a resolution 'declaring opposition to any assistant master serving under a headmistress', others claiming it was 'impossible for a man to serve under a woman and retain his self respect and manhood'.[28]

The small National Association of Women Teachers challenged the NAS, arguing that the emphasis on masculinity and femininity should be broken down, and girls' needs should be given more consideration. Committed women like these strove to put teaching on a professional footing for women, shifting it away from a 'moral vocation for which little material reward was expected'. Sarah Burstall, Headmistress of Manchester High School for Girls, claimed 'parents have to realize that the teacher is an expert professional and is therefore entitled to the deference shown to the skilled professional opinion of the doctor, lawyer or architect'. Such women probably prevented teaching from falling into the same trap as nursing, while an influx of middle-class women helped to upgrade it. Nevertheless, despite equal pay and grades, vertical segregation at all levels persists. For example, in 1993 in England and Wales, 82 per cent of primary teachers were women but only 16 per cent of women held headships or deputy headships. However, while 18 per cent of primary teachers were men, 57 per cent were heads or deputy heads. In higher education, the differential was even more pronounced. In Imperial Germany no woman obtained a university chair; in 1934 there were only five university professors in France. In the late 1960s only 9 per cent of full-time academic staff in British universities were women and by 1992–93, still only 22 per cent, with women concentrated in lower grades, only 5 per cent of professors and 11 per cent of readers and senior lecturers.[29] Thus, despite different structures and developmental routes, the effect in nursing and teaching was similar in that women are less likely to attain high rank and status vis-à-vis men.

WOMEN AS WORKERS

Repeatedly historians cite the emergence of the service sector, the complexity of the economy, and the widening sphere of government as key factors in the employment of women in white-collar work throughout Europe. Two features contributed to this perception: gradual change in attitudes towards hiring women, promoted by women actively arguing the case for middle-class females; and educational improvements which increased availability of qualified women. Better education also meant that some were unprepared to become seamstresses and domestics. A certain educational standard was important in white-bloused work, of course, although growth took place mainly in routine tasks. Yet, this was not the whole truth. Undoubtedly, gender contributed heavily to hiring women, and helped determine specifically the kind of work they did. Concerns about male staffing, wages and promotion structure pushed employers to think creatively. Hiring women seemed the answer. Employers could limit the number of men, and continue to offer the career path they expected. Women could be kept in lower-paid jobs with no career route. Instead of hiring boys who were released when they came of age as many firms did, the Prudential employed women to work at the lower end of the scale, 'thus preserving the male career structure'. The practice was followed in banks, insurance companies, shipping firms and large merchant houses from the 1870s, where 'both the companies and the male employees profited from this; hiring an increasing number of low paid women for menial work saved expenses and kept the male clerks in good mood because the more interesting and better paid work became their exclusive domain'. Similarly, the Union Marine Insurance Company wished to pay male underwriters well to prevent them being poached, so, to keep staff costs down, hired women typists from 1905. Specialization also played a part. 'Scientific management', centralization and striving towards increased efficiency created pockets of routinized work which could be seen as 'natural' work for women.[30]

Gender and sex were potent reasons for hiring female shop assistants. Employers played not only on female 'glamour, luxury and charm', but on women knowing what other women wanted:

> The other reason for the increased temptation to spend money is the large numbers of women which are now employed. Women . . . understand so much more readily what other women want; they can enter into the little troubles of their customers; they can fathom the agony of despair as to the arrangement of colours, the alternative trimmings, the duration of a fashion, the depths of a woman's purse,

and, more important than all, the question of the becomingness of a dress . . . to the wearer.[31]

The importance of women as sellers to women was reflected in the relatively high ratio of women senior staff by the interwar period. For example, at Fenwicks in 1932, twenty-eight of forty-seven top managers were women. Femininity was also closely linked to a sense of propriety, and a Dundee draper told Parliament, 'A great deal more of the goods are made up now though than they used to be, and it is much more suitable for females to sell made-up garments to ladies than for males.' It was argued in offices 'where the staff is mixed, the female clerks will raise the tone of the whole staff'. They also impressed employers with their personal qualities of 'politeness', sobriety and even a 'talent for calculation'. Despite low wages, assistants were expected to dress attractively and fashionably. According to a young woman in a Russian pastry shop, 'The bosses want only good-looking girls . . . Most shop girls are from seventeen to twenty years old, and a girl over thirty can very seldom be encountered, and then never in shops on the main streets.'[32] The close link between femininity, glamour and female attractiveness is apparent, so that youth and physical beauty became more important than intelligence or expertise.

Clearly women's perceived 'work culture' was a central consideration. They were seen as more docile, quiescent, less likely to become politically active, less likely to seek promotion and willing to accept lower wages. The 'tradition' of women's wages being lower than men's has been evident throughout this book, so it is no wonder that it was accepted as a truism by employers. They were also engaging a 'new' workforce, one without any real work culture behind them. Middle-class women did not bring a sense of the workplace with them, nor did they have the customs of clerking as part of their cultural tradition. In this sense they were 'green' workers. The British Treasury, for example, claimed women were better qualified, cheaper, less experienced, and supposedly less interested in trade union activities. A Post Office official echoed this view: 'They are also less disposed than men to combine for the purpose of extorting higher wages, and this is by no means an unimportant matter.' Similarly, after the Paris shopworkers' strikes of 1869, employers responded by hiring women in numbers for the first time who were described as docile, 'lacking in tradition' and less eager to strike.[33] They were also not expected to have a career, but to work for a short time and leave on marriage. Thus a lack of responsibility and promotion was justified.

Underlying employer assumptions were ideas about gender and their construction of the female. For example, when women were first hired, an International Telegraph Company employee argued that he was 'perfectly satisfied that the girls are not only more teachable, more attentive, and quicker-eyed than the men clerks formerly employed, but also . . . more trustworthy, more easily managed, and . . . sooner satisfied with lower wages'. Many claimed females were better suited temperamentally to routine clerical work, they worked harder and with more interest in their work than 'youths whose minds are still full of football and cricket'. However, the continual reference to lower wages echoes Crompton and Mann's suggestion that emphasis on feminine characteristics may have been 'mere glosses for their cheapness'.[34] Clearly notions of the feminine and the character of women's work came together with the need for more staff and a need to protect the male's position in the workplace to predispose employers to hire women.

Significantly, women were proactive in claiming white-collar work. The British Society for Promoting the Employment of Women and the Dutch women's movement demanded better training and jobs for middle-class women from the 1860s. The Women's Educational Association of Leipzig similarly organized to educate middle-class women for work. The British Society scored their greatest success placing women in offices: in 1892–93, 430 of 619 temporary posts obtained were clerical. In *Hilda van Suylenburg*, 'the most successful Dutch feminist novel', the debate on men's and women's work focused on office work, depicted as attractive and liberating for women. As such it was seen as an occupation worth fighting for. Careers guides similarly advocated professions and office work as 'suitable' and as a means of independence, such as Paquet-Mille's *Nouveau guide pratique des jeunes filles dans le choix d'une profession* (New Practical Guide for Girls in the Choice of a Profession), 1891. The Dutch guide, *Wat kan mijne dochter worden?* (What Can my Daughter Do?), 1878, listed stenography, postal service and telegraph operator as appropriate occupations, though the latter was not formally open to women. This guide, like *Lucratieve betrekkingen voor vrouwen uit den beschaafden stand* (Lucrative Jobs for Women from Civilized Classes), 1884, by Catharina Alberdingk Thijm, centred on the struggle to extend clerical jobs to women by opening training and competitive exams. Feminists also claimed typewriting. As new work, it avoided competition with men and held promise, since educated and trained middle-class women were 'eager to seize the opportunity of earning a livelihood which is neither degrading to self-respect nor trying to their physical powers'. It is significant that women perceived clerking as a viable option, that they were not simply 'recruited' or 'introduced' but that many voices claimed white-collar work for women at a time when the workplace was undergoing radical expansion and redefinition. That they specifically identified 'new' areas of work, such as typing, as a route to better jobs is also pertinent. By 1912, 17 per cent of the typists employed by the British Civil Service between 1894 and 1906 had left to work in private firms, while Collet's survey showed that 23 per cent of ordinary typists in private firms earned more than the maximum for the Civil Service.[35]

For many working-class girls, shopwork represented a step up while for the middle classes it signified respectable work: 'They were part of the store's public image, and its class and reputation was also theirs.' For example, the upmarket Plummer Rodis store in Folkestone sacked a clerk because 'nice

Plummer's girls did not allow themselves to be seen in such a place as a public skating rink'. Young women in Stirling valued shopwork over domestic service, 'I didnae like [domestic service] much, so I moved on – to better things I hope. I went to the grocer shop as a message girl, that was ten shillings a week.' Retail was popular because it was perceived as skilled, requiring training. Trainee drapery assistants had to learn the technical skills of alterations as well as the personal skills needed to serve customers. The sense of pride comes out: 'You were dying to serve customers . . . but it was your job. You were being trained.' Vocational advisers in Weimar Germany reported that ever more girls wanted to become clerical workers or shop assistants, and that shop assistants regarded themselves as 'a cut above' factory workers who, 'did not know how to behave'. Woodward's study of British department stores in the 1950s demonstrated the common attraction of store reputation and women's awareness of status. The study also reveals that assistants reflected high self-esteem and self-appreciation of their value to employers. Such attitudes enhanced a woman's confidence and opportunities, which were mirrored in high turnover rates. There were clear differences between the motives of young unmarried and married women and older and single, widowed or divorced women. The former were relatively uninterested in careers, while the latter, besides economic need, were highly motivated and more career orientated. This group was more likely to aspire to and gain senior sales positions, occasionally becoming buyers.[36]

Clerks and secretaries regarded themselves as above shop assistants, because their work was more worthwhile and better remunerated. Social attributes and prestige of clerical work were highly valued. Such attractions consequently created a large, willing, cheap labour force. It was initially perceived as good work with good prospects, and there were far more applicants than jobs. For example, 5,000 applied for 20–25 posts at the Banque de France, while British Post Office posts were regularly oversubscribed. In 1874, 700 candidates applied for 5 women clerk positions; in 1901, when more opportunities existed, there were still 329 applicants for 25 posts. Women saw clerical work as an outlet for their abilities and skills with the advantages of a safe job, and for some, a career with a pension. The importance of cachet and status attracted many women despite its routine and boring character. It looked like liberation, opportunity and independence. A low-grade option for men, it was a positive step for women. For women workers anxious about respectability, strict discipline and sexually segregated employment were positive features, while oral evidence shows that considerable pride was taken in their work.[37]

A shift in attitudes took place early in the twentieth century, when it was clear that women were not allowed equal access to pay, or to the most interesting work, and were not given opportunities to utilize their intelligence. As Zerner points out, 'recruitment to office work was not the point of departure for a rise in society, but on the contrary it was its end point . . . The female office *employée* . . . is now as distanced from the management as she believes herself to be from the workers.' Most women clerks recognized that their position was contextualized by notions of inferiority, with resulting low pay, dull work and patronizing interference. For British female civil servants, the white-collar sector held promise without challenging their ability: 'what I really wanted was to be an analytical chemist, but to do that you had to take a job at a very low salary and study in your spare time, and I thought it was about time I earned some money, so I entered the Civil Service exam'.[38] Women responded to their sense of injustice by developing strategies to gain better access to interesting work and promotions. As early as 1889, the Aid Association for Female Salaried Employees in Commerce and Trade was formed in Berlin, recruiting 600 members in four months. Typists in the British Civil Service demanded a more fluid approach to postings and gradings, arguing for the complexity and value of their work. In 1903, rates of pay and treatment by the National Union of Clerks (male) led to the formation of the Association of Women Clerks and Secretaries. In the interwar period, they, like their sisters in the *PTT*, argued that women and men should be recruited by the same procedures, to the same grades, with the same opportunities for promotion and the same financial rewards. 'In large measure women . . . accepted the idea of "a woman's job and a woman's rate", just as they accepted responsibility for home and family. But, they did not necessarily also accept the low value accorded their work – either in the workplace or at home.' Women's clerical work remained contested by employers, unions and governments, while many women saw themselves as defining 'women's freedom to labour'. The most rehearsed argument against their employment was men's unemployment, since men as breadwinners were seen as having a right to work, and employers were therefore justified in limiting women to specific 'female' jobs, while assuming that men were suitable for office work.[39] At the same time the policy of many employers was precisely to utilize the skills and willingness of the female workforce to resolve problems of staffing and cost.

That sales and office work grew as domestic service declined was no accident, but they did not involve the same absolute cohort of females. The attractions of shop work led to a widely mixed social grouping, 'the daughters of artisans, of agricultural labourers, of skilled mechanics, of struggling and prosperous shopkeepers, of clerks and professional men'. However, urban and rural women had different choices. While servants were largely rural, white-blouse workers were far more likely to be urban, where their knowledge and confidence in the urban setting contributed to their desire for and usefulness in clerical work. Notably, servants started work younger than most clerks, who required education and poise. There were important constraints of class and education which shaped the route a young woman could take. The first female clerical office workers, factory inspectors and professionals tended to be drawn from middle-class families, often from high echelons, of a good educational standard, usually higher than men in similar positions. They were able to gain posts partly for socio-economic reasons and partly because they offered the correct educational and social profile to employers. In this respect they were sig-nificantly different from servants, factory girls and even sales assistants. Sales assistants were likely to be modestly educated, and in Britain and France were drawn from lower middle-class and even working-class girls.[40] Girls served a training period and could expect to assist with cleaning the shop, and some-times the home of the shopkeeper, tidying shelves and so on, tasks not far removed from the duties of servants. For example,

> I had to come to Edinburgh to get a job and I got a job in a fruit shop and I lived in and I helped the lady who owned the fruit shop in the house, and I used to go down and I used to have to help her in the shop after that.[41]

Gradually the educational and social structure of white-blouse work became more complex. It was unusual in requiring education beyond elementary level, though professions put even more educational demands on applicants. Female civil servants increasingly pushed against occupational structures which pre-vented their advancement, presenting themselves as from the same class back-ground and holding the same educational qualifications as men in administrative grades, often with better pass levels. As demand increased, more women of other classes, with less education, began to enter. In the Civil Service, open competitive examinations became more usual than patronage, opening the door to more females from lower classes. Improving education also enabled more young women to compete for available posts. Similarly, sales assistants increasingly were drawn from young women at all levels, and Lockwood reflects that by 1900 in Britain they were drawn from the same groups as domestic servants, dressmakers and even factories.[42]

THE WORK EXPERIENCE

White-blouse work was, of course, extremely variable, including jobs at the low end of status and pay as well as those at the pinnacle of professional work. From the first, most white-blouse work was better paid than other women's, and most jobs were salaried, especially in offices and professions, rather than waged. Workers saw this as a mark of distinction and status, so even when they received less than factory women, the gentility and status of the job were com-pensations. Salaries, however, meant that they were not paid for overtime which was rife. Some had pensions from the outset, though in most firms these were gained only after a case was made. Since employers expected women to stay only a short time, pensions seemed ridiculous. The Bank of England offered them to women at age fifty or if they retired due to ill health but the Civil Service resisted. Notably, of 89 women hired between 1894 and 1907, 59 were still in service; most left for marriage. Nevertheless, comparing women in

251

offices, shops and professions with their male peers, the similarities in women's experience becomes apparent. On balance they were paid less and had lower-status work than men, and both issues continue to exercise feminists and other women today.

McBride calculated that women in department stores earned well in comparison to other female workers. The average store worker earned 75 francs per week while a woman in industry earned only 75 francs a month. However, the range in female salaries is apparent when a department store is compared to a small shop. Miller estimated an annual female salary of 3,000 francs per year at the Bon Marché, twice the best in a small shop. Saleswomen also earned less than office workers. German firms paid different rates depending on their perception of a worker's need: women in families were paid less than those living independently. German male clerical workers earned 1,941 marks on average and females 997 marks in 1913, and Weimar wage agreements for commercial workers stipulated women's pay should be 10 to 25 per cent lower than men's, because men had more clothing and living costs, since women could sew and cook! While this practice acknowledged the difficulties of surviving on such wages, it assumed that girls living at home worked for 'pin money'.[43] Janet Hogarth, a supervisor at the Bank of England, summed up the experience of white-blouse workers across Europe:

> Thirty shillings after several years' experience was considered a good rate of pay. Yet, allowing for her expenses in fares and food out, it barely sufficed to keep a girl of good middle-class origin and decent standard of living in one of the smaller hostels or boarding houses . . . Nothing to speak of was left for clothes, less than nothing for recreation. In fact, though it might mean comfortable pocket-money for daughters living at home, even when they contributed to home expenses, it was bare subsistence and nothing more to a girl on her own.[44]

In the interwar period, over half of the female members of the German Union of Female Retail and Office Staff under twenty-five earned a maximum of 100 marks per month, which after national insurance put them below the poverty line. The staff list of John Lewis (London) in 1931 confirms a gendered pattern of pay. Seventy-two per cent of females earned £3 or less per week, while only 27 per cent of males did; 20 per cent of the males earned £6 per week or more, but only 5.5 per cent of females did. Zimmeck estimates that female wages in Britain were 25 to 50 per cent lower than men's in comparable work, and that highly experienced women earned less than male juniors in the same firms. Thus, the notion of the family wage for men also permeated white-collar work. Equal pay for equal work was not claimed until very late in the nineteenth century and even then it was forestalled by segregated pay and promotion scales which permeated white-collar structures.[45]

Hours of work also show important divergence. Office workers gained, since most worked eight hours, except during inventory or rush periods. Women at Barings Bank, Pearl Assurance and the Prudential worked from 10 a.m. to 5 p.m. with an hour for lunch, and had twenty-four days' annual leave after 1901. *Dames employées* in France worked fewer hours than most salaried women, seven to eight hours a day, but split by shifts. Shopworkers' hours were far more variable, and longer than they appeared since they had to come in early and stay after shops closed to sort stock and make things ready for morning, while eight or ten o'clock closing was common, with small shops far likelier to close late and open early. However, in Britain by the 1880s, and in France by 1901, many large stores closed by 7 p.m., some claiming that long hours were not profitable. Also hours may have been balanced against employees' goodwill and public opinion.[46]

Working arrangements were strictly segregated for some time. Indeed, segregation was welcomed by many women as preservation of respectability, which helped make work appropriate for middle-class women. At the Prudential and Pearl insurance companies, women entered and left by separate entrances, and worked different hours from men so as not to encounter them arriving or leaving. In department stores where employees were fed, dining rooms were strictly segregated. When the Bon Marché opened offices to women in 1899, they too were in a separate bureau, as were women in telegraph offices. The rationale was not only morality, since division of labour was easier to maintain if the sexes were separated. Paternalism led to close control and supervision. Many women were fed in-house, enjoined to eat in silence, often locked into the dining room, conversation regulated, and prevented from leaving the store during working hours. Breach of strict rules was punished by fines or dismissals. Examples included talking, lateness, wearing flowers, or allowing customers to get away without buying. Russian women reported bullying and abuse, while a Berlinerin reported being slapped by a warehouse chief for leaving stock disordered. Her employer replied 'she probably deserved it'. Siemens demanded employees take no second job, including voluntary work, and not marry or move house without notification. The Bon Marché sacked a woman because 'Good employee. Fired because we learned that she was living in marital fashion and not with her parents.' Women usually wore distinctive dress, sometimes a uniform. In Paris, the general rule was black silk.[47] One English girl described a small shop:

> I mean, he wanted to rule your life . . . If he knew I was going any-where, he'd find me all sorts of jobs . . . I was invited to the Friends' School Christmas Party, and this was considered a great honour . . . He decided after tea that we would start packing currants, . . . The shop officially closed at seven but he didn't think I should go . . . He insisted on me wearing black stockings. I mean absolutely ridiculous . . . he bought me some, didn't reckon anything to these silk stockings.[48]

Paternalism meant that benefits often cost workers in interference and control over private lives. In other cases, women were simply 'less eligible', predicated on their perceived inferiority. For example, a survey in 1901 in London found that roughly half of fifty-five offices had no separate lavatory facilities for women. In the German Civil Service, though hours were the same as men's, women had no holidays and had to pay for replacements at an exorbitant rate if they were ill.[49] The importance of a contented and disciplined workforce was recognized by some employers, and McBride argues this is why paternal practices continued long after size of operations had destroyed traditional relationships. A range of 'good practices' was introduced by large stores, including savings plans, provident funds, vacation homes for employees by the Louvre, hospitals, doctor's care, sports grounds and other recreational facilities and day nurseries. Both the Samaritaine and the *PTT* introduced crèches. The *PTT* also introduced thirty-five days' maternity leave after 1903. By the First World War many salaried staff had paid holidays and commission was replaced by staff discounts.

Reform movements attempted to alter conditions, but despite attempts to include shops and offices in factory and workshop statutes, little legislation affected employees until the beginning of the twentieth century. The pressure on early closing was organized by female consumers, and implementation was largely voluntary. The ten-hour maximum day for women was in effect in the Parisian department stores by the turn of the century, but legislation did not apply in Britain until 1911. As late as the 1930s, in Britain, legislation only required definite meal times, a weekly half-day holiday and a seventy-four hour week for those under eighteen years old. There is evidence that female staff resisted reform because they feared it would exclude them from shift work and therefore from access to the workplace altogether. Enforcement was ineffectual in many instances, since there were not enough inspectors. One of the more interesting campaigns was the movement to provide seating, and in Germany, France and Britain it enlisted female customers. In Berlin it achieved an Ordinance in 1896 and an amendment to the industrial code in 1900. In 1899, the British Shops Act required provision of one seat for every three female assistants. However, there is extensive evidence that employers complied with the letter of the law, but fined employees if they sat on the chairs.[50]

SKILL, STATUS AND SEGREGATION

Capitalist expansion is charged with creating specialization which led to fragmented, routinized and potentially deskilled work in the white-collar sector. In some areas, a limited range of specific skills was needed, while quite complex understanding and skill was required by some grades and professions. Arguably, work was 'degraded' and not 'deskilled' because women did it. As argued earlier, the question of skill cannot be separated from status, nor from gender. Specialization and division of tasks had an impact on both. Within new hierarchies, a managerial class of white-collar workers in business and Civil Service emerged who saw themselves belonging to the ranks of professionals. Specialization helped to solidify these hierarchies, making promotion between levels increasingly difficult. Similar dichotomies existed in teaching and medicine, as well as other professions. Tasks and ranks became more closely associated with different levels of education, and because of limited on-the-job training, bridging gaps became more difficult. These changes undermined the prestige associated with the older-style clerk by eroding the special position, educational advantage, and ultimately the chance of reaching the pinnacle of an organization, or becoming an independent businessman. Since rationalization and creation of the white-collar workforce happened together, causal links are not transparent.[51] Thus as white-blouse women workers became more ubiquitous, issues of gender reflected a number of perceived threats to males which in reality emanated from a complex set of shifts in the workplace of the 'traditional' clerk or professional man.

White-collar work was contested on two levels, first, what was appropriate for women to do to retain their gentility with regard to mixing with men and other undesirables, and whether to work or not; and second, what abilities and character women had and what they were capable of. Both proponents and opponents of women clerks engaged with issues of gender and class. Cultural constraints were difficult for women and feminists to overcome, and to some extent they used them to claim white-collar work for women. For example, the *English Woman's Journal* posed 'that in several departments of government young women might be employed as clerks, especially to copy and draught . . . As, however, it would not answer to mix up clerks of both sexes, there should of course be apartments for each.'[52] Three key principles emerged:

1   only unmarried women should work outside the home;
2   young women should not work with or mix with men at work;
3   young women should be supervised by older women.

Segregation was key. Since it was inappropriate in principle for women to work, those that did so broke out of their allotted domain. Segregation, at least, made them invisible, and, it was argued, preserved their respectability. It was reluctantly accepted that some middle-class women needed income, but the money and the work that created it was never intended to become more desirable than their rightful place. Segregation also addressed the second problem which was preservation of the male clerical culture. It mattered less whether the work done by each sex was different, but segregation allowed there to be no comparison and permitted preservation of male hierarchies and promotion routes.[53]

The coherence of views on women's place confirmed that work should be suitable to their delicacy and to their ability. Thus, in 1876, the *International*

255

Postal Union warned 'immediate contact with the public mass . . . was irreconcilable with a woman's vocation'. A careful decision placing women in urban post offices in France meant they were not located in working-class areas, nor near railway stations, which were unsuitable for women's 'naturally high-strung' nature. Gender was invoked to women's disadvantage in an equal-pay dispute centring on Norwegian women telegraphers in 1898. The director reported to parliament that women were less competent and physically weaker than men, particularly when operating more complicated equipment and in technical work. His statement was made in the context that women had equal training, equal work loads and on the whole better marks on training courses. An anonymous female telegrapher retorted, 'The primary reason why female telegraphers manifest little interest in the technical aspects of their work is that our lords and masters, men, have since time immemorial regarded themselves as the only ones competent in this field.' In Britain, the MacDonnell Commission on the Civil Service recommended in 1914, confirmed by the Gladstone Commission (1918), that women continue to be recruited on separate lines, because in 'powers of sustained work, in continuity of service, in adaptability to varying service conditions, the advantage lay with men'. It is clear that women's clerical work was highly politicized.[54]

Technology operated alongside economic and social changes to provide opportunities for women in white-collar work. New work patterns, such as the division of labour, were prompted by the telegraph, typewriter, telephone, cash register and 'point of sale' systems. Initially, typing was gender free, as was shorthand, but 'men steered clear of being labelled shorthand typists, fearful of becoming mere letter-writing machines'. Women, in contrast, eagerly became typists. Indeed, the term 'typewriter' was synonymous with the machine and the female operator.[55] Importantly, as Zimmeck has pointed out, 'women were neither the first choice nor the "natural" candidates for employment on typewriting duties'. Conflicting views of 'appropriateness' and market value as well as tensions inherent in the Civil Service meant that men, boys, women and girls coexisted as a copying and typing force. Gendered views prompted departments to assume 'that men typists . . . would be failures', boys tended to engage in 'all sorts of merry japes', required training and sought promotion at the first opportunity, so departments voiced a pronounced preference for women, whose promotion prospects were of no concern. Thus it was not the typewriter but gendered images of work which gave women an opening.[56] Other factors linked women with typewriters from an early stage. Many employers relied on firms which provided typewriters together with trained operators, as legal stationers had supplied copyists. Similarly, women could buy a machine and hire out their services. Miss Cliston from Liverpool was 'the pioneer of this kind of work for women', opening 'the first type-writer office', and from 1892 a similar firm existed in Amsterdam, offering courses in stenography and typing. Jo Brouwer explained,

Now . . . I move my typewriter hither and thither, now here for a short time, now there for a somewhat longer time and on and off at my own office, in order to relieve people of a mass of paperwork . . . Typewriting is a job admirably suited to ladies.[57]

De Haan points out 'this way of organizing the work . . . may have helped people 'to get used' to women in offices'. Davin thus conjured the image of the typewriter 'as Trojan Horse, [so that] many a city sanctum was invaded by females, and the normal system of controlling entrance to clerical posts by advertisements, interviews and references was completely bypassed'.[58] Certainly, the typewriter, and indeed other technology, was relevant to women entering the office, and while not the cause, women did, for better or worse, claim it and the skill associated with it.

White-blouse work changed significantly after the Second World War, largely due to the rapid development of computers. Initially they were seen either as saviours or as harbingers of doom. Proponents argued that they would remove 'drudgery' and boredom, allowing workers to take more control and to have more time for administration, while opponents saw them as deskilling work, and potentially replacing workers. The related emphasis on Taylorism and an urge to apply scientific principles to the office were seen by many as leading to further routinization and degradation of work. From the 1980s, however, a more optimistic view began to emerge from specific case studies. Research in Norway, for example, suggested the impact had not been as dramatic as foreseen and identified no relationship between computerization and loss of employment. Crompton and Jones confirmed that deskilling depends on a broader and longer process of rationalization, and may not be directly related to computerization itself.[59]

The effect of technical change seems to depend on the type of workplace into which it is introduced and the way it is implemented. In large firms where typing pools were the norm, it tended to intensify work and impose more restrictions and less variety. In Bremen, despite promises of upgraded tasks and of splitting up typing pools, after three years 'hardly any changes had been planned or carried out in the organizational structure . . . hardly any of the typing pools had been reorganized into an upgraded mixed work office. The work contents of the great majority of typists had not changed at all.' In contrast, Tijdens identified the positive influence of the microcomputer as opposed to earlier systems based on terminals linked to central mainframes, which enhanced women's control of their work and led to greater access to the technology of the new office. Though only a third were involved in making decisions about the hardware and software purchase, this was greater than pessimists predicted. However, Tijdens indicated that the use of computers and women's involvement in the decision-making process marked out differentials in status between women workers. Using a computer all day typified a young, little-educated woman, earning relatively low wages and working in poor conditions. In contrast, women who used one for a few hours daily represented women who were well educated, earning well and operating in good working conditions. The latter were also more likely to be better trained, with more prospects of promotion, and had already made career moves. Indeed, they were likely to be part of the supervisory and managerial staff. Gender relations and male control of technology form an important area of analysis. For some, computers represented 'unqualified work for women and new qualified jobs for men'. One difficulty besets the historian who steps into the virtual present: there is little opportunity of gaining hindsight and perspective, and a range of different answers and projections present themselves. Many of the studies of the 1970s and early 1980s focused on expectations of employees and trade unions, and extrapolated their findings to the future, rather than postulating on the basis of evidence.[60] Thus time and more detailed research is needed to understand the effect on women's work and their work experience. Anecdotal evidence from an office in Aberdeen suggests that female staff see the computer as a status symbol and demand training to expand the range of their abilities. They feel their work is valued if they have a better machine with more software, which allows them to do more interesting tasks.

Within the tertiary sector women and men were occupationally and physically separated by practices of segregation and stratification. Pay scales and grading were designed to provide two quite separate gendered hierarchies, preventing women from moving into administrative and higher-level work. Initially, high-status men's jobs such as bookkeeping were 'deskilled' and taken over by women; second, men transferred out of low-level office jobs filled by women, and new routine jobs were created for women. For example, the managerial side of bookkeeping became accountancy and financial management, while routine accounting became female dominated. Lower-grade work was increasingly mechanized by calculating and adding machines between the wars, and women became 'Jills of all trades', handling, processing and filing quantities of paper. Men were redeployed in the office hierarchy, and substantial new white-collar employment opportunities opened for them in sales, marketing, management, and a promotion ladder was created for men who continued to enter.

From the beginning, women were largely confined to lowest-status jobs, and all-female grades were implemented. For example, the British Civil Service opened a grade for 'women clerks' in 1881, and in 1883 the Post Office created a grade of 'women sorters'; neither mixed with male workers. At the Prudential, women were employed in a very narrow range of activities, and the career ladder open to males was closed to them, as was true in the Dutch telegraph and the French postal service. In the 1890s, a new structure in the Norwegian Telegraph Service created a lower category for women, 'female assistants', while a higher telegraph course gave men access to senior technical or administrative positions. Also, the new training scheme meant it was very difficult for women to become highly experienced telegraphers adept at more complicated machinery. Similarly, women were less likely to gain posts in retailing, as supervisors, buyers, floor managers or window dressers, and the majority of department heads and assistants were male, though gradually women succeeded.[61] Even as physical divisions broke down, separate classifications persisted and survived the rationalization and fragmentation of clerical work. Thus gendered changes in white-collar work coincided with and contributed to the continuous and major reclassification of jobs which led to large-scale vertical segregation of men and women. Jordan argues it was a deliberate policy to placate men, which was willingly accepted:

> The way gender was experienced in middle-class households in the 1870s, the meaning it gave to everyday actions and relationships, meant that the aspirations and life paths of the mothers, wives, sisters and daughters of the men who pursued careers in organizations like the Prudential Assurance Company were seen as quite distinct from those of their male relatives. This in turn made it almost mandatory that they should be offered different working conditions and career paths if they entered such an organization. These conditions thus made the introduction of vertical segregation seem the natural and inevitable way of organizing a workforce composed of male and female clerks.[62]

De Haan agrees in that relations in the Dutch office were hierarchically structured, and modelled on the gender order. 'The world of the office was part of a larger cultural context in which men dominated. This hierarchy did not cease to exist on crossing the office's threshold.'[63]

The interwar and post-war eras saw only modest amelioration of occupational segregation, even with legislation against sex discrimination and for equal pay. After the First World War, women in the *PTT* did not gain upgrading, despite their wartime contribution, while men, promoted during hostilities, tended to retain posts. The new competitive Civil Service exam was opened to women, so that some gained more senior jobs, though very much a minority, which decreases as one looks up the hierarchy. They were partially successful in 1928 when women who had entered administrative work before the war as *dames employées* were integrated into clerk grades. However, fewer people were hired as clerks, being recruited instead to new 'manipulative' grades as sorters and operators with lower status, pay and mobility than in the same jobs before the war. The Gladstone Commission invoked the classic distinction between mechanical or clerical work and intellectual or administrative work, constructing a pyramid of grades whereby women were confined to the lowest-grade clerical work. The border between clerical and administrative grades was carefully policed throughout interwar years by a series of formal and informal devices. The Civil Service delayed open competition for women, added new barriers, made the marriage bar virtually absolute, if not retrospective, and managed to avoid the terms of the Sex Disqualification (Removal) Act, 1919. In the private sector, the 'executive' who emerged was almost always a man. The effect of the discourse of the 1930s, regarding both home and work, male and female, was to reconfirm higher managerial functions as male and lower-grade routine jobs as female. Reynolds thus calls the 'triumph of the female office worker' a 'two-edged concept: the new generations of women who came in at the bottom of the hierarchy generally stayed there'.[64]

After the Second World War, the structure of the white-collar hierarchy retained the profile of segregation and higher-status jobs for men established at the end of the nineteenth century. In West Germany between 1961 and 1987, women increased as administrators in the office from 28 per cent to 44 per cent, but still retained predominance in what Kolinsky calls the 'infrastructure' or as 'dog's bodies' in the office. In France, a slight increase of women in 'middle management' from 36.7 per cent to 40.6 per cent between 1954 and 1968 suggests an improvement in status, but the category also included primary school teachers and social workers, thus rendering conclusions about women's supervisory roles impossible. However, 'department stores were the first institutions that opened the door of middle and high management to women, thereby creating perhaps the first career structure with genuine prospects of promotion for women in the modern period'. And retailing was one area where women have gained access to female careers; in 1981, there were 24,000 female sales managers and 10,000 men.[65] Occupational segregation

> has been an important mechanism via which systematic differences in the levels of economic reward between men and women have persisted without violating an ideological commitment to the principles of formal equality. Women are not paid less for the same work (this would in any case be illegal), rather, women do different kinds of work, and this work is poorly paid.[66]

Occupational segregation also reinforces gendered stereotypes. It operates in the same way that physical segregation did in the early years of white-collar work. It stifles women's resentment of poor promotion prospects by keeping them from sectors where 'fast-track' men prevail. Crompton argues for shifts particularly in the last two decades, when more women acquired job-related qualifications, and in a climate where sex discrimination was illegal, qualifications obtained have universality, and where the excessively child-centred mother of the 1950s and 1960s was no longer the prevailing model, newer patterns of women's employment and promotion occurred.[67]

12

CONCLUSION
Gender, skill and status

gender has been a central dimension of the social practices and power relations that have had profound consequences for people's lives.[1]

GENDERING THE WORKPLACE; GENDERING THE WORKER

A fundamental problem with the public/private dichotomy is that it was a model to delineate woman's place. Nineteenth-century thought formulated it to *create* separate spheres. However, substantial evidence indicates that it was not a reality, particularly when we consider women as workers. The proportion of working women and the range of their activities is clear confirmation that they were not sequestered or protected in a private place. Also, the public sphere that so much has been written about, and which so often has been the area of historical interest, was itself constructed on exclusions, particularly the exclusion of women, who were simply defined away.[2] The realms of work and home were not separate and oppositional, but sites of gendered co-operation and conflict. Both men and women worked to contribute to households, whether of a single person or a family. However, other ideologies contributed to creating gendered meanings for work and the workplace. Across the period covered by this book, the home was increasingly defined in terms of the female. The workplace was increasingly constructed in a male idiom and work constructed by male definitions, which derived from increasing waged labour and emerging from debate about a 'family wage'. These not only subordinated women's work, but contributed to identifying women as not workers, and specifically female tasks, including activities at home, as not work. Redefinitions tended to make women's work even more invisible, while the visible woman worker had to be controlled, categorized and constructed as a temporary worker or not a worker.

Concentration on measurable statistics obscured women who were rarely counted. Recorders missed the part-time char, laundress, homeworker. While they picked up odd bits of work as they needed it, some working almost continually, they assured researchers that they 'don't go out to work no more'.

261

A ribbon-maker in St Etienne, asked whether her mother worked after marriage, responded, 'No, never. She stayed at home, but she did mending for other people. *She was never without some work in her hands.*' Similarly, a married Welsh woman in the 1920s said, 'No, never worked no more. Oh – I went out working in *houses* to earn a few shillings, yes, I worked with a family, my mother's and my sister's, and took in washing ... I'd do *anything* to earn money.' The belief that this was not real work because it was occasional and not done in a proper 'workplace' was coupled with a perception that married women did not work. Here we see the confusion between work and home. What looked like housework was not work. Recorders also miss the farm wife and the 'housewife' simply because what they were doing was 'natural' and not work. Though domestic responsibility is timeless for women, it has historical and cultural specificity. What is done, when and how it is done, alters as meanings and contexts of keeping house change. Attitudes to tasks and the meanings associated with them as well as definitions of social roles for men, women and children determined what it consisted of. Practices of men and children going home for a main meal at midday shaped women's workday. In late nineteenth-century Tourcoing, factory women rushed out to prepare meals for children and men. A German textile worker in the 1920s explained, 'We women have mostly extended our lunch time by a quarter or half an hour. I have also done this because I go home in the lunchtime. Most days my son must go to school in the afternoon. He can thus eat properly and I can get him ready.' In the late 1950s, half-day school attendance and no cafeterias in Italy meant that mothers had to be at home to prepare a meal.[3] Not only do household responsibilities shape ideas about women's work, they shape the time discipline of her day and week. While for many women domestic obligations remained important to them, a pressure on time, and crucial to the household, they are probably more disguised today than when they were subsumed into a working day, as visible and as valued as gardening, knitting and earning.

It is too simplistic to identify the pre- or proto-industrial family as the ideal worker family in the way many proto-industrialists have done. Conflict and cooperation shaped responses, as did individualism and collaboration. The significance of home and family on the working woman has been to define her place in terms of status, hierarchy, tasks and role. It was fluid, and certainly not consistent, but for much of the last 300 years women have been defined first in terms of domestic responsibilities. They were working *women*, not women *workers*. In many respects the notion of woman as not worker derived from the married woman or mother, who was perceived as having domestic responsibilities. Where the location of work and home was nearly contiguous, these tasks blended, and the idea of male or female workers was underplayed. Tensions which arose with the shifting location of work, its identity as waged, and more capitalistic control of work contributed to defining gendered locations for men and women. In the case of women, the married woman/mother was the model, whereas numerous females were not married or mothers at any point in time. Thus central ideas which emerged about one point in the female life cycle tended to colour the position of all women. It was not quite this simple, however, since ideas of patriarchy and male control had a very long history, and the importance of controlling women and maintaining male status were significant factors in determining how culture defined men and women in relation to the workplace. These factors together meant that women were often seen as casual workers, as assistants, and as not real workers. They were also seen as a flexible workforce, 'a reserve army of labour' to be drawn on when needed and released when not needed. In some ways fact and myth come together, since women often worked to a different time discipline from the regimented factory, workshop or office. Nevertheless, women have defined themselves as workers, increasingly so as time passed and work itself became more clearly defined, identified and crystallized as a specific entity rather than as part of a collection of activities. As time has become controlled more centrally, women have needed to respond either by remaining in the informal economy or a 'casual' workforce or by joining the 'male' mainstream structures that have emerged. That they have increasingly matched their work patterns to the mainstream and that they are more prominent in recorded work are evidence of this shift. It does not mean their work was any more casual or unimportant in the past.

When society has needed women as workers, it has always been adept at redefining their nature to fit new demands. The world wars are obvious examples. Female nature and so-called female skills were regularly redefined to adjust to the changing workplace. For example, women's household role made them eminently suitable as a workforce for domestic industry. Their domestic role led to their industrial role insofar as they already had the skills to transfer to the labour market. Almost all women made things for the household. An important shift was to make things for the market, and initially the products for sale were indistinguishable from those made for household consumption. Precisely this close association between domestic manufacture and the home led to a long struggle by men to establish their artisanal work as distinct from and more 'esteemed' than domestic production which became defined as 'women's work.[4] With changes in organization of industrial work, particularly the use of more mechanization, there was again a reworking of the gendered division of labour. Assumptions about women's weaker physical capacity and inferior intelligence justified male monopoly of high-status positions. Perceptions about the meaning of women's work and their wage levels meant that these remained low, often explicitly to reflect a percentage of the male wage while the latter remained consistent with the idea of a 'family wage'.

GENDERING SKILL

A feature of how work was allocated was its identity as skilled or unskilled. As has been said before, notions of skill are historically and culturally specific. The meanings of skill in the craft-based society of the eighteenth century are not the same as those in the twentieth century. The cultural traditions of trades and their consequent implications for standing in the community and citizenship in the polity were tied up with the meanings of value and worth, and occupational status was central to working people. In the twentieth century, far more emphasis has been placed on the relationship of men to knowledge and expertise, and in many cases, control of technology. Women were most restricted in those areas where men could claim a craft component for the work, which allowed them to align it with masculine notions of skill, custom and control. Iron, steel, sawmills, wood production and motor vehicles retained this identity for men, to the exclusion of women. It did not matter if women had the 'skill' or ability; it was assumed that they did not. For example, male compositors in Edinburgh 'were adamant . . . that women were *not* skilled workers'.[5] This view can be a protective mechanism; protective of a male preserve which they can mystify and control. It speaks not only of maleness, but of men's place in the hierarchy and their patriarchal right to command power and authority in the workplace as well as at home. As a toolmaker in Coventry explained:

> Going from one toolroom to another, when you talk to toolmakers . . . you talk the same language. And it all stems from the sort of training in your earlier years as an apprentice . . . I think in teaching your craft you become associated to the people who are doing the teaching and I think they also pass on their knowledge of other things as well.

These distinctions contributed to shaping male identity, 'in producing and reproducing a model of masculinity which implicitly constructs a model of femininity'.[6] They describe the dignity and status men derive from work, which contributes to their construction of gender. As Glucksmann said, 'If gender was basic to the organization of the work process so too was work fundamental to the construction of gender relations.' Clearly notions of skill are not just about the time to learn a task, nor its complexity; they are about meanings that become associated with it. These meanings are social features which affect perceptions of self. While the converse of skill is often described as deskilling, it is frequently unclear what is meant. Cockburn pointed out that we can measure degradation in terms of hours, earnings, conditions, control or division of labour. Though these improved for newspaper workers, they still complained about loss of craft and skill. They probably meant their status had declined. The ultimate drop in status was an association with females. Typesetters, for example, faced the problem of using keyboards while trying to retain the status and 'skill' that went with their self-perception as craftsmen.[7]

Skill is constructed and reconstructed, just as jobs and their meaning are constructed and reconstructed to suit the dominant powers, what de Groot and Schrover have called the 'social negotiations that surround definitions of jobs and skills'. The process is highly gendered from the outset. Employers and men often assumed that women were quick, nimble, patient, docile and presumably not easily bored, so that assembly work, like needlework or weeding, was suitable for them. 'For example, [it] was perceived as light, clean, monotonous and unskilled because women did it and conversely women were perceived as the appropriate gender for the job because it was light, clean, monotonous and unskilled.' They were not 'making' or creating anything, and their work was fragmented. Similarly, machine tending, whether looms or light machine presses, was appropriate to women's special talents. The specialities of female typesetters, such as small type, foreign languages and keyboarding, were not acknowledged, for example. Men, however, handled heavier equipment, continuing the association of strength with skill. At Magneti Marelli, gendered definitions of abilities were clear: 'men were generally thought to be good at "intellectual" or physically heavy work. They alone were seen as capable of highly skilled technical work or craft work . . . Women, on the other hand, were presented as possessing specific female skills of endurance, nimble-fingeredness, and patience and were thought to be good at any task that was delicate, repetitive, and monotonous.' Light industry is not a gender-neutral term. The workplace was an important site 'for the formation of gender, gender identity, gender inequality and gender subordination'.[8] Skill and work are both gendered terms, which have meaning in terms of male attributes, not female ones. Skill is regularly described as something which belongs to men, and is part of male essence. Women's skills, particularly those abilities which women 'naturally' demonstrated, were not skills. Men become workers and artisans; women become assistants and working women.

Division of labour is dependent on constructions of sexual difference. Gendered division of labour was the result of perceptions of women's special and usually unrecognized skills of dexterity, speed and ability to withstand monotony and handle simple, light work, and men's particular ability to handle heavy, difficult, dirty or even 'real' skilled work. It was the rationale for placing women in the 'posher' end of pottery, away from the 'mucky noisy world of men'. In tobacco men took over the heavier larger machinery and new machinery 'where technological knowledge is seen as relevant'. De Groot and Schrover, however, argue that this rationale is inadequate, simply because women did do heavy work. Indeed, feminine characteristics are often assigned to a task *after* it has been labelled as female work. In new industries, employers could have had a free hand to hire workers of either sex, and jobs could have emerged which were not sex-typed. However, it didn't happen. Many tasks were gendered from the outset, because they related to older activities, like crating in the margarine industry linked to cooperage. Also, in some new industries, old traditions persisted, as in tobacco whereby men brought in their own female assistants. As de Groot and Schrover argue, work in new industries branched out to include auxiliary tasks that embraced work which was not new. It was already coded as male, and because employers faced resistance from organized men if they 'tampered' with the gendered character of these jobs, the pre-existent coding restricted women's entry to these areas.[9] This is clearly not gender blindness, but overt gender awareness. It is about seeing the sex of the worker associated with the nature of the task regardless of time and place.

Training and access to knowledge are important elements of the process, and male solidarity colluded to prevent women gaining access to knowledge. Guilds and apprenticed trades constrained female participation in high-status work throughout the eighteenth century. In the twentieth century, in the Coventry car industry, women were excluded from apprenticeships, which theoretically would have allowed access to the plant, because they were simply the wrong sex. It was like joining a club, to which women had no access. Reynolds says, 'there was no such thing as a timeserved journeywoman' in printing, and girls were not apprentices but 'learners', 'indicating that they were not really acquiring a skill, just "learning on the job"'. In St Etienne metalworks, women usually entered through family members and learned from them: 'The apprenticeship was done quickly, on the job.'[10] The views of employers and men reflect the reason given to vocational counsellors in interwar Germany to explain the few apprenticeships for girls:

> We will have to revise our one-sided emphasis on artisan and trades skills for girls in favor of semiskilled work ... Many a girl with mediocre or weak intelligence will prefer a semiskilled trade, in which she will find greater satisfaction than in a skilled trade whose requirements are too difficult ... The skilled trades can only use lively and intelligent *people* ... less talented *girls* will be happier with simple assembly work. [Her emphasis.][11]

The situation was little different in post-war France. Electrical industries had apprenticeships for 10,040 boys and only 341 girls in 1959/60; 3,353 boys and only 93 girls attended technical colleges.[12] Not only did the lack of training opportunities reflect the masculine character of skill and the notion of a closed shop; it epitomized the view that women's work required little training, and women workers were temporary and interchangeable. The perception that women did not have 'careers' was itself a reason for not giving training. Such notions were fundamental to restricting and gendering education, white-blouse work and professions.

GENDERING TECHNOLOGY

The relationship of women to machines was not straightforward. On the one hand, increasing mechanization supposedly allowed more women to be employed, and to replace skilled and expensive men. On the other hand, women were not supposed to understand machines and were only to tend and operate them. Technology has often provided an opportunity to re-gender work, and to mean that work was deskilled and thus feminized. Although automation and the application of machinery were associated with hiring women, paradoxically women did not get 'technical work', and equipment and tools belonged to men. Men repaired and maintained machinery, while women fed it, 'start and stop the manufacturing cycle at maximum speed but never do anything on the machine. This is the job of qualified men.' Simone Weil's memory of working in metal components in the mid-1930s confirms that 'the men . . . were either skilled experts who came to fix the machine or they were performing heavy tasks . . . When the machines on which she worked went wrong she was powerless to fix them, being dependent on the male fitter's arrival (and any loss of time lowering the wages of the woman operator).' Indeed, she wrote, 'I have never seen a woman touch a machine except to operate it.'[13] This association of men with mechanical aptitude was seldom questioned, and was perceived as an inherent characteristic of the sex, not possessed by women.

The sex of the operator is frequently a precondition for the definition and application of technology. 'Technology is created with the gender of the operator in mind.' Berg argued this for the eighteenth century, Rose for the nineteenth, and in the twentieth century perceptions and not technology itself remain central to gendering technology. Some machines were men's machines and the process was defined as skilled, while others were female machines and the process defined as unskilled, such as sewing machines and typewriters. The female machine and task thus was inferior, poorer paid and low in status. The converse was true of men's machines and tasks. Manual tasks also had a duality in that sometimes women were designated the laborious fiddly hand work; other times hand work was coded as craft work and claimed for men. Certainly not all hand work, nor all machine work, requires the same abilities, training, expertise or judgement, but no consistency existed in defining either hand or machine work, except by gender, and sometimes by age. 'The precise nature of the relationship between women and technology remains elusive.' Cockburn's summation that 'women may push the buttons but they may not meddle with the works' aptly describes technological gender relations. The link between the terms, and consequently the concepts, of skill and technology is not surprising. As Braverman and others linked technology to deskilling in partial explanation of the division of labour, then male control of technology and by implication their control of 'skill' has been an essential element in analysing the gendered nature of white-collar work. Tijdens, however, takes an optimistic view from the vantage point of the 1990s office. She argues that gender relations used to be hierarchical in that men designed and controlled the computer production process, while women entered data or performed clerical tasks. However, this changed with the spread of microcomputers instead of centralized computer systems. The decentralized structure led to a change in the gender relations and the share of jobs, and the increased use of microcomputers superseded the male sex-typing of computers. The majority of female office workers have become skilled computer workers, superseding the view that the supervisor knows how to handle software while the 'non-technical' secretary does not.[14] Two images remain. One is the persistence of an association of men with technical 'know-how', whether justified or not, and a sense of control and increased status. The other is the growing confidence and practical experience of female office workers with computerized technology, which gives them a certain amount of control over the work itself. Concepts of skill and gender are fluid, constantly redefining the social meaning of the workplace. Technology was only one factor which interacted with a range of variables to reshape the sexual division of labour in a multiplicity of workplaces. Culture and economy, as well as different workplace structures, meant that technology can only be seen in context. Firms working in the same industry employed different practices and took different decisions about gender, while the pace of change varied from site to site.

GENDERING CONTROL

A fact of the gendered workplace is the allocation of control to men resulting from gendered division of labour and notions of skill and status ascribed within the workplace. Common where household and work overlapped and the male was head of household, and again in many nineteenth-century workplaces, male control was a feature of the designation of the spinning mule as a male machine. Such practices persisted into the twentieth century and were particularly embedded in the occupational structures of white-bloused work. Also, in British hosiery, 62 per cent of the workforce were female, but over 92 per cent of foremen and overlookers were men in the interwar period. Similarly, at the velvet factory at Maroeuil in Artois, the Bremen jute works, Courtaulds and Viennese factories women did hands-on work and men supervised, thus investing men with authority—or recognizing the patriarchal view of society towards men's inherent authority. Only in 1910 did Anjte Jongbloed become the first female supervisor in the Dutch Cotton Mill Company. These were textile works, which could have relied on older traditional practice, derived from the patriarchal working household of the putting-out system. However, evidence from 'new' industries is little different, though in a number of plants, women acted as supervisor over women, answering ultimately to a male overseer. For example, in Dutch rayon, there was one mistress to every fourteen female workers, three headmistresses and two male overseers in every department. At Magneti Marelli, introduction of assembly lines altered foremen's jobs, and some women became overlookers, or *maestra*. However, Luigia Pedroni, who commanded the virtually all-female winding shop, was the only female head. Willson pointed out that women often resisted advancement, partly because they were reluctant to take on additional problems at work. As one explained, 'I'm not refusing to work, I'm just refusing to do this job because I've got a home to take care of.' In interwar Germany, the larger the establishment the less likely it was that a woman would hold a management position, and between 1907 and 1925 the percentage of female managers in industry halved, double the overall drop.[15] Men were 'in charge' and the practices of the workplace continued to operate on this basis, confirmed by perceptions that women did not have the ability and 'strength' to control the workforce, that they did not have the management skills required. Like skill, supervision derives from preconceived notions of gender and is intimately linked to the male need to retain status and standing, not only with regard to other men and the workplace, but with respect to women, and the home. Not only did men need to control, women 'needed' to be controlled.

THE WOMAN WORKER; THE WORKING WOMAN

Importantly, natural differences ascribed to men and women in the workplace are precisely that: ascribed. They are not necessarily real. Women can and did do the same tasks as men; they were even better at some of them, such as using the scythe. They were not all frail, delicate and weak. In fact the history of women's work is about their strength, both physical and mental. It is also about claiming space. Space was often gendered, whether fields or farmyard; office or shops; factories or workshops. It was not necessarily about home and work in the physical sense of claiming place.

A range of variables determined whether a woman went out to work. Much depended on the perception of a woman's contribution to the labour market by family members, other workers and employers, as well as her place in the life cycle. Clearly the workplace was a gendered context in which women often encountered a hostile environment. But self-perception and their own needs, whether contextualized in family or personal terms, were significant. The way women related to their work reflected a range of choices and the decisions they made. They used a range of strategies to earn income, and made decisions based on complex considerations. Several shifts in the structure of the workforce indicate that women chose the work they wanted to do. Females left agriculture, particularly when they could migrate to towns. There they might take up domestic service either temporarily or as a career. They might choose to leave to marry, or to take up other work, not always better paid, in factories or homework. They demanded education, created voluntary work and ultimately social work, and they claimed shop and office work. They shaped their own context, worked for their own reasons and enjoyed it. The effect was, as Kolinsky described, that women became more employment orientated and less inclined to live their lives in separate phases as the twentieth century moved on.[16] Women were agents in the conception of their own work experience and in fashioning themselves as workers with an identity based in the workplace, and not as women who happened to be working.

NOTES

1 INTRODUCTION

1 John (1986) p. 10; Cockburn (1985) p. 12; Braverman (1982) pp. 148–56; Hartmann (1982) pp. 446–69; Linn (1987) pp. 128–29.
2 Milward and Saul (1973) p. 30.
3 Hudson and Lee (1990) pp. 34–35.
4 Fox-Genovese (1984b) p. 113.
5 Shorter (1976) p. 520; Fox-Genovese (1984a) p. 11.

2 WOMEN, HOUSEHOLD AND FARM

1 Kleinbaum (1977) pp. 219, 220. That the Philosophes' view of women is problematic, highly complicated and not in the least uniform is confirmed by their writing and by the wealth of literature on the issue. Useful examples of the latter are Jacobs, *et al.* (1979); Graham (1976); Pope (1987); Wexler (1976); and Williams (1971).
2 Frevert (1988) p. 12.
3 Brown (1764) pp. 4–12.
4 Quoted in Frevert (1988) p. 13.
5 Brown (1765) p. 6; Fénelon (1843) vol. 2, p. 495.
6 Horne (1796) p. 5; Rousseau quoted in Wexler (1976) p. 270.
7 Frevert (1988) p. 14; Horne (1796) p. 8; Rousseau quoted in Pope (1987) p. 140.
8 Chapman (1752) p.15; Moir (1784) p. 49 and More (1799); Trimmer (1787) pp. 66–67; Wollstonecraft (1792) pp. 286–89.
9 Richards (1974) pp. 335–57.
10 Hudson and Lee (1990) p. 5. See various descriptions of 'family economy' in Hufton (1975) p. 1; Snell (1985) p. 62; Tilly and Scott (1978) p. 12; McBride (1977) p. 283; Rule (1981) p. 42. See also Clarkson's critique (1985) p. 48.
11 Berg (1989) pp. 65–66.
12 On plebeian culture, custom and control see Berg (1985) chapter 7; Medick (1976) p. 303 and (1983) pp. 84–113; Thompson (1971) 76–136 and (1974) 382–405.
13 Fox-Genovese (1984b) pp. 112, 118; Wiesner (1987a) pp. 70-71; Boxer and Quataert (1987) p. 40 and Houston (1989) p. 122; Middleton (1978) pp. 163–65.
14 Segalen (1983) p. 9; Pope (1987) p. 138; Frevert (1988) pp. 23–24; Cowan (1989) pp. 16–18; *Compact Oxford English Dictionary* (1979) vol. 1, p. 425.
15 Quoted in Frevert (1988) p. 23.
16 Quotes in Tilly and Scott (1978) p. 45; Pinchbeck (1930) pp. 8, 9. See Boxer and

Quataert (1987) p. 40; Houston (1989) pp. 121–22; Hasbach (1908) p. 97; Fox-Genovese (1984b) pp. 114–15; Shorter (1976) pp. 515–17; Hufton (1995) pp. 154–55.

17 See Boxer and Quataert (1987) p. 40; Shorter (1976) pp. 515, 518, 526; McBride (1977) p. 286; Frevert (1988) p. 13; Hufton (1975) p. 16; Fussell and Fussell (1953) p. 54.

18 Quote from Pahl (1984) p. 29; see also Hufton (1975) p. 11; Shorter (1976) p. 516; Fox-Genovese (1984b) p. 115. See on the preparation of food Cullen (1991) pp. 265–76.

19 Fox-Genovese (1984b) p. 116; Boxer and Quataert (1987) p. 40; Davis (1986) pp. 173–74; Wiesner (1987b) p. 66; Frevert (1988) p. 41.

20 Haywood (1743).

21 Lee (1990) p. 54; Fox-Genovese (1984b) p. 116; Sogner (1984) pp. 125–26; Hufton (1971) p. 92, (1975) pp. 19–21 and (1974) p. 109.

22 Berg (1991) pp. 10, 14. See also Cowan (1989) p. 31; Weatherill (1988); McKendrick (1974) pp. 152–210 and McKendrick, Brewer and Plumb (1983) pp. 1, 10, 23. See also Cunningham (1980) on commercialization of popular leisure, p. 9.

23 Berg (1985) p. 170.

24 Thompson (1974) p. 42.

25 McBride (1977) p. 282.

26 Schlumbohm (1980) p. 79–80; Simonton (1988) pp. 250ff; on schooling and the role of housewifery in the curriculum, pp. 138–57, on girls going into service on leaving school, pp. 169–72 and on mothers as educators, pp. 284–97; Frevert (1988) pp. 24–25; Hufton (1981) p. 190.

27 Simonton (1988) p. 266.

28 Wall (1978) pp. 190–91; Kussmaul (1981) pp. 70–72; Simonton (1988) pp. 264–67; see also Laslett (1977) pp. 34, 44; Cerutti (1992) pp. 108–11; Hufton (1981) p. 197.

29 Kussmaul (1981) pp. 83–84; Hasbach (1908) p. 97.

30 Laslett (1977) p. 43; Bourdieu (1979) p. 134n.

31 Shorter (1976) p. 517.

32 See Hartwell (1981) pp. 390–408. For example Shorter (1975) p. 168 and Stone (1977) p. 81. See Cunningham (1995) and Pollock (1983) for revision of the earlier views of childhood. Two thought-provoking articles are by Jordanova (1987) and Minge-Kalman (1978).

33 Laslett (1977) p. 42; Wrigley and Schofield (1981) pp. 232–34, 254; Laslett and Wall (1972) p. 154.

34 Schlumbohm (1980) p. 78; Frevert (1988) pp. 23–24; Tilly and Scott (1978) p. 59; Sussman (1982); Hufton (1975) p. 12; Fox-Genovese (1984b) p. 121.

35 Wall (1981) p. 312, 314 and (1978) pp. 197–98; Hufton (1984) and (1975) pp. 17–18.

36 Anderson and Zinsser (1988) vol. 1, p. 87.

37 Snell (1981 and 1985); Lee (1990); Pollard (1981) pp. 46–56; Braudel (1985).

38 Abensour (1923) p. 240; Fox-Genovese (1984b) p. 115; Hufton (1995) p. 152; Hasbach (1908) p. 97; Frevert (1988) pp. 23–24; Wiesner (1993) pp. 86–87; Shorter (1976) p. 515.

39 The most comprehensive work on English agricultural servants is Kussmaul (1981). See also Hufton (1981); Pinchbeck (1930) pp. 7, 16–19; Hasbach (1908) pp. 77, 97; Blum (1978) p. 110; Hammond and Hammond (1911) p. 25. The terms of service between apprentices and farm servants were significantly different, see discussion in Kussmaul (1981) and Simonton (1988) pp. 343–49, 174 and

unpublished raw data; Sogner (1984) pp. 118–19; Ankarloo (1979) p. 114; Frevert (1988) p. 26.
40 Hufton (1981) p. 190 and (1995) pp. 71–75; Gray (1984) p. 11; Fox-Genovese (1984b) p. 116; Pinchbeck (1930) pp. 16–19, 53–65; Kussmaul (1981) p. 15; see also Hasbach (1908) p. 69; Sogner (1984) p. 118; Ankarloo (1979) p. 114; Hufton (1993) p. 17; Hill (1989) chapter 5; Whyte and Whyte (1988) p. 93.
41 Abensour (1923) p. 243; Scottish Record Office CH2/471/3: May 1661, quoted in Houston (1989) p. 121; Smout (1969) p. 298; Bailey and Gulley (1794) p. 53 and Pringle, p. 291 quoted in Hasbach (1908) p. 87; Gray (1984) p. 11 and (1988) p. 66.
42 Wiesner (1993) p. 91; Blum (1978) pp. 52–57, 74, 386–88; Pollard (1981) pp. 48–56; Lee (1990) p. 52; Lough (1960) pp. 17–20; Abensour (1923), p. 240.
43 Quotes in Lee (1990) p. 54 and Sogner (1984) pp. 125–26; Shorter (1976) p. 515.
44 Shorter (1976) p. 517; Wiesner (1993) p.87; Hufton (1995) pp. 8, 73 and (1975) p. 3; Frader (1987) p. 314; Lee (1990) p. 55; Hill (1989) pp. 28–37; Bradley (1989) p. 79; Smout (1969) p. 299; Cammarosano (1991) pp. 153–54.
45 Pinchbeck (1930) p. 17; P. P. (1843a) XII, p. 109.
46 Hufton (1975) p. 3 and (1995) p. 153; King (1991) p. 474; Hill (1989) pp. 37–38.
47 Frevert (1988) p. 23; Gullickson (1981) pp. 178, 181, 185; Fox-Genovese (1984b) p. 115; Blum (1978) 111; Hasbach (1908) p. 82.
48 Sommestad (1995) pp. 155–56 and (1992) p. 36; Valenze (1991), pp. 144, 145–48, 152; Segalen (1983) pp. 97–98; Devine (1984) p. 99; Hansen (1982) p. 225; Hufton (1995) pp. 73–74.
49 Wiesner (1993) p. 86.
50 Lee (1990) p. 54.
51 Hufton (1995) p. 154; also Hill (1989) p. 35 on the lack of clear demarcation of tasks.
52 Graham (1812), p. 313; Staatsarchiv für Oberbayern, Hofmark Thalhausen, Rechnungen, 1812–13, quoted in Lee (1990) p. 56.
53 Young (1929) p. 40.
54 Gray (1984) p. 13; Houston (1989) p. 121; Devine (1984) pp. 99–100; Blum (1978) pp. 131–32; Pringle quoted in Hill (1984) p. 186 and Clarke quoted in Hill (1989) p. 35; Bradley (1989) pp. 78–81; Frader (1987) p. 314; Lee (1990) pp. 51–52, 55; Roberts (1979); Boxer and Quataert (1987) p. 40; Wiesner (1993) p. 87.
55 Roberts (1979); Howatson (1984) pp. 126–32; Lee (1990) pp. 54–55; Blum (1978) pp. 132–33; Hufton (1995) p. 154; Wiesner (1993) p. 87; Shorter (1976) p. 517; Goody (1976), p. 35; Roberts (1979) p. 8.
56 Pringle (1794) p. 293; Hill (1989) p. 75; Berg (1985); Hasbach (1908) among others. Marshall quoted in Bradley (1989) p. 80.
57 Lee (1990) p. 52; Hufton (1981) p. 195; Blum (1978) p. 111.
58 Kussmaul (1981) p. 37; Snell (1981) p. 414 and (1985) pp. 29–47; Hufton (1995) p. 74; Robson (1984) pp. 81–82.

3 MAKING, SELLING, SERVING

1 Mendels (1972) pp. 241–62, quote p. 241. See Berg (1991) p. 4, for a discussion of the relationship of proto-industrial theory to the development of the market; Medick (1976) pp. 291–315; Berg (1985); Snell (1985); Tilly (1979) pp. 137–52; Hufton (1975) pp. 1–22.
2 Davis (1989) p. 63; Hudson (1982) pp. 35–37; Schlumbohm (1980) pp. 95–98 and (1983) pp. 92–123. For a survey of the debate see Clarkson (1985); Berg, Hudson and Sonenscher (1983), and Houston and Snell (1984) pp. 473–92. See

also Coleman (1983); Kreidte, Medick and Schlumbohm (1981); Gullickson (1986); Anderson (1980) p. 75; and Medick (1976) p. 307.

3 Hudson (1982) p. 37.

4 Hufton (1981) p. 187; Whyte (1989) pp. 234, 246; Gullickson (1991) p. 209 and (1981) p. 185; George (1931) pp. 132–33.

5 Gullickson (1987) p.1.

6 Richards (1974) pp. 338, 346; Young (1929) p. 99.

7 Gullickson (1991) pp. 208–10; Lynch (1991) p. 381; Whyte (1989) p. 243; Houston (1989) p. 124; Durie (1979); Blum (1978) pp. 172–73; Lis and Soly (1979) pp. 143–45, 151; Reddy (1984) p. 68.

8 Ogilvie (1990) pp. 84–85, 88–89; Whyte (1989) p. 243; Houston (1989) p. 124; Collins (1982) pp. 132–34; Gullickson (1981) pp. 183–84 and (1986) p. 213; Flandrin (1979) pp. 106–10; Hufton (1981) p. 199.

9 Rothstein (1961); Hufton (1975) p. 4 and (1981) p. 192.

10 Ogilvie (1990) pp. 89, 92–99; Schlumbohm (1983) pp. 104–07; Boxer and Quataert (1987) p. 43; Pinchbeck (1930) p. 121; Brown (1969) pp. 16–26.

11 The *maire* of Osnabrück, May 1812, quoted Schlumbohm (1983) pp. 106–07.

12 Medick (1976) pp. 310–12.

13 Hufton (1975) pp. 14–15.

14 Lis and Soly (1979) p. 144; Berg (1989) p. 71; Whyte (1989) pp. 247–48; Bradley (1989) p. 133; Levine (1977) pp. 46–57.

15 Snell (1985) p. 279; John (1980) pp. 20–25; Pinchbeck (1930) pp. 244–46, 269; Rule (1992) p. 205; Berg (1985) pp. 307–13; Simonton (1988) pp. 250–52, 349 and (1991) pp. 240–41 and unpublished data; Hufton (1975) p. 14; Blum (1978) p. 173; Lis and Soly (1979) pp. 143–45; Reddy (1984) p. 68.

16 Hutton (1817) p. 158.

17 Keele University Library, Wedgwood Archives 46–29123, 95–17476 to 95–17510; 29111–46 to 29245–46; 133–26816; Wedgwood quoted in Bradley (1989) p. 119.

18 Hufton (1981) p. 188; Medick (1976) pp. 303–04; Whyte (1989) pp. 242, 247.

19 Ogilvie (1990) p. 91; Whyte (1989) p. 240; Gullickson (1991) p. 212; Dunlop and Denman (1912) ch. 9.

20 Quoted in Whyte (1989) p. 247.

21 Fox-Genovese (1984a) p. 11; Hufton (1981) pp. 188–89 and (1975) pp. 11, 13; McKendrick (1974) p. 187; Whyte (1989) p. 240; Pinchbeck (1930) p. 138; Houston (1989) p. 123.

22 Berg (1985) p. 158; Gullickson (1987) p. 2; Rudolph (1980) pp. 111–18.

23 Monter (1980) p. 203. Passementerie was silk usually woven with gold threads. See also Wiesner (1989); Quataert (1985) p. 1124.

24 Abensour (1923) pp. 184–89; Tilly and Scott (1978) p. 49; Fox-Genovese (1984b) pp. 117–18.

25 Abensour (1923) p. 186; Goodman and Honeyman (1988) p. 112; Prior (1985) pp. 111–13; Rendall (1990) p. 28. For lacemakers see Lis and Soly (1979) p. 170.

26 The following paragraphs draw on: Sheridan (1992) pp. 51–52; Hufton (1995) pp. 91–93 and (1984) p. 364; Prior (1985) pp. 103, 108–110; Wiesner (1993) pp. 103–06 and (1987b) p. 67; Fox-Genovese (1984b) p. 117; Abensour (1923) pp. 184–92, 208; Kingston Upon Thames KB 11/1/4, KB 1/2, KB 8/1/3; Daly (1974) pp. ix, 165; Dunlop and Denman (1912); Pinchbeck (1930) p. 293; Hill (1989) p. 94; Snell (1985) p. 299.

27 Monter (1980) pp. 201–02; Howell (1986). See also DuPlessis and Howell (1982) pp. 49–63.

28 Dobson (1980) p. 63; Pinchbeck (1930) pp. 160–61; Hufton (1995) p. 94;

Wiesner (1987b) p. 66 and (1987a) pp. 230–33; Power (1975); Clark (1919) pp. 10, 150; Sheridan (1992) pp. 52–53; Abensour (1923) p. 205; Lane (1977) p. 122; Dale (1961) p. xv; Dunlop and Denman (1912) pp. 150–51; Simonton (1991) pp. 244–46.

29 This discussion is based on Simonton (1988) chapter 5, drawing on over 18,000 apprentices. Although the original research included Poor Law apprentices, they are largely excluded because of their lack of comparability with most European examples.

30 Monter (1980) p. 200.

31 Although seven years is commonly identified as the traditional period of apprenticeship, there are enough exceptions to remind us that it was an ideal. In Turin, the tailors' guild did not have rules for the age apprenticeship began and five years was thought to be needed to learn the art, although there was a request to make it eight (Cerutti (1992) p. 106). Davis (1986) p. 169 cites apprenticeships ranging from three to five years. See the discussion of age distribution and length of terms in Simonton (1988) pp. 230–49, which shows variation across the century and trades, and also differences by type of apprenticeship and sex. See also Rule (1981) p. 97; Wiesner (1987b) pp. 65–66.

32 Gilbert (1874) p. 114; Dunlop and Denman (1912) pp. 148–49; Pinchbeck (1930) pp. 126, 160, 1802–03, vol. 8, pp. 343, 344, 383; Sheridan (1992) p. 53; Wiesner (1987a) p. 231; Simonton (1988) pp. 143–48; Quataert (1985) p. 1137; Smout (1969) p. 435.

33 Ogilvie (1990); Whyte (1989); Wiesner (1987b) pp. 67–68; Reddy (1984) p. 31; Hufton (1975) pp. 14–16 and (1981) pp. 191–92; Lown (1990) pp. 9–15; Lis and Soly (1979) p. 170.

34 Goubert (1960) p. 344; Sheridan (1992) pp. 56–57; Hufton (1975) p. 9 and (1995) pp. 92, 94; Farge (1993) pp. 114–15; Wiesner (1987b) p. 66; Ogilvie (1990) p. 84; Lis and Soly (1979) p. 170; Berg (1985) p. 311; Lown (1990) p. 18.

35 Sheridan (1992) pp. 53–55; Abensour (1923) pp. 168, 200–04; Houston (1989) p. 122; Fox-Genovese (1984b) p. 116.

36 Reddy (1984) p. 22; Gibson (1989) p. 105; Pinchbeck (1930) p. 282.

37 Campbell (1747) p. 23.

38 Farge (1993) pp. 114–15.

39 Wrigley and Schofield (1981) p. 263; Hufton (1984) p. 357; Wall (1981) pp. 303–07; Gullickson (1991) p. 216 and (1981) p. 187; Malcolmson (1981) p. 176.

40 Sharpe (1991) pp. 68–69; Ogilvie (1990) pp. 86–97; Houston (1989) pp. 132–33; Fox-Genovese (1984b) p. 114.

41 Kussmaul (1981) p. 71; Hufton (1975) pp. 3–8 and (1995) p. 77.

42 Simonton (1988) pp. 169–74; ERO D/Q 24/2.

43 Reddy (1984) pp. 24–27, 31; see also Gullickson (1991) p. 212.

44 Reddy (1984) pp. 31–33; Gullickson (1991) pp. 212, 215 and (1981) p. 187; Hufton (1975) pp. 14–15; Whyte (1989) p. 240; Collins (1982) p. 133; Sharpe (1991) pp. 58–60.

45 Reddy (1984) pp. 24, 31–32; Wiesner (1987b) p. 68; Lis and Soly (1979) p. 166; Sheridan (1992) pp. 55, 63–64; Berg (1994) p. 278; Monter (1980) p. 200; see also Quataert (1985).

46 Monter (1980) p. 201; Hufton (1984) pp. 364–65; Prior (1985) pp. 105–07.

47 Simonton (1988).

48 Simonton (1988) pp. 353–55; Campbell (1747) pp. 206, 208, 227, 336.

49 Hufton (1981) pp. 196–97; Houston (1989) p. 122; Wiesner (1987b) pp. 72–73.

50 Hufton (1995) pp. 183, 497; Ramsey (1988) p. 35; Wiesner (1987b) p. 71; Anderson and Zinsser (1988) I, p. 110; Andrew (1991) pp. 88–97.

51 Boxer and Quataert (1987) pp. 44–45; Gibson (1989) pp. 117–19; Hudson and Lee (1990) p. 15; Abensour (1923) pp. 215–21; Pinchbeck (1930) pp. 300–02; Ramsey (1988) p. 50.

52 The important collection edited by Marland (1993) explores and explodes a number of myths about midwifery in this period across Europe. See also Schnorrenberg (1981); Versluysen (1981); Donnison (1977).

53 Harley (1993) pp. 28–31; Simonton (1988) pp. 249, 351; Burnby (1977) pp. 154–55; Ortiz (1993) pp. 100–01.

54 Harley (1993) p. 42.

55 Filippini (1993) pp. 152–75; see generally Marland (1993).

56 Berg (1985) p. 157. See Simonton (1988) p. 356 and chapter 3A; Hufton (1995) pp. 83, 236, 253.

57 ERO, D/P 50/25/42 (c. 1785).

58 SRO, D1157/1/5/1; Simonton (1988) p. 131.

59 Sheridan (1992) pp. 57–63; Hufton (1984) pp. 364–65; Prior (1985) pp. 105–06; Corfield (1985) p. 13; Pinchbeck (1930) pp. 284–85; Hill (1989) chapter 13; Todd (1985) pp. 54–92.

60 Quoted in Hufton (1984) p. 366.

61 Hufton (1975) pp. 17–18, 20–21, (1974) pp. 115–17 and (1984) pp. 365–66; Marshall (1926); Wiesner (1987b) p. 67 and (1989) pp. 131–33.

62 Hufton (1974) pp. 306–17 and (1995) pp. 299–331; Hill (1989) p. 173.

63 Wiesner (1987b) p. 67; Davis (1986) p. 169.

64 See Cerutti (1992) pp. 121–25; Davis (1986) pp. 183–84; Hufton (1995) pp. 168–70; Gibson (1989) p. 112; Schlumbohm (1980).

4 LOCATION, SKILL AND STATUS

1 McBride (1977) p. 282; Hudson and Lee (1990) p. 16; Berg (1989) p. 76.

2 See Thompson (1974) pp. 42–43, 55.

3 Collier (1740) pp. 8–9.

4 Berg, Hudson and Sonenscher (1983) p. 10.

5 *Ibid.*, pp. 9–10; Reddy (1984) p. 33.

6 McBride (1977) p. 283.

7 Berg (1985) p. 155.

8 Sharpe (1991) p. 55.

9 Probably the best examinations of issues related to the introduction of new technologies in textile and metal trades in the early stages of English industrialization are Berg (1989) pp. 64–98 and (1994) pp. 144–55.

10 Reddy (1984) pp. 55, 58–59; Young (1929) pp. 252–53, 300; Rule (1992) pp. 205–06; Berg (1989) p. 143 and (1985) pp. 146–49; Brown (1969) pp. 22–46; Rendall (1990) p. 21; Richards (1974) pp. 345–46.

11 Phillips and Taylor (1986) p. 55.

12 Williams (1983) p. 315. Mechanical should not be narrowed exclusively to the practical and 'manual', relating as it does to theories of laws of motion and its implications for religious thought during the Enlightenment, p. 202.

13 Defoe (1726) p. 11.

14 Sonenscher (1989) p. 50; see Rule (1989) pp. 99–118.

15 Quataert (1985) pp. 1126–27, 1134–35.

16 Wiesner (1989) pp. 127, 128, 131.

17 Prior (1985) pp. 110–13; Abensour (1923) p. 185.

18 See Dunlop and Denman (1912); Rule (1981); Behagg (1979).

19 Simonton (1988) and (1991).

20 Berg (1989) p. 76 and (1985) pp. 155, 173; Hufton (1981) p. 188; Pinchbeck (1930) p. 2; Gillis (1986) p. 117; Ogilvie (1990) p. 93.
21 Hudson and Lee (1990) p. 15.
22 Gamarnikow (1978) p. 100.
23 *Ibid.*, p. 101; Berg, Hudson and Sonenscher (1983) p. 19.
24 Reddy (1987) p. 12; Gullickson (1991) pp. 217–19.
25 Berg (1985) pp. 149–50; Davis (1979).

5 DOMESTICITY, THE INVENTION OF HOUSEWORK, AND DOMESTIC SERVICE

1 This phrase is from Welter (1978).
2 McMillan (1981) p. 9.
3 Welter (1978) p. 313.
4 Schlegel-Schelling (1980) p. 75.
5 Blackbourn and Evans (1991) p. 10.
6 Jules Simon, *La Femme au vingtième siècle* (1892), quoted in McMillan (1981) p. 12.
7 John Ruskin, *Sesame and Lilies: Of Queen's Gardens* (1865) quoted in Bédarida (1979) pp. 118–19.
8 Daniel Lesueur, *L'Evolution féminine: ses résultats économiques* (1900), quoted in McMillan (1981) p. 13.
9 Frevert (1988) pp. 89, 91; John (1986) p. 3; Blackbourn and Evans (1991) p. 11; Rose (1988) p. 191.
10 Quoted in Bédarida (1979) p. 120.
11 Quoted in Frevert (1988) pp. 56–57.
12 Davidoff (1976) p. 123. The following discussion is heavily indebted to this article.
13 Gray (1987) pp. 413, 422; Davidoff and Hall (1987), especially pp. 358–87; Oakley (1974) pp. 43, 49.
14 Davidoff and Hall (1987) p. 13; McBride (1976) p. 27; Smith (1981) pp. 42–43.
15 Ellis (1843) p. 242.
16 Quotes in Smith (1981) p. 72, see also pp. 71, 187, and Davidoff and Hall (1987) pp. 124, 281; Meyer (1987) pp. 186–87; Frevert (1988) p. 110.
17 See Davidoff (1976) on new definitions of dirt. In 'Der Wäscheschrank,' *Schweizer Frauenheim*, no. 21, pp. 291–92, gave a detailed description of how to adorn the linen closet. Smith (1981) p. 67, also pp. 66–69, 75; Davidoff and Hall (1987) pp. 90–93; Meyer (1987) pp. 179–80, 185–87.
18 Keith Thomas, 'Cleanliness and Godliness in the Eighteenth Century,' Public Lecture, University of Aberdeen, June 1993; Simonton (1988) 109–11.
19 Hausen (1987) p. 275.
20 Davidoff (1976) p. 128; see p. 124 on the cultural perception of dirt and disorder; Hansen (1982) p. 236.
21 Davidoff (1976); Frevert (1988) pp. 102–05; Smith (1981) pp. 156–58.
22 Neff (1929) p. 251; Rendall (1990) p. 89; Davidson (1982) p. 128; Davidoff and Hall (1987) pp. 381–82; McBride (1976) p. 30; Ravetz (1987) p. 201; Cowan (1989) pp. 44–49, 53; Bose (1979) pp. 295–304; Hardyment (1990) pp. 33, 39, 55.
23 Quoted in Gerhard (1978) pp. 282–83.
24 Davidoff and Hall (1987) pp. 284, 385.
25 Meyer (1987) and (1982); see critique, Frevert (1988) p. 103n8. Quote in Davidoff and Hall (1987) p. 52.
26 Quoted in Frevert (1988) p. 110.
27 Ravetz (1987) p. 203; Barrett and McIntosh (1980) pp. 51–72.

28 Davidoff (1976) p. 136; Nipperdey (1983) p. 123.
29 Cammarosano (1991) p. 175; Tilly and Scott (1978) p. 38n5, p. 79; Dauphin (1993) p. 433; Frevert (1988) pp. 68, 83; Lynch (1991) p. 352; Pinchbeck (1930) p. 36; Bourke (1993) p. 62; Price (1987) p. 154.
30 My calculations and McBride (1976) pp. 35–36; Wierling (1987) p. 146; Sagarra (1980) p. 237; Armstrong (1988) p. 95; Bairoch *et al.* (1968) and Mitchell (1978).
31 Bourke (1993) p. 61; McBride (1976) p. 86; Schlegel (1983) p. 75; Dauphin (1993) p. 433; Alexander (1983) p. 50; Davidson (1982) p. 165.
32 Wierling (1987) pp. 148–49; LePlay (1877–79) vol. V, p. 442, vol. VI, p. 202.
33 McBride (1976) p. 90.
34 McBride (1974) pp. 63–78; Willcox (1982) pp. 31–32; Gullickson (1986) p. 78.
35 Higgs (1986) p. 139; Tilly and Scott (1978) p. 108; McBride (1976) pp. 35–44; McPhee (1992) p. 202; Schlegel (1983) pp. 60–63; Weber (1899) pp. 276–80, 375; Cammarosano (1991) p. 175; Davidoff and Hall (1987) p. 389; Alexander (1983) p. 50; Darrow (1989) p. 181; 'Madame Elise Blanc' in Hellerstein *et al.* (1981) p. 347; Tilly (1982) p. 171.
36 Schlegel (1983) p. 63; Davidoff and Hall (1987) p. 389; Armstrong (1988) p. 95; Pinchbeck (1930) p. 80; McBride (1976) p. 38; Smith (1981) p. 76.
37 Cammarosano (1991) p. 175.
38 Nipperdey (1983) p. 123. *Herrschaft* translates as power or rule, or as a collective noun for 'ladies and gentlemen' or 'masters and mistresses'. In the context of domestic service, it carries a sense of the 'domain' or bourgeois household. English does not convey the sense of the German.
39 Wierling (1987) pp. 146, 148, 165; Lown (1990) p. 60; Gullickson (1986) p. 78.
40 McPhee (1992) p. 202; McBride (1976) pp. 39, 45; McDougall (1977) p. 267; Bourke (1993) p. 60; McMillan (1981) p. 70; Schlegel (1983) pp. 62–63; Sagarra (1980) p. 237; Darrow (1989) p. 86; Meyer (1987) p. 182; Burnett (1974) p. 185.
41 Darrow (1989) pp. 86–87; Higgs (1986) p. 136; McBride (1976) p. 20; Schlegel (1983) p. 64; Nipperdey (1983) p. 123; Wierling (1987) pp. 151, 161.
42 Davidoff and Hall (1987) p. 388; McBride (1976) pp. 20–21; Higgs (1986) pp. 133–34; Jamieson (1990) pp. 138–39; Bourke (1993) pp. 75–77; Davidoff (1976) pp. 136–37; Smith (1981) p. 74.
43 Schlegel (1983) p. 61.
44 Wierling (1987) pp. 152–53; Schlegel (1983) p. 61.
45 Hardyment (1990) p. 33.
46 Higgs (1986) pp. 137–38. His data are expressed in decimals not in £ s d. For French servants see McBride (1976) pp. 60–64 and for Irish see Bourke (1993) pp. 72–74. See the discussions about data in Bourke and McBride. Frevert (1988) p. 86; Wierling (1987) pp. 148–49; Anderson (1971) p. 128.
47 Darrow (1989) p. 237n; *Suffrage Speeches from the Dock* (1912) in Riemer and Fout (1980) pp. 76–77.
48 Twenty-one editions were published, Hellerstein *et al.* (1981) p. 295.
49 Darrow (1989) p. 237n; Scott and Tilly (1975) p. 54.
50 Wierling (1987) p. 150; Davidoff and Hall (1987) p. 389; Schlegel (1983) p. 65; Lown (1990) p. 21; Hall (1982) p. 18.
51 Schlegel (1983) p. 69.
52 Darrow (1989) pp. 183–84.
53 G.B. Parliamentary Papers, Police Reports, 1816, V, p. 229.
54 Pierre Guiral and Guy Thuillier, *La Vie Quotidienne des domestiques en France au XIXe siècle* (Paris, 1978), cited in McPhee (1992) p. 202; McBride (1976) p. 105; Frevert (1988) p. 120; Mahood (1990) p. 35.
55 Pinchbeck (1930) pp. 310–11; I do not intend to deal in detail with prostitution

as women's work, but it must be placed in its context of discourse and in relation to other forms of work. For more thorough studies of prostitution see Walser (1985) pp. 99–111; Evans (1976); Walkowitz (1980) and (1993); Finnegan (1979); Mahood (1990) and Littlewood and Mahood (1991); Harsin (1985); Corbin (1990).

56 Walser (1985); P.P. (1831–32) XV, p. 467; (1833) XX, C i, p. 26; (1843) XIV, p. 58; Thompson and Yeo (1984) pp. 142, 200–01.
57 Littlewood and Mahood (1991) pp. 162, 164.
58 Smith (1981) p. 75; Wierling (1987) pp. 147, 157, 165–66.
59 Quoted in Dyhouse (1986) p. 32.
60 Henriette Davidis 'Treues Dienen' in Dülmen (1991) pp. 133–34.
61 Smith (1981) pp. 76–77.
62 Schlegel (1983) pp. 61, 62; Davidoff and Hall (1987) p. 392; Jamieson (1990) pp. 146–47.
63 Dyhouse (1986) p. 29; Schlegel (1983) p. 64; Davidoff and Hall (1987) p. 390.
64 Schlegel (1983) pp. 70–72; Cammarosano (1991) pp. 175–76; 'Modern Domestic Service,' *Edinburgh Review* 115 (1862) 414–15, quoted by McClelland (1989) p. 202; Wierling (1987) pp. 167–69.
65 Rendall (1990) p. 101; Frevert (1988) p. 89; Davidson (1982) p. 178; Lown (1990) p. 48.
66 Mayhew, vol. 1 p. 39, *The City Missionary Magazine* 10 (1836) p. 127, quoted in Alexander (1983) p. 51.
67 Mayhew, quoted in Alexander (1983) p. 51.
68 McMillan (1981) p. 69.
69 Tristan (1973) pp. 216–17.
70 McMillan (1981) p.69; Alexander (1983) pp. 51–52.

6 RURAL WOMEN – FARMHOUSE AND AGRICULTURE

1 Bairoch *et al.* (1968); Armstrong (1988) pp. 94–95; Horn (1984) pp. 95–96; Devine (1984) p. 112. Data for the period before mid-century is either non-existent or misleading, as in Britain where large numbers of married women were recorded as unemployed in 1841; see Miller (1984) pp. 139–61.
2 Pierre du Maroussem, *Fermiers montagnards du Haut-Forez* (1894) p. 421, quoted in Lehning (1980) p. 130.
3 In Hellerstein *et al.* (1981) p. 294.
4 Smout (1987) p. 18; Bourke (1993) p. 149; Gullickson (1986) p. 115; Horn (1980) p. 30; Reed (1984) p. 60; McDermid (1990) p. 214; Mattosian (1992) p. 19; Cammarosano (1991) p. 167; Gabaccia (1987) p. 169; Henri Baudrillart, quoted in Weber (1976) p. 202; Roubin (1976) pp. 158–59; Price (1987) p. 166.
5 Tilly and Scott (1978) p. 118.
6 Mrs Murray, quoted in Howkins (1991) p. 42.
7 Rosa Kempf, *Arbeits- und Lebensverhältnisse der Frauen in der Landwirtschaft Bayerns* (1918), quoted in Shulte (1987) pp. 123, also pp. 117–19.
8 Sayer (1993) p. 186.
9 Miller (1984) pp. 123–38.
10 P.P. (1843) XII, p. 3; Culley, quoted in Devine (1984) p. 98; Nadaud, quoted in McPhee (1992) p. 154; Gullickson (1986) pp. 53, 114–15; Roubin (1976) p. 155; Gabaccia (1987) pp. 171–73; Cammarosano (1991) p. 169; Hilden (1993) p. 193.
11 Lee (1990) pp. 59–60; Gabaccia (1987) pp. 171–73; Schneider and Schneider (1992) p. 153; Gullickson (1986) p. 114; Lehning (1980) p. 106; Devine (1984) p. 109; Hasbach (1908) pp. 82, 413; Fussell and Fussell (1953) p. 171;

Armstrong (1988) pp. 27, 97; Tilly and Scott (1978) p. 118; Mingay (1977) pp. 99–100, 109.

12 Snell (1985) p. 155; Miller (1984) p. 151; Devine (1984) p. 101; Gray (1984) pp. 11, 18; Orr (1984) p. 39; Hainer (1986) pp. 113–15; Bourke (1993) p. 145; Mingay (1977) p. 79; Howkins (1991) p. 95.

13 Lehning (1980) p. 47; Gabaccia (1987) pp. 169, 173; Sommestad (1994) p. 62; Houston (1989) p. 121; Howatson (1984) pp. 126–28, 130; Bradley (1989) p. 85; Lee (1990) pp. 54–55, 60, 71n34; Blum (1978) pp. 132–33; Price (1987) p. 166; Glickman (1992) p. 56; Schulte (1987) p. 119.

14 Stephen, quoted in Hostettler (1977) pp. 95-96, also p. 97; Howatson (1984) p. 132; Lee (1990) p. 71n34; Roberts (1979) p. 13 and n60; Fenton (1977) p. 54.

15 King (1991) pp. 462–63, 465, 471–73; Weber (1976) p. 129; Schneider and Schneider (1992) p. 153; Gabaccia (1987) p. 170; Snell (1985) pp. 157–58.

16 Bourke (1993) p. 147; Lehning (1980) pp. 139, 144–45.

17 Guiseppe Daniele, quoted in Cammarosano (1991) p. 169. See also Gabaccia (1987) p. 169.

18 Fussell and Fussell (1953) p. 172; Schulte (1987) pp. 112–13; Gullickson (1986) pp. 114–15; Gray (1984) pp. 19, 21; Bailey and Culley (1794) p. 53; Howkins (1991) p. 50.

19 Armstrong (1988) p. 95; the figures for men are 32 per cent, 14 per cent and 29 per cent respectively; Gullickson (1986) pp. 114–15; Devine (1984) pp. 106, 109.

20 P.P. (1867) XVI, pp. 85, 89, 91–92.

21 Fussell and Fussell (1953) pp. 172, 176–78; Mingay (1977) p. 82; Sayer (1993) p. 187; Howkins (1991) pp. 106–08; Bradley cites gangs still being used to harvest celery, beets, potatoes and weeding today (1989) p. 84; Hilden (1993) pp. 156, 171.

22 Sturrock (1866-67) p. 89; Bourke (1993) p. 83; Hansen (1982) p. 227; Annika Osterman, 'Kvinnor och kor', *Fataburen* (1986) p. 67, quoted in Sommestad (1994) p. 60 also (1992) p. 36; Fussell and Fussell (1953) pp. 194-95; Campbell (1984) p. 66.

23 Schulte (1987) pp. 118–19; Devine (1984) p. 103; Hansen (1982) pp. 227–31; Sommestad (1994) p. 47n8 and (1992) p. 36.

24 Middleton's *Middlesex* (1807) p. 409, quoted in Pinchbeck (1981) pp. 40–41.

25 P.P. (1881) XVII, pp. 918–19, 941 and (1893) XXXVI, part 1, p. 52; Bourke (1993) pp. 82–83; Sommestad (1992) p. 36 and (1994) p. 57; Bradley (1989) p. 86.

26 Bradley (1989) p. 86; Sommestad (1992) pp. 36–37 and (1994) pp. 59, 62–63.

27 O.S.A. XIII, pp. 423–24; Gray (1978) p. 13; Dorian (1985) p. 33; Thompson *et al.* (1983) pp. 173–75; Gunda (1984). The novel by Neil Gunn, *The Silver Darlings* (1941), is a good illustration of the association of masculinity with fishing and describes the role of women in the combined fishing and crofting communities.

28 Munby, Diary, 15–16 October 1867, extract in Hiley (1979) pp. 105–09; Delitala (1984) p. 112.

29 O.S.A. XIII, p. 424.

30 Dorian (1985) p. 69.

31 Quote in Bradley (1989) p. 99 and Charles Weld, *Two Months in the Highlands* (1860) in Smout and Wood (1990) p. 88.

32 Thompson *et al.* (1983) p. 173; Dorian (1985) pp. 33–37.

33 Johansson (1989) p. 202; Schulte (1987) p. 120; Gullickson (1986) p. 31.

34 Smith (1811) p. 521; P.P. (1843) XII, pp. 27, 166; Bradley (1989) pp. 82–83; Gullickson (1986) p. 31; Graham (1812) p. 313; Bourke (1993) p. 149; Fussell and Fussell (1953) p. 172; Price (1987) p. 166; Houston (1989) p. 121; Devine (1984) pp. 99–100.

35 Johansson (1989) p. 201; Weber (1976) p. 172; Price (1987) p. 167; Roubin (1976) pp. 158–59.
36 Schulte (1987) pp. 122–23.
37 Ingeborg Weber-Kellermann in Dülmen (1991) pp. 142-43.
38 Quoted in Bourke (1993) p. 38.
39 Verney (1888) p. 98.
40 P.P. (1867–68) XVII, p. 95.
41 Howkins (1991) p. 44; Jefferies (1880) p. 110; P.P. (1843) XII, p. 141; Price (1987) p. 154.
42 McPhee (1992) p. 255; David Lafford, *Gloucester Journal* 27 April 1872, quoted in Miller (1984) p. 152; Gullickson (1986) p. 116; *Labourers' Union Chronicle* 7 June 1873, quoted in Sayer (1993) p. 193.
43 Gray (1984) p. 21; see also Orr (1984) p. 40; Devine (1984) p. 106.
44 Jefferies (1880) p. 235.
45 *The Agricultural Labourer, Ireland*, quoted in Bourke (1993) p. 38; Weber (1976) p. 174; Frederick Clifford (1874), cited in Fussell and Fussell (1953) p. 174; also Heath (1874); P.P. (1893–94) XXXV, I, part iv, p. 102.
46 P.P. (1843) pp. 65–68.

7 INDUSTRY, COMMERCE AND PUBLIC SERVICE

1 Berg and Hudson (1992) p. 24; Tilly and Scott (1978); Holmes and Quataert (1986) pp. 200–03; Accampo (1989) pp. 12, 16; Boxer and Quataert (1987) p. 98.
2 Berg, in her extensively rewritten second edition of *Age of Manufactures* (1994), explores many issues which underpin the structures of women's work in Britain, providing a crucial analysis of the relationship between technologies, labour and capital during industrialization. Gullickson (1981) p. 199; Holmes and Quataert (1986) pp. 200–03.
3 Cammarosano (1991) pp. 158–61, 165, 173–74; Berg (1989) p. 80, (1993) p. 3 and (1994) pp. 139–40, 153, 213, 228–29, 242–43, 252; Sheridan (1979) p. 113; Lehning (1980) pp. 40, 46, 107–09, 136–37; Quataert (1986) p. 12; Holmes and Quataert (1986) p. 201; Pinchbeck (1930) pp. 162–64, 174–75; Collins (1982); Gullickson (1981) pp. 190–99 and (1986) pp. 98–99; Heywood (1976) pp. 95–98, 108–09; Darrow (1989) p. 146; Hilden (1993) pp. 41, 69.
4 Richards (1974) p. 345; Heywood (1988) p. 98; Gullickson (1986) p. 104; Mitchell (1978) p. 61; Lown (1990) p. 20; Frevert (1988) p. 328.
5 Barlee (1863) p. 32.
6 Gullickson (1986) pp. 101–04, 128; Accampo (1989) p. 89.
7 Desama, *Population et révolution* p. 227, cited in Hilden (1993) p. 71.
8 Lown (1990) pp. 36, 59; Morgan (1992) p. 30; Reddy (1984) pp. 163–64; Heywood (1988) p. 103; Cento Bull (1991) pp. 20–24; Cammarosano (1991) p. 162; Berg (1994) p. 276; P.P. (1843b) XIII, p. 16; Dupree (1989) p. 556.
9 Lehning (1980) p. 159; Cento Bull (1991) pp. 19–20; Accampo (1989) pp. 23, 81–84; Reddy (1984) p. 164; Heywood (1988) p. 102; Boxer and Quataert (1987) p. 101; Lown (1990) p. 86; Tilly and Scott (1978) pp. 83, 113–14.
10 McPhee (1992) p. 201; Tilly and Scott (1978) p. 109; Dauphin (1993) p. 435; Accampo (1989) pp. 82–83.
11 Tilly and Scott (1978) p. 82; Lehning (1980) pp. 41, 45; Accampo (1989) pp. 83–85; quote p. 95; Hilden (1993) p. 71; Frevert (1988) p. 329; Evans (1990) p. 249; Reddy (1984) p. 164; Dupree (1989) pp. 556–57, 562–64.
12 Tilly and Scott (1978) pp. 134–35; Evans (1990) p. 251.
13 Cento Bull (1991) pp. 29–30.

14 Scott (1993) p. 413; Hilden (1993) pp. 74–75; Lown (1990) pp. 36, 81; Ellena, 'La statistica', quoted in Cammarosano (1991) p. 182.
15 P.P. (1818) IX, p. 7 and (1840) XXIV, p. 40; Rendall (1990) pp. 22–23; Berg (1989) pp. 80–81 and (1994) p. 228; Pinchbeck (1930) pp. 170–71; Accampo (1989) pp. 29–31; Osterud (1986) pp. 51–52.
16 Bock (1991) p. 3; Cento Bull (1991) p. 17; Osterud (1986) p. 50. See also Alexander (1983) pp. 25–27.
17 Gullickson (1987) p. 17, also pp. 11–12, 15–16.
18 P.P. (1845) XV, Minutes I, p. 194.
19 Gullickson (1986) pp. 199–201; Rose (1992) pp. 22–23; Collyer (1761); Lown (1990) pp. 14–17; Accampo (1989) pp. 29–31; Pinchbeck (1930) p. 169.
20 Rose (1992) p. 29.
21 Berg (1993) p. 34, (1989) p. 83 and (1994) pp. 151–52, 277, 279; Heywood (1988) p. 101; Jordan (1989) pp. 284–85; Simonton (1988).
22 Jordan (1989) pp. 292–93; Freifeld (1986) pp. 334–35.
23 Freifeld (1986) p. 331; Reddy (1984) p. 165; Gullickson (1986) p. 107.
24 Rose (1986) pp. 118–19 and (1992) pp. 24–25.
25 Bradley (1989) p. 135; Lown (1990) pp. 45–58; Accampo (1989) pp. 23–24, 79–80, 86; Rose (1992) pp. 27–28.
26 John (1980); Hilden (1993) pp. 86–153; Bradley (1989) pp. 104–15; Pinchbeck (1981) pp. 240–69; Burke (1980) pp. 179–204; Mark-Lawson and Witz (1988) pp. 151–74; Cammarosano (1991) p. 181.
27 Rose (1992) pp. 24, 159; Reddy (1984) p. 163; Lown (1990) p. 57; Lazonick (1979) pp. 236, 239; Heywood (1988) p. 117.
28 Hilden (1993) pp. 86–153.
29 Lown (1990) p. 54.
30 Berg (1994) p. 231; Quataert (1986) p. 6.
31 Franzoi (1987) p. 150; Morris (1986) pp. 95–96; Albert (1990) p. 158.
32 Aminzade (1979) p. 101.
33 Gullickson (1986) p. 128; Cammarosano (1991) p. 175; Aminzade (1979) pp. 100–01; Glickman (1992) p. 60; Jordan (1989) p. 292.
34 Scott (1984) p. 76; LePlay (1877–79) vol. 5, pp. 9, 16–17, 45, 50–54; Hilden (1993) pp. 71–77; Frevert (1988) p. 90; Franzoi (1987) pp. 147–48; Cammarosano (1991) pp. 175–76; Tilly and Scott (1978) p. 108; Alexander (1983) pp. 82–83; Tilly (1982) pp. 184–85.
35 Quataert (1985) pp. 1141–42.
36 Hunt (1986) p. 73; see Johnson (1975) pp. 87–114 and (1979) pp. 65–84; Scott (1984) pp. 67–94; Morris (1986); Taylor (1983) pp. 101–17; Alexander (1983) pp. 30, 56–61; Albert (1990) p. 60; Cammarosano (1991) pp. 174–75; Collins (1991) pp. 139–40.
37 Quataert (1985) pp. 1135–43; quote in Scott (1984) p. 70.
38 Scott (1984) pp. 75–76; see also Taylor (1983) pp. 94–116.
39 Scott (1984) pp. 77–79; Alexander (1983) pp. 34–40, 43–44; Thompson and Yeo (1984) pp. 519, 527–29.
40 Quataert (1985) pp. 1139–42; Collins (1991) pp. 141–42, 148–50; Smout (1987) p. 20.
41 Cammarosano (1991) p. 178; Mingay (1977) pp. 116–17; Pinchbeck (1930) pp. 224–26; P.P. (1843) XVI, pp. d35, d39 and (1860) XXII, p. 246; Glickman (1992) p. 61; Bradley (1989) p. 149.
42 Collins (1991) p. 149; Tilly (1982) p. 172; Quataert (1985) p. 1144; Cammarosano (1991) pp. 177–79.
43 Franzoi (1987) p. 148; Anderson and Zinsser (1988) II, p. 271; Scott and Tilly (1975) p. 59; Quataert (1985) pp. 1122–23.

44 Davidoff and Hall (1987) pp. 52, 57–58, 301; Darrow (1989) pp. 117–18; Smith (1981) pp. 35–38, 43–48; Hall (1990) pp. 113.
45 Darrow (1989), quote p. 169, also p. 150; Accampo (1989) p. 68; Tilly (1982) p. 182; LePlay (1877–79) vol. 3, pp. 161, 281; Krünitz, quoted in Frevert (1988) pp. 31, 68.
46 Pinchbeck (1930) pp. 294–95; Hilden (1993) p. 186; Tilly (1982) p. 182; Darrow (1989) p. 160; Hall (1990) p. 111; Davidoff and Hall (1987) pp. 302–04; Alexander (1983) p. 52; Wedgwood Archives.
47 Tilly and Scott (1978) p. 125 and Scott and Tilly (1975) p. 47; Davidoff and Hall (1987) pp. 299–301. Davidoff (1979) provides a sensitive exploration of gender issues tied up with lodging, and this discussion relies heavily upon it.
48 Mayhew quoted in Alexander (1983) pp. 52–53; Pinchbeck (1930) p. 299; LePlay (1877–79) vol. 3, pp. 106–07; Darrow (1989) p. 200.
49 Darrow (1989) p. 171.
50 Reddy (1986) p. 379.
51 More and Nightingale, quoted in Anderson and Zinsser (1988) II, p. 176; Summers (1979) pp. 38, 58; Frevert (1988) p. 70.
52 Perrot (1993) pp. 451–57; Summers (1979); Prochaska (1974); Frevert (1988) pp. 69–71; Anderson and Zinsser (1988) II pp. 176–85.
53 Hughes (1993); Gorham (1982) p. 126.
54 Eugène Buret, *The Misery of the Working Classes* (1840), cited in Scott (1989) pp. 125–26.

8 CONTINUITY AND CHANGE

1 Ellena, quoted in Cammarosano (1991) p. 165; Accampo (1989) p. 82; quote in Berg (1993) p. 34.
2 P.P. (1842) XV, p. 387; XVII, pp. 215, 217.
3 Cento Bull (1991) pp. 24, 31; Gaskell (1833) pp. 184–85; Lazonick (1979) p. 234.
4 John (1980); Hilden (1993) pp. 86–153, quote p. 111; Bradley (1989) pp. 104–15; Pinchbeck (1930) pp. 240–69; P.P. (1842) XV, p. 27; XVI, pp. 460, 475; XVII, p. 217.
5 Munby, *Diary*, 29 September 1860 and 1 September 1862, quoted in Hiley (1979) pp. 83–84, 100.
6 *Enquête*, 1846, pp. 40, 63, 437, quoted in Hilden (1993) pp. 64, 73; see also p. 58; P.P. (1843a) XII, pp. 65–68; Heller and Imhof (1983) pp. 147–52; Lee (1990) p. 68.
7 Scott (1993) p. 399.
8 Lown (1990); Alexander (1984) p. 139.
9 Nardinelli (1990) p. 59. I am grateful for comments by Hugh Cunningham on this line of thought.
10 Gray (1989) p. 177; Reddy (1986) p. 374; P.P. (1843) pp. 65–68; Hutchins (1915) p. 51; Gaskell (1833).
11 McPhee (1992) p. 203. It is worth questioning his suggestion that 'separation' caused domesticity among working-class women. Accampo (1989) p. 76; Gullickson (1986) p. 149. The authors cited do not argue in such a simplistic way, but the 'shorthand' of separation of home and work often appears unproblematized in historical accounts. See Berg (1989) pp. 64–66.
12 Dupree (1989) p. 552.
13 Scott (1993) pp. 400–01, 404–05.
14 Beier (1991) pp. 217–18; Frevert (1988) p. 90; Franzoi (1987) pp. 147–48.
15 Quataert (1985) p. 1144; Beier (1991) pp. 217ff; Taylor (1983) p. 112; Tilly (1985) p. 199 and (1982) pp. 170–71; Franzoi (1987) p. 148; B[rocher] (1976) p. 61.

16 Thompson and Yeo (1984) pp. 145, 251; Pinchbeck (1930) pp. 209–15, 237.
17 Jury, 'L'Industrie des lacets', p. 18, quoted in Accampo (1989) p. 85.
18 Scott (1993) p. 401.
19 Higgs (1987) p. 60.
20 Reddy (1984) p. 162. See Scott (1993) p. 408.
21 Heywood (1988) p. 114; Berg (1993) p. 31.
22 P.P. (1802–03) VII, pp. 22, 268, 297; Pinchbeck (1930) pp. 157–58, 312–13; Heywood (1988) p. 115.
23 Land (1981) p. 16.
24 Frevert (1988) p. 96; John (1986) p. 25; Winters, quoted in Osterud (1986) p. 54; Humphries (1977) pp. 241–58; Fine (1992) p. 105; Rose (1992) p. 130. See also Cento Bull (1991) p. 12.
25 Frevert (1988) pp. 94-95; Valverde (1987/8) p. 628; Cento Bull (1991) p. 12; Osterud (1986) p. 52.
26 Rose (1992) p. 130; *Concordia: Organ der Association der Cigarrenarbeiter*, no. 34, December 1849, quoted in Frevert (1988) p. 97.
27 G.B. Hansard, 15 March 1844, pp. 1088–100.
28 Thompson (1968) pp. 340–41; Rose (1992) pp. 175, 188; Barrett and McIntosh (1980) p. 74; Gray (1980).
29 Quoted in Barrett and McIntosh (1980) p. 75.
30 Frevert (1988) pp. 96, 99; *Northern Star*, quoted in John (1986) p. 24; Rose (1992) pp. 187–88.
31 Taylor (1983) pp. 110–11.
32 P.P. (1876), quoted in Rose (1992) p. 70.
33 *Ibid.*
34 Barrett and McIntosh (1980) p. 74.
35 *Ibid.* p. 81.
36 Hudson and Lee (1990) p. 18.
37 Berg (1989) p. 84; Rose (1986) p. 120; Osterud (1986); Alexander (1983) p. 28.
38 Jordan (1989) pp. 274, 276–78, 287, 289; see Heywood (1988) pp. 105–06.
39 Bairoch *et al.* (1968) p. 174; Osterud (1986) p. 58; Ehmer (1986); Bradley (1989) pp. 146–51.
40 Freifeld (1986) pp. 320–21.
41 Reddy (1984) pp. 81, 136, 166.
42 Rule (1989) pp. 103, 108.
43 P.P. (1845) XV, Minutes, p. 180; Rose (1986) p. 125.

9 HOME AND WORK

1 Reynolds (1996) pp. 83–84; Zerner (1987) p. 10.
2 Mason (1976) 1, p. 78; Glucksmann (1990) p. 39; Bairoch *et al.* (1968); Mitchell (1978); Bridenthal (1973) p. 150.
3 Boxer and Quataert (1987) pp. 191–93; Bairoch *et al.* (1968); Mitchell (1978).
4 Mason (1976) I, p. 77; Bridenthal (1973) p. 150; Reynolds (1996) p. 102; Hatton and Bailey (1988) p. 695.
5 Lagrave (1994) pp. 467–68; Tipton and Aldrich (1987) p. 174; Ambrosius and Hubbard (1989) p. 55.
6 Lagrave (1994) p. 458.
7 Marwick (1970) p. 12.
8 Marwick (1977) pp. 157–58.
9 See Pope (1991) pp. 9–18; Tipton and Aldrich (1987) pp. 48–49.

10 Bougle, quoted in Hause (1987) p. 102; Montague, quoted in Marwick (1977) p. 166; Higonnet *et al.* (1987) pp. 6–7.
11 Hause (1987) p. 104.
12 Thébaud (1994) pp. 30, 33; Hause (1987) p. 104; Anderson and Zinsser (1988) II p. 309; see also Braybon and Summerfield (1987).
13 Hause (1987) pp. 102, 104; Thébaud (1994) pp. 29–30, 33; Reynolds (1996) p. 99; Pope (1991) p. 21; Braybon and Summerfield (1987) p. 167.
14 Taylor (1977) p. 54; Frevert (1988) p. 267; Adams (1988) p. 23; Gittins (1986) pp. 260–61; Jalland (1986).
15 Webb (1907) pp. 8–15; 'The Declining Birth-Rate', *The Times*, 31 October 1913; Lewis (1980) p. 15; Boxer and Quataert (1987) pp. 200–03, 210; Bland *et al.* (1978) pp. 49–50; Blom (1991) p. 21; Ohlander (1991) p. 63; Cova (1991) p. 120; Bridenthal (1977) pp. 439–40; Ross (1993) pp. 135, 181–84, 198ff; Gittins (1982) pp. 56–60, 136, 139–41; McMillan (1981) pp. 191–92.
16 Hall (1977) p. 68; Lewis (1980) p. 16 and (1991) pp. 76–79; Anderson and Zinsser (1988) II pp. 299–300; Rosenbeck (1987) p. 49; Manning (1992) pp. 206–35; Offen (1991); Farnsworth (1992) pp. 145–66.
17 Saraceno (1992) pp. 258–59; Caldwell (1991) pp. 43–45, 55; Kolinsky (1989) pp. 14–20; Weyrather (1993); Koonz (1988); Bridenthal (1977) p. 441; Frevert (1985) p. 232; Boxer and Quataert (1987) p. 213.
18 Richardson (1993) pp. 28–32; Stearns (1972) p. 101; Tilly and Scott (1978) p. 211; Kaelble (1990) pp. 134–35.
19 Quoted in Frevert (1985) p. 263, also pp. 257–58, 262–63; Kolinsky (1989) pp. 12, 26–27.
20 *Woman,* 1968, p. 45, quoted in Winship (1987) p. 32; also pp. 28–35; Ambrosius and Hubbard (1989) p. 101; Wilson (1980); Saraceno (1992) p. 261–65; Tipton and Aldrich (1987).
21 Thane (1991) p. 114; Pfeil (1961) p. 79; Pross (1975) p. 13; Frevert (1985) p. 266; Kolinsky (1989) pp. 77, 264.
22 Glickman (1984) pp. 89–96.
23 Gittins (1982) pp. 69–73.
24 Tipton and Aldrich (1987) pp. 184–85; Ambrosius and Hubbard (1989) pp. 55, 101; Pennington and Westover (1989) pp. 11–12; Bourke (1993) p. 271; Tenfelde (1992) pp. 200–01; Roberts (1984) pp. 136, 137; Tilly and Scott (1978) pp. 194–95, 198–201, 208; Reddy (1975) p. 111; Leleu (1981) pp. 662–63; Hilden (1986) pp. 278–79; Sussman (1982) p. 163.
25 Saraceno (1992) pp. 257–58; Allart (1981) p. 704; Burdy *et al.* (1987) pp. 29–32; Mason (1976) 2, pp. 9–12; Hakim (1979) pp. 11–12; Beddoe (1989) pp. 57–59, 87; Glucksmann (1990) p. 42; Gittins (1982) p. 105.
26 Lefaucheur (1994) p. 438; McIvor (1992) p. 142; Lagrave (1994) p. 456.
27 McIvor (1992) p. 142; Lagrave (1994) p. 468; see Kolinsky (1989) pp. 153–59; Bairoch *et al.* (1968); Pollert (1981) pp. 93–103.
28 Glucksmann (1990) p. 43; McIvor (1992) p. 142; Lagrave (1994) p. 481.
29 Boxer and Quataert (1987) p. 217.
30 Glucksmann (1995) p. 277.
31 Seager and Olson (1986) p. 109.
32 Kolinsky (1989) pp. 156–57.
33 Gittins (1982) pp. 104–05.
34 Sommestad (1995) p. 162.
35 Rowntree and Lavers (1951) p. 56.
36 Pollert (1981) pp. 121, 98.
37 Saraceno (1992) p. 263; Rosenbeck (1987) pp. 49–50; Davidoff and Westover (1986) pp. 26–27; Frevert (1988) pp. 152–53, 194.

38 Allart (1981) p. 718; Kolinsky (1989) p. 29; Leyret (1895) pp. 49–50; Orthmann (1986) p. 29; Adams (1988) p. 24; Fout (1986) pp. 50, 51, 53; Ross (1983) pp. 7, 11–12; Leleu (1981) pp. 650–51; Stearns (1972) p. 106; Roberts (1984) p. 179; Frevert (1988) p. 260.
39 Royle (1987) pp. 31–33; Bédarida (1979) pp. 231–35; Bourke (1993) pp. 206–12; Allart (1981) p. 717; Stearns (1975) pp. 191–92; Gittins (1982) p. 41; Pahl (1984) p. 74; Davidson (1982) pp. 30–31, 112, 125; Tilly (1979) p. 142.
40 Williams (1982) pp. 58, 65; Bowden and Offer (1994) 730, 732–34, 744; Saraceno (1992) p. 262; Robinson et al. (1972) p. 125; Frevert (1988) p. 195; Hausen (1987) p. 278; Bourke (1993) pp. 217–18.
41 Allart (1981) p. 719; Davidson (1982) p. 163; Bourke (1993) p. 225; Hausen (1987) pp. 278–89.
42 Leleu (1981) p. 649; Ross (1993) pp. 69–72, 80; Bourke (1994) p. 186 and (1993) pp. 213, 216; Wedel (1986) pp. 305–20.
43 Saraceno (1992) pp. 261–62; Winship (1987) p. 43; Wilson (1980) p. 22; Kolinsky (1989) p. 76; Gershuny (1983) p. 149; Davidoff and Westover (1986) p. 30; Baumet (1954) p. 115; Frevert (1988) pp. 67–68.
44 Mrs Gardiner, quoted in Hall (1977) pp. 73, 75, 77; Tilly and Scott (1978) p. 212.
45 Armstrong (1988) p. 113; Schlegel (1983); Bourke (1993) pp. 65–67, 71–72, 77–78.
46 Schlegel (1983) p. 66.
47 My calculations and McBride (1976) pp. 35–36, 118; Mitchell (1978); Braybon (1981) pp. 26, 180–84; Jamieson (1990) p. 138; Beddoe (1989) p. 59; Frevert (1988) p. 334; Wilson (1980) p. 24; James (1962) p. 291. Changes in recording mean data are not strictly comparable, but the trend is obvious.
48 Dyhouse (1981) p. 84; Hardyment (1990) p. 36; Bourke (1993) p. 74.
49 Tilly and Scott (1978) pp. 153–55; McBride (1976) p. 113; Bourke (1993) p. 61; Roberts (1984) pp. 54, 56; Sanderson (1988) p. 28.
50 Tilly and Scott (1978) p. 154.
51 Treble (1986) p. 37; Allart (1981) p. 211; Gittins (1982) pp. 46, 76; Chinn (1988) pp. 105–06; Taylor (1977) p. 54; McBride (1976) pp. 111–13.
52 Leleu (1981) pp. 654–55; Allart (1981) pp. 705, 709; Burnett (1974) pp. 139–40; Tilly and Scott (1978) p. 153.
53 Seidl, in Riemer and Fout (1980) p. 20; Leleu (1981) p. 654; McMillan (1981) pp. 73–74; Horn (1975) p. 163; Beddoe (1989) p. 60; Saraceno (1992) p. 254.
54 Boxer and Quataert (1987) pp. 212–13; Frevert (1988) p. 200; Anderson and Zinsser (1988) II p. 184; Dyhouse (1981) p. 83.
55 Quoted in Beddoe (1989) p. 61.
56 Collet (1894) pp. 25–30; Gittins (1986) p. 78; Sauget et Mouillon, in Riemer and Fout (1980) pp. 143–44; Leleu (1981) p. 654; Hearn (1990) pp. 168–69; Schlegel (1983) p. 75; Bourke (1993) p. 70.
57 Drake (1917); Braybon (1981) p. 49; Daily Chronicle, 7 December 1918, quoted in Beddoe (1989) p. 51; Frevert (1988) p. 153; Jamieson (1990) pp. 142–43.
58 Braybon (1981) pp. 182–83.
59 Labour Woman, from Braybon (1981) pp. 180–82; Daily Mail, 23 May 1919, from Beddoe (1989) pp. 51–52; Frevert (1988) pp. 195, 218, 227–28; Boxer and Quataert (1987) p. 213; 'Das Deutsche Mädel,' Zeitschrift des BDM, December 1936, from Kolinsky (1989) pp. 19, 33; Wilson (1980) p. 23.

NOTES

10 CONTINUITIES IN COUNTRY AND TOWN

1 Bridenthal (1973) pp. 151–52; Mason (1976) 2, p. 17; Armstrong (1988) pp. 123, 143; Newby (1980) p. 123; Bradley (1989) p. 91; Hoggart *et al.* (1995) pp. 63, 206.

2 Orr (1984) p. 40; Campbell (1984) p. 56; Armstrong (1988) p. 175; Sommestad (1994) p. 66; Dodge and Feshbach (1992) p. 238; Bridger (1991) pp. 192–99; Hansen (1982) p. 238; Dunn (1978) p. 180; Mason (1976) 2, p. 17; Hoggart *et al.* (1995) pp. 192, 206; Bridenthal (1973) p. 153; Ingold (1984) p. 128; Pfeffer (1989) p. 71.

3 Greenwood (1976); Golde (1975); Pina-Cabral (1986); Pescatello (1976); Sacks (1978); Moulin (1981); Dunn (1978); Mørkeberg (1978); Cernea (1978); First-Dilic (1978); Holmes and Quataert (1986); Pfeffer (1989); Besteman (1989); Bleksaune *et al.* (1993); Arensberg and Kemball (1971) pp. 22–23; Bridenthal (1973) p. 152; Golde (1975) p. 117; Blom (1990) p. 166; Robertson (1990) p. 131; Segalen (1985) pp. 63–67.

4 Pina-Cabral (1986) p. 83; Pescatello (1976) p. 44; Abrahams (1984) p. 108; Roubin (1970); Hostettler (1977) p. 99; Ingold (1984) pp. 125–27; Abrahams (1984) p. 108; Zonabend (1984) p. 121; Pfeffer (1989) p. 63; Sacks (1978) p. 156; Wylie (1957) pp. 157–63; Mørkeberg (1978) p. 101; Allart (1981) pp. 708–09.

5 Farnsworth and Viola (1992) p. 142; Dodge and Feshbach (1992) p. 250; Dunn (1978) p. 174; Mason (1976) 2, pp. 17–18; Koonz (1988) pp. 394–98; Wylie (1957) p. 159.

6 Bradley (1989) pp. 90–91; Robertson (1990) p. 132; Dodge and Feshbach (1992) p. 250; Kolinsky (1989) p. 159.

7 First-Dilic (1978) p. 130; Bleksaune *et al.* (1993) p. 114; Besteman (1989) p. 130; Moulin (1981) p. 187; Sacks (1978) p. 150; Cernea (1978) pp. 110–13; Golde (1975) p. 115. Half of Protestant women thought machines made work easier, and two-thirds of Catholic women thought not, illustrating the effect of customs in farm life.

8 Sommestad (1994) pp. 55, 60, 70; Allart (1981) p. 709; Bridenthal (1973); Hansen (1982) pp. 234–35; Bleksaune *et al.* (1993) pp. 114, 121; Bouquet (1984) pp. 143–44; Besteman (1989) p. 134.

9 Thompson *et al.* (1983) pp. 11, 173.

10 Thompson *et al.* (1983) pp. 168, 173–74; Dorian (1985); Butcher (1987); Johnson (1984) p. 165.

11 Moulin (1981) p. 186; Wilke (1986) p. 175; Griepentrog (1986); Pescatello (1976) p. 44; Cernea (1978) p. 110; Mørkeberg (1978) pp. 96–98; Pina-Cabral (1986) pp. 18–19; Besteman (1989) pp. 130–31; Greenwood (1976) pp. 50–51; Engel (1980) pp. 69–70; Levi (1982); Holmes and Quataert (1986) p. 210; Inhetveen (1982) pp. 246–61; First-Dilic (1978) p. 134; Mason (1976) 2, p. 17; Hoggart *et al.* (1995) p. 22; Blom (1990) p. 166; Gordon (1990) p. 212; Golde (1975) p. 114.

12 Mørkeberg (1978) pp. 95–98; Bleksaune *et al.* (1993) pp. 118–19; Hillebrand and Blom (1993) pp. 179, 181; Pfeffer (1989) p. 65; Besteman (1989) pp. 132–34; Gasson (1984) p. 220; Shortall (1992) p. 439; Stebbing (1984) pp. 202–05; Bouquet (1984) pp. 146–49; Johnson (1984); Gilligan (1984) pp. 102–04; Allart (1981) p. 712.

13 Thompson *et al.* (1983) pp. 175–79; Cernea (1978) p. 118; Tryfan (1972).

14 Pina-Cabral (1986) p. 85; Shortall (1992) pp. 431–37; Hillebrand and Blom (1993) pp. 180–81.

15 Pescatello (1976) pp. 44–45; Wylie (1957) pp. 268, 70–73; Stebbing (1984) p. 206; Hoggart *et al.* (1995) p. 222; Johnson (1984) p. 171.

287

NOTES

16 Zerner (1987) p. 18; Boxer (1986) pp. 47, 48–50, 59n12 and (1981) pp. 404, 413; Morris (1986) pp. 105, 110; Schmiechen (1984); Hudson and Lee (1990) p. 30; Oliunina (1983) p. 163; Franzoi (1987) pp. 149, 153; Beier (1983) pp. 37–38; Collins (1991) p. 152; Albert (1990) p. 162.
17 Bairoch *et al.* (1968).
18 Collins (1991) pp. 155–56n36; Blom (1990) p. 162; Boxer (1981) pp. 412–14; Albert (1990) pp. 162–63; Glickman (1984) p. 43.
19 Pennington and Westover (1989) pp. 126, 132; Hausen (1986) p. 4; Pope (1991) p. 22; Bythell (1978) p. 148; Reynolds (1996) pp. 87–88; Boxer (1981) p. 415n37; Allart (1981) p. 712; Zerner (1987) pp. 17–18; Bairoch *et al.* (1968); Roberts (1984) p. 205.
20 Hope *et al.* (1976) pp. 89, 101; Lagrave (1994) pp. 482–83.
21 McMillan (1981) pp. 66–67; Beier (1983) pp. 38–39, 61, 75–79; Albert (1990) p. 165, also pp. 159, 163–66; Boxer (1986) pp. 52, 54; Treble (1986) pp. 39, 46; Cadbury (1906).
22 Treble (1986) p. 38.
23 *Ibid.*; Pennington and Westover (1989) pp. 18–19, 144–45; Beier (1983) pp. 39–40, 86, 88; Boxer (1981) p. 407.
24 Pennington and Westover (1989) pp. 160, 162; Hope *et al.* (1976) pp. 88–89, 94–95, 97, 107–08; Lagrave (1994) pp. 482–83; Owen (1994) pp. 49, 157.
25 Boxer (1981) pp. 404, 408, 417, 418, 422.
26 *Ibid.* pp. 409, 412.
27 Oliunina (1983) p. 171.
28 Fout (1986) p. 53.
29 McMillan (1981) pp. 61, 63; Oliunina (1983) pp. 162–63, 168; Boxer (1981) p. 409; Albert (1990) p. 166.
30 Oliunina (1983) p. 164.
31 Allart (1981) p. 712; Pennington and Westover (1989) pp. 145, 148–49.
32 Glickman (1984) pp. 38, 41–42, 63; Tilly and Scott (1978) pp. 162–63; Schrover (1995) p. 172; Morris (1986) pp. 104, 110; Baader (1991) p. 160; Boxer (1981) p. 414 and quote in (1986) p. 49; Collins (1991); McMillan (1981) p. 61; Franzoi (1987) p. 151; Beier (1983) p. 114.
33 Beier (1991) p. 162 and (1983) p. 109; Morris (1986) pp. 105, 111; Roberts (1984) pp. 66, 67; Hope *et al.* (1976) 95.
34 Baader (1991) pp. 161, 162.
35 Albert (1990) p. 161; Pennington and Westover (1989) pp. 139, 143.
36 Boxer (1981) p. 413; Taylor (1977) p. 52; Treble (1986) p. 37; P.P. (1909) p. 247, quoted in Albert (1990) p. 160; Hudson and Lee (1990) p. 30; P.P. (1908) p. vii.
37 Quoted in Pennington and Westover (1989) p. 163.
38 Boxer (1986) pp. 46, 51; Franzoi (1987) pp. 152–53; Hilden (1993) p. 191; Hausen (1986) pp. 3–4; Albert (1990) pp. 161, 169–70; Pennington and Westover (1989) pp. 134–35, 146. See Bythell (1978) p. 148 who contradicts.
39 Boxer (1981) pp. 416–17 and (1986) p. 51; Roberts (1984) pp. 137, 139; Chinn (1988) p. 102; Pennington and Westover (1989) p. 163; Albert (1990) p. 164; McMillan (1981) p. 65.
40 Braverman (1974) p. 62; Allen and Wolkowitz (1987) pp. 243–49.
41 Definitions of work are not strictly comparable between countries. Bairoch *et al.* (1968); Mitchell (1978). See statistics reported by Mason (1976) 2, pp. 6–9, 17; Bock (1994) p. 158; Frevert (1988) pp. 155–56; Grant (1990) p. 223; Reynolds (1996) p. 102; Beddoe (1989) p. 64; Tilly and Scott (1978) p. 152; Sohn (1994) pp. 98–99; Bridenthal (1977) pp. 430–31; Stockmann (1985) p. 449; McIvor (1992) p. 140; Tilly (1993) pp. 34–35, 40; Lagrave (1994) p. 459; Hilden (1986) pp. 22–24.

42 Stockmann (1985) p. 450; Zerner (1987) p. 22; Frevert (1988) p. 86; Hilden
   (1993) p. 181; Leleu (1981) pp. 658, 660; Ellerkamp and Jungmann (1987)
   pp. 130–31. For example, see Tilly (1993) pp. 34, 41, 42; Chenut (1996) p. 84;
   Glickman (1984) pp. 76–78, 82; Burdy *et al.* (1987) pp. 37–38.
43 Glickman (1984) p. 76.
44 Bairoch *et al.* (1968); Tilly and Scott (1978) p. 155; Whipp (1990) p. 13; Hilden
   (1993) pp. 186–87, 192–93; Glickman (1984) p. 84; Reynolds (1989) p. 88;
   Frader (1996) pp. 149–51; Stockmann (1985) p. 461; Glucksmann (1990)
   pp. 48–49.
45 See Braybon and Summerfield (1987); Zerner (1987) p. 20; Shrover (1995);
   Sommestad (1994); Reynolds (1996) p. 101; Bridenthal (1973) p. 157 and (1977)
   p. 430.
46 Savage (1988) p. 214; Beddoe (1989) pp. 66–67.
47 Stockmann (1985) pp. 455–56, 461, 467; Bridenthal (1973) pp. 157–58; Tilly and
   Scott (1978) pp. 154–55; Thébaud (1994) p. 70; Reynolds (1996) pp. 102–03;
   Lagrave (1994) pp. 459–60; Duchen (1994) p. 139; Savage (1988) p. 210;
   Glucksmann (1990) p. 34; Zerner (1987) p. 20; Willson (1993) pp. 11, 129.
48 Reynolds (1996) p. 103; Fridenson (1979); Grant (1990) pp. 222–23; Willson
   (1993) p. 103.
49 Anderson and Zinsser (1988) 2, p. 259; Orthmann (1986) pp. 29–36; Willson
   (1993) p. 104.
50 Duchen (1994) p. 140; Mason (1976) 2, p. 9; Hilden (1993) pp. 191–92; Beddoe
   (1989) p. 66; Fridenson (1986) pp. 516–18; Fourcaut (1982) pp. 103, 109; McIvor
   (1992) p. 149.
51 Schrover (1995) pp. 181–84; Willson (1993) p. 103, 103n7; Glucksmann (1990)
   pp. 61, 233; see also Savage (1988) p. 222; Ellerkamp and Jungmann (1987)
   p. 132; McIvor (1992) p. 158.
52 Leleu (1981) pp. 659, 662; Mason (1976) 2, p. 16; Glickman (1984) pp. 86–87;
   Guilbert (1966) p. 208; Thébaud (1994) p. 70.
53 Guilbert (1966) pp. 133–35; P.P. 1919, quoted by Bradley (1989) p. 127;
   Bridenthal (1973) p. 159; Zerner (1987) pp. 20–21; Willson (1993) pp. 132–33;
   Fout (1986) p. 45.
54 Reynolds (1996) p. 100.
55 Glucksmann (1990) p. 277.
56 Willson (1993) p. 131, 152; Bradley (1989) pp. 130, 142.
57 A description of women's assembly-line work is in Cavendish (1982); Zerner, cited
   by Reynolds (1996) pp. 103–104; Pollert (1981) p. 30; McIvor (1992) p. 149;
   Beauchamp (1937) p. 42; Beddoe (1989) p. 68; Willson (1993) p. 132; de Groot
   and Schrover (1995a) pp. 283–84; Glucksmann (1990) pp. 199–202; Bradley
   (1989) pp. 168–70.
58 Leleu (1981) pp. 658, 662; Bradley (1989) p. 139; Chenut (1996) p. 79; *Monthly
   Report of the National Union of Boot and Shoe Operatives*, March 1910, quoted in
   Greenfield (1995) p. 88; Willson (1993) pp. 132, 139–40.
59 Frevert (1988) pp. 184–85; Reynolds (1996) p. 104; Frader (1987); Willson (1993)
   pp. 141–42.

11 NEW WORK

1 Miller (1981) p. 20.
2 McBride (1977a) p. 665.
3 Benson and Shaw (1992) pp. 153, 173–75, 179; Lancaster (1995) pp. 24, 37–38;

NOTES

Pasdermadjian (1954) p. 65; Adams (1988) p. 8; Miller (1981) p. 43; Goodman and Honeyman (1988) p. 117; see also Crossick (1996).

4 Bédarida (1979) pp. 50–51, 205–06; Royle (1987) pp. 104–05; Leroux-Hugon (1987), p. 56; Stearns (1975) pp. 218–19.

5 See, for example, Bachrach (1987) pp. 69–88; Reynolds (1996) p. 93; Adams (1988). De Haan disputes this terminology (1992); Bridenthal (1977) p. 434.

6 Bradley (1989) pp. 175–76; Tilly and Scott (1978) p. 183; Winstanley (1983) p. 67; Bachrach (1983) pp. 7–15; 'Célestine' (1870) p. 10 and Storm-van der Chijs (1863) p. 466, quoted in de Haan (n.d.) p. 3.

7 Bairoch *et al.* (1968); Lockwood (1989) p. 122.

8 Bradley (1989) pp. 178, 181, 186; P.P. (1894) LXXXI, part 1, p. 10, (1908) LIX, vol. 1, pp. 209, 296, and (1919) XXXI, p. 146; Miller (1981) pp. 193–94; Perrot (1987) p. 52; Frevert (1988) p. 76; McIvor (1992) pp. 141–42.

9 Holcombe (1973) pp. 104–06; McBride (1977a) p. 668; Winstanley (1983) p. 68; Bradley (1989) p. 178; Lancaster (1995) p. 138.

10 Bradley (1989) p. 183.

11 Holcombe (1973); Adburgham (1964) p. 146; P.P. (1919) XXXI, p. 110.

12 Smith (1982); S. Webb, 'Gender and Authority in the Workplace,' paper presented at BSA Annual Conference, 1982, cited in Bradley (1989) p. 186; see also pp. 182–83.

13 Miller (1981) p. 64; Cockburn (1985) pp. 79–80, 86–91.

14 Jordan (1996) pp. 65–66; Zerner (1987) p. 15; Anderson (1988) p. 5; Adams (1988) pp. 14–15; Lewis (1988) p. 35; Riemer and Fout (1980) pp. 40–41; MBYLA Annual Report, 1884, p. 8, quoted in Kirrane (1987) p. 9.

15 De Haan (n.d.) p. 3; Bachrach (1987) pp. 71–73, 75–76; Kirrane (1987) p. 6; Zimmeck (1995) pp. 71–72 and (1988) p. 90.

16 Frevert (1988) pp. 177, 179, 182; Reynolds (1996) pp. 93–94; Zerner (1987) p. 15; de Haan (1996) p. 4; Anderson (1988) p. 12.

17 Crompton (1988) pp. 123–27; Hakim (1979); Kolinsky (1989) pp. 159–74; Lewis (1988) pp. 32–34; Frevert (1988) pp. 177, 270, 276; Duchen (1994) p. 131, 134–35, 153; Bachrach (1983) p. 106; Tijdens (1994) p. 135.

18 Riemer and Fout (1980) p. 47.

19 Howe (1996) pp. 16, 18; Offen (1983) pp. 257, 270–71, 277; Duchen (1994) pp. 143–44; Albisetti (1986) p. 94.

20 Suzanne Bidault (née Borel), *Par une Porte entre-baillée* (1972) p. 20, quoted in Reynolds (1996) p. 95; Duchen (1994) p. 144; Crompton and Sanderson (1990) p. 67; Lagrave (1994) p. 472.

21 Booth (1996) p. 267; Reynolds (1996) pp. 95–96; Duchen (1994) p. 143; Haupt (1992) pp. 150, 154; Crompton and Sanderson (1990) pp. 74–75.

22 Russell (1996) p. 293.

23 Geyer-Kordesh and Ferguson (1996) p. 304.

24 Booth (1996) pp. 272–73.

25 Ibid., pp. 268, 270; Duchen (1994) p. 143; Albisetti (1986) p. 95.

26 Leroux-Hugon (1987) p. 55.

27 Gamarnikow (1978) pp. 97, 106, 109; Bradley (1989) p. 194; Leroux-Hugon (1987) pp. 56, 60–62.

28 Hunt (1987) p. 101; Albisetti (1986) pp. 97–98, 100; Corr (1983) pp. 138, 140, 142, 143, 147; Widdowson (1983); Bradley (1989) pp. 203–04, 206–08, 210; Reynolds (1996) p. 98; Adams (1996) p. 208; P.P. (1919) XXXI, p. 21; Brittain (1928) p. 65; Partington (1976) p. 36.

29 Hunt (1987) p. 101; Bradley (1989) p. 209; Burstall, quoted in Vicinus (1985) p. 175; Widdowson (1983); Blackstone (1996) pp. 10–11; Albisetti (1986) pp. 100–01; Moore (1991) p. 51; Reynolds (1996) p. 97.

30 Jordan (1996) p. 66; Anderson (1988) p. 5; Dohrn (1988) pp. 49, 52; Zerner (1987) p. 15.

31 Adburgham (1964) p. 236.

32 Lancaster (1995) p. 177; P.P. (1879) XXX, pp. 797–98, 800; Anderson (1976) p. 3; McBride (1977a) p. 669; Gudvan (1925) p. 195.

33 Anderson (1976) p. 3; Reynolds (1996) p. 93; Bachrach (1987); Zimmeck (1988) p. 90; Miller (1981) p. 90; McBride (1977a) p. 668; Goodman and Honeyman (1988) p. 117; Silverstone (1976).

34 Quotes in Kirrane (1987) p. 6 and Holcombe (1973) p. 146; Crompton and Mann (1986) p. 21.

35 'Vereinsnachrichten,' *Neue Bahnen: Organ des Allgemeinen Deutschen Frauenvereins* (1866) and Paquet-Mille in Riemer and Fout (1980) pp. 39, 43–44, also p. 31; Holcombe (1973) p. 210; de Haan (1996) p. 3, (1992) p. 480 and (n.d.) pp. 2, 5–7; 'Passing Notes' (1889) p. 63.

36 M. Corina, *Fine Silks and Oak Counters*, pp. 80–81, quoted in Lancaster (1995) p. 141; Stephenson and Brown (1990) pp. 13–15, 17–18; Winstanley (1983) p. 69; Pentland and Calton Reminiscence Group, *Friday Night was Brasso Night* (1987), quoted in McIvor (1992) p. 147, also p. 156; Lau (1925), in Frevert (1988) p. 181; Woodward (1960) pp. 11, 29, 50–51.

37 McMillan (1981) p. 57; Zimmeck (1986) pp. 164, 167; Lewis (1988) p. 43; Sanderson (1986) pp. 145–60, also (1988) p. 30; Frevert (1988) p. 181; Reynolds (1996) p. 94.

38 Zerner (1987) p. 16; Zimmeck (1986) p. 165; Sanderson (1988) p. 30.

39 Lewis (1988) pp. 43, 45; Adams (1988) p. 53; Zimmeck (1995) p. 84 and (1988) p. 92; Bachrach (1983) p. 105; de Haan (1996) p. 5 and (1992) p. 483.

40 Holcombe (1973) p. 107; McMillan (1981) p. 64; McBride (1977a).

41 'Jane' in Jamieson (1990) p. 139.

42 Lockwood (1989) pp. 106–07.

43 McBride (1977a) p. 675; Miller (1981) p. 195n; Holcombe (1973) p. 111; Adams (1988) p. 17.

44 Hogarth (1926) pp. 147–48.

45 Frevert (1988) pp. 179, 183; Zimmeck (1986) p. 163; Lancaster (1995) p. 150; my calculations. 'Briefe' (1878) in Riemer and Fout (1980) pp. 40–42.

46 Dohrn (1988) p. 59; Bachrach (1987) p. 83; Miller (1981) p. 147; Lancaster (1995) pp. 132–33; McIvor (1992) p. 148; Winstanley (1983) p. 57; McBride (1977a) pp. 673–74; Gudvan (1925) p. 195; Tilly and Scott (1978) p. 183.

47 Dohrn (1988) pp. 57–61; Adams (1988) p. 10; McBride (1977a) pp. 672–73, 377; Lancaster (1995) p. 130; Bradley (1989) pp. 179–80; Miller (1981) pp. 86, 220; Goodman and Honeyman (1988) p. 117.

48 Roberts (1984) p. 64.

49 McBride (1977a) pp. 672, 675–76; Dohrn (1988) p. 60; Bachrach (1987) p. 83; Miller (1981) pp. 99–107; Lancaster (1995) p. 142; Zimmeck (1995) p. 82; Lewis (1988) p. 43; 'Briefe' (1878) in Riemer and Fout (1980) pp. 40–42.

50 Anderson (1988) p. 22; Tilly and Scott (1978) p. 183; McIvor (1992) p. 48; McBride (1977a) pp. 673, 678; Adams (1988) pp. 57–58; Lancaster (1995) p. 135; Miller (1981) p. 147.

51 Adams (1988) pp. 9–10.

52 'How to Utilize the Powers of Women,' *English Woman's Journal*, 3 (1859) p. 43.

53 Jordan (1996) pp. 76, 78; Bachrach (1987) p. 72 and (1983) pp. 46–50; de Haan (n.d.) p. 3.

54 Bachrach (1987) pp. 72, 78; Hagemann (1985) pp. 146–47; Lewis (1988) p. 39; Zimmeck (1988) p. 91.

55 Reynolds (1996) p. 93; SPRU (1985) p. 211; Bradley (1989) p. 186; Anderson

(1988) pp. 6–7; also Reynolds (1996) p. 93; de Haan (1992) p. 480; Carnaffan (1988) p. 81.

56 Zimmeck (1995) pp. 74–75, 77–78; Reynolds (1996) p. 93.

57 Van Woude, *Typewriting*, p. 9, quoted in de Haan (n.d.) p. 7.

58 de Haan (n.d.) pp. 7–8; Anna Davin, 'Genteel Occupations in Late Nineteenth-century London, Class and Employment of Women' (n.d.), p. 32; quoted in Carnaffan (1988) p. 82.

59 See, for example, Softley (1985) pp. 222–51; see overview in Bird (1980); Zmroczek and Henwood (1983); Braverman (1974); Barker and Downing (1980) pp. 64–99; Lie and Rasmussen (1985) pp. 43–52; Buchanan and Boddy (1982) pp. 1–11; Crompton and Jones (1984).

60 Tijdens (1994) p. 138; Winker (1994) p. 144; Softley (1985) p. 235.

61 Anderson (1988) p. 17; Sanderson (1988) p. 30; Lancaster (1995) p. 177.

62 Jordan (1996) pp. 66–67, 75; Lewis (1988) pp. 35–36, 39; Hagemann (1985) pp. 148–49, 151; de Haan (n.d.) p. 19n27; Bachrach (1987) p. 76.

63 De Haan (1996) p. 5.

64 Bachrach (1983) p. 105; Lewis (1988) pp. 35–36; Reynolds (1996) pp. 93–94. Zimmeck's research on the British Civil Service provides a well-focused look at one influential employer of female clerical workers during this period: Zimmeck (1984).

65 Bradley (1989) p. 187; McBride (1977a) p. 668; Kolinsky (1989) p. 167; Duchen (1994) p. 134.

66 Crompton (1988) p. 122.

67 Ibid., pp. 134–36.

12 CONCLUSION

1 Frader and Rose (1996) p. 2.

2 *Ibid.*, p. 11.

3 Quotes in Reynolds (1996) p. 88, Gittins (1982) p. 115; Abelhauser, in Dülmen (1991) p. 168; Hilden (1986) p. 36; Saraceno (1992) p. 253.

4 Quataert (1985) pp. 1125–27.

5 Reynolds (1989) p. 63. For example, see Chenut (1996) p. 82 on the interaction of *métier* and worker identity in France. As she argues, 'the meanings attached to métier were contested and have evolved over time'.

6 Quotes in Grant (1990) pp. 226, 230.

7 Glucksmann (1990) p. 277; Cockburn (1983) pp. 117–18.

8 de Groot and Schrover (1995b) p. 5; Glucksmann (1990) p. 277; Lagrave (1994) p. 459; Reynolds (1989) p. 63; Willson (1993) p. 144.

9 Sarsby (1995) p. 131; Bradley (1989) pp. 162–64; de Groot and Schrover (1995a) pp. 284, 296 and (1995b) p. 12.

10 Reynolds (1989) pp. 51–52, 128, 137; Grant (1990) p. 226; Burdy et al. (1987) p. 49.

11 Quoted in Bridenthal (1973) p. 159.

12 Duchen (1994) p. 152.

13 de Groot and Schrover (1995a) p. 294; Zerner (1987) p. 22; Bradley (1989) p. 139; Weil, quoted in Reynolds (1996) p. 103; Burdy et al. (1987) pp. 42–43; Leleu (1981) p. 660.

14 de Groot and Schrover (1995b) p. 11; Willson (1993) p. 105; Burdy et al. (1987) pp. 50–51; Honeyman (1996) p. 455; Cockburn (1985) p. 12; Braverman (1974); Tijdens (1994) p. 138.

15 Allart (1981) p. 710; Brittain (1928) p. 4; Ellerkamp and Jungmann (1987)

NOTES

p. 133; Fout (1986) p. 47; Tilly (1993) p. 43; de Groot (1995) p. 62; de Groot and Schrover (1995a) pp. 289, 291; Willson (1993) pp. 133, 151, 161–62; Bridenthal (1973) p. 160.
16 Kolinsky (1989) p. 152.

BIBLIOGRAPHY

Abbreviations

P.P.	Great Britain. Parliamentary Papers
O.S.A.	Old Statistical Account of Scotland
E.R.O.	Essex Record Office
S.R.O.	Staffordshire Record Office
KB	Kingston Upon Thames Borough Archives

Abensour, Léon. (1923; 1966) *La Femme et le Féminisme en France avant la Révolution*. Geneva: Slatkine-Maganotis.

Abrahams, Ray G. (1984) 'Cooperation on and between Eastern Finnish Family Farms.' *Family and Work in Rural Societies, Perspectives on Non-wage Labour*. Norman Long, ed. London: Tavistock Publications.

Accampo, Elinor. (1989) *Industrialization, Family Life and Class Relations: Saint Chamond, 1815–1914*. Berkeley: University of California Press.

Adams, Carole Elizabeth. (1988) *Women Clerks in Wilhelmine Germany; Issues of Class and Gender*. Cambridge: Cambridge University Press.

Adams, Catherine. (1996) 'Public legislation, private decisions: The Life of Miss Anywoman, Scottish Teacher, Born 1909.' *Women and Higher Education: Past Present and Future*. Mary R. Masson and Deborah Simonton, eds, pp. 204–10. Aberdeen: University of Aberdeen Press.

Adburgham, Alison. (1964) *Shops and Shopping*. London: George Allen and Unwin.

Albert, Alice J. (1990) 'Fit Work for Women: Sweated Home-workers in Glasgow, c. 1875–1914.' *The World is Ill Divided: Women's Work in Scotland in the Nineteenth and Early Twentieth Centuries*. Eleanor Gordon and Esther Breitenbach, eds, pp. 158–77. Edinburgh: Edinburgh University Press.

Albisetti, James. (1986) 'Women and the Professions in Imperial Germany.' *German Women in the Eighteenth and Nineteenth Centuries. A Social and Literary History*. Ruth-Ellen B. Joeres and Mary Jo Maynes, eds, pp. 94–109. Bloomington: Indiana University Press.

Alexander, Sally. (1983) *Women's Work in 19th Century London: A Study of the Years 1820–50*. London: Journeyman Press.

Alexander, Sally. (1984) 'Women, Class and Sexual Difference in the 1830s and 1840s: Some Reflections on the Writing of a Feminist History.' *History Workshop*, 17, pp. 125–49.

Allart, Marie Christine. (1981) 'Les Femmes de trois villages de l'Artois: travail et vécu quotidien (1919–1939).' *Histoire des femmes du nord; special issue of Revue du Nord.* Marcel Gillet, ed., 63, 250, pp. 703–24.

Allen, Sheila and Carol Wolkowitz. (1987) *Homeworking Myths and Realities.* London: Macmillan Education.

Ambrosius, Gerold and William H. Hubbard. (1989) *A Social and Economic History of Twentieth Century Europe.* London: Harvard University Press.

Aminzade, Ronald. (1979) 'The transformation of social solidarities in nineteenth-century Toulouse.' *Consciousness and Class Experience in Nineteenth-century Europe.* John M. Merriman, ed., pp. 85–105. London: Holmes and Meier Publishers, Inc.

Anderson, Bonnie S. and Judith P. Zinsser, (1988) *A History of Their Own: Women in Europe from Prehistory to the Present.* 2 vols. London: Penguin.

Anderson, Gregory. (1976) *Victorian Clerks.* Manchester: Manchester University Press.

Anderson, Gregory. (1988) 'The White-blouse Revolution.' *The White-blouse Revolution, Female Office Workers since 1870.* Gregory Anderson, ed., pp. 1–26. Manchester: Manchester University Press.

Anderson, Michael. (1971) *Family Structure in Nineteenth-century Lancashire.* Cambridge: Cambridge University Press.

Anderson, Michael. (1980) *Approaches to the History of the Western Family, 1500–1914.* London: Macmillan Press Ltd.

Andrew, Donna. (1991) 'Two Medical Charities in Eighteenth-century London: The Lock Hospital and the Lying-in Charity for Married Women.' *Medicine and Charity before the Welfare State.* Jonathan Barry and Colin Jones, eds, pp. 82–97. London: Routledge.

Ankarloo, Bengt. (1979) 'Agriculture and Women's Work: Directions of Change in the West, 1700–1900.' *Journal of Family History,* 4, pp. 111–20.

Arensberg, C. M. and S. T. Kemball. (1971) 'The Small Farm Family in Rural Ireland.' *Sociology of the Family, Selected Readings.* Michael Anderson, ed., Harmondsworth: Penguin Books Ltd.

Armstrong, Alan. (1988) *Farmworkers in England and Wales. A Social and Economic History, 1770–1980.* London: BT Batsford Limited.

Augustine, Dolores L. (1991) 'Arriving in the Upper Class: The Wealthy Business Elite of Wilhelmine Germany.' *The German Bourgeoisie.* David Blackbourn and Richard Evans, eds, pp. 46–86. London: Routledge.

B[rocher], Victorine. (1976) *Souvenirs d'une morte vivante.* Paris: F. Maspero.

Baader, Ottilie. (1991) 'Factory and Home Work as a Seamstress: End of Nineteenth Century.' *Frauen, ein historisches Lesebuch.* Andrea van Dülmen, ed., pp. 160–62. München: Verlag C. H. Beck.

Bachrach, Susan. (1983) 'Dames Employées, the Feminization of Postal Work in Nineteenth-century France.' *Women and History,* 8.

Bachrach, Susan. (1987) 'La Féminisation des PTT au tournant du siècle.' *Mouvement Social,* 140, pp. 69–87.

Bailey, W. and G. Culley. (1794) *General View of the Agriculture of Northumberland, Cumberland and Westmoreland.* London: Board of Agriculture.

Bairoch, P., T. Deldycke, H. Gelders and J.-M. Limbor. (1968) *The Working Population and Its Structure.* Brussels: Institut de Sociologie, Université Libre de Bruxelles.

Barker, Jane and Hazel Downing. (1980) 'Word Processing and the Transformation of the Patriarchal Relations of Control in the Office.' *Capital and Class,* 10, pp. 64–99.

Barlee, Ellen. (1863) *A Visit to Lancashire in December 1862.* London: Seely.

Barrett, Michelle and Mary McIntosh. (1980) 'The Family Wage.' *Changing Experience of Women*. Elizabeth Whitelegg *et al.*, eds, pp. 71–85. Oxford: Blackwell.

Baumert, G. (1954) *Deutsche Familien nach dem Krieg*. Darmstadt: E. Roether.

Beauchamp, Jean. (1937) *Women who Work*. London: Lawrence and Wishart.

Bédarida, François. (1979) *A Social History of England, 1851–1975*. London: Methuen & Co, Ltd.

Beddoe, Deirdre. (1989) *Back to Home and Duty: Women between the Wars, 1919–1939*. London: Pandora.

Behagg, Clive. (1979) 'Custom, Class and Change: The Trade Societies of Birmingham.' *Social History*, 4 , 3, pp. 455–80.

Beier, Rosemarie. (1983) *Frauenarbeit und Frauenalltag in Deutschen Kaiserreich Heimarbeiterinnen in der Berliner Bekleidungsindustrie, 1880–1914*. Frankfurt: Campus.

Beier, Rosemarie. (1991) 'Textilarbeiterinnen.' *Frauen, ein Historisches Lesebuch*. Andrea van Dülmen, ed., pp. 162–64. München: Verlag C. H. Beck.

Benson, John and Gareth Shaw, eds. (1992) *The Evolution of Retail Systems, c. 1800–1914*. Leicester: Leicester University Press.

Berg, Maxine. (1985; 1994) *The Age of Manufactures: Industry, Innovation and Work in Britain, 1700–1820*. London: Fontana Press, 2nd edn Routledge.

Berg, Maxine. (1989) 'Women's Work, Mechanisation and the Early Phases of Industrialisation in England.' *The Historical Meanings of Work*. Patrick Joyce, ed., pp. 64–98. Cambridge: Cambridge University Press.

Berg, Maxine, ed. (1991) *Markets and Manufacture in Early Industrial Europe*. London: Routledge.

Berg, Maxine. (1993) 'What Difference Did Women's Work Make to the Industrial Revolution?' *History Workshop Journal*, 35, pp. 22–44.

Berg, Maxine and Pat Hudson. (1992) 'Rehabilitating the Industrial Revolution.' *Economic History Review*, 45, 1, pp. 24–50.

Berg, Maxine, Pat Hudson and Michael Sonenscher, eds. (1983) *Manufacture in Town and Country before the Factory*. Cambridge: Cambridge University Press.

Besteman, Catherine. (1989) 'Economic Strategies of Farming Households in Penabranca, Portugal.' *Economic Development and Cultural Change*, 37, pp. 129–93.

Bird, E. (1980) *Information Technology in the Office: The Impact on Women's Jobs*. London: Equal Opportunities Commission.

Blackbourn, David and Richard Evans, eds. (1991) *The German Bourgeoisie: Essays on the Social History of the German Middle Class from the Late Eighteenth to the Early Twentieth Century*. London: Routledge.

Blackstone, Tessa. (1996) 'Education and Careers: A Rough Road to the Top.' *Women and Higher Education: Past Present and Future*. Mary R. Masson and Deborah Simonton, eds, pp. 5–14. Aberdeen: University of Aberdeen Press.

Bland, Lucy, Charlotte Brunsdon, Dorothy Hobson and Janice Winship. (1978) 'Women "Inside and Outside" the Relations of Production.' *Women Take Issue, Aspects of Women's Subordination*. Women's Studies Group, pp. 35–78. London: Hutchinson.

Bleksaune, Arild, Wava G. Haney, and Marit S. Hougen. (1993) 'On the Question of Feminization of Production on Part-time Farms: Evidence from Norway.' *Rural Sociology*, 58, pp. 111–29.

Blom, Ida. (1990) '"Hun er den Raadende over Husets økonomiske Angliggender", Changes in Women's Work and Family Responsibilities in Norway since the 1860s.' *Women's Work and the Family Economy in Historical Perspective*. Pat Hudson and W. R. Lee, eds, pp. 157–82. Manchester: Manchester University Press.

Blom, Ida. (1991) 'Voluntary Motherhood 1900–1930; Theories and Politics of a Norwegian Feminist in an International Perspective.' *Maternity and Gender Policies, Women and the Rise of the European Welfare States, 1880s–1950s.* Gisela Bock and Pat Thane, eds, pp. 21–39. London: Routledge.

Blum, Jerome. (1978) *The End of the Old Order in Europe.* Princeton, N.J.: Princeton University Press.

Bock, Gisela. (1991) 'Challenging Dichotomies: Perspectives on Women's History.' *Writing Women's History; International Perspectives.* Karen Offen and Jane Rendall, eds, pp. 1–24. London: Macmillan.

Bock, Gisela. (1994) 'Nazi Gender Policies and Women's History.' *A History of Women in the West, V. Toward a Cultural Identity in the Twentieth Century.* François Thébaud, ed., pp. 149–76. Cambridge, Mass.: The Belknap Press of Harvard University.

Booth, Margaret. (1996) 'Women as Lawyers.' *Women and Higher Education: Past Present and Future.* Mary R. Masson and Deborah Simonton, eds, pp. 267–73. Aberdeen: University of Aberdeen Press.

Bose, Christine. C. (1979) 'Technology and Changes in the Division of Labour in the American Home.' *Women's Studies International Quarterly,* 2, pp. 295–304.

Bouquet, Mary. (1984) 'Women's Work in Rural South-west England.' *Family and Work in Rural Societies, Perspectives on Non-wage Labour.* Norman Long, ed., pp. 142–59. London: Tavistock Publications.

Bourdieu, Pierre. (1979) 'Marriage Strategies as Strategies of Social Reproduction.' *Family and Society: Selections from the 'Annales'.* R. Forster, and O. Ranum, eds, pp. 117–44. Baltimore: The Johns Hopkins University Press.

Bourke, Joanna. (1993) *Husbandry to Housewifery: Economic Change and Housework in Ireland, 1890–1914.* Oxford: Clarendon Press.

Bourke, Joanna. (1994) 'Housewifery in Working-class England, 1860–1914.' *Past and Present,* 143, pp. 167–97.

Bowden, Sue and Avner Offer. (1994) 'Household Appliances and the Use of Time: The United States and Britain since the 1920s.' *Economic History Review,* XLVII, 4, pp. 725–48.

Boxer, Marilyn J. (1981) 'Women in Industrial Work: The Flowermakers of the Parisian Belle Epoque.' *French Historical Studies,* 12, pp. 401–23.

Boxer, M. J. (1986) 'Protective Legislation and Home Industry: The Marginalization of Women Workers in Late Nineteenth Century and Early Twentieth Century France.' *Journal of Social History,* 19, pp. 45–65.

Boxer, M. J. and J. H. Quataert, eds. (1987) *Connecting Spheres, Women in the Western World, 1500 to the Present.* Oxford: Oxford University Press.

Bradley, Harriet. (1989) *Men's Work, Women's Work.* Oxford: Polity Press.

Braudel, Fernand. (1985) *The Wheels of Commerce.* London: Fontana Press.

Braverman, Harry. (1974) *Labor and Monopoly Capital.* New York: Monthly Review Press.

Braverman, Harry. (1982) 'Capitalism and the Division of Labour.' *Classes, Power and Conflict.* A. Giddens and D. Held, eds, pp. 148–56. Basingstoke: The Macmillan Press Ltd.

Braybon, Gail. (1981) *Women Workers in the First World War.* London: Croom Helm.

Braybon, Gail and Penny Summerfield. (1987) *Out of the Cage. Women's Experiences in Two World Wars.* London: Routledge and Kegan Paul.

Bridenthal, Renate. (1973) 'Beyond "Kinder, Küche, Kirche": Weimar Women at Work.' *Central European History,* VI, 2, pp. 148–66.

Bridenthal, Renate. (1977) 'Something Old, Something New: Women between the Two World Wars.' *Becoming Visible, Women in European History*. Renate Bridenthal and Claudia Koonz, eds, 1st edn pp. 422–44. Boston: Houghton, Mifflin Company.

Bridger, Sue. (1991) 'Young Women and Perestroika.' *Women and Society in Russia and the Soviet Union*. Linda Edmondson, ed., pp. 178–201. Cambridge: Cambridge University Press.

Brittain, Vera. (1928) *Women's Work in Modern England*. London: Noel Douglas.

Brown, A. F. J. (1969) *Essex at Work, 1770–1815*. Chelmsford: Essex Record Office.

Brown, John. (1764) *Sermons on Various Subjects*. London: L. Davis and C. Reymers.

Brown, John. (1765) *On the Female Character and Education*. London.

Buchanan, D. A. and D. Boddy. (1982) 'Advanced Technology and the Quality of Working Life: the Effects of Word Processing on Video Typists.' *Journal of Occupational Psychology*, 55, pp. 1–11.

Burdy, J. P., M. Dubesset and M. Zancarini-Fourner. (1987) 'Rôles, travaux et métiers de femmes dans une ville industrielle: Saint-Etienne, 1900–1950.' *Mouvement Social*, 140, pp. 27–54.

Burke, Gill. (1986) 'The Decline of the Independent Bâl Maiden: the Impact of Change in the Cornish Mining Industry.' *Unequal Opportunities, Women's Employment in England, 1800–1918*. Angela John, ed., pp. 179–204. Oxford: Basil Blackwell.

Burnby, J. G. L. (1977) 'Apprenticeship Records: An Examination of Inland Revenue Apprenticeship Records between the Years 1710 and 1811 with Particular Reference to Medicine and Pharmacy.' *Transactions of the British Society for the History of Pharmacy*, 1, pp. 145–94.

Burnett, John, ed. (1974) *Useful Toil: Autobiographies of Working People from the 1820s to the 1920s*. London: Allen Lane.

Butcher, David. (1987) *Following the Fishing*. London: David and Charles.

Bythell, Duncan. (1978) *The Sweated Trades*. London: Batsford.

Cadbury, Edward. (1906) *Women's Work and Women's Wages: A Phase of Life in an Industrial City*. London: T. Fisher Unwin.

Caldwell, Lesley. (1991) 'Madri d'Italia: Film and Fascist Concern with Motherhood.' *Women and Italy, Essays on Gender, Culture and History*. Zygmut Baraǹsky and Shirley Vinall, eds, pp. 43–63. London: Macmillan.

Cammarosano, Simonetta Ortaggi. (1991) 'Labouring Women in Northern and Central Italy in the Nineteenth Century.' *Society and Politics in the Age of the Risorgimento: Essays in Honour of Denis Mack Smith*. John A. Davis and Paul Ginsborg, eds, pp. 152–83. Cambridge: Cambridge University Press.

Campbell, Robert. (1747; 1969) *The London Tradesman*. London: T. Gardner.

Campbell, R. H. (1984) 'Agricultural Labour in the South-west.' *Farm Servants and Labour in Lowland Scotland, 1740–1914*. T. M. Devine, ed., pp. 55–70. Edinburgh: John Donald Publishers.

Carnaffan, Gladys. (1988) 'Commercial Education and the Female Office Worker.' *The White-blouse Revolution, Female Office Workers since 1870*. Gregory Anderson, ed., pp. 67–87. Manchester: Manchester University Press.

Cavendish, Ruth. (1982) *Women on the Line*. London: Routledge and Kegan Paul.

Cento Bull, Anna. (1991) 'Lombard Silk Spinners in the Nineteenth Century: An Industrial Workforce in a Rural Setting.' *Women and Italy, Essays on Gender, Culture and History*. Zygmut Baraǹsky and Shirley Vinall, eds, pp. 11–42. London: Macmillan.

Cernea, Michael. (1978) 'Macrosocial Change, Feminization of Agriculture and Peasant Women's Threefold Economic Role.' *Sociologica Ruralis*, 18, pp. 107–20.

Cerutti, Simona. (1992) 'Group Strategies and Trade Strategies.' *Domestic Strategies: Work and Family in France and Italy, 1600–1800: Studies in Modern Capitalism.* Stuart Woolf, ed., pp. 102–47. Cambridge: Cambridge University Press.

Chapman, John. (1752) *The Ends and Uses of Charity Schools.* London.

Chenut, Helen Harden. (1996) 'The Gendering of Skill as Historical Process: The Case of French Knitters in Industrial Troyes, 1880–1939.' *Gender and Class in Modern Europe.* Laura Frader and Sonya O. Rose, eds, pp. 77–110. London: Cornell University Press.

Chinn, Carl. (1988) *They Worked all Their Lives: Women of the Urban Poor in England, 1880–1939.* Manchester: Manchester University Press.

Clark, Alice. (1919; 1982) *Working Life of Women in the Seventeenth Century.* London: George Routledge and Sons Ltd.

Clarkson, L. A. (1985) *Proto-industrialisation: The First Phase of Industrialisation?* London: Macmillan.

Cockburn, Cynthia. (1983) *Brothers.* London: Pluto Press Limited.

Cockburn, Cynthia. (1985) *Machinery of Dominance, Women, Men and Technical Know-how.* London: Pluto Press Limited.

Coleman, D. C. (1983) 'Protoindustrialisation: A Concept Too Many.' *Economic History Review*, 36, 3, pp. 435–48.

Collet, C. E. (1894) *Report on the Statistics of Employment of Women and Girls.* H.C. [Cmd. 7564].

Collier, Mary. (1740) *The Woman's Labour, an Epistle to Mr Stephen Duck, in Answer to his Late Poem Entitled The Thresher's Labour.* London: J. Roberts.

Collins, Brenda. (1982) 'Proto-industrialization and Pre-famine Emigration.' *Social History*, 7, 2, pp. 127–46.

Collins, Brenda. (1991) 'Sewing Outwork in Ulster.' *Markets and Manufacturers in Early Industrial Europe.* Maxine Berg, ed., pp. 121–42. London: Routledge.

Collyer, R. (1761) *Parents' Directory.* London.

Corbin, Alain. (1990) *Women for Hire: Prostitution and Sexuality in France after 1850.* Cambridge, Mass.: Harvard University Press.

Corfield, Penelope. (1985) 'Tinker, Tailor, Bleeder, Grieve: On the Division of Labour in the 18th Century.' *Times Higher Education Supplement*, 13 September, p. 13.

Corr, Helen. (1983) 'The Sexual Division of Labour in the Scottish Teaching Profession, 1872–1914.' *Scottish Culture and Scottish Education, 1800–1980.* W. Humes and H. Paterson, eds, pp. 137–50. Edinburgh: Donald.

Cova, Anne. (1991) 'French Feminism and Maternity: Theories and Policies 1890–1918.' *Maternity and Gender Policies, Women and the Rise of the European Welfare States, 1880s–1950s.* Gisela Bock and Pat Thane, eds, pp. 119–37. London: Routledge.

Cowan, Ruth Schwartz. (1989) *More Work for Mother, the Ironies of Household Technology from the Open Hearth to the Microwave.* London: Free Association Books.

Crompton, Rosemary. (1988) 'The Feminisation of the Clerical Labour Force since the Second World War.' *The White-blouse Revolution, Female Office Workers since 1870.* Gregory Anderson, ed., pp. 121–42. Manchester: Manchester University Press.

Crompton, Rosemary and Gareth Jones. (1984) *White Collar Proletariat: Deskilling and Gender in Clerical Work.* London: Macmillan Press.

Crompton, Rosemary and Michael Mann. (1986) *Gender and Stratification.* Cambridge: Polity Press.

Crompton, Rosemary and Kay Sanderson. (1990) *Gendered Jobs and Social Change*. London: Unwin Hyman.

Crossick, Geoffrey. (1996) 'Review of Lancaster, *The Department Store.*' *Economic History Review*, 44, 2, pp. 400–02.

Cullen, Nuala. (1991) 'Women and the Preparation of Food in Eighteenth-century Ireland.' *Women in Early Modern Ireland*. Margaret MacCurtain and Mary O'Dowd, eds, pp. 265–76. Dublin: Wolfhound Press.

Cunningham, Hugh. (1980) *Leisure in the Industrial Revolution, c. 1780–c. 1880*. London: Croom Helm.

Cunningham, Hugh. (1995) *Children and Childhood in Western Society since 1500*. London: Longman.

Dale, Christabel. (1961) *Wiltshire Apprentices and Their Masters*. Devizes: Wiltshire Archaeology and Natural History Society.

Daly, Anne, ed. (1974) *Kingston Upon Thames Register of Apprentices, 1563–1713*. XXVIII. Guildford: Surrey Record Society.

Darrow, Margaret. (1989) *Revolution in the House: Family, Class and Inheritance in Southern France, 1775–1825*. Princeton: Princeton University Press.

Dauphin, Cecile. (1993) 'Single Women.' *A History of Women in the West, Vol. IV, Emerging Feminism from Revolution to World War*. Geneviève Fraisse and Michelle Perrot, eds, pp. 427–42. Cambridge, Mass.: The Belknap Press of Harvard University Press.

Davidoff, Leonore. (1976) 'The Rationalisation of Housework.' *Dependence and Exploitation in Work and Marriage*. Diana Leonard Barker and Sheila Allen, eds, pp. 121–51. London: Longman Group Limited.

Davidoff, Leonore. (1979) 'The Separation of Home and Work? Landladies and Lodgers in Nineteenth and Twentieth Century England.' *Fit Work for Women*. Sandra Burman, ed., pp. 64–97. London: Croom Helm.

Davidoff, Leonore, and Catherine Hall. (1987) *Family Fortunes, Men and Women of the English Middle Class, 1780–1850*. London: Hutchinson.

Davidoff, Leonore and Belinda Westover. (1986) 'Women's World in England, 1880–1939.' *Our Work, Our Lives, Our Words, Women's History and Women's Work*. Leonore Davidoff and Belinda Westover, eds. London: Macmillan Education.

Davidson, Caroline. (1982) *A Woman's Work is Never Done: A History of Housework in the British Isles*. London: Chatto and Windus.

Davis, John A. (1989) 'Industrialization in Britain and Europe before 1850: New Perspectives, Old Problems.' *The First Industrial Revolutions, the Nature of Industrialization*. Peter Mathias and John A. Davis, eds, pp. 44–68. Oxford: Basil Blackwell.

Davis, Natalie Zemon. (1979) 'Women in the Arts Mécaniques of Sixteenth Century Lyon.' *Mélanges Richard Gascon*. Lyon: Presses Universitaires de Lyon.

Davis, Natalie Zemon. (1986) 'Women in the Crafts in Sixteenth Century Lyon.' *Women and Work in Preindustrial Europe*. Barbara Hanawalt, ed., pp. 167–97. Bloomington: Indiana University Press.

'The Declining Birth-Rate.' *The Times*, 31 October 1913.

de Groot, Gertjan. (1995) 'Foreign Technology and the Gender Division of Labour in a Dutch Cotton Spinning Mill.' *Women Workers and Technological Change in Europe in the Nineteenth and Twentieth Centuries*. Gertjan de Groot and Marlou Schrover, eds, pp. 52–66. London: Taylor and Francis.

de Groot, Gertjan and Marlou Schrover. (1995a) 'Between Men and Machines: Women Workers in New Industries, 1870–1940.' *Social History*, 20 3, pp. 279–96.

de Groot, Gertjan and Marlou Schrover, eds. (1995b) *Women Workers and Technological Change in Europe in the Nineteenth and Twentieth Centuries*. London: Taylor and Francis.

de Haan, Francisca. (1992) *Sekse op Kantoor, Over vrouwelijkeid, Mannelijkheid en macht, Nederland 1860–1940*. Hilversum: Verloren.

de Haan, Francisca. (1996) 'The Meaning of Office Work for Women, 1860–1940: Some Observations from a Dutch Perspective.' Unpublished paper presented at Social History Conference, 'Social History of the Workplace.' University of Strathclyde, Glasgow.

de Haan, Francisca. (forthcoming) *Gender and the Politics of Office Work in the Netherlands, 1860–1940*. Amsterdam: Amsterdam University Press.

de Haan, Francisca (n.d.) 'The Women's Labor Movement and the Office (1860–1940).' Unpublished manuscript.

Defoe, Daniel. (1726, 1969) *Complete English Tradesman*. London: Augustus M. Kelly Publishers.

Delitala, Enrica. (1984) 'Lobster Fishing in a Sardinian Fishing Village: Stintino.' *The Fishing Culture of the World*. Béla Gunda, ed., pp. 105–19. Budapest: Akadémiai Kaidó.

'Der Wäscheschrank.' *Schweizer Frauenheim*, May 25 1895, p. 21.

Devine, T. M. (1984) 'Women Workers, 1850–1914.' *Farm Servants and Labour in Lowland Scotland, 1740–1914*. T. M. Devine, ed., pp. 98–123. Edinburgh: John Donald Publishers.

Dobson, C. R. (1980) *Masters and Journeymen: A Prehistory of Industrial Relations, 1717–1800*. London: Croom Helm.

Dodge, Norton D. and Murray Feshbach. (1992) 'The Role of Women in Soviet Agriculture.' *Russian Peasant Women*. Beatrice Farnsworth and Lynne Viola, eds, pp. 236–70. Oxford: Oxford University Press.

Dohrn, Susanne. (1988) 'Pioneers in a Dead-end Profession: The First Women Clerks in Banks and Insurance Companies.' *The White-blouse Revolution, Female Office Workers since 1870*. Gregory Anderson, ed., pp. 48–66. Manchester: Manchester University Press.

Donnison, Jean. (1977) *Midwives and Medical Men*. London: Heinemann.

Dorian, Nancy. (1985) *Tyranny of Tide*. Ann Arbor: Karoma.

Drake, Barbara. (1917) *Women in Engineering Trades*. London: Fabian Research.

Duchen, Claire. (1994) *Women's Rights and Women's Lives in France, 1944–1968*. London: Routledge.

Dülmen, Andrea van, ed. (1991) *Frauen: Ein Historisches Lesebuch*. München: Verlag C. H. Beck.

Dunlop, O. J. and R. D. Denman. (1912) *English Apprenticeship and Child Labour – A History*. London: Fisher Unwin.

Dunn, Ethel. (1978) 'Russian Rural Women.' *Women in Russia*. Dorothy Atkinson, Alexandra Dallin and Gail Lapidus, eds, pp. 167–88. Hassocks: The Harvester Press.

DuPlessis, R. and M. C. Howell. (1982) 'Reconsidering the Early Modern Urban Economy: The Cases of Leiden and Lille.' *Past and Present*, 94, pp. 49–89.

Dupree, Marguerite. (1989) 'The Community Perspective in Family History: The Potteries during the Nineteenth Century.' *The First Modern Society*. A. R. Beier,

D. Cannadine and J. M. Rosenheim, eds, pp. 549–73. Cambridge: Cambridge University Press.

Durie, A. J. (1979) *The Scottish Linen Industry in the Eighteenth Century*. Edinburgh: John Donald.

Dyhouse, Carol. (1981) *Girls Growing up in Late Victorian and Edwardian England*. London: Routledge and Kegan Paul Ltd.

Dyhouse, Carol. (1986) 'Mothers and Daughters in the Middle-class Home, c. 1870–1914.' *Labour and Love, Women's Experience of Home and Family, 1850–1940*. Jane Lewis, ed., pp. 27–48. Oxford: Basil Blackwell.

Ehmer, Josef. (1986) 'Master's Household or Journeyman's Family: the Units of Artisan Outwork Production in Central Europe and England in the Mid-19th Century.' ESRC Workshops on Proto-industrial Communities, University of Essex.

Ellerkamp, Marlene and Brigitte Jungmann. (1987) 'Unendliche Arbeit. Frauen in der "Jutespinnerei und -weberei Bremen" 1888–1914.' *Frauen Suchen Ihre Geschichte*. Karin Hausen, ed. pp. 130–45. München: Verlag C. H. Beck.

Ellis, Sarah Stickney. (1843) *Wives of England*. London.

Engel, Barbara. (1980) 'The Woman's Side: Male Outmigration and the Family Economy in Kostroma Province.' *The World of the Russian Peasant: Post Emancipation Culture and Society*. Ben Eklof and Stephen P. Franks, eds, pp. 65–80 London: Unwin Hyman.

Engel, Barbara Alpern. (1996) *Between the Fields and the City, Women, Work and Family in Russia*, 1861–1914. Cambridge: Cambridge University Press.

Essex Record Office. 'Romford Charity School Minutes and Accounts, 1762–1803.' D/Q 24/2. Chelmsford.

Evans, Clare. (1990) 'Unemployment and the Making of the Feminine during the Lancashire Cotton Famine.' *Women's Work and the Family Economy in Historical Perspective*. P. Hudson, and W. R. Lee, eds, pp. 248–70. Manchester: Manchester University Press.

Evans, Richard J. (1976) 'Prostitution, State and Society in Imperial Germany.' *Past and Present*, 70, pp. 106–29.

Farge, Arlette. (1993) *Fragile Lives: Violence, Power and Solidarity in Eighteenth-century Paris*. London: Polity Press.

Farnsworth, Beatrice. (1992) 'Village Women Experience the Revolution.' *Russian Peasant Women*. Beatrice Farnsworth and Lynne Viola, eds, pp. 145–66. Oxford: Oxford University Press.

Farnsworth, Beatrice, and Lynne Viola, eds. (1992) *Russian Peasant Women*. Oxford: Oxford University Press.

Fénelon, François de Salignac de la Mothe. (1843) *Œuvres*. Paris: Didot.

Fenton, Alexander. (1977) *Scottish Country Life*. Edinburgh: Donald.

Filippini, Nadia Maria. (1993) 'The Church, the State and Childbirth: The Midwife in Italy during the Eighteenth Century.' *The Art of Midwifery: Early Modern Midwives in Europe*. Hilary Marland, ed. pp. 152–75. London: Routledge.

Fine, Ben. (1992) *Women's Employment and the Capitalist Family*. London: Routledge.

Finnegan, F. (1979) *Poverty and Prostitution*. London: Cambridge University Press.

First-Dilic, Ruza. (1978) 'The Productive Role of Farm Women in Yugoslavia.' *Sociologica Ruralis*, 18, pp. 125–37.

Flandrin, Jean-Louis. (1979) *Families in Former Times. Kinship, Household and Sexuality*. Cambridge: Cambridge University Press.

Fourcaut, Anna. (1982) *Femmes à l'usine dans l'entre-deux-guerres.* Paris: F. Maspero.

Fout, John. (1986) 'The Viennese Enquête of 1896 on Working Women.' *German Women in the Eighteenth and Nineteenth Centuries. A Social and Literary History.* Ruth-Ellen B. Joeres, and Mary Jo Maynes, eds, pp. 42–60. Bloomington: Indiana University Press.

Fox-Genovese, Elizabeth. (1984a) 'Introduction.' *French Women and the Age of Enlightenment.* Samia L. Spencer, ed., pp. 1–29. Bloomington: Indiana University Press.

Fox-Genovese, Elizabeth. (1984b) 'Women and Work.' *French Women and the Age of Enlightenment.* Samia L. Spencer, ed., pp. 111–27. Bloomington: Indiana University Press.

Frader, Laura Levine. (1987) 'Women in the Industrial Capitalist Economy.' *Becoming Visible, Women in European History.* Renate Bridenthal, Claudia Koonz and Susan Stuard, eds, 2nd edn pp. 279–308. Boston: Houghton, Mifflin Company.

Frader, Laura. (1996) 'Engendering Work and Wages: the French Labor Movement and the Family Wage.' *Gender and Class in Modern Europe.* Laura Frader and Sonya O. Rose, eds, pp. 142–64. London: Cornell University Press.

Frader, Laura and Sonya O. Rose, eds. (1996) *Gender and Class in Modern Europe.* London: Cornell University Press.

Franzoi, Barbara. (1985) *At the Very Least She Pays the Rent, Women and German Industrialization, 1871–1914.* London: Greenwood Press.

Franzoi, Barbara. (1987) '. . . with the wolf always at the door. Women's Work in Domestic Industry in Britain and Germany.' *Connecting Spheres.* Marilyn Boxer and Jean H. Quataert, eds, pp. 146–55. Oxford: Oxford University Press.

Freifeld, M. (1986) 'Technological Change and the "Self-acting" Mule: A Study of Skill and the Sexual Division of Labour.' *Social History,* 11, 3, pp. 319–43.

Frevert, Ute. (1985) '"Fürsorgliche Belagerung": Hygienebewegung und Arbeiterfrauen im 19. und frühen 20. jahrhundert.' *Geschichte und Gesellschaft,* 11, pp. 420–46.

Frevert, Ute. (1988) *Women in German History, from Bourgeois Emancipation to Sexual Liberation.* Oxford: Berg Publishers Limited.

Fridenson, Patrick. (1979) 'Les Premiers Ouvriers français de l'automobile (1890–1914).' *Sociologie du Travail,* 21, pp. 297–325.

Fridenson, Patrick. (1986) 'Automobile Workers in France and Their Work, 1914–1983.' *Work in France.* Steven Kaplan and Cynthia Koepp, eds, pp. 514–47. London: Cornell University Press.

Fussell, G. E. and K. R. Fussell. (1953) *The English Countrywoman, a Farmhouse Social History, The Internal Aspect of Rural Life, AD 1500–1900.* London: Andrew Melrose.

Gabaccia, Donna. (1987) 'In the Shadows of the Periphery: Italian Women in the Nineteenth Century.' *Connecting Sphere.* Marilyn Boxer and Jean H. Quataert, eds, pp. 166–76. Oxford: Oxford University Press.

Gamarnikow, Eva. (1978) 'Sexual Division of Labour: The Case of Nursing.' *Feminism and Materialism, Women and Modes of Production.* Annette Kuhn and Ann Marie Wolpe, eds, pp. 97–123. London: Routledge and Kegan Paul.

Gaskell, Peter. (1833) *Manufacturing Population of England.* London: Baldwin and Craddock.

Gasson, R. (1984) 'Farm Women in Europe: Their Need for Off-Farm Employment.' *Sociologia Ruralis,* 24, 3/4, pp. 216–29.

G.B. Parliamentary Papers. (1802–03) *Report on Disputes between Masters and Workmen Engaged in the Cotton Manufacture*. VIII.

G.B. Parliamentary Papers. (1802–03) *Report on Petitions of Persons Concerned in the Woollen Trade and Manufactures*. VII.

G.B. Parliamentary Papers. (1818) *Reports on Ribbon Weavers' Petitions*. IX.

G.B. Parliamentary Papers. (1831–32) *Report on the Bill to Regulate the Labour of Children in the Mills and Factories*. XV.

G.B. Parliamentary Papers. (1833) *Factories Employment Commission, First Report*. XX.

G.B. Parliamentary Papers. (1840) *Reports from Commissioners on the State of the Handloom Weavers*. XXIII, XXIV.

G.B. Parliamentary Papers. (1842) *Report of Commissioners, Children's Employment Commission*. XV, XVI, XVII.

G.B. Parliamentary Papers. (1843a) *Report from Commissioners on Employment of Women and Children in Agriculture*. XII.

G.B. Parliamentary Papers. (1843b) *Second Report of Commissioners on Trade and Manufactures*. XIII, XIV.

G.B. Parliamentary Papers. (1845) *Royal Commission on the Condition of the Framework Knitters*. XV.

G.B. Parliamentary Papers. (1860) *Select Committee on Masters and Operatives*. XXII.

G.B. Parliamentary Papers. (1867) *Children's Employment Commission*. XVI.

G.B. Parliamentary Papers. (1867–68) *Royal Commission on the Children; Young Persons' and Women's Employment in Agriculture, 1st Report*. XVII.

G.B. Parliamentary Papers. (1893–94) *Royal Commission on Labour: Report on the Employment of Women*. XXXVI, XXXVII.

G.B. Parliamentary Papers. (1919) *Report of the War Cabinet of Women in Industry*. XXXI.

George, Dorothy. (1931; 1953) *England in Transition, Life and Work in the Eighteenth Century*. Harmondsworth: Penguin Books Ltd.

Gerhard, Ute. (1978) *Verhältnisse und Verhinderungen. Frauen arbeit, Familie und Rechte der Frauen ins 19. Jahrhundert. Mit Dokumenten*. Frankfurt am Main: Suhrkamp.

Gershuny, Jonathan. (1983) *Social Innovation and the Division of Labour*. Oxford: Oxford University Press.

Geyer-Kordesh, J. and R. Ferguson. (1996) 'Medical Careers: Historical Dilemmas.' *Women and Higher Education: Past Present and Future*. Mary R. Masson and Deborah Simonton, eds, pp. 303–10. Aberdeen: University of Aberdeen Press.

Gibson, Wendy. (1989) *Women in Seventeenth-century France*. London: The Macmillan Press Ltd.

Gilbert, Ann Taylor. (1874) *Autobiography and Other Memorials of Mrs Gilbert, Formerly Ann Taylor*. Josiah Gilbert, ed. London: Henry S. King and Co.

Gilligan, J. Herman. (1984) 'The Rural Labour Process: A Case Study of a Cornish Town.' *Locality and Rurality: Economy and Society in Rural Regions*. Tony Bradley and Philip Lowe, eds, pp. 91–114. Norwich: Geo Books.

Gillis, John. (1986) *For Better, For Worse: British Marriages, 1600–present*. Oxford: Oxford University Press.

Gittins, Diana. (1982) *Fair Sex, Family Size and Structure, 1900–39*. London: Hutchinson.

Gittins, Diana. (1986) 'Marital Status, Work and Kinship' *Labour and Love: Women's*

Experience of Home and Family, 1850–1940. Jane Lewis, ed. pp. 249–67. Oxford: Basil Blackwell.

Glickman, Rose L. (1984) *Russian Factory Women: Workplace and Society, 1880–1914.* Berkeley: University of California Press.

Glickman, Rose L. (1992) 'Peasant Women and Their Work.' *Russian Peasant Women.* Beatrice Farnsworth and Lynne Viola, eds, pp. 54–72. Oxford: Oxford University Press.

Glucksmann, Miriam. (1990) *Women Assemble: Women Workers and New Industries in Inter-war Britain.* London: Routledge.

Glucksmann, Miriam. (1995) 'Some do, Some Don't . . .' *Gender and History*, 7, 2, p. 277.

Golde, Günter. (1975) *Catholics and Protestants, Agricultural Modernization in Two German Villages.* London: Academic Press.

Goodman, Jordan and Katrina Honeyman. (1988) *Gainful Pursuits: The Making of Industrial Europe, 1600–1914.* London: Edward Arnold.

Goody, Jack. (1976) *Production and Reproduction, a Comparative Study of the Domestic Domain.* Cambridge: Cambridge University Press.

Gordon, Eleanor. (1990) 'Women's Spheres.' *People and Society in Scotland. II: 1830–1914.* W. Hamish Fraser and R. J. Morris, eds, pp. 206–35. Edinburgh: John Donald Publishers Ltd.

Gorham, Deborah. (1982) *The Victorian Girl and the Feminine Idea.* London: Croon Helm.

Graham, Patrick. (1812) *General View of the Agriculture of Stirlingshire.* Edinburgh: G. and W. Nicol.

Goubert, Pierre. (1960) *Beauvais et le Beauvaisis de 1600 à 1730.* Paris: SEVPEN.

Graham, Ruth. (1976) 'Rousseau's Sexism Revolutionized.' *Women in the Eighteenth Century and Other Essays.* Paul Fritz and Richard Morton, eds, pp. 127–40. Toronto: Hakkert and Co.

Grant, Linda. (1990) 'Women in a Car Town: Coventry 1920–45.' *Women's Work and the Family Economy in Historical Perspective.* P. Hudson, and W. R. Lee, eds, pp. 220–46. Manchester: Manchester University Press.

Gray, Malcolm. (1978) *The Fishing Industries of Scotland, 1790–1914, a Study in Regional Adaptation.* Oxford: Oxford University Press.

Gray, Malcolm. (1984) 'Farmworkers in North East Scotland.' *Farm Servants and Labour in Lowland Scotland.* T. M. Devine, ed., pp. 10–28. Edinburgh: John Donald Publishers.

Gray, Malcolm. (1988) 'The social impact of agrarian change in the rural lowlands.' *People and Society in Scotland, 1760–1830.* T. M. Devine and Rosalind Mitchison, eds, pp. 53–69. Edinburgh: John Donald Publishers.

Gray, Marion W. (1987) 'Prescriptions for Productive Female Domesticity in a Transitional Era: Germany's Hausmütterliterature, 1780–1840.' *History of European Ideas*, 8, 4/5, pp. 413–26.

Gray, Robert. (1980) *The Aristocracy of Labour in Nineteenth-century Britain, c. 1850–1900.* London: Macmillan.

Gray, Robert. (1989) 'The Languages of Factory Reform in Britain, c. 1830–1860.' *The Historical Meanings of Work.* Patrick Joyce, ed., pp. 143–79. Cambridge: Cambridge University Press.

Greenfield, J. (1995) 'Technology, Gender and Labour Organization in the East

Midlands Boot and Shoe Industry, 1850–1911.' *New Directions in Economic and Social History*. Ian Blanchard, ed., pp. 85–100. Edinburgh: Economic History Society.

Greenwood, Davydd J. (1976) *Unrewarding Wealth, the Commercialization and Collapse of Agriculture in a Spanish Basque Town*. Cambridge: Cambridge University Press.

Griepentrog, Gisela. (1986) 'Peasants, Poverty and Population: Economic and Political Factors in the Family Structure of the Working People in the Magdeburg Region, 1900–39.' *The German Peasantry*. Richard Evans and W. R. Lee, eds, pp. 205–23. London: Croom Helm.

Gudvan, A. M. (1925, 1983) 'Essays on the History of the Movement of Sales-Clerical Workers in Russia.' *The Russian Worker*. Victoria E. Bonnell, ed., pp. 186–208. Berkeley: University of California Press.

Guilbert, Madeleine. (1966) *Les Fonctions des femmes dans l'industrie*. The Hague: Mouton.

Gullickson, Gay. (1981) 'The Sexual Division of Labor in Cottage Industry and Agriculture in the Pays de Caux 1750–1850.' *French Historical Studies*, 12, pp. 177–99.

Gullickson, Gay. (1986) *Spinners and Weavers of Auffay*. New York: Cambridge University Press.

Gullickson, Gay. (1987) 'Women and Proto-industrialization: A Review of the Literature and the Case of the Caux.' Conference on Custom and Commerce, University of Warwick.

Gullickson, Gay. (1991) 'Love and Power in the Proto-industrial Family.' *Markets and Manufactures in Early Industrial Europe*. Maxine Berg, ed., pp. 205–26. London: Routledge.

Gunda, Béla, ed. (1984) *The Fishing Culture of the World, Studies in Ethnology, Cultural Ecology and Folklore*. Budapest: Akadémiai Kaidó.

Hagemann, Gro. (1985) 'Feminism and the Sexual Division of Labour. Female Labour in the Norwegian Telegraph Service around the Turn of the Century.' *Scandinavian Journal of History*, 10, pp. 143–54.

Hainer, Paul. (1986) 'The Rural Proletariat: The Everyday Life of Rural Labourers in the Magdeburg Region, 1830–1880.' *The German Peasantry, Conflict and Community in Rural society from the Eighteenth to the Twentieth Centuries*. Richard Evans and W. R. Lee, eds, pp. 102–28. London: Croom Helm.

Hakim, Catherine. (1979) *Occupational Segregation*. Research Paper No. 9. London: Department of Employment.

Hall, Catherine. (1977) 'Married Women at Home in Birmingham in the 1920's and 1930's.' *Oral History*, 5, 2, pp. 42–82.

Hall, Catherine. (1982) 'The Home Turned Upside Down? The Working Class Family in Cotton Textiles 1780–1850.' *The Changing Experience of Women*. Elizabeth Whitelegg *et al.*, eds, pp. 17–29. Oxford: Basil Blackwell.

Hall, Catherine. (1990) '"Strains in the Firm of Wife, Children and Friends"? Middle-class Women and Employment in Early Nineteenth-century England.' *Women's Work and the Family Economy in Historical Perspective*. P. Hudson, and W. R. Lee, eds, pp. 105–31. Manchester: Manchester University Press.

Hammond, Barbara and J. L. Hammond (1911; 1978) *The Village Labourer*. London: Longman.

Hansen, Bodil. (1982) 'Rural Women in Late Nineteenth Century Denmark.' *Journal of Peasant Studies*, 9, 2, pp. 225–40.

Hardyment, Christina. (1990) *From Mangle to Microwave, the Mechanization of Household Work*. Cambridge: Polity Press.

Harley, David. (1993) 'Provincial Midwives in Seventeenth-century London.' *The Art of Midwifery: Early Modern Midwives in Europe*. Hilary Marland, ed., pp. 27–48. London: Routledge.

Harsin, Jill. (1985) *Policing Prostitution in Nineteenth-century Paris*. Princeton: Princeton University Press.

Hartmann, Heidi. (1982) 'Capitalism, Patriarchy and Job Segregation by Sex.' *Classes, Power and Conflict*. Anthony Giddens and David Held, eds, pp. 446–69. Basingstoke: The Macmillan Press Ltd.

Hartwell, R. M. (1981) *The Industrial Revolution and Economic Growth*. London: Methuen and Co. Ltd.

Hasbach, W. (1908) *A History of the English Agricultural Labourer*. London: Frank Cass Ltd.

Hatton, T. J. and R. E. Bailey. (1988) 'Female Labour Force Participation in Interwar Britain.' *Oxford Economic Papers*, 40, pp. 695–718.

Haupt, Heinz-Gerhard. (1992) 'Männliche und weibliche BerufsKarrierer im deutschen Bürgertum in der Zwerten Hälfte des 19. jahrhunderts: Zum Verhältnis von Klasse und Geschlecht. *Geschichte und Gesellschaft*, 18, pp. 143–60.

Hause, Stephen C. (1987) 'More Minerva than Mars: The French Women's Rights Campaign and the First World War.' *Behind the Lines, Gender and the Two World Wars*. Margaret R. Higonnet, Jane Jenson, Sonya Michel and Margaret Collins Weitz, eds, pp. 99–113. New Haven: Yale University Press.

Hausen, Karin. (1986) 'Ideology as Reality. Investigations into Outwork during the 1920s in Germany.' Paper presented to the ESRC workshop, 'The Artisan and Outwork Family.' University of Essex.

Hausen, Karin. (1987) 'Grosse Wäsche: Technischer Forschritt und sozialer Wandel in Deutschland vom 18 bis ims 20. jahrhundert.' *Geschichte und Gesellschaft*, 13, pp. 273–303.

Haywood, Eliza. (1743) *A Present for a Servant Maid*. London.

Hearn, Mona. (1990) 'Life for Domestic Servants in Dublin, 1880–1920.' *Women Surviving: Studies in Irish Women's History in the Nineteenth and Twentieth Centuries*. Maria Luddy and Cliona Murphy, eds, pp. 148–79. Dublin: Poolbeg Press Ltd.

Heath, Francis George. (1874) *The English Peasantry*. London.

Heller, Geneviève and Arthur E. Imhof. (1983) 'Körperliche Uberlastung von Frauen im 19. Jahrhundert.' *Der Mensch und sein Körper von der Antike bis Heute*. A. E. Imhof, ed., pp. 137–56. München: Friedrich-Meinecke Inst.

Hellerstein, Erna Olafson, Leslie Parker Hume and Karen Offen, eds. (1981) *Victorian Women, a Documentary Account of Women's Lives in Nineteenth-century England, France and the United States*. Brighton: Harvester Press.

Heywood, Colin. (1976) 'The Rural Hosiery Industry of the Lower Champagne Region, 1750–1850.' *Textile History*, 7, pp. 89–111.

Heywood, Colin. (1988) *Childhood in Nineteenth-century France: Work, Health and Education among the Classes Populaires*. Cambridge: Cambridge University Press.

Higgs, Edward. (1986) 'Domestic Service and Household Production.' *Unequal Opportunities, Women's Employment in England, 1800–1918*. Angela John, ed. pp. 125–52. Oxford: Basil Blackwell.

Higgs, Edward. (1987) 'Women, Occupations and Work in the Nineteenth Century Censuses.' *History Workshop*, 23, pp. 59–80.

Higonnet, Margaret R., Jane Jenson, Sonya Michel and Margaret Collins Weitz, eds. (1987) *Behind the Lines, Gender and the Two World Wars*. New Haven: Yale University Press.

Hilden, Patricia. (1986) *Working Women and Socialist Politics in France 1880–1914, a Regional Study*. Oxford: Clarendon Press.

Hilden, Patricia Penn. (1993) *Women, Work and Politics, Belgium 1830–1914*. Oxford: Clarendon Press.

Hiley, Michael. (1979) *Victorian Working Women: Portraits from Life*. London: Gordon Fraser.

Hill, Bridget. (1989) *Women, Work and Sexual Politics in Eighteenth-century England*. Oxford: Basil Blackwell.

Hill, Bridget, ed. (1984) *Eighteenth-century Women: An Anthology*. London: Allen and Unwin.

Hillebrand, Hans and Ursula Blom. (1993) 'Young Women on Dutch Family Farms.' *Sociologia Ruralis*, 33, pp. 178–89.

Hogarth, Janet. (1926) *Recollected in Tranquillity*. London: W. Heinemann.

Hoggart, Keith, Henry Butler and Richard Black. (1995) *Rural Europe, Identity and Change*. London: Arnold.

Holcombe, Lee. (1973) *Victorian Ladies at Work: Middle Class Working Women in England and Wales, 1850–1914*. Newton Abbot: David and Charles.

Holmes, Douglas and Jean Quataert. (1986) 'An Approach to Modern Labor: Worker Peasantries in Historic Saxony and the Friuli Region over Three Centuries.' *Comparative Studies in Society and History*, 28, 2, pp. 191–216.

Honeyman, Katrina. (1996) 'Review of de Groot and Schrover, *Women Workers and Technological Change in Europe in the Nineteenth and Twentieth Centuries*.' *Women's History Review*, 5, 3, pp. 454–55.

Hope, Emily, Mary Kennedy and Anne de Winter. (1976) 'Homeworkers in North London.' *Dependence and Exploitation in Work and Marriage*. Diana Leonard Barker and Sheila Allen, eds pp. 88–108. London: Longman Group Limited.

Horn, Pamela. (1975) *The Rise and Fall of the Victorian Domestic Servant*. Dublin: Gill and Macmillan.

Horn, Pamela. (1980) *The Rural World, 1780–1850. Social Change in the English Countryside*. London: Hutchinson and Co. Ltd.

Horn, Pamela. (1984) *The Changing Countryside in Victorian and Edwardian England and Wales*. London: The Athlone Press.

Horne, John. (1796) *Reflections on the Importance of Forming the Female Character by Education*. Dublin: W. Watson and Son.

Hostettler, Eve. (1977) 'Gourlay Steell and the Sexual Division of Labour.' *History Workshop*, 4, pp. 95–100.

Houston, Rab. (1989) 'Women in the Economy and Society of Scotland.' *Scottish Society, 1500–1800*. R. A. Houston and I. A. Whyte, eds, pp. 118–47. Cambridge: Cambridge University Press.

Houston, Rab and K. D. M. Snell. (1984) 'Proto-industrialization? Cottage Industry, Social Change, and Industrial Revolution.' *Historical Journal*, 27, 2, pp. 473–92.

Howatson, William. (1984) 'Grain Harvesting and Harvesters.' *Farm Servants and Labour in Lowland Scotland, 1740–1914*. T. M. Devine, ed., pp. 124–42. Edinburgh: John Donald Publishers.

Howe, Elspeth. (1996) 'Equal Opportunities: Past Present and Future.' *Women and*

Higher Education: Past Present and Future. Mary R. Masson and Deborah Simonton, eds, pp. 22–28. Aberdeen: University of Aberdeen Press.

Howell, Martha C. (1986) 'Women, the Family Economy and the Structures of Market Production in Cities of Northern Europe during the Late Middle Ages.' *Women and Work in Preindustrial Europe.* Barbara Hanawalt, ed., pp. 198–222. Bloomington: University of Indiana Press.

Howkins, Alun. (1991) *Reshaping Rural England. A Social History, 1850–1925.* London: HarperCollins Academic.

Hudson, Pat. (1982) 'Proto-industrialisation: The Case of the West Riding Wool Textile Industry in the 18th and Early 19th Centuries.' *History Workshop Journal,* 12, pp. 34–61.

Hudson, Pat and W. R. Lee, eds. (1990) *Women's Work and the Family Economy in Historical Perspective.* Manchester: Manchester University Press.

Hufton, Olwen. (1971) 'Women in Revolution, 1789–1796.' *Past and Present,* 53, pp. 90–108.

Hufton, Olwen. (1974) *The Poor of Eighteenth Century France, 1750–1789.* Oxford: Oxford University Press.

Hufton, Olwen. (1975) 'Women and the Family Economy in Eighteenth Century France.' *French Historical Studies,* 9, pp. 1–22.

Hufton, Olwen. (1981) 'Women, Work and Marriage in Eighteenth-century France.' *Marriage and Society, Studies in the Social History of Marriage.* R. B. Outhwaite, ed., pp. 186–203. London: Europa.

Hufton, Olwen. (1984) 'Women without Men: Widows and Spinsters in Britain and France in the Eighteenth Century.' *Journal of Family History,* 9, pp. 355–76.

Hufton, Olwen. (1993) 'Women, Work and Family.' *A History of Women in the West, III, Renaissance and Enlightenment Paradoxes.* Natalie Zemon Davies and Arlette Farge, eds, pp. 15–45. Cambridge, Mass.: The Belknap Press of Harvard University.

Hufton, Olwen. (1995) *The Prospect before Her, a History of Women in Western Europe.* London: Fontana Press.

Hughes, Kathryn. (1993) *The Victorian Governess.* London: The Hambledon Press.

Humphries, Jane. (1977) 'Class Struggle and the Persistence of the Working-class Family.' *Cambridge Journal of Economics,* 1, 1, pp. 241–58.

Hunt, Audrey. (1968) *A Survey of Women's Employment.* London: HMSO.

Hunt, Felicity. (1986) 'Opportunities Lost and Gained.' *Unequal Opportunities, Women's Employment in England, 1800–1918.* Felicity Hunt, ed., pp. 71–94. Oxford: Basil Blackwell.

Hunt, Felicity. (1987) 'Inequalities in the Teaching Profession: The Effect on Teachers and Pupils, 1910–39.' *Lessons for Life: The Schooling of Girls and Women, 1850–1950.* Angela John, ed., pp. 101–23. Oxford: Basil Blackwell.

Hutchins, B. L. (1915) *Women in Modern Industry.* London: G. Bell and Sons Ltd.

Hutton, William. (1817) *History of Derby.* Birmingham.

Ingold, Tim. (1984) 'The Estimation of Work in a Northern Finnish Farming Community.' *Family and Work in Rural Societies, Perspectives on Non-wage Labour.* Norman Long, ed., pp. 116–34. London: Tavistock Publications.

Inhetveen, Heide. (1982) 'Nie fertig mit Anschaffen und Anpassen: Kleinbäuerinen zwischen Tradition und Fortschrift.' *Sociologia Ruralis,* 22, 3, pp. 246–61.

Jacobs, Eva, W. H. Barber and Jean Block, eds. (1979) *Women and Society in Eighteenth Century France: Essays in Honour of John Stephenson Spink.* London: The Athlone Press.

Jalland, Pat. (1986) 'Dutiful Daughters, Desperate Rebels and the Transition to the New Woman.' *Women, Marriage and Politics, 1860–1914.* Oxford: Clarendon Press.

James, Edward. (1962) 'Women at Work in Twentieth Century Britain.' *The Manchester School of Economics and Social Studies,* 30, 3, pp. 283–99.

Jamieson, Lynn. (1990) 'Rural and Urban Women in Domestic Service.' *The World is Ill Divided: Women's Work in Scotland in the Nineteenth and Early Twentieth Centuries.* Eleanor Gordon and Esther Breitenbach, eds, pp. 136–57. Edinburgh: Edinburgh University Press.

Jefferies, Richard. (1880; 1979) *Hodge and His Masters.* London: Quartet Books.

Johansson, Ella. (1989) 'Beautiful Men, Fine Women and Good Workpeople: Gender and Skill in Northern Sweden. 1850–1950.' *Gender and History,* 1, 2, pp. 200–12.

John, A. V. (1980) *By the Sweat of Their Brow: Women Workers at Victorian Coal Mines.* London: Croom Helm.

John, Angela V., ed. (1986) *Unequal Opportunities, Women's Employment in England, 1800–1918.* Oxford: Basil Blackwell.

Johnson, Christopher. (1975) 'Economic Change and Artisan Discontent: The Tailors' History, 1800–48.' *Revolution and Reaction: 1848 and the Second French Republic.* Roger Price, ed., pp. 87–114. London: Croom Helm.

Johnson, C. (1979) 'Patterns of Proletarianization: Parisian Tailors and Lodève Woollens Workers.' *Consciousness and Class Experience in Nineteenth-century Europe.* John M. Merriman, ed., pp. 65–84. London: Holmes and Meier.

Johnson, Marie. (1984) 'Domestic Work in Rural Iceland: An Historical Overview.' *Family and Work in Rural Societies, Perspectives on Non-wage Labour.* Norman Long, ed., pp. 160–74. London: Tavistock Publications.

Jordan, E. (1989) 'The Exclusion of Women from Industry in Nineteenth-century Britain.' *Comparative Studies in Society and History,* 31, pp. 273–96.

Jordan, Ellen. (1996) 'The Lady Clerks at the Prudential: The Beginning of Vertical Segregation by Sex in Clerical Work in Nineteenth-century Britain.' *Gender and History,* 8, 1, pp. 65–81.

Jordanova, Ludmilla. (1987) 'Conceptualizing Childhood in the Eighteenth Century: The Problem of Child Labour.' *British Journal for Eighteenth-century Studies,* 10, 2, pp. 201–10.

Kaelble, H. (1990) *A Social History of Western Europe, 1880–1980.* Dublin: Gill and Macmillan.

King, Peter. (1991) 'Customary Rights and Women's Earnings: The Importance of Gleaning to the Rural Labouring Poor, 1750–1850.' *Economic History Review,* 44, 3, pp. 461–76.

Kingston Upon Thames Borough Archives. 'Ordinances of the Corporation Governing the Trading Companies.' KB 8/1/3.

Kingston Upon Thames Borough Archives. 'Roll of Admission to the Freedom of . . . Companies, 1746–1835.' KB 11/1/4.

Kingston Upon Thames Borough Archives. 'Court of Assembly Minutes, 1725–1776.' KB 1/2.

Kirrane, Mary. (1987) 'Early Women Office Workers.' *North West Labour History,* 12, pp. 3–16.

Kleinbaum, Abby. (1977) 'Women in the Age of Light.' *Becoming Visible, Women in European History.* Renate Bridenthal and Claudia Koonz, eds, pp. 217–35. Boston: Houghton, Mifflin Company.

Kolinsky, Eva. (1989) *Women in West Germany, Life, Work and Politics*. Oxford: Berg Publishers Limited.

Koonz, Claudia. (1988) *Mothers in the Fatherland, Women, the Family and Nazi Politics*. London: Methuen London Limited.

Kreidte, Peter, Medick, Hans and Jürgen Schlumbohm, eds. (1981) *Industrialization before Industrialization, Rural Industry in the Genesis of Capitalism*. Cambridge: Cambridge University Press.

Kussmaul, Ann. (1981) *Servants in Husbandry in Early Modern England*. Cambridge: Cambridge University Press.

Lagrave, Rose-Marie. (1994) 'A Supervised Emancipation.' *A History of Women in the West, V. Toward a Cultural Identity in the Twentieth Century*. François Thébaud, ed., pp. 453–89. Cambridge, Mass.: The Belknap Press of Harvard University.

Lancaster, Bill. (1995) *The Department Store, a Social History*. Leicester: Leicester University Press.

Land, Hilary. (1981) 'The Family Wage.' *New Statesman*, 18 December, pp. 16–18.

Lane, Joan. (1977) 'Apprenticeship in Warwickshire, 1700–1834.' PhD thesis, University of Birmingham.

Laslett, Peter, ed. (1977) *Family Life and Illicit Love in Earlier Generations*. Cambridge: Cambridge University Press.

Laslett, Peter and Richard Wall, eds. (1972) *Household and Family in Past Time*. Cambridge: Cambridge University Press.

Lazonick, William. (1979) 'Industrial Relations and Technical Change: The Case of the Self-acting Mule.' *Cambridge Journal of Economics*, 3, pp. 231–62.

Lee, W. R. (1990) 'Women's Work and the Family: some Demographic Implications of Gender-specific Rural Work Patterns in Nineteenth-century Germany.' *Women's Work and the Family Economy in Historical Perspective*. Pat Hudson and W. R. Lee, eds, pp. 50–75. Manchester: Manchester University Press.

Lefaucheur, Nadine. (1994) 'Maternity, Family and the State.' *A History of Women in the West, V. Toward a Cultural Identity in the Twentieth Century*. François Thébaud, ed., pp. 433–52. Cambridge, Mass.: The Belknap Press of Harvard University.

Lehning, James. (1980) *The Peasants of Marlhes: Economic Development and Family Organization in Nineteenth-century France*. London: The Macmillan Press Ltd.

Leleu, Thierry. (1981) 'Scènes de la vie quotidienne: les femmes de la vallée de la Lys (1870–1920).' *Histoire des Femmes du Nord; Special Issue of Revue du Nord*. Marcel Gillet, ed. 63, 250, pp. 637–66.

LePlay, Frédéric, ed. (1877–79) *Les Ouvriers Européens, Études sur les travaux, la vie domestique et la condition morale des populations ouvrières de l'Europe*. 2nd edn. Tours: Alfred Mame et Fils, Libraires-Éditeurs.

Leroux-Hugon, Véronique. (1987) 'L'Infirmière au début du xxe siècle: nouveau métier et tâches traditionnelles.' *Mouvement Social*, 140, pp 55–68.

Levi, Carlo. (1982) *Christ Stopped at Eboli*. Harmondsworth: Penguin Books.

Levine, David. (1977) *Family Formation in an Age of Nascent Capitalism*. Cambridge: Cambridge University Press.

Lewis, Jane. (1980) *The Politics of Motherhood: Child and Maternal Welfare in England, 1900–1939*. London: Croom Helm.

Lewis, Jane. (1991) 'Models of Equality for Women: The Case of State Support for Children in Twentieth-century Britain.' *Maternity and Gender Policies, Women and the Rise of the European Welfare States, 1880s–1950s*. Gisela Bock and Pat Thane, eds, pp. 73–92. London: Routledge.

Lewis, Jane E. (1988) 'Women Clerical Workers in Late Nineteenth and Early Twentieth Centuries.' *The White-blouse Revolution, Female Office Workers since 1870.* Gregory Anderson, ed. pp. 27–47. Manchester: Manchester University Press.

Leyret, Henry. (1895) *En plein faubourg; moeurs ouvrières.* Paris: Charpentier.

Lie, M. and B. Rasmussen. (1985) 'Office Work and Skills.' *Women, Work and Computerization, Opportunities and Disadvantages.* A. Olerup *et al.,* eds, pp. 95–104. Amsterdam: North-Holland.

Linn, Pam. (1987) 'Gender Stereotypes, Technology Stereotypes.' *Gender and Expertise.* Maureen McNeil, ed. pp. 127–51. London: Free Association Books.

Lis, Catherina and Hugo Soly. (1979) *Poverty and Capitalism in Pre-industrial Europe.* Atlantic Highlands, N. J.: Humanities.

Littlewood, Barbara and Linda Mahood. (1991) 'Prostitutes and Wayward Girls: Dangerous Sexualities of Working Class Women in Victorian Scotland.' *Gender and History*, 3, 2, pp. 160–75.

Lockwood, David. (1989) *The Blackcoated Worker, a Study in Class Consciousness.* Oxford: Clarendon Press.

Lough, John. (1960) *An Introduction to Eighteenth Century France.* London: Longmans.

Lown, Judy. (1990) *Women and Industrialization: Gender at Work in Nineteenth-century England.* London: Polity Press.

Lynch, Michael. (1991) *Scotland, A New History.* Edinburgh: Century.

Mahood, Linda. (1990) 'The Wages of Sin: Women, Work and Sexuality in the Nineteenth Century.' *The World is Ill Divided: Women's Work in Scotland in the Nineteenth and Early Twentieth Centuries.* Eleanor Gordon and Esther Breitenbach, eds, pp. 29–48. Edinburgh: Edinburgh University Press.

Malcolmson, Robert W. (1981) *Life and Labour in England 1700–1800.* London: Hutchinson.

Manning, Roberta T. (1992) 'Women in the Soviet Countryside on the Eve of World War II, 1935–40.' *Russian Peasant Women.* Beatrice Farnsworth and Lynne Viola, eds, pp. 206–35. Oxford: Oxford University Press.

Mark-Lawson, Jane and Witz, Anne. (1988) 'From "Family Labour" to "Family Wage"? The Case of Women's Labour in Nineteenth-century Coal-mining.' *Social History*, 13, pp. 151–74.

Marland, Hilary, ed. (1993) *The Art of Midwifery: Early Modern Midwives in Europe.* London: Routledge.

Marshall, Dorothy. (1926) *The English Poor in the Eighteenth-century: A Study in Administrative History.* London: George Routledge and Sons, Ltd.

Marwick, Arthur. (1970) *Britain in the Century of Total War.* Harmondsworth: Penguin.

Marwick, Arthur. (1977) *Women at War.* London: Croom Helm.

Mason, Tim. (1976) 'Women in Germany, 1925–40: Family, Welfare and Work.' *History Workshop*, 1, pp. 74–113; 2, pp. 5–32.

Mattosian, Mary. (1992) 'The Peasant Way of Life.' *Russian Peasant Women.* Beatrice Farnsworth and Lynne Viola, eds, pp. 11–40. Oxford: Oxford University Press.

McBride, Theresa. (1974) 'Social Mobility for the Lower Classes: Domestic Servants in France.' *Journal of Social History*, 7, pp. 63–78.

McBride, Theresa. (1976) *The Domestic Revolution: The Modernisation of Household Service in England and France, 1820–1920.* London: Croom Helm.

McBride, Theresa. (1977) 'The Long Road Home, Women's Work and

Industrialization.' *Becoming Visible, Women in European History*. Renate Bridenthal and Claudia Koonz, eds, pp. 280–93. Boston: Houghton, Mifflin Company.

McBride, T. (1977a) 'A Woman's World: Department Stores and the Evolution of Women's Employment, 1870–1920.' *French Historical Studies*, 10, pp. 664–83.

McClelland, Keith. (1989) ' Time to Work, Time to Live: Some Aspects of Work and the Reformation of Class in Britain, 1850–1880.' *The Historical Meanings of Work*. Joyce Patrick, ed., pp. 180–209. Cambridge: Cambridge University Press.

McDermid, Jane. (1990) 'Women in Urban Employment and the Shaping of the Russian Working Class, 1880–1917.' *Women's Work and the Family Economy in Historical Perspective*. Pat Hudson and W. R. Lee, eds, pp. 204–19. Manchester: Manchester University Press.

McDougall, Mary Lynn. (1977) 'Working-class Women during the Industrial Revolution, 1780–1914.' *Becoming Visible, Women in European History*. Renate Bridenthal and Claudia Koonz, eds, pp. 251–79. Boston: Houghton, Mifflin Company.

McIvor, Arthur J. (1992) 'Women and Work in Twentieth-century Scotland.' *People and Society in Scotland, Vol. 3, 1914–1990*. A. Dickson and J. H. Treble, eds, pp. 138–73. Edinburgh: John Donald Publishers.

McKendrick, Neil, ed. (1974) 'Home Demand, Women and Children.' *Historical Perspectives, Studies in English Thought and Society*. Neil McKendrick, ed., pp. 152–210. London: Europa Publications.

McKendrick, Neil, John Brewer and J. H. Plumb, eds. (1983) *The Birth of a Consumer Society, The Commercialization of Eighteenth Century England*. London: Hutchinson and Co. Ltd.

McMillan, James. (1981) *Housewife or Harlot: The Place of Women in French Society, 1870–1940*. New York: Saint Martin's Press.

McPhee, Peter. (1992) *A Social History of France, 1780–1880*. London: Routledge.

Medick, Hans. (1976) 'The Proto-industrial Family Economy: The Structural Function of Household and Family during the Transition from Peasant Society to Industrial Capitalism.' *Social History*, 3, pp. 291–315.

Medick, Hans. (1983) 'Plebeian Culture in the Transition to Capitalism.' *Culture, Ideology and Politics, Essays for Eric Hobsbawm*. Raphael Samuel and Gareth Stedman Jones, eds pp. 84–113. London: Routledge.

Mendels, F. (1972) 'Proto-industrialization: The First Phase of the Industrialization Process.' *Journal of Economic History*, 32, pp. 241–61.

Merson, A. L. (1968) 'Apprenticeship at Southampton in the Seventeenth Century.' *A Calendar of Southampton Apprenticeship Registers, 1609–1740*. A. L. Merson, ed., vol. XII ix–lxxvi. Southampton: Southampton University Press.

Meyer, Sibylle. (1982) *Das Theatre mit der Hausarbeit: Bürgerliche Repräsentation in der Familie der wilhelminishen Zeit*. Frankfurt: Campus.

Meyer, Sybille. (1987) 'Die mühsame Arbeit des demonstrativen Müssiggangs. Uber die häuslichen Pflichten der Beamtenfrauen im Kaiserreich.' *Frauen Suchen Ihre Geschichte*. Karin Hausen, ed. pp. 175–97. München: Verlag C. H. Beck.

Middleton, Chris. (1978) 'The Sexual Division of Labour in Feudal England.' *New Left Review*, 113–14, pp. 147–68.

Miller, C. (1984) 'The Hidden Workforce: Female Fieldworkers in Gloucestershire, 1870–1901.' *Southern History*, 6, pp. 139–61.

Miller, Michael. (1981) *The Bon Marché, Bourgeois Culture and the Department Store, 1869–1920*. Princeton: Princeton University Press.

Milward, A. and S. B. Saul. (1973) *Development of the Economies of Continental Europe*. London: George Allen and Unwin Ltd.

Mingay, G. E. (1977) *Rural Life in Victorian England*. London: Heinemann.

Minge-Kalman, Wanda. (1978) 'The Industrial Revolution and the European Family: The Institutionalization of Childhood as a Market for Family Labour.' *Comparative Studies in Society and History*, 20, 2, pp. 454–68.

Mitchell, B. R. (1978) *European Historical Statistics, 1750–1970*. Abridged edn. London: Macmillan Press Ltd.

Moir, John. (1784) *Female Tuition, or an Address to Mothers on the Education of Daughters*. London.

Monter, E. (1980) 'Women in Calvinist Geneva, 1550–1800.' *Signs*, 6, pp. 189–209.

Moore, Lindy. (1991) *Bajanellas and Semilinas, Aberdeen University and the Education of Women, 1860–1920*. Aberdeen: Aberdeen University Press.

More, Hannah. (1799) *Strictures on the Modern System of Female Education with a View of the Principles and Conduct Prevalent among Females of Rank and Fortune*. London: T. Cadell Jun. and W. Davies.

Morgan, Carol E. (1992) 'Women, Work and Consciousness in the Mid Nineteenth-century English Cotton Industry.' *Social History*, 17, pp. 23–41.

Mørkeberg, Henrik. (1978) 'Working Conditions of Women Married to Selfemployed Farmers.' *Sociologica Ruralis*, 18, pp. 95–105.

Morris, Jenny. (1986) 'The Characteristics of Sweating: The Late Nineteenth Century London and Leeds Tailoring Trade.' *Unequal Opportunities, Women's Employment in England, 1800–1918*. Angela John, ed. pp. 95–121. Oxford: Basil Blackwell.

Moulin, Annie. (1981) *Peasantry and Society in France since 1789*. Cambridge: Cambridge University Press.

Nardinelli, Clark. (1990) *Child Labour and the Industrial Revolution*. Bloomington: Indiana University Press.

National Council of Public Morals – for the Regeneration – Spiritual, Moral and Physical. (1917) *The Declining Birth-rate, its Causes and Effects (Being the Report and the Chief Evidence Taken by the National Birth-rate Commission, Instituted with Official Recognition)*. London: Chapman and Hall.

Neff, Wanda. (1929; 1966) *Victorian Working Women, a Historical and Literary Study of Women in British Industries and Professions, 1832–1850*. London: Frank Cass & Co. Ltd.

Newby, H. (1980) *Green and Pleasant Land*. Harmondsworth: Penguin.

Nipperdey, Thomas. (1983) *Deutsche Geschichte, 1800–1866, Bürgerwelt und starker Staat*. München: Verlag C. H. Beck.

Oakley, Ann. (1974) *Housewife*. London: Allen Lane.

OED (1979) *The Compact Edition of the Oxford English Dictionary*. 2 vols. London: Book Club Associates.

Offen, Karen. (1983) 'The Second Sex and the Baccalauréat in Republican France 1880–1924.' *French Historical Studies*, 13, pp. 252–86.

Offen, Karen. (1991) 'Body Politics: Women, Work and the Politics of Motherhood in France, 1920–1950.' *Maternity and Gender Policies, Women and the Rise of the European Welfare States, 1880s-1950s*. Gisela Bock and Pat Thane, eds, pp. 138–59. London: Routledge.

Ogilvie, Sheilagh. (1990) 'Women and Proto-industrialisation in a Corporate Society: Württemberg Woollen Weaving, 1590–1760.' *Women's Work and the Family Economy in Historical Perspective.* Pat Hudson and W. R. Lee, eds, pp. 76–103. Manchester: Manchester University Press.

Ohlander, Ann-Sophie. (1991) 'The Invisible Child? The Struggle for a Social Democratic Family Policy in Sweden, 1900–1960s.' *Maternity and Gender Policies, Women and the Rise of the European Welfare States, 1880s-1950s.* Gisela Bock and Pat Thane, eds. London: Routledge.

Oliunina, E. A. (1914; 1983) 'The Tailoring Trade in Moscow and the Villages of Moscow and Riazan Provinces: Material on the History of the Domestic Industry in Russia.' *The Russian Worker: Life and Labour under the Tsarist Regime.* Victoria E. Bonnell, ed. pp. 154–84. Berkeley: University of California Press.

Orr, Alastair. (1984) 'Farm Servants and Farm Labour in the Forth Valley and the South East Lowlands.' *Farm Servants and Labour in Lowland Scotland, 1740–1914.* T. M. Devine, ed. Edinburgh: John Donald Publishers.

Orthmann, Rosemary. (1986) 'Labor Force Participation, Life Cycle, and Expenditure Patterns: The Case of Unmarried Female Factory Workers in Berlin (1902).' *German Women in the Eighteenth and Nineteenth Centuries. A Social and Literary History.* Ruth-Ellen B. Joeres, and Mary Jo Maynes, eds, pp. 24–41. Bloomington: Indiana University Press.

Ortiz, Teresa. (1993) 'From Hegemony to Subordination: Midwives in Early Modern Spain.' *The Art of Midwifery: Early Modern Midwives in Europe.* Hilary Marland, ed., pp. 95–114. London: Routledge.

Osterud, Nancy Grey. (1986) 'Gender Divisions and the Organization of Work in the Leicester Hosiery Industry.' *Unequal Opportunities, Women's Employment in England, 1800–1918.* Angela John, ed. pp. 45–70. Oxford: Basil Blackwell.

Owen, David. (1994) *Ethnic Minority Women and the Labour Market: Analysis of the 1991 Census.* Centre for Research in Ethnic Relations, University of Warwick. Manchester: Equal Opportunities Commission.

Pahl, R. (1984) *Divisions of Labour.* Oxford: Basil Blackwell.

Partington, G. (1976) *Women Teachers in the Twentieth Century.* London: NFER.

Pasdermadjian, Hrant. (1954) *The Department Store: Its Origins, Evolution and Economics.* London: Newman Books.

Pennington, Shelley and Belinda Westover. (1989) *A Hidden Workforce: Women Homeworkers in Britain, 1850–1985.* London: Macmillan.

Perrot, Michelle. (1987) 'The New Eve and the Old Adam: French Women's Condition at the Turn of the Century.' *Behind the Lines, Gender and the Two World Wars.* Margaret Randolph Higonnet, Jane Jenson, Sonya Michel, Margaret Collins Weitz, eds, pp. 51–60. New Haven: Yale University Press.

Perrot, Michelle. (1993) 'Stepping Out.' *A History of Women in the West, Vol. IV, Emerging Feminism from Revolution to World War.* Geneviève Fraisse and Michelle Perrot, eds, pp. 449–81. Cambridge, Mass.: The Belknap Press of Harvard University.

Pescatello, Ann M. (1976) *Power and Pawn, the Female in Iberian Families, Societies and Cultures.* London: Greenwood Press.

Pfeffer, Max J. (1989) 'The Feminization of Production on Part-time Farms in the Federal Republic of Germany.' *Rural Sociology,* 54, 1, pp. 60–73.

Pfeil, Elisabeth. (1961) *Die Berufstätigkeit von Müttern.* Tübingen: J. C. B. Mohr.

Phillips, Anne and Barbara Taylor. (1986) 'Sex and Skill.' *Waged Work, a Reader.* [Collection of articles from *Feminist Review*], pp. 54–66. London: Virago Press.

315

Pina-Cabral, Joaode. (1986) *Sons of Adam, Daughters of Eve, the Peasant World View of the Alto Minho.* Oxford: Clarendon Press.

Pinchbeck, Ivy. (1930; 1981) *Women Workers and the Industrial Revolution 1750–1850.* London: Routledge and Sons; Virago.

Pollard, Sidney. (1981) *Peaceful Conquest, the Industrialization of Europe 1760–1970.* Oxford: Oxford University Press.

Pollert, Anna. (1981) *Girls, Wives, Factory Lives.* London: The Macmillan Press.

Pollock, Linda. (1983) *Forgotten Children. Parent–Child relations from 1500–1900.* Cambridge: Cambridge University Press.

Pope, Barbara Corrado. (1987) 'The Influence of Rousseau's Ideology of Domesticity.' *Connecting Spheres.* Marilyn Boxer and Jean H. Quataert, eds, pp. 136–45. Oxford: Oxford University Press.

Pope, Rex. (1991) *War and Society in Britain, 1899–1948.* London: Longman.

Power, Eileen. (1975) *Medieval Women.* Cambridge: Cambridge University Press.

Price, Roger. (1987) *A Social History of Nineteenth-century France.* London: Hutchinson Education.

Pringle, A. (1794) General View of the County of Westmorland. London: Board of Agriculture.

Prior, Mary. (1985) 'Women in the Urban Economy: Oxford, 1500–1800.' *Women in English Society, 1500–1800.* Mary Prior, ed., pp. 93–117. London: Methuen and Co. Ltd.

Prochaska, F. K. (1974) 'Women in English Philanthropy 1790–1830.' *International Review of Social History,* 19, 3, pp. 426–45.

Pross, Helge. (1975) *Die Wirklichkeit der Hausfrau. Die erste repräsentative Untersuchung über nichterwerbstätige Ehefrauen.* Reinbek: Rowohlt.

Quataert, Jean. (1985) 'The Shaping of Women's Work in Manufacturing Guilds, Households and the State in Central Europe, 1648–1870.' *American Historical Review,* 90, pp. 1122–48.

Quataert, Jean H. (1986) 'Teamwork in Saxon Homeweaving Families in the Nineteenth Century, a Preliminary Investigation into the Issue of Gender Work Roles.' *German Women in the Eighteenth and Nineteenth Centuries. A Social and Literary History.* Ruth-Ellen B. Joeres and Mary Jo Maynes, eds, pp. 3–23. Bloomington: Indiana University Press.

Ramsey, Matthew. (1988) *Professional and Popular Medicine in France, 1770–1830.* Cambridge: Cambridge University Press.

Ravetz, Alison. (1987) 'Housework and Domestic Technologies. An Essay Review.' *Gender and Expertise.* Maureen McNeil, ed., pp. 198–208. London: Free Association Books.

Reddy, William. (1975) 'Family and Factory – French Linen Weavers in the Belle-Epoque.' *Journal of Social History,* 8, pp. 102–12.

Reddy, William. (1984) *The Rise of Market Culture, the Textile Trade and French Society, 1750–1900.* Cambridge: Cambridge University Press.

Reddy, William M. (1986) 'The Moral Sense of Farce: The Patois Literature of Lille Factory Laborers, 1848–70.' *Work in France: Representations, Meaning, Organization and Practice.* Steven Kaplan and Cynthia Koepp, eds, pp. 364–92. London: Cornell University Press.

Reddy, William M. (1987) 'Protoentrepreneurship: the Inadequacy of Numerical Measurement in the Study of Eighteenth-century Household Manufacturing.'

Unpublished paper presented to Conference on Custom and Commerce, University of Warwick.

Reed, Mick. (1984) 'The Peasantry of Nineteenth-century England: A Neglected Class?' *History Workshop Journal*, 18, pp. 52–76.

Rendall, Jane. (1990) *Women in an Industrializing Society: England, 1750–1880*. Oxford: Basil Blackwell.

Reynolds, Siân. (1989) *Britannica's Typesetters, Women Compositors in Edwardian Edinburgh*. Edinburgh: Edinburgh University Press.

Reynolds, Siân. (1996) *France between the Wars: Gender and Politics*. London: Routledge.

Richards, Eric. (1974) 'Women in the British Economy since about 1700, an Interpretation.' *History*, 59, 197, pp. 337–57.

Richardson, Diane. (1993) *Women, Motherhood and Childrearing*. London: The Macmillan Press.

Riemer, Eleanor S. and John Fout, eds. (1980) *European Women, a Documentary History, 1789–1945*. New York: Schocken Books.

Roberts, Elizabeth. (1984) *A Woman's Place, an Oral History of Working-class Women, 1890–1940*. Oxford: Blackwell's Publishers Limited.

Roberts, Michael. (1979) 'Sickles and Scythes: Women's Work and Men's Work at Harvest Time.' *History Workshop*, 7, pp. 3–29.

Robertson, Barbara W. (1990) 'In Bondage: The Female Farm Worker in South-east Scotland.' *The World is Ill Divided: Women's Work in Scotland in the Nineteenth and Early Twentieth Centuries*. Eleanor Gordon and Esther Breitenbach, eds, pp. 117–35. Edinburgh: Edinburgh University Press.

Robinson, J., P. Converse and A. Szalai. (1972) 'Everyday Life in Twelve Countries.' *The Use of Time*. Alexander Szalai, ed. The Hague: UNESCO.

Robson, Michael. (1984) 'The Border Farm Worker.' *Farm Servants and Labour in Lowland Scotland, 1740–1914*. T. M. Devine, ed., pp. 71–96. Edinburgh: John Donald Publishers.

Rose, Sonya O. (1986) 'Gender at Work: Sex, Class and Industrial Capitalism.' *History Workshop*, 21, pp. 113–31.

Rose, Sonya O. (1988) 'Proto-industry, Women's Work and the Household Economy in the Transition to Industrial Capitalism.' *Journal of Family History*, 13, pp. 181–93.

Rose, Sonya O. (1992) *Limited Livelihoods: Gender and Class in Nineteenth-century England*. Berkeley: University of California Press.

Rosenbeck, Bente. (1987) 'Boundaries of Femininity, Denmark, 1880–1980.' *Scandinavian Journal of History*, 12, pp. 47–62.

Ross, Ellen. (1983) 'Survival Networks: Women's Neighbourhood Sharing in London before World War I.' *History Workshop*, 15, pp. 4–27.

Ross, Ellen. (1993) *Love and Toil, Motherhood in Outcast London 1870–1918*. Oxford: Oxford University Press.

Rothstein, N. K. (1961) 'The Silk Industry in London, 1702–1766.' Unpublished MA thesis, London University.

Roubin, Lucienne. (1970; 1976) 'Espace masculin, espace féminin.' *Rural Society in France, Selections from the Annales, Economies, Sociétés, Civilisations (from Annales E.S.C. 2 (1970)*. Robert Forster and Orest Ranum, eds, pp. 152–80. Baltimore: The Johns Hopkins University Press.

Rowntree, Benjamin Seebohm and G. R. Lavers. (1951) *Poverty and the Welfare State*. London: Longmans Green.

Royle, Edward. (1987) *Modern Britain: A Social History, 1750–1985*. London: Edward Arnold.

Rudolph, Richard L. (1980) 'Family Structure and Proto-industrialization in Russia.' *Journal of Economic History*, 40, pp. 111–18.

Rule, John. (1981) *Experience of Labour in Eighteenth Century Industry*. London: Croom Helm.

Rule, John. (1989) 'The Property of Skill in the Period of Manufacture.' *The Historical Meanings of Work*. Patrick Joyce, ed., pp. 99–118. Cambridge: Cambridge University Press.

Rule, John. (1992) *The Vital Century, England's Developing Economy, 1714–1815*. London: Longman Group UK Limited.

Russell, Elizabeth. (1996) 'Women and Medicine.' *Women and Higher Education: Past Present and Future*. Mary R. Masson and Deborah Simonton, eds, pp. 295–96. Aberdeen: University of Aberdeen Press.

Sacks, Michael Paul. (1978) 'Women in the Industrial Labor Force.' *Women in Russia*. A. Atkinson, A. Dallin and G. Lapidus, eds, pp. 189–204. Hassocks: The Harvester Press.

Sagarra, Eda. (1980) *An Introduction to Nineteenth-century Germany*. London: Longman Group Limited.

Sanderson, Kay. (1986) 'A Pension to Look Forward to . . .? Women Civil Servants in London, 1925–1939.' *Our Work, Our Lives, Our Words*. Leonore Davidoff and Belinda Westover, eds, pp. 145–60. London: Macmillan Education.

Sanderson, Kay. (1988) 'Women's Lives: Social Class and the Oral Historian.' *Life Stories/Récits de vie*, 4, pp. 27–34.

Saraceno, Chiara. (1992) 'Constructing Families, Shaping Women's Lives: The Making of Italian Families between Market Economies and State Intervention.' *The European Experience of Declining Fertility*. John Gillis, Louise Tilly and David Levine, eds, pp. 251–69. Oxford: Basil Blackwell.

Sarsby, Jacqueline. (1995) 'Gender and Technological Change in the North Staffordshire Pottery Industry.' *Women Workers and Technological Change in Europe in the Nineteenth and Twentieth Centuries*. Gertjan de Groot and Marlou Schrover, eds, pp. 119–34. London: Taylor and Francis.

Savage, Mike. (1988) 'Trade Unionism, Sex Segregation, and the State: Women's employment in "New Industries" in Interwar Britain.' *Social History*, 13, 2, pp.209–30.

Sayer, Karen. (1993) 'Field-faring Women: the Resistance of Women who Worked in the Fields of Nineteenth-century England.' *Women's History Review*, 2, 2, pp. 185–98.

Schlegel, Katharina. (1983) 'Mistress and Servant in Nineteenth-century Hamburg: Employer/Employee Relationships in Domestic Service, 1880–1914.' *History Workshop*, 15, pp. 60–77.

Schlegel-Schelling, Caroline. (1980) *'Lieber Freund, ich komme weit her schon an diesem fruher Morgen': Caroline Schlegel-Schelling in ihren Briefen*. Sigrid Damm, ed. Darmstadt: Luchterhand.

Schlumbohm, Jürgen. (1980) '"Traditional" Collectivity and "Modern" Individuality: Some Questions and Suggestions for the Historical Study of Socialization. The Examples of the German Lower and Upper Bourgeoisies around 1800.' *Social History*, 5, 1, pp. 71–103.

Schlumbohm, Jürgen. (1983) 'Seasonal Fluctuations and Social Division of Labour: Rural Linen Production in the Osnabrück and Bielefeld Regions and the Urban Woollen Industry in the Niederlausitz, c. 1770–c. 1850.' *Manufacture in Town and Country before the Factory.* Maxine Berg, Pat Hudson and Michael Sonenscher, eds, pp. 92–123. Cambridge: Cambridge University Press.

Schmiechen, James. (1984) *Sweated Industries and Sweated Labour.* London: Croom Helm.

Schneider, Jane and Schneider, Peter. (1992) 'Going Forward in Reverse Gear: Culture, Economy and Political Economy in the Demographic Transitions of a Sicilian Town.' *The European Experience of Declining Fertility, 1850–1970.* John Gillis, Louise Tilly and David Levine, eds, pp. 146–74. Oxford: Basil Blackwell.

Schnorrenberg, Barbara Brandon. (1981) 'Is Childbirth any Place for a Woman? The Decline of Midwifery in Eighteenth-century England.' *Studies in Eighteenth-century Culture.* Harry C. Payne, ed., vol. 10. pp. 393–408. Madison: University of Wisconsin Press.

Schrover, Marlou. (1995) 'Cooking up Women's Work: Women Workers in the Dutch Food Industries, 1889–1960.' *Women Workers and Technological Change in Europe in the Nineteenth and Twentieth Centuries.* Gertjan de Groot and Marlou Schrover, eds, pp. 170–92. London: Taylor and Francis.

Schulte, Regina. (1987) 'Bauernmägde in Bayern am Ende des 19. Jahrhunderts.' *Frauen Suchen Ihre Geschichte.* Karin Hausen, ed., pp. 112–29. München: Verlag C. H. Beck.

Scott, Joan. (1984) 'Men and Women in the Parisian Garment Trades.' *The Power of the Past.* Pat Thane, Geoffrey Crossick and Roderick Floud, eds, pp. 67–93. Cambridge: Cambridge University Press.

Scott, Joan W. (1989) '"L'Ouvrière! Mot Impie, sordide . . .": Women Workers in the Discourse of French Political Economy, 1840–1860.' *The Historical Meanings of Work.* Patrick Joyce, ed., pp. 119–42. Cambridge: Cambridge University Press.

Scott, Joan W. (1993) 'The Woman Worker' *A History of Women in the West, Vol. IV, Emerging Feminism from Revolution to World War.* Geneviève Fraisse and Michelle Perrot, eds, pp. 399–426. Cambridge, Mass.: The Belknap Press of Harvard University Press.

Scott, Joan and Louise Tilly. (1975) 'Women's Work and the Family in Nineteenth Century Europe.' *Comparative Studies in Society and History,* 17, pp. 36–64.

Seager, Joni and Ann Olson. (1986) *Women in the World, an International Atlas.* London: Pan Books Ltd.

Segalen, Martine. (1983) *Love and Power in the Peasant Family: Rural France in the Nineteenth Century.* Oxford: Basil Blackwell.

Segalen, Martine. (1985) 'The Household at Work.' *The Experience of Work.* Craig Littler, ed. Aldershot: Gower Publishing Company Limited.

Sharpe, Pam. (1991) 'Literally Spinsters: A New Interpretation of the Local Economy and Demography in Colyton in the Seventeenth and Eighteenth Centuries.' *Economic History Review,* 46, 1, pp. 46–65.

Sheridan, George J. Jr. (1979) 'Household and Craft in an Industrializing Economy. The Case of the Silk Weavers of Lyon.' *Consciousness and Class Experience in Nineteenth-century Europe.* John M. Merriman ed., pp. 107–28. London: Holmes and Meier Publishers, Inc.

Sheridan, Geraldine. (1992) 'Women in the Booktrade in Eighteenth-century France.' *British Journal for Eighteenth-century Studies*, 15, 1, pp. 51–70.

Shortall, Sally. (1992) 'Power Analysis and Farm Wives, an Empirical Study of the Power Relationships Affecting Women on Irish Farms.' *Sociologica Ruralis*, 32, 4, pp. 431–51.

Shorter, Edward. (1975) *The Making of the Modern Family*. New York: Basic Books.

Shorter, Edward. (1976) 'Women's Work: What Difference Did Capitalism Make?' *Theory and Society*, 3, pp. 513–28.

Silverstone, R. (1976) 'Office Work for Women: An Historical Review.' *Business History*, 18, pp. 98–110.

Simonton, Deborah. (1988) 'The Education and Training of Eighteenth-century English Girls, with Special Reference to the Working Classes.' PhD Thesis, University of Essex.

Simonton, Deborah. (1991) 'Apprenticeship: Training and Gender in Eighteenth-century England.' *Markets and Manufacture in Early Industrial Europe*. Maxine Berg, ed. pp. 227–58. London: Routledge.

Smith, Bonnie. (1981) *Ladies of the Leisure Class: The Bourgeoises of Northern France in the Nineteenth Century*. Princeton: Princeton University Press.

Smith, Diana. (1982) 'Women in the Local Labour Market.' *Diversity and Decomposition in the Labour Market*. G. Day, ed. Aldershot: Gower.

Smith, George Skene. (1811) *A General View of the Agriculture of Aberdeenshire*. Aberdeen.

Smout, T. C. (1969) *A History of the Scottish People, 1560–1830*. London: Fontana Press.

Smout, T. C. (1987) *A Century of the Scottish People, 1830–1950*. London: Fontana Press.

Smout, T. C. and Sydney Wood. (1990) *Scottish Voices, 1745–1960*. London: Fontana Press.

Snell, Keith. (1985) *Annals of the Labouring Poor, Social Change and Agrarian England, 1660–1900*. Cambridge: Cambridge University Press.

Snell, K. D. M. (1981) 'Agricultural Seasonal Unemployment, the Standard of Living and Women's Work in the South and East.' *Economic History Review*, 34, pp. 107–437.

Softley, Elena. (1985) 'Word Processing: New Opportunities for Women Office Workers.' *Smothered by Invention*. Wendy Faulkner and E. Arnold, eds, pp. 222–51. London: Pluto Press Ltd.

Sogner, Sølvi. (1984) '". . . a Prudent Wife is from the Lord." The Married Peasant Women of the Eighteenth-century: Demographic Perspective.' *Scandinavian Journal of History*, 9, 2, pp. 113–33.

Sohn, Ann-Marie. (1994) 'Between the Wars in France and England.' *A History of Women in the West, V. Toward a Cultural Identity in the Twentieth Century*. François Thébaud, ed., pp. 92–119. Cambridge, Mass.: The Belknap Press of Harvard University.

Sommestad, Lena. (1992) 'Education and De-feminization in the Swedish Dairy Industry.' *Gender and History*, 4, 1, pp. 34–48.

Sommestad, Lena. (1994) 'Gendering Work, Interpreting Gender: The Masculinization of Dairy Work in Sweden, 1850–1950.' *History Workshop Journal*, 37, pp. 57–75.

Sommestad, Lena. (1995) 'Creating Gender: Technology and Femininity in the Swedish Dairy Industry.' *Women Workers and Technological Change in Europe in the*

Nineteenth and Twentieth Centuries. Gertjan de Groot and Marlou Schrover, eds, pp. 151–69. London: Taylor and Francis.

Sonenscher, M. (1989) 'Mythical Work: Workshop Production and the Compagnonnages of Eighteenth-century France.' *The Historical Meanings of Work*. Patrick Joyce, ed., pp. 31–63. Cambridge: Cambridge University Press.

SPRU Women and Technology Studies. (1985) 'Microelectronics and the Jobs Women Do.' *Smothered by Invention*. Wendy Faulkner and E. Arnold, eds, pp. 200–21. London: Pluto Press Ltd.

Stearns, Peter. (1975) *European Society in Upheaval, Social History since 1750*. London: Collier Macmillan Publishers.

Stearns, Peter N. (1972) 'Working-class Women in Britain, 1890–1914.' *Suffer and Be Still*. Martha Vicinus, ed., pp. 100–20. Bloomington: Indiana University Press.

Stebbing, Sue. (1984) 'Women's Roles and Rural Society.' *Locality and Rurality: Economy and Society in Rural Region*. Tony Bradley and Philip Lowe, eds, Rural Economy and Society Series 1, pp. 199–208. Norwich: Geo Books.

Stephenson, Jayne D. and Callum G. Brown. (1990) 'The View from the Workplace: Women's Memories of Work in Stirling *c.* 1910–*c*.1950.' *The World is Ill Divided: Women's Work in Scotland in the Nineteenth and Early Twentieth Centuries*. Eleanor Gordon and Esther Breitenbach, eds, pp. 7–28. Edinburgh: Edinburgh University Press.

Stockmann, Reinhard. (1985) 'Gewerbliche Frauenarbeit in Deutschland, 1875–1980, Zur Entwichlung der Beschäftigtenstruktur.' *Geschichte und Gesellschaft*, 11, pp. 447–75.

Stone, Lawrence. (1977) *The Family, Sex and Marriage in England*. London: Weidenfeld and Nicolson.

Sturrock, Archibald. (1866–67) 'Report of the Agriculture of Ayrshire.' *Prize Essays and Transactions of the Highland Society of Scotland*, 4.

Summers, Ann. (1979) 'A Home from Home – Women's Philanthropic Work in the Nineteenth Century.' *Fit Work for Women*. Sandra Burman, ed., pp. 33–63. London: Croom Helm.

Sussman, George. (1982) *Selling Mothers' Milk: The Wet-nursing Business in France, 1715–1914*. Urbana: University of Illinois Press.

Taylor, Barbara. (1983) *Eve and the New Jerusalem*. London: Virago.

Taylor, Sandra. (1977) 'The Effect of Marriage on Job Possibilities for Women and the Ideology of the Home: Nottingham, 1890–1930.' *Oral History*, 5, 5, pp. 46–61.

Tenfelde, Klaus. (1992) 'Arbeiter Familier und Geschlechter beziehungen im Deutschen Kaiserreich.' *Geschichte und Gesellschaft*, 18, pp. 179–203.

Thane, Pat. (1991) 'Visions of Gender in the Making of the British Welfare State: The Case of Women in the British Labour Party and Social Policy, 1906–1945.' *Maternity and Gender Policies, Women and the Rise of the European Welfare States, 1880s–1950s*. Gisela Bock and Pat Thane, eds, pp. 93–118. London: Routledge.

Thébaud, Françoise. (1994) 'The Great War and the Triumph of Sexual Division.' *A History of Women in the West, V. Toward a Cultural Identity in the Twentieth Century*. Françoise Thébaud, ed., pp. 21–75. Cambridge, Mass.: The Belknap Press of Harvard University.

Thompson, E. P. (1968) *Making of the English Working Class*. Harmondsworth: Penguin Books Ltd.

Thompson, E. P. (1971) 'Moral Economy of the English Crowd in the Eighteenth Century.' *Past and Present*, 50, pp. 75–136.

Thompson, E. P. (1974) 'Time, Work, Discipline, and Industrial Capitalism.' *Essays in Social History*. M. W. Flinn and T. C. Smout, eds, pp. 39–77. Oxford: Clarendon Press.

Thompson, P. and Eileen Yeo. (1984) *Unknown Mayhew: Selections from the* Morning Chronicle, *1849–1850*. Harmondsworth: Penguin.

Thompson, Paul, T. Wailey and Trevor Lummis. (1983) *Living the Fishing*. London: Routledge and Kegan Paul.

Tijdens, Kea. (1994) 'Behind the Screens: The Foreseen and Unforeseen Impact of Computerization on Female Office Workers' Jobs.' *Feminist Perspectives on Technology, Work and Ecology, Conference Proceedings, 2nd European Feminist Research Conference, Graz, Austria*, pp. 132–39.

Tilly, Louise. (1979) 'Individual Lives and Family Strategies in the French Proletariat.' *Journal of Family History*, 4, pp. 137–52.

Tilly, Louise. (1982) 'Three Faces of Capitalism; Women and Work in French Cities.' *French Cities in the Nineteenth Century*. J. H. Merriman, ed., pp. 165–92. London: Hutchinson and Co. Ltd.

Tilly, Louise. (1985) 'Family, Gender and Occupation in Industrial France.' *Gender and the Life Course*. Alice Rossi, ed., pp. 193–212. New York: Aldine Publishing Company.

Tilly, Louise A. (1986) 'Rural England, Poverty, and the Institution of Service. A Review Article.' *Journal of Comparative Studies in Society and History*, 28, pp. 239–47.

Tilly, Louise A. (1993) 'Gender and Jobs in Early Twentieth-century French Industry.' *International Labor and Working-class History*, 43, pp. 31–47.

Tilly, Louise and Joan Scott. (1978) *Women, Work and Family*. New York: Holt, Rinehart and Winston.

Tipton, Frank B. and Robert Aldrich. (1987) *An Economic and Social History of Europe in the Twentieth Century*. London: Macmillan Education Ltd.

Todd, Barbara. (1985) 'The Remarrying Widow: A Stereotype Reconsidered.' *Women in English Society, 1500–1800*. Mary Prior, ed., pp. 54–92. London: Methuen and Co. Ltd.

Treble, James H. (1986) 'The Characteristics of the Female Unskilled Labour Market and the Formation of the Female Casual Labour Market in Glasgow, 1891–1914.' *Scottish Economic and Social History*, 6, pp. 33–46.

Trimmer, Sarah. (1787) *The Oeconomy of Charity; or an Address to Ladies Concerning Sunday Schools*. London: J. Johnson.

Tristan, Flora. (1973) *Le Tour de France: Journal inédit (1843–1844)*. Paris: F. Maspero.

Tryfan, Barbara. (1972) 'The Role of Rural Women in the Family.' Paper presented at the 3rd World Congress of Rural Sociology, Baton Rouge, Louisiana.

Valenze, Deborah. (1991) 'The Art of Women and the Business of Men: Women's Work and the Dairy Industry, *c.*1740–1840.' *Past and Present*, 130, pp. 142–69.

Valenze, Deborah. (1995) *The First Industrial Woman*. Oxford: Oxford University Press.

Valverde, M. (1987/8) '"Giving the Female a Domestic Turn": The Social, Legal and Moral Regulation of Women's Work in British Cotton Mills, 1820–50.' *Journal of Social History*, 21, pp. 619–34.

Verney, Lady. (1888) *How the Peasant Owner Lives in Parts of France, Germany, Italy, Russia*. London: Macmillan and Co.

322

Versluysen, Margaret Connors. (1981) 'Midwives, Medical Men and "Poor Women of Labouring Child" Lying-in Hospitals in Eighteenth-century London.' *Women's Health and Reproduction*. Helen Roberts, ed. London: Routledge.

Vicinus, M. (1985) *Independent Women: Work and Community for Single Women, 1850–1920*. London: Virago.

Walkowitz, Judith. (1980) *Prostitution and Victorian Society, Women, Class and the State*. Cambridge: Cambridge University Press.

Walkowitz, Judith. (1993) 'Dangerous Sexualities.' *A History of Women in the West. IV. Emerging Feminism from Revolution to World War*. Geneviève Fraisse and Michelle Perrot, eds, pp. 371–98. Cambridge, Mass.: The Belknap Press of Harvard University.

Wall, Richard. (1978) 'The Age at Leaving Home.' *Journal of Family History*, 3, pp. 181–202.

Wall, Richard. (1981) 'Woman Alone in English Society.' *Annales de Démographie Historique*, pp. 303–16.

Walser, Karin. (1985) 'Prostitutions verdacht und Geschlechterforschung. Das Beispiel der Dienstmädchen um 1900.' *Geschichte und Gesellschaft*, 11, pp. 99–111.

Weatherill, Lorna. (1988) *Consumer Behaviour and Material Culture in Britain, 1660–1760*. London: Routledge.

Webb, Sidney. (1907) *The Decline in the Birth-rate*. Fabian Tract no. 131. London: Fabian Society.

Weber, Adna Ferrin. (1899) *The Growth of Cities in the Nineteenth Century, a Study in Statistics*. Ithaca, N. Y.: Cornell University Press.

Weber, Eugen. (1976) *Peasants into Frenchmen, the Modernization of Rural France, 1870–1914*. London: Chatto and Windus Ltd.

Wedel, Gudrun. (1986) '. . . Nothing More than a German Woman.' *German Women in the Eighteenth and Nineteenth Centuries. A Social and Literary History*. Ruth-Ellen B. Joeres and Mary Jo Maynes, eds. pp. 305–20. Bloomington: Indiana University Press.

Wedgwood Archives, Keele University Library.

Welter, Barbara. (1978) 'The Cult of True Womanhood, 1820–1860.' *The Family in Social-historical Perspective*. Michael Gordon, ed., 2nd edn pp. 313–33. New York: Saint Martin's Press Inc.

Wexler, Victor G. (1976) 'Made for Man's Delight, Rousseau as an Antifeminist.' *American Historical Review*, 81, pp. 266–91.

Weyrather, Irmgard. (1993) *Muttertag und Mutterkreuz; der Kult um die "deutsche Mutter" im Nationalsozialismus*. Frankfurt-am-Main: Fischer Taschenbuch Verlag GmbH.

Whipp, Richard. (1990a) *Patterns of Labour, Work and Social Change in the Pottery Industry*. London: Routledge.

Whyte, Ian. (1989) 'Protoindustrialisation in Scotland.' *Regions and Industries: A Perspective on the Industrial Revolution in Britain*. Pat Hudson, ed., pp. 228–51. Cambridge: Cambridge University Press.

Whyte, Ian D. and Kathleen A. Whyte. (1988) 'The Geographical Mobility of Women in Early Modern Scotland.' *Perspectives in Scottish Social History*. Leah Leneman, ed., pp. 83–106. Aberdeen: Aberdeen University Press.

Widdowson, Frances. (1983) *Going up into the Next Class*. London: Hutchinson.

Wierling, Dorothee. (1987) '"Ich hab meine Arbeit gemacht – was wollt sie mehr?"' Dienst Mädchen im städtischen Haushalt der Jahrhundertwende.' *Frauen Suchen Ihre Geschichte*. Karin Hausen, ed., pp. 146–74. München: Verlag C. H. Beck.

Wiesner, Merry. (1987a) 'Spinning Out Capital.' *Becoming Visible, Women in European History*. Renate Bridenthal, Claudia Koonz and Susan Stuard, eds, 2nd edn pp. 221–50. Boston: Houghton, Mifflin Company.

Wiesner, Merry. (1987b) 'Women's Work in the Changing City Economy, 1500–1650.' *Connecting Spheres*. Marilyn Boxer and Jean H. Quataert, eds, pp. 64–74. Oxford: Oxford University Press.

Wiesner, Merry. (1989) 'Guilds, Male Bonding and Women's Work in Early Modern Germany.' *Gender and History*, 1, 2, pp. 125–37.

Wiesner, Merry E. (1993) *Women and Gender in Early Modern Europe*. Cambridge: Cambridge University Press.

Wilke, Gerard. (1986) 'The Sins of the Fathers, Village Society and Social Control in the Weimar Republic.' *The German Peasantry, Conflict and Community in Rural Society from the Eighteenth to the Twentieth Centuries*. Richard Evans and W. R. Lee, eds, London: Croom Helm.

Willcox, Penelope. (1982) 'Marriage, Mobility, and Domestic Service in Victorian Cambridge.' *Local Population Studies*, 29, pp. 19–34.

Williams, David. (1971) 'The Politics of feminism in the French Enlightenment.' *The Varied Pattern: Studies in the Eighteenth Century*. Peter Hughes and David Williams, eds, pp. 333–51. Toronto: Hakkert.

Williams, Rosalind. (1982) *Dream Worlds: Mass Consumption in Late Nineteenth-century France*. Berkeley: University of California Press.

Williams, Raymond. (1983) *Keywords, A Vocabulary of Culture and Society*. London: Fontana.

Willson, Perry R. (1993) *The Clockwork Factory, Women and Work in Fascist Italy*. Oxford: Clarendon Press.

Wilson, Elizabeth. (1980) *Only Halfway to Paradise, Women in Postwar Britain, 1945–1968*. London: Routledge.

Winker, Gabriele. (1994) 'A Gendered View on Computer Supporter Work in the Office.' *Feminist Perspectives on Technology, Work and Ecology, Conference Proceedings, 2nd European Feminist Research Conference, 5–9 July 1994, Graz, Austria*, pp. 144–51.

Winship, Janice. (1987) *Inside Women's Magazines*. London: Pandora.

Winstanley, M. (1983) *The Shopkeepers' World, 1830–1914*. Manchester: Manchester University Press.

Wollstonecraft, Mary. (1792; 1978) *Vindication of the Rights of Woman*. Miriam Kramnick, ed. Harmondsworth: Penguin.

Woodward, J. (1960) *The Saleswoman: A Study of Attitudes and Behaviour in Retail Distribution*. London: Pitman.

Wrigley, E. A. and R. S. Schofield. (1981) *The Population History of England, 1541–1871*. A Reconstruction. London: Edward Arnold.

Wylie, Laurence. (1957) *Village in the Vaucluse*. Cambridge, Mass.: Harvard University Press.

Young, A., ed. (1784–1815) *Annals of Agriculture*. London: Board of Agriculture.

Young, Arthur. (1929) *Travels in France, during the Years 1787, 1788 and 1789*. Constantia Maxwell, ed. Cambridge: Cambridge University Press.

Zerner, Sylvie. (1987) 'De la Couture aux presses: l'emploi féminin entre les deux guerres.' *Le Mouvement Social*, 140, pp. 9–26.

Zimmeck, M. (1986) 'Jobs for the Girls: The Expansion of Clerical Work for Women,

1850–1914.' *Unequal Opportunities, Women's Employment in England, 1800–1918.* Angela John, ed., pp. 153–78. Oxford: Basil Blackwell.

Zimmeck, Meta. (1984) 'Strategies and Strategems for the Employment of Women in the British Civil Service, 1919–39.' *Historical Journal*, 27, pp. 901–24.

Zimmeck, Meta. (1988) '"Get out and Get under": The Impact of Demobilisation on the Civil Service, 1919–32.' *The White-blouse Revolution, Female Office Workers since 1870*. Gregory Anderson, ed. pp. 88–120. Manchester: Manchester University Press.

Zimmeck, Meta. (1995) '"The Mysteries of the Typewriter": Technology and Gender in the British Civil Service, 1870–1914.' *Women Workers and Technological Change in Europe in the Nineteenth and Twentieth Centuries*. Gertjan de Groot and Marlou Schrover, eds, pp. 67–96. London: Taylor and Francis.

Zmroczek, C. and F. Henwood. (1983) *New Information Technology and Women's Employment*. Brighton: Science Policy Review Unit.

Zonabend, Françoise. (1984) *The Enduring Memory, Time and History in a French Village*. Manchester: Manchester University Press.

INDEX

Abensour, Léon 4, 29, 49, 55
Accampo, Elinor 135, 140, 167
Adams, Carol Elizabeth 238
agricultural gangs 121–2
agriculture 16–18; British Commission
   on 166; Belgium 113, 116, 122;
   capitalist 112; collectivized 210;
   commercialized 27; day labour 29,
   116, 117, 120; employment of women
   27–30, 112–13, 114, 183, 207;
   enclosure 112, 120; family labour
   120–1; farm management 19, 20;
   female strength 164–5; femininity
   115–16; feudal service 29; fieldwork
   115, 116, 117–18, 132; Finland 209;
   gendered labour divisions 27, 30–6,
   127–8, 209; Germanic countries 29,
   118–19, 123; horse work 33, 128;
   labour-intensive 112, 113, 115;
   mechanization 210–11; Netherlands
   29; second incomes 212–13; specialist
   jobs 33; stigmatized 208; subsistence
   39; training 27–8; unpaid work 207;
   wages 35–6, 118, 119; wartime 210;
   see also England, agriculture; France,
   agriculture; Germany, agriculture;
   Italy, agriculture; Scotland, agriculture
Alexander, Sally 165, 176
Allen, Sheila 222
Ambrosius, Gerold 183
Aminzade, Ronald 149, 150
Anderson, Bonnie S. 6, 27
androcentrism 176–7
Ankarloo, Bengt 28
apprenticeships: class 52; England 50–1;
   France 51, 266; gender 51–2, 61–2,
   79–80, 266; Germany 51, 266; girls
   48, 49–53, 80, 81; mystery 76, 79;

parish 80–1; as rite of passage 80;
   trade distributions 51–3
Armentières 228, 231
Army and Navy Stores 238
Ashley, Lord 174
assembly lines 231
Association of Women Clerks and
   Secretaries 250
automobile industry 226–7
Auvergne 20

Baader, Ottilie 219
baking trade 62
Banffshire, fisherwives 126
barriers to employment 185, 242
Bavaria, dairying 123
Beddoe, Deirdre 193, 231
Beeton, Isabella Mary 92
begging 22
Behagg, Clive 79
Beier, Rosemarie 168, 219
Belgium: agriculture 113, 116, 122;
   factory work 227; female garment-
   makers 215; female strength 163–4;
   glassware 224; linen manufacture 136;
   manufacturing 222, 223, 224; marital
   status of women workers 193; mining
   140, 148, 164; spinning 54; women
   in workforce 113, 116, 134, 193, 222,
   223, 224; woollen mills 138; working
   mothers 141
Berg, Maxine 17, 22, 81, 83, 144, 170,
   267
Besteman, Catherine 210
Birmingham charwomen 203
birth: see childbirth
black economy 216
Bloquel, Simon 92

INDEX

Blum, Jerome 33
Bon Marché 236, 153
book trade 49, 53, 55, 61, 66
bookbinding 151
bookkeeping 156
Borel, Suzanne 242
Bose, Christine C. 95
Bougle, Célestin 185
Bouquet, Mary 214
bourgeoisie 13, 88
Bourke, Joanna 200
Bouvier, Jeanne 104
Boxer, M. J. 5, 215, 220, 221
boys: apprenticeships 51–2, 53, 80, 81;
    domestic chores 23; life cycle patterns
    23–4
Bradley, Harriet 124, 245
braid industry 139, 140
Braudel, Fernand 27
Braverman, Harry 3, 222, 267
breastfeeding 189
brewing industry 62
Bridenthal, Renate 225, 237
Britain: Agricultural Commission 166;
    Children's Employment Commission
    144; civil service 248, 256, 258, 259;
    clerical work 240; employment
    statistics 134, 181–2, 184; female
    garment-makers 215; higher education
    241; housework 19; manufacturing
    222, 223; marital status of women
    workers 192, 193; Mass Observation
    survey 227; mining 42–3, 147, 74–5;
    National Insurance Act 203; Old Age
    Pensions Act 203; outwork 215–16;
    Poor Law 100; Select Committee on
    Homework 220; Sex Disqualification
    (Removal) Act 260; Shops Act 254;
    Society for Promoting the
    Employment of Women 248; welfare
    provision 188–9; see also England;
    Ireland; Scotland; Wales
Broadhurst, Henry 174
Brouwer, Jo 256–7
Brown, John 14
Buret, Eugène 161
Burstall, Sarah 245
businesswomen 155–61
butler 109
Butler-Schloss, Elizabeth 243

Cadbury, Elizabeth Head 96, 156–7
Cadbury's Chocolates 231

calico printing 144–5, 163
calico weaving 143
Cammarosano, Simonetta Ortaggi 110,
    150
Campbell, Robert 56, 62, 76
capitalism: agriculture 112; craft
    traditions 176; opposed 172;
    production 37; and specialization
    254–5; trade 37; and womanhood
    162; women's roles 4, 7
career breaks, childcare 193, 195
careers guides for women 248
casual work 263
catalogue houses 238
Caux: agriculture 39, 116, 117, 121;
    calico weaving 143; power looms 131;
    spinning 40, 60, 145–6; weaving
    82–3, 136, 143; yarn selling 41
censuses 181, 182
centralization of workforce 135
Cernea, Michael 212, 213
Chadwick, Sir Edwin 94
charitable work 91, 159–60, 236
charity, for widows 66–7
Chartism 172, 175
charwomen 110, 202–3
cheesemaking 123, 124, 195
Chenut, Helen Harden 231
childbirth 25, 188
childcare: career breaks 193, 195; France
    25; Germany 26; and homework
    150–1; middle-class 96; mothers
    15–16, 25–6, 168, 189–90;
    networking 214
childhood as concept 2, 15
children as social investment 25
Children's Employment Commission 144
Chinn, Carl 221
Christianity 13, 14
cigar-making 173, 174
civil service: Gladstone Commission 256,
    259; MacDonnell Commission 256;
    professionals 255; typists 248; women
    239, 240, 258
Clark, Alice 4, 8
class: apprenticeships 52; childcare 96;
    cleanliness 93, 94; clerical work 255;
    domesticity 168, 171–2; education 16,
    89; family 165; family wage 89–90,
    171–2; femininity 8, 87, 89;
    housework 95–6, 199–200; housing
    197; labour division 19; life cycle
    patterns 23–4; midwives 64; mothers

327

15–16; shopwork 248–9, 250; women
workers 190
cleanliness 20–1, 93–4, 164, 198–9
clerical work: as career 249; gender/class
241, 255; status 238–9, 240, 250;
typing 233–4, 248; *see also* office work
clockmaking 49–50
clothes traders, second-hand 68–9
clothing trade 79, 150, 214–15, 218–19
coaching trade 158
Cockburn, Cynthia 3, 264, 267
Collier, Mary 71
Collins, Brenda 40
Collyer, R. 76
Colyton 74
Comasco 140
commercialization: agriculture 27;
dairying 122–3; fishing 127, 211–12;
household goods 19, 22, 95
Como 142
compagnonnages 77, 83
computers 257–8
confection: see ready made clothes
consumer durables 197–8, 199–200
consumerism 22, 196, 214
contraceptives 188
control, gendered 268–9
cook 103, 109
Cornwall 213
cottage industries 39, 45, 137
cotton mills 74, 136, 141
Courtauld's 138, 146, 147, 148, 165
Cowan, Ruth Schwartz 96
craft traditions 7, 140, 176, 177–8
Crompton, Rosemary 242, 260
Culley, George 116
culture: labour divisions 32; segregation
226; technology 4; women in
profession 243
cutlery workers 157

dairying: Bavaria 123; cheesemaking
123, 124, 195; commercial 122–3;
Denmark 31, 122, 123; England 31,
123–4; Finland 122; France 31;
Ireland 31, 122, 124; masculinization
124–5, 211; mechanization 208, 211;
Norway 208; skill 30, 127; Sweden
31, 122, 123, 124, 195; as woman's
task 31, 114, 122–3
daughters: agricultural training 27–8;
household tasks 23, 114; sent to
service 29, 100–1; working at home 55

Davidis, Henriette 92, 108
Davidoff, Leonore 91, 92, 110, 156, 158
Davin, Anna 257
Davis, John A. 38
Davis, Natalie Zemon 68, 83
day labouring 29, 116, 117, 120
de Groot, Gertjan 5, 265–6
de Haan, Francisca 257, 259
Defoe, Daniel 76
Denman, R. D. 44
Denmark: cleanliness 94; dairying 31,
122, 123; employment statistics 182;
feudal service 29; marital status of
women workers 193; postnatal care
189
department stores 183, 214, 234, 236–7,
252
Derry 154
deskilling 3–4, 9, 178, 257, 267
dexterity 144–5, 162, 163, 209, 265
discrimination 183–4, 188, 245
divorce 194
docility 163, 247
domestic appliances 104
domestic finances 196–7
domestic industry: *see* homework
domestic roles 2, 14, 23
domestic servants 96–8, 102, 103–4;
backgrounds 99–102, 203; in decline
183, 200–1; and employers 103,
108–9, 201, 204; England 59, 97–9,
100, 101; France 20, 59, 97, 99, 100,
101, 104–5; Germany 97, 98, 99,
100, 101, 104, 109, 206; hierarchy
109–10; length of service 204; living
out 110–11; male/female 102; marital
status 99–100; prostitution 106–7;
sexually vulnerable 59–60, 106; single
women 59; tasks 114–15, 204–5;
wages 60, 97, 104–5; working
conditions 102–6, 203; working hours
105–6; world wars 205
Domestic Servants Union 204
domestic work: *see* housework
domesticity 87–9, 165, 168, 171–2,
187–8, 190
dowry 55, 129, 134
dressmaking 153; *see also* clothing trade
du Maroussem, Pierre 113
dual spheres doctrine 87
Duchen, Claire 243–4
Dunlop, O. J. 44, 79
Dupree, Marguerite 167

Halstead mills 141
Hansen, Bodil 122, 123
Hardyment, Christina 104
Harley, David 64
harvesting 118
hatmaking 150
Hause, Stephen C. 185
Hausen, Karin 93
hay-making 132
Heller, Geneviève 164
herring gutting 126
Heywood, Colin 170
Higgs, Edward 104
higher education 63, 241, 245–6
Higonnet, Margaret R. 185
Hilden, Patricia 164, 227
Hogarth, Janet 252
Holcombe, Lee 237
Holmes, Douglas 133, 135
home and work separation 167–8,
   169–70, 174
homemaking 93, 196; *see also*
   domesticity; housework
homework: acceptability 217; catalogue
   selling 238; as cheap labour 46–7; and
   childcare 150–1; clothing trade
   214–15, 218–19; dangers 221; ethnic
   minorities 217; flower-makers
   217–18, 220, 221–2; Germany
   148–9, 153, 215; Glasgow 214,
   216–17; Italy 150–1; London 214;
   marital status 216–17; and
   mechanization 220; Moscow 219;
   needlework 151–4; sewing machines
   154–5; Vienna 218; wages 46, 155,
   168–9, 218–19, 220; working
   conditions 221; *see also* outwork;
   putting-out system
horse work 33, 128
hosiery 142, 146, 268
hospitals 63
Hostettler, Eve 119
household, female ranking 24
household goods 19, 22, 95
household management 196–7
housewives 190, 191, 262
Housewives Union 204, 205
housework 2–3, 18–23, 91–2, 195–200;
   appliances 94–5, 198; childcare 96;
   class 95–6, 199–200; cleanliness
   93–4; daughters/sons 23, 114; on farm
   114, 210; femininity 19; financial
   management 196–7; gender divisions

72–3; and paid work 22–3;
   professionalized 92; Sweden 21–2;
   technology 198
housework manuals 92–3
housing conditions 197
Houston, Rab 45, 55
Howell, Martha C. 50
Hubbard, William H. 183
Hudson, Pat 5, 17, 38–9
Hufton, Olwen 6, 22, 24, 26, 39, 41,
   45, 49, 51, 55, 57, 59, 65, 81, 197
Hutton, William 43

identification with work 77, 78
identity, gender 33, 264
Imhof, Arthur E. 164
independence 48, 57–8, 60–1, 74, 135
industrial revolution 4, 7
industrialization 73, 74, 135, 168
industry 38–9, 43, 61; *see also* light
   industry
inequality of wages 247, 248, 252, 256
informal economy 181–2
innkeeping 158
International Postal Union 255–6
Ireland: Belfast 215; dairying 31, 122,
   124; Derry 154; emigration 132;
   family farms 120; female strength
   130; linen 40, 60; second incomes
   212–13; shirtmaking 153–4; women's
   status on farms 214
Italy: Comasco 140; Como 142; female
   strength 130; homeworking 150–1;
   manufacturing 222, 223; motherhood
   189; poverty 200; protective
   legislation 203–4; silk mills 140, 142,
   162–3; women workers 222, 223;
   working mothers 141
Italy, agriculture: gendered labour 30,
   120; gleaning 120; labour migration
   212; seasonal work 112, 113

Jefferies, Richard 131–2
Johansson, Ella 127, 128, 129
John, Angela V. 3
John Lewis Partnership 252
Jordan, Ellen 145, 176–7, 238, 259
Judaism 13

King, Peter 31
Kingston upon Thames 49
kitchen garden 114, 127
Kleinbaum, Abby 13

widows: as businesswomen 156; charity 66–7; independence 61; as proportion of population 57; remarriage 66; retailing 157; status 26

Wierling, Dorothee 101, 103, 108, 110

Wiesner, Merry 6, 31, 53, 68, 78

Willson, Perry R. 232, 269

wives: of farmers 27–8, 212–13, 262; of masters 56; *see also* married women

Wolkowitz, Carol 222

Wollstonecraft, Mary 16

Woman Worker 205

Woman 220–1

womanhood 87, 88, 162

Woman's Leader 204

women: abilities 255–6; capitalism 4, 7; class 8, 89, 96, 156, 190, 191, 233, 247; as consumers 22; as evil 13; exclusion 49, 177; housework 18–23; independence 48, 57–8, 74; live births 25; private sphere 88–9; roles 6–7, 14, 165; self-perception 2, 187, 214, 269–70; sexual protection 14–15; social constructions 1–2, 181; status 81, 147–8; substituting for absent men 20, 35, 57, 171, 183, 185–6; *see also* married women; single women; women workers

women-headed households 60–1, 67

women returners 194

women workers 71–2, 230; agriculture 27–30, 112–13, 114, 116–17, 128, 183, 207–8; Belgium 113, 116, 134, 193, 222, 223, 224; as casual workers 263; as cheap labour 52, 74, 75, 136, 170, 220, 228–9, 232, 239–40, 246; class 190, 247; flexible labour 44; France 134, 184, 222, 223, 260; full/part time work 45; Germany 134, 184, 222, 223; as green workers 226, 247; in industry 61; location 70; marital status 192–3; mechanization 144, 145–6, 229; professions 183–4, 242–3, 244; by sectors 134, 184; as

threat 231–2, 243; traders 47, 68–9; wartime 184–6

Women's Advisory Committee 204–5

Women's Educational Association of Leipzig 248

women's movement 91, 160, 248

women's rights 242

Woodward, J. 249

woollen industry 41, 136, 138

work: casual 263; conditions 102–6, 165, 203, 221; discipline 169; flexibility 71; full/part time 45; honourable/ dishonourable 78, 141, 153; hours 105–6, 169, 221, 253, 254; identity 77, 78; labour intensive 112, 113, 115, 136, 145, 231; life cycle 23, 55, 68, 140, 169–70; location 70, 73; male exclusivity 78–9; modern 6–7; paid/unpaid 2–3, 17, 22–3, 26, 70–2, 165–6, 193; part-time 194, 236; repetitious 187, 219, 231; shifting practices 133–5; and time 26, 71, 169, 221–2; use/exchange values 2; *see also* employment; labour; wage work

work satisfaction 195

workers: centralization 135; hidden 149, 261–2; status 128; *see also* women workers

working-class: family wage/domesticity 171–2; girls 16; housing conditions 197; life cycle patterns 23–4; mothers 15–16; women 89, 191

workplaces, gendered 148

World War I 184–6, 205, 239–40

World War II 185–6, 260

Württemberg 41, 44, 58

Young, Arthur 32, 40

Zerner, Sylvie 181, 231, 249

Zimmeck, Meta 252, 256

Zinsser, Judith P. 6, 27

Zola, E. 236